DATE DUE

NOV 1 2 2018	
WITHDRAWN	

The Ethics of Immigration

The Ethics of Immigration

JOSEPH H. CARENS

OXFORD
UNIVERSITY PRESS

OXFORD
UNIVERSITY PRESS

Oxford University Press is a department of the University of Oxford.
It furthers the University's objective of excellence in research, scholarship,
and education by publishing worldwide.

Oxford   New York

Auckland   Cape Town   Dar es Salaam   Hong Kong   Karachi
Kuala Lumpur   Madrid   Melbourne   Mexico City   Nairobi
New Delhi   Shanghai   Taipei   Toronto

With offices in

Argentina   Austria   Brazil   Chile   Czech Republic   France   Greece
Guatemala   Hungary   Italy   Japan   Poland   Portugal   Singapore
South Korea   Switzerland   Thailand   Turkey   Ukraine   Vietnam

Oxford is a registered trademark of Oxford University Press
in the UK and certain other countries.

Published in the United States of America by
Oxford University Press
198 Madison Avenue, New York, NY 10016

Library of Congress Cataloging-in-Publication Data
Joseph H. Carens
The ethics of immigration / Joseph H. Carens.
pages cm
Includes bibliographical references and index.
ISBN 978–0–19–993383–9 (hardback : alk. paper)   1. United States—Emigration and immigration—
Government policy.   2. Illegal aliens—United States—Government policy.   3. Emigration and
immigration—Moral and ethical aspects.   I. Title.
JV6477.C37 2013
172'.2—dc23
2013011943

3 5 7 9 8 6 4
Printed in the United States of America
er

For Jenny, Michael, and Daniel

CONTENTS

ACKNOWLEDGMENTS

It is customary to save the dedication to the end of one's acknowledgments, but I have over thirty years' worth of people to thank, and I fear some readers might not make it to the end. So, I'll begin with what is most important to me. I get great satisfaction from my work, but I have always known that my family mattered more. I have tried to live in accordance with that knowledge and not to sacrifice time with them to my work. For the most part, I have succeeded in that endeavor, and my life has been much the richer for it. I dedicate this book with love and gratitude to Jenny and Michael and Daniel.

I first started thinking about the ethics of immigration in 1980. I had been invited to participate in an APSA faculty seminar directed by Nan Keohane. The price of admission to the seminar was a commitment to write a paper on citizenship. While casting around for a topic, I found myself reading stories about Haitians trying to get to Florida to ask for asylum as refugees. I had no preconceptions about what Americans (or anyone else) should do about the Haitians, but I felt intuitively torn between the feeling that there was something wrong in excluding people in such obvious need and the worry that admitting everyone with comparable claims would be overwhelming and would be especially harmful to those already most disadvantaged in America. I wanted to look at the political theory literature on immigration to help me think about this topic, but I discovered, to my surprise, that there was no such literature. So, I decided to think about what the leading liberal theories of the day would entail if applied to this topic. Again I was surprised. I concluded that all of the theories I was considering (Rawls, Nozick, utilitarianism) should support open borders (with minor qualifications). For various reasons, I put the paper aside for a few years. By the time I returned to it, Michael Walzer had published his seminal piece on membership. In that essay Walzer argued that states are morally entitled to exercise discretionary control over immigration, at least for the most part.

Engaging with Walzer's essay clarified my thinking, but it only served to confirm my earlier view that liberal democratic principles entail a commitment to open borders. So, I added a critical discussion of Walzer, spent a long time polishing and refining my paper, and then sent it off. It was promptly—or, sometimes, not so promptly—turned down by three leading journals: *American Political Science Review*, *Ethics*, and *Philosophy & Public Affairs*. I'll admit to finding these rejections discouraging. I persisted, however, and on my fourth try the paper found a home in *Review of Politics*.

I thought that my open borders argument was getting at an important truth. At the same time, I recognized that it was not a practical proposal and that it did not provide much guidance for actual policy issues (like the question of how to respond to the Haitians). I was not quite sure how to go about pursuing the ethics of immigration further. Then, in 1987, I was invited to a conference on comparative citizenship and naturalization policies organized by the German Marshall Fund. This conference involved administrators and policymakers from several European states along with academics who were mainly lawyers or empirical scholars. I was the only political theorist. I knew that this audience would not be much interested in an abstract philosophical discussion of Rawls, Nozick, and open borders. They wanted to know what European states should do about the immigrants in their midst, people who had arrived as temporary workers but had settled permanently. Fortunately, I had a political theorist to rely upon in addressing this issue: Michael Walzer. In the very same article in which he defended discretionary control over immigration, Walzer argued that if democratic states do admit immigrants, they have to put the immigrants on a path to citizenship. I found Walzer's argument compelling and used it as the foundation for my own analysis in my contribution to the conference.

My agreement with Walzer on access to citizenship did not change my views about our disagreement over admissions. Instead it set me to wondering about how to connect these two quite different sorts of argument and how best to identify the moral issues raised by immigration. Some of these moral issues seemed to grow out of immediate, contingent circumstances. Others seemed more enduring and more tied to the central requirements of democratic principles. For some issues (like access to citizenship), what I thought justice required was already practiced by some democratic states and was not unimaginable in most of the others. For other issues (like open borders), what I thought justice required seemed far removed from anything feasible in the foreseeable future. And so I began to try to sort out these puzzles, hoping to provide an overview of the normative issues raised by immigration and to say something about the different ways in which one might approach such a topic.

I did not think that it would take me as long as it has to produce this book. By the early 1990s I had already written several papers on immigration. Indeed, in 1993 Philippe van Parijs organized a workshop on my draft manuscript at Louvain-la-Neuve in Belgium. The workshop was helpful, but I felt that my manuscript did not fully hang together. I wanted to produce a sustained and coherent analysis, not just a collection of articles. In retrospect I can see that it was a mistake not to publish what I had then. That manuscript already advanced some of the key themes about social membership and open borders that are found in this book. The earlier version did not solve all of the problems, but then no book does, including this one. If I had published a book then, it would have advanced the conversation, and it certainly would have advanced my career. Still, one is fortunate indeed in life if one's mistakes have such limited negative consequences as this mistake had for me. I did not keep my thoughts to myself but published them as articles. So, my ideas did reach a part of the scholarly community, if not the wider audience that a book can command. Moreover, I already had a secure position in a department that I regarded then (and still regard) as the best place in the world for a political theorist. So, whatever professional opportunities I missed by not publishing the book sooner were not all that important in the end.

I don't mean to suggest that I did not care about whether or not the book came out, however. On the contrary, the fact that it was not finished has been weighing on me for the better part of two decades. I have a colleague who was told as a graduate student, "Don't get it right, get it done." I regard this as good, anti-perfectionist advice, which I pass on to my own graduate students, and which I have followed myself in publishing articles. I was unable to follow it when it came to this book, however. When I published a book on multiculturalism in 2000 (and, in that case, I was quite satisfied to produce a collection of revised essays), I wrote in the preface that my book on the ethics of immigration would follow within a couple of years. I thought that this public commitment would make it too humiliating for me not to finish my immigration book right away. As it turned out, I was wrong. I kept working on it. I had one workshop on the manuscript in 2006 and two more in 2008, and still I could not quite let it go. If you wonder why I finally did so now, I have no simple answer. I'm certainly not under the illusion that this is a perfect book. I do think, however, that I have, at long last, written the book I wanted to write.

Over the course of thirty plus years, one acquires a lot of debts, more than I can possibly acknowledge here, and indeed, more than I can remember. I will do my best, however, starting with the most recent.

Over the past two summers, as I was preparing the manuscript for submission and then as I was finishing the final revisions, my wife Jenny Nedelsky read many of the revised sections and chapters and helped me to see what worked and what didn't, what was needed and what was too much. (I have a tendency to overwrite.) Her advice mattered a lot to me and made this a much better book. My sons Michael Carens-Nedelsky and Daniel Carens-Nedelsky also helped. Daniel read large parts of the manuscript, giving me a valuable perspective on what was accessible to bright non-specialists. Michael also read some chapters, but more importantly, he offered an entire theory about what a book cover should do (a topic that I had never actually considered) and gave me some crucial guidance on the design of the cover.

Dave McBride, my editor at OUP, followed this project from a distance for years, and then when I submitted it, made the decision to publish with Oxford easy. He also read the entire manuscript and offered valuable advice about some key issues. I also want to thank Niko Pfund for taking a personal interest in the project. That helped to persuade me that OUP was the place for this book. Lynn Childress was an ideal copyeditor.

I owe an especially deep intellectual debt to Rainer Bauböck, Will Kymlicka, David Miller, and David Owen, the four people who served as readers for OUP and another press in the fall of 2011. I have been discussing the ethics of migration with Rainer for almost twenty years. While we don't agree on everything, there is no one whose basic judgments are closer to my own and no one who has helped me more to think about this topic. Will Kymlicka's work has shaped my own thinking for a long time. His characteristically lucid reactions to the manuscript really helped me to clarify the nature of my project. Above all, Will pressed me to make my underlying theory more explicit. The discussion of social membership in chapter 8 and the discussion of why freedom of movement matters morally in the last half of chapter 11 are a response to his challenges (though I suspect that what I wrote may not satisfy him). In the book, I probably have more explicit arguments with David Miller than with anyone else, and that is precisely why I was so happy that he served as a reviewer. He gave me many criticisms and challenges in his report, but all of them were fair-minded and helped me to improve my text. President Obama likes to say that we should be able to disagree without being disagreeable. David exemplifies that capacity. (The debt goes deeper, too. He was one of the reviewers for the first book that I published, back in 1981, thus helping to make my academic career possible.) My connections to David Owen do not stretch back as far in time as my connections to the other three, but his role in the publication process was crucial. Indeed, the review process might have floundered if he had not been willing to read the manuscript and submit a report in record time. That report helped me (and others) see strengths in certain parts of the manuscript that I might otherwise have considered cutting. I'm grateful for his encouragement and his insight. I made substantial changes in the book in response to the comments of all four readers, and it is clear to me that the book is much better as a result.

This is a long book, but it could easily be longer still. I have left at least half as much again on the cutting room floor. (My apologies to those whose scenes were deleted.) I was inspired to trim in part by a remark from Josh Cohen after

I presented a paper at Stanford in the fall of 2009. He liked the paper, he said, but as an editor he felt it had "too many nails." This was a phrase that stayed in my mind while I worked on the revisions, because I had had the experience earlier that year of working with Josh and especially with Deb Chasman on an article about amnesty for irregular migrants for *Boston Review*. They helped me to turn a somewhat convoluted academic piece into something much more accessible and enabled me to see that less can be more. I tried to use what I learned from that experience in revising the rest of the book. Fewer nails, but, I hope, a better finished product.

I want next to express my appreciation for the various workshops on my manuscript. I often tell graduate students that they should enjoy their Ph.D. defense because it may be the only occasion in their academic lives when several scholars will sit around a table for a couple of hours with the sole purpose of discussing and improving their work. Contrary to this prediction, I have had the good fortune to have had several occasions on which people devoted even more than two hours to discussing my work.

The most recent was also the one in the most beautiful location: a two-day event organized by Rainer Bauböck at the European University Institute in Fiesole (just outside Florence) in May 2012. In addition to Rainer himself, the participants included Costica Dumbrava, Iseult Honohan, Joseph Lacey, Eléonore Lépinard, Kieran Oberman, David Owen, Ruth Rubio-Marin, Bas Schotel, Andrei Stavila, Anna Triandafilidou, Inès Valdez, and Jonathan Zaragoza. I want to thank all of them and to communicate my particular gratitude to Iseult, Kieran, David, and Bas who traveled a long way for the event (though I recognize that coming to Florence in May is not quite as burdensome as, say, traveling to Toronto in January). This workshop came late in the game, but as I worked on revisions to the manuscript throughout the summer and fall, I had the comments of the participants in mind.

In the spring of 2008, Melissa Williams organized a one-day manuscript workshop for me at the Centre for Ethics at the University of Toronto. Will Kymlicka came from Queen's to offer an overall reaction to the manuscript and several colleagues from political science, law, and philosophy provided responses to individual chapters. My thanks to Simone Chambers, David Dyzenhaus, Mohammad Fadel, Randall Hansen, Audrey Macklin, Jenny Nedelsky, and Phil Triadafilopoulos and especially to Melissa and Will for devoting so much time and thought to the discussion of my work. The book is much better as a result.

Eamonn Callan and David Miller conducted a postdoc institute at Stanford in late June 2008 and generously invited me to spend a day with the fellows discussing my manuscript. Unfortunately, I no longer have a list of the participants, though I do remember that Helder de Schutter and Kieran Oberman served as the formal commentators. It was a stimulating session.

In the fall of 2006, Andrew Altman and Andrew I. Cohen of the Jean Beer Blumenfeld Center for Ethics at Georgia State University organized a manuscript workshop that included both of them, their Georgia State colleagues A. J. Cohen, William Edmundson, Christie Hartley, Peter Lindsay (a former student of mine), and George Rainbolt, and three colleagues from elsewhere: Don Moon from Wesleyan, Jeff Spinner-Halev from the University of North Carolina at Chapel Hill, and Kit Wellman from Washington University in St. Louis. Again, I am grateful to all of the participants for their willingness to engage so thoughtfully with my work, and especially to Don, Jeff, and Kit for traveling such a distance to do so. This workshop really helped me to see what was working in the manuscript and what needed to be changed. Among other things, when I told the people at the workshop that I was trying to reach a wider audience than just specialists in the field, Jeff said, "Tell more stories." Again, that is advice that has stuck with me through the subsequent revisions and that I've tried to follow. I'm sure that the participants in this workshop thought (as did I) that the book would be out soon after. Better late than never.

I no longer have the list of the people involved in the 1993 workshop that Philippe van Parijs organized at Louvain-la-Neuve, but I do remember that this was the occasion on which I first met Veit Bader with whom I have been in conversation about these issues ever since. That alone made the trip worthwhile.

In addition to these formal workshops, I have presented papers containing some version of the arguments in this book at dozens of conferences and I have given talks on the topic at Boston University, Cornell University, Harvard University, Institut d'Études Politiques (Paris), Institute for Advanced Studies (Vienna), London School of Economics, Massachusetts Institute of Technology, McGill University, New School for Social Research, New York University, Northwestern University, Oxford University, Queen's University (Kingston), Princeton University, Rutgers University, Stanford University, Université de Montreal, University of Alberta, University of Amsterdam, University of California at Berkeley, University of California at Davis, University of California at Irvine, University of California at Los Angeles, University of California at San Diego, University of Chicago, University of Nijmegen (Netherlands), University of North Carolina at Chapel Hill, University of North Carolina at Charlotte, University of Pennsylvania, University of Texas at San Antonio, Wilfred Laurier University, Yale University, and York University (Toronto). I benefited from the exchanges on all these occasions.

I want to express my appreciation to the colleagues and friends who offered comments at these conferences and talks or in other contexts, often on more than one occasion. I won't repeat the names of any of those whom I thanked previously, although many of them were participants in one or more of these other exchanges as well. Merely mentioning names on a list cannot capture my deep debt to some of those who follow. It would be harder, however, to draw distinctions. So, my sincere thanks to: Arash Abizadeh, Yasmeen Abu-Laban, Howard Adelman, Alex Aleinikoff, Bridget Anderson, Ed Andrew, Ryan Balot, Sot Barber, the late Brian Barry, Christian Barry, Ronnie Beiner, Chuck Beitz, Daniel Bell, Seyla Benhabib, Nancy Bertoldi, Michael Blake, Jon Blazer, Erik Bleich, Linda Bosniak, Wendy Brown, Christina Boswell, Rogers Brubaker, Kathy Bullock, Wibren van der Burg, Martin Chamorro, Phil Cole, Cathryn Costello, Frank Cunningham, Michael Doyle, the late Ronald Dworkin, John Ejobowah, Jean Bethke Elshtain, Walter Feinberg, Sarah Fine, Don Forbes, Chaim Gans, Matt Gibney, Bob Goodin, Amy Gutmann, James Hampshire, Phillip Harvey, Nicole Hassoun, Burke Hendrix, Peter Higgins, Jennifer Hochschild, Nils Holtug, Bonnie Honig, Adam Hosein, Henk van Houtum, the late Richard Iton, John Isbister, Christian Joppke, Courtney Jung, Gerald Kernerman, Rebecca Kingston, Peggy Kohn, Nick Kompridis, Christine Korsgaard, Chandran Kukathas, Sune Laegaard, Gara LaMarche, Steve Legomsky, Patti Lenard, Jacob Levy, Kasper Lippert-Rasmussen, Matt Lister, Mary Liston, Willem Maas, Steve Macedo, David Martin, Phil Martin, Andy Mason, Doug Massey, Jon Medow, Peter Meilaender, Chuck Miller, Marit Hovdal Moan, Tariq Modood, Margaret Moore, Thomas Nagel, Gerald Neuman, Mae Ngai, Shmulik Nili, Carla Norrlof, Cliff Orwin, Bhikhu Parekh, Serena Parekh, Alan Patten, Shirley Pendlebury, Nahshon Perez, Anne Phillips, Roland Pierik, Thomas Pogge, Sean Rehaag, Mathias Risse, Marc Rosenblum, Nancy Rosenblum, Martin Ruhs, Sam Scheffler, Peter Schuck, Liza Schuster, Ayelet Shachar, Molly Shanley, Stephanie Silverman, Abe Singer, Rogers Smith, Sarah Song, Christine Straehle, Roberto Suro, Carol Swain, Dennis Thompson, Ronald Tinnevelt, Guido Tintori, Varun Uberoi, Diego von Vacano, Jeremy Waldron, Michael Walzer, Patrick Weil, the late Myron Weiner, Daniel Weinstock, James Woodward, the late Iris Marion Young, Lea Ypi, Ricard Zapata, Giovanna Zincone, and Simone Zurbuchen. I know that there are other people who belong on this list but whom I have not included due to the flaws in my record-keeping and my memory. My apologies to them. I also want to assure those whose names do appear on the list that their presence here does not make them responsible for anything in the text. Indeed, some are here precisely because they have explained why they disagree with me. Over the years, I have also subjected a number of classes of students at the University of Toronto to parts of this project, and I appreciate both their feedback and their forbearance.

I have had the benefit of several excellent research assistants. My thanks to Jon Blazer, Catherine Frost, Margaret Haderer, Chelsea Bin Han, Petr Kafka, Mary Liston, Jon Medow, Iffat Sajjad, Caitlin Tom, Catherine Tomas, and Abe Singer. I have a back problem that might have been incapacitating without the help of Jerry Cott, Judith Neilly, and Susan Sinclair. Marcia Weiner and Nancy Ross helped with other, less tangible problems.

The Social Sciences and Humanities Research Council of Canada and the Department of Political Science at the University of Toronto provided financial support that enabled me to hire those research assistants and go to many of the conferences among other things. Writing this book would have been even harder without this assistance.

As I explained at the outset, I have been working on this project for many years. Everything in the book was rewritten to some extent and large chunks of it are entirely new, but parts of the book have appeared previously in print in many different forms. Sometimes I have used just a few paragraphs from an earlier article, sometimes much more. I wish to thank the various publishers for permission to use the following previously published materials here. "Immigration and Citizenship" in Francisco Gonzalez, ed., *Values and Ethics for the 21st Century* (Madrid: BBVA 2012), 121–164. "The Case for Amnesty," *Boston Review* 34 (May, June 2009): 7–10, 24. Slightly revised version published as *Immigrants and the Right to Stay* (Cambridge, MA: MIT Press, 2010). "Fear vs. Fairness: Migration, Citizenship and the Transformation of Political Community," in Kasper Lippert-Rasmussen, Nils Holtug, and Sune Lægaard, eds., *Nationalism and Multiculturalism in a World of Immigration* (Houndmills, UK: Palgrave Macmillan, 2009), 174–193. "The Rights of Irregular Migrants," *Ethics & International Affairs* 22 (2) (Summer 2008): 163–186. "Live-In Domestics, Seasonal Workers, and Others Hard to Locate on the Map of Democracy," *Journal of Political Philosophy* 16 (4) (2008): 419–445. "Immigration, Democracy, and Citizenship," in Oliver Schmidtke and Saime Ozcurumez, eds., *Of States, Rights, and Social Closure: Governing Migration and Citizenship* (New York: Palgrave Macmillan, 2008), 17–36. "Wer gehört dazu? Migration und die Rekonzeptualisierung der Staatsbürgerschaft," in Simone Zurbuchen, ed., *Bürgerschaft und Migration: Einwanderung und Einbürgerung aus ethisch-politischer Perspektive* (Münster: LIT, 2007), 25–51. "Fear vs. Fairness: Migration, Citizenship and the Transformation of Political Community," *Philosophy of Education*, 2006: 36–48. "On Belonging: What We Owe People Who Stay," *Boston Review* 30 (3–4) (Summer 2005): 16–19. "The Integration of Immigrants," *Journal of Moral Philosophy* 2 (1) (April 2005): 29–46. "La integración de los inmigrantes" in Gemma Aubarell and Ricard Zapata, eds., *Inmigración y procesos de cambio: Europa y el Mediterráneo en el contexto global* (Barcelona: Icaria- Institut Europeu de la Mediterrània, 2004) , 393–420. "Who Should Get In? The Ethics of Immigration Admissions," *Ethics & International Affairs* 17 (1) (Spring 2003): 95–110. "Immigación y justicia: A quien dejamos pasar?" *Isegoria* 26 (June 2002): 5–27. "Citizenship and Civil Society: What Rights for Residents?" in Randall Hansen and Patrick Weil, eds., *Dual Nationality, Social Rights and Federal Citizenship in the US and Europe: The Reinvention of Citizenship* (Oxford: Berghahn Books, 2002), 100–118. "Cosmopolitanism, Nationalism, and Immigration: False Dichotomies and Shifting Presuppositions," in Ronald Beiner and Wayne Norman, eds., *Canadian Political Philosophy: Contemporary Reflections* (Toronto: Oxford University Press, 2001), 17–35. "Open Borders and Liberal Limits: A Response to Isbister," *International Migration Review* 34 (2) (Summer 2000): 636–643. "Per a una ètica de la immigració: Els drets dels residents," *Idees: Revista de temes contemporanis* 8 (October/December 2000): 90–102. "Reconsidering Open Borders," *International Migration Review* 33 (4) (Winter 1999): 1082–1097. "Why Naturalization Should Be Easy: A Response to Noah Pickus," in Noah Pickus, ed., *Immigration and Citizenship in the 21st Century* (Totowa, NJ: Rowman and Littlefield, 1998), 141–146. "The Philosopher and the Policymaker: Two Perspectives on the Ethics of Immigration with Special Attention to the Problem of Restricting Asylum," in Kay Hailbronner, David Martin, and Hiroshi Motomura, eds., *Immigration Admissions: The Search for Workable Policies in Germany and the United States* (Oxford: Berghahn Books, 1997), 3–51. "Realistic and Idealistic Approaches to the Ethics of Immigration," *International Migration Review* 30 (1) (Spring 1996): 156–170. "The Rights of Immigrants," in Judith Baker, ed., *Group Rights* (Toronto: University of Toronto Press, 1994), 142–163. "Migration and Morality: A Liberal Egalitarian Perspective," in Brian Barry and Robert Goodin, eds., *Free Movement* (London: Harvester-Wheatsheaf, 1992), 25–47. "Refugees and the Limits of Obligation," *Public Affairs Quarterly* 6 (1) (January 1992): 31–44. "Membership and Morality: Admission to Citizenship in Liberal Democratic States," in William Rogers Brubaker, ed., *Immigration and the Politics of Citizenship in Europe and North America* (Lanham, MD: German Marshall Fund and University Press of America, 1989), 31–49. "Aliens and Citizens: The Case for Open Borders," *Review of Politics* 49 (2) (Spring 1987): 251–273.

Parts of two of the chapters will appear more or less simultaneously in other publications. Part of chapter 2 will appear as "In Defense of Birthright Citizenship," in Sarah Fine and Lea Ypi, eds., *Migration in Political Theory: The Ethics of Movement and Membership* (Oxford: Oxford University Press, forthcoming) and part of chapter 4 will appear as "Beyond Rules and Rights: Multiculturalism and the Inclusion of Immigrants" in Tariq Modood and Varun Uberoi, eds., *Multiculturalism Reconsidered* (Cambridge: Cambridge University Press, forthcoming).

The Ethics of Immigration

Introduction

Mapping the Ethics of Immigration

Miguel Sanchez could not earn enough to pay the bills in his hometown. He tried for several years to obtain a visa to come to the United States and was rejected every time. In 2000 he entered on foot with the help of a smuggler. He made his way to Chicago where he had relatives and friends and started working in construction, sending money to his father. Sanchez worked weekends at Dunkin Donuts and went to school in the evening to learn English. In 2002 he met an American-born US citizen who lived in his neighborhood. They married in 2003, and now have a 6-year-old son.

Sanchez, his wife, and son live under constant fear of his deportation. Driving to the funeral of a relative in another city causes high stress: a traffic stop or an accident can lead to Sanchez's removal from the country. Nor can the family travel by plane. Their son has never met his grandparents in Mexico. Meanwhile, they have an ordinary life in the neighborhood: they own a home and pay taxes; their child attends school, and they have become friends with other parents. Current US law provides Sanchez and his family no feasible path to regularize his status.

Miguel Sanchez's story is true, but for a few identifying details. And there are millions of similar stories. Some eleven million irregular migrants—noncitizens living within the territory without official authorization—now live in the United States.

How should the United States respond to irregular migrants like Sanchez? Should it expel as many of these migrants as it can? Should it accept such migrants as members of the community, at least if they have been present for an extended period, and grant them legal authorization to stay? Should it pursue some third alternative, with a path to permanent residence mixed with penalties and restrictions?

Now consider Faiza Silmi a Moroccan woman who married a French citizen of Moroccan descent and moved to France with him where they had four children, all of whom are French citizens. She speaks French and has lived in France for several years. Silmi is a devout Muslim. Out of religious conviction, she wears a niqab, the garment that covers the entire body except for the eyes. She applied for French citizenship but was denied on grounds of "insufficient assimilation" to France. When she appealed, the ruling was upheld by the highest court with authority over this issue. It stated that her application was denied because "She has adopted a radical practice of her religion, incompatible with essential values of the French community, particularly the principle of equality of the sexes."[1]

What should we think of the decision to deny citizenship to Faiza Silmi? Was it a morally objectionable refusal to grant formal citizenship to someone who deserves it? Was it a legitimate choice by a democratic state to restrict citizenship to those whom public officials judge to be committed to the state's fundamental values?

The questions I have asked about Sanchez and Silmi are moral questions. They are just a few of the ethical issues raised by immigration.[2] Everywhere in Europe and North America we find heated debates about what states should do to regulate entry and about how those who have arrived should be treated. In this book I try to take a step back from the political passions and practical policy concerns that usually animate these debates in order to reflect upon the deeper moral issues that they entail. I want to show that debates about immigration raise ethical questions, that many of these ethical questions are interconnected, and that a commitment to democratic principles greatly constrains the kinds of answers we can offer to these questions.

I use the term "democratic principles" in a very general sense to refer to the broad moral commitments that underlie and justify contemporary political institutions and policies throughout North America and Europe—things like the ideas that all human beings are of equal moral worth, that disagreements should normally be resolved through the principle of majority rule, that we have a duty to respect the rights and freedoms of individuals, that legitimate government depends upon the consent of the governed, that all citizens should be equal under the law, that coercion should only be exercised in accordance with the rule of law, that people should not be subject to discrimination on the basis of characteristics like race, religion, or gender, that we should respect norms like fairness and reciprocity in our policies, and so on. Others might use the terms "liberal" or "liberal democratic" or "republican" to characterize the principles and ideas for which I use the term "democratic." While these alternative terms sometimes mark off important lines of debate, those disagreements play no role in this book. Nothing substantive hinges on my choice of the term "democratic" rather than one of the others. These democratic principles can be interpreted in many different ways, and they can even conflict with one another. Nevertheless, on a wide range of topics there is no serious disagreement among those who think of themselves as democrats. For example, (almost) no democrat today thinks that it is morally acceptable to force someone to convert from one religion to another or to discriminate on the basis of race.

I want to use that broad moral consensus to explore some of the ethical questions raised by immigration. I think of my enterprise as providing a map of the ethics of immigration with this democratic normative framework as my moral compass. I identify some important moral questions that immigration raises from a democratic perspective, I show how the key questions are related to one another, and I provide some directions for navigating the terrain.

My focus is on questions of principle, but I should caution that these are not the only sort of questions one can ask about what we ought to do. In thinking about what to do in a particular situation, we have to consider questions of priority and questions of political feasibility, among other factors. One cannot always move directly from principles to a plan of action.

Every book is an imaginary conversation between an author and his or her readers. It is a one-sided conversation, of course, because the author gets to do all the talking. Still, to communicate effectively, one has to have some sense of who is listening—what they know and what needs to be explained, what assumptions they will bring and what questions they will want to ask, and so on.

I write with multiple audiences in view. First, I am addressing ordinary men and women in North America and Europe who think of themselves as people who believe in democracy and individual rights and who want to understand the challenges posed by immigration into their societies.[3] Some of these readers may find my way of talking unsettling. I am a political philosopher and I speak about things like morality, ethics, and democratic principles. I know from experience that language like this sometimes makes people uncomfortable. Some think that talk about ethics is suited only for the classroom (or perhaps only for the pulpit). Some see moral claims either as authoritative pronouncements designed to command the listener's adherence or as subjective preferences not really open to reasoned evaluation. Doubtless there are versions of political philosophy that fit these descriptions, but I hope that my readers will experience this book differently. The kind of political philosophy that I undertake in this book is intended to invite reasoned reflection, discussion, and contestation.

In everyday political conversations, we all talk about what is fair and unfair, right and wrong, good and bad, just and unjust in our policies and in our public life, even if we do not always use those precise words. The questions that I ask in this book grow out of our ordinary conversations with one another about immigration. I give reasons for my answers to these questions, and I try to show that my reasons are connected to norms and standards that most people in contemporary democratic societies accept, at least in principle. But I do not claim any special authority for my views.

I know that I will not persuade every reader to accept everything I claim. Indeed, I would be surprised if anyone agreed with all of my arguments. I do hope, however, to persuade many readers that my account helps them to think more clearly about the questions raised by immigration. That is what matters most to me.

I do not pretend that I am neutral in my basic stance on immigration. I write from a particular point of view. I see it as our responsibility to include those immigrants who have already arrived and to be open to more. Broadly speaking, in my view, immigrants belong, and democratic states and populations ought to adjust their policies and self-understandings to make that belonging more of a social reality. Nevertheless, I am trying to contribute to an ongoing conversation, not to have the last word. To that end, I have tried my best to articulate as many questions, objections, and concerns as I could, and I have tried not to sweep issues under the rug even when I knew that my own understanding of these issues was not fully satisfactory. This book is not a polemic, and persuasion is not its only goal. I hope that even readers who disagree with my conclusions will find that this book helps them to reflect more deeply about the ethics of immigration.

In addition to the general audience, I have a range of specific academic audiences in mind. First, I want the book to appeal to all those in the fields of sociology, law, geography, political science, international studies, and public policy who study immigration. Most of these scholars use empirical rather than normative approaches, and most will not be deeply familiar with the existing philosophical literature on the topic. That is one further reason why I have tried to write in an accessible way and to focus on the central issues. Second, I aspire to reach empirical scholars who have not turned their minds to immigration at all. With respect to my own discipline of political science, I hope that the book will help scholars in comparative politics, international relations, and public policy with no special interest in immigration to see why normative and empirical inquiries can be complementary and mutually beneficial (and also to see why they should care about immigration). Third, I want to persuade scholars already engaged in normative inquiries to pay more attention to immigration. I hope to show those who study human rights that immigration raises a range of important human rights questions and that thinking about immigration can challenge some of the familiar categories that people use in talking about human rights. For those who study the ethics of public policy, my goal is to generate discussions about the challenges of exploring tensions between what is feasible and what is right. I hope that my fellow political theorists will find that this book leads them to re-examine some of the ways in which they talk about citizenship and democracy and also that they will see some virtue in the theoretical approach that I employ. Finally, and most obviously, I am also writing for fellow specialists in the ethics of immigration. I hope they will find that the book identifies the main issues in our field and discusses them fruitfully.

Having multiple audiences in view inevitably creates certain tensions for a writer, because what is needed for one audience may be different from what is needed for another. In this case, I think that the tensions are manageable. General readers should be able to understand the book, but I have not left out any important substantive arguments for the sake of making the text more accessible. A few of the later chapters may be somewhat harder going for non-theorists, but I hope that by then these readers will have been seduced by the pleasures of political philosophy and so will be willing to bear a bit of pain for the sake of those pleasures.

One feature of my audience that may puzzle some is that it includes both Europeans and North Americans. When it comes to immigration, Americans tend to think only of their own problems and to see those as unique, while Europeans tend to assume that the problems posed by immigration for them are utterly different from those faced in North America. But the story of Miguel Sanchez could just as easily be a story of a migrant from some country in Africa to some country in Europe, and debates about the inclusion of Muslim immigrants like Faiza Silmi make headlines in North America as well as in Europe. We will all gain if we are more open to conversations across borders, whatever we do about letting people cross them. I hope to show that for the most important issues in immigration, both the problems and the solutions travel. There are moral guidelines and moral constraints that greatly limit the options open to any state or any population committed to democratic principles.

This claim obviously presupposes that there is some sort of agreement about fundamental democratic principles. Many will want to deny that any such shared understanding exists. It is true that there is no fully worked out theoretical account of democracy that everyone accepts. I think that it is possible, however, to show that any plausible version of basic democratic ideas like equality and freedom has concrete and significant implications for immigration. In many areas, democratic states already recognize these implications in their practices. Indeed, practice sometimes even runs ahead of theory so that in some cases we have found ways of treating immigrants fairly without having managed to articulate fully to ourselves why this way of doing things is right. One of the goals of this book is to bring these sorts of implicit understandings to the surface and to connect them consciously and explicitly to basic principles. I contend in this book that there is already a wide area of agreement about immigration among democratic states in Europe and North America, an agreement that is largely, if imperfectly, reflected in policy and practice. We tend not to notice this agreement because we focus on what is disputed. Nevertheless, as we shall see, on many key issues, there is no serious debate. One part of my task then is just to articulate what everyone already thinks and to show what that consensus entails.

I do not mean to suggest, however, that democratic states always live up to their own principles or that there is no disagreement about what those principles require. I devote much of the book to challenging existing practices and to arguing that democratic states ought to act differently in order to be true to their most basic commitments. The success of this sort of critical enterprise will depend on whether I can persuade readers that I am appealing to norms and principles that they themselves actually accept and that my way of resolving conflicts and inconsistencies is more faithful to their basic commitments than any alternative account.

The Challenge of Sovereignty and Democratic Self-Determination

There is one challenge that would stop this whole project in its tracks if I could not meet it, namely the claim that immigration and citizenship are not fit topics for moral discussion. Some people resist the idea of using words like "right" and "wrong" or "just" and "unjust" in talking about these matters. These are political issues, not moral ones, they say.[4] One way to elaborate this position is to say that the use of moral language in discussing immigration and citizenship is incompatible with the norm of state sovereignty. On this view, states must be free to construct their own immigration and citizenship policies, free from external interference. Another version of the critique emphasizes the ideal of democratic self-determination. From this perspective, questions about immigration and citizenship should be left to self-governing peoples to answer for themselves. Ultimately, it must be up to the American people to say who may become an American, the Swiss who may become Swiss, and the French who may become French, even if that works out badly for someone like Silmi.

This sort of attempt to shield immigration and citizenship policies from moral scrutiny is misguided. It confuses the question of who ought to have the authority to determine a policy with the question of whether a given policy is morally acceptable. One can think that someone has the moral right to make a decision and still think that the decision itself is morally wrong. That applies just as much to a collective agent like a democratic state as it does to individuals.

Consider some specific examples relating to immigration and citizenship. In the late nineteenth century, the United States passed the Chinese Exclusion Act, which prohibited people from China from immigrating to the United States and stipulated that those Chinese immigrants who were already legally present could not become American citizens. Until the 1960s, Canada's immigration laws discriminated against people from outside Europe. In the 1930s, several European states stripped large numbers of people of their citizenship, often (though not always) people who had acquired citizenship through naturalization. Many were left stateless. The infamous Nuremberg Laws depriving German Jews of their citizenship were the most prominent example of this phenomenon. Until late in the twentieth century, many liberal democratic states permitted fathers, but not mothers, to pass on their nationality to their children. In all these cases, the policies were enacted by a sovereign state and the policies enjoyed widespread popular support.

Should we say that respect for state sovereignty or democratic self-determination prevents us from saying that these laws and policies were unjust? I treat this as a rhetorical question. There is no plausible account of democratic principles today that can reconcile them with the Chinese Exclusion Act and the Nuremberg Laws. But if it is appropriate to describe these laws as unjust, then we cannot say that it is always inappropriate to use moral language about immigration and citizenship policies. State sovereignty and democratic self-determination are morally constrained. The decisions of a sovereign state may be morally wrong even if the state is morally entitled to make those decisions. The actions of a democratic community may be unjust even if the community has not violated any democratic procedures.

The general point that I am making here should be familiar from contemporary discussions of human rights. Every claim about human rights is subject to the objection that it sets moral limits to state sovereignty and democratic self-determination. But the whole point of human rights talk is to assert that some exercises of state power are morally wrong. That does not necessarily mean that we should create new institutions or reconfigure political authority (although that may sometimes be appropriate). We can think that states are morally obliged to behave in certain ways without thinking that there should be an international authority to make them do so. For example, moral criticism of the Chinese Exclusion Act does not imply that some other state should have intervened to change American policy. My critical approach to immigration and citizenship in this book does not entail the view that we should try to create some international body to assess and regulate immigration and citizenship policies.

The claim that something is a human right or a moral obligation says nothing about how that right or obligation is to be enforced. In fact, in the world today where human rights have come to play an important role, most human rights claims are enforced by states against themselves. That is, states themselves are expected to (and often do) limit their own actions and policies in accordance with the human rights norms that they recognize and respect. The very idea of constitutional democracy is built upon the notion of self-limiting government, that is, that states have the capacity to restrict the exercise of their power in accordance with their norms and values. And that is the framework within which I am pursuing the discussion of immigration and citizenship in this book.

Ultimately, there is no way to escape the terrain of moral argument in discussing immigration and citizenship, at least so long as we approach the issue from the perspective of democratic principles. Indeed, to say that states are morally free to adopt whatever policies they want with respect to citizenship is itself a moral argument, a claim about what justice permits. It is a claim that must be supported with normative arguments.

I don't want to overstate my position. I am saying that immigration and citizenship are appropriate topics for ethical reflection and that immigration and citizenship policies may sometimes be unjust. This is not the same as saying that moral principles can settle all the details of immigration and citizenship policy.

There is something to the claim that freedom from external criticism is an important component of state autonomy and democratic self-determination. As John Stuart Mill famously insisted, individual liberty depends not just on a person having a legal right to do what she wants but also on the recognition by others that her choices are her own to make, that they are not anyone else's business. That is true of collective freedom as well. The familiar international norm that one state should not criticize the domestic policies of another reflects this view that what a state does within its own borders is normally no other state's business. When the state is governed democratically, the norm is even stronger. So, it may be plausible to argue, from a moral perspective, that states should enjoy wide latitude in setting their immigration and citizenship policies. But no one thinks this sort of freedom is unlimited.

The example of human rights discourse may again be helpful in clarifying this issue. Human rights set minimum standards that states are morally obliged to respect but there may be vastly different laws and policies that are compatible with these minimum standards. In this book I am primarily concerned with the minimum standards that flow from democratic principles. These will constrain immigration and citizenship policies but they will not determine all of their content. Many issues will remain which states are morally free to resolve on the basis of their own self-understandings and interests.

Some Brief Comments on Methods

Nothing is more boring to non-specialists than discussions of methods, but I have to say two things here so as to try to avoid misunderstandings. First, I know from previous reactions to my work that some people will assume that when I make claims about democratic principles I must be drawing, at least implicitly, on some general theory of democracy, and they will want to know what that theory is. That is not my approach, however. There are plenty of well worked out theories of democracy, from John Stuart Mill in the nineteenth century to John Rawls and Jürgen Habermas in the twentieth, with lots of other candidates as well. Each of these theories has its virtues and limitations, well explored through extensive critical discussion. I do not want to offer an account of the ethics of immigration that depends on any one of these theories, and even less one that depends on some democratic theory of my own which would undoubtedly be more flawed than the ones already out there. Instead, I want to base my analysis on principles and ideas that all of these democratic theorists would accept, and for the same reasons that non-theorists accept these principles and ideas, namely that they fit so closely with our ordinary understanding of democracy. John Rawls has argued that the political principles that govern liberal democratic societies can find justifications in many different moral views. He calls this an overlapping consensus.[5] One way to describe the approach in this book is to say that it relies upon an overlapping consensus among different political theorists and among ordinary people from different democratic societies about the moral principles that I appeal to in my arguments. Rather than try to give a general list of such principles and ideas in advance, I try to identify them when they are needed to address some particular question or problem. Then I connect the principle to some practice that I wish to defend or criticize.

You might call my approach "political theory from the ground up." The idea is to start with actual problems and questions such as these: Under what conditions should immigrants be able to become citizens? What legal rights should residents have? What can a receiving state legitimately ask (or demand) of immigrants with respect to cultural adaptation? In exploring such questions, I try to say something about our practices and our principles and how they narrow the range of morally acceptable answers to these questions. For example, I will appeal to the principle of religious freedom to argue that, whatever sort of cultural adaptation we may ask of immigrants, it cannot include conversion to a new religion. Readers may or may not accept any particular claim I make about what democratic principles are and what they imply. When it comes to something like the principle that no one should be forced to convert to a new religion, I can be quite confident that most of my readers will accept that principle. That's an easy case. But other claims about principles or about the implications of principles are more likely to be contested. My task as an author is to anticipate what claims are likely to be accepted and what ones are likely to be challenged. Then I have to provide further supporting arguments for the claims that are likely to be challenged. But at no point will I appeal to some comprehensive general theory of democracy. Instead, I will simply try to address what I take to be the most plausible objections to the position I am trying to defend by appealing to principles and ideas that I think those making the objections will accept.

Of course, I have to keep an eye out to see how well later arguments fit with earlier ones. If the arguments fit together well, then the theoretical contribution of the book will come from the overall picture of the ethics of immigration that emerges from the various particular arguments. This overall picture won't be a full democratic theory and it won't depend on any particular theoretical account of democracy. It will, however, be a general account of how democrats should think about immigration. As such, it will give us reasons to challenge and modify some of the existing democratic theories and it will set limits to the plausibility of any more comprehensive account.

The second methodological point is that there is a big difference between the way I frame the inquiry in the first ten chapters and the way I frame it in the last few. In the first ten chapters I presuppose (1) the contemporary international order which divides the world into independent states with vast differences of freedom, security, and economic opportunity among them and (2) the conventional moral view on immigration, i.e., that despite these vast differences between states, each state is morally entitled to exercise considerable discretionary control over the admission of immigrants.

I take the existing international order as a given because that order is deeply entrenched and it is the context within which moral questions about immigration and citizenship first arise for us. I accept the conventional moral view on immigration because it is, as the name implies, widely held, and I want to explore what normative conclusions we can reach about immigration and citizenship within the constraints that this view imposes. In the last few chapters of the book, however, I step back from these presuppositions. I challenge the conventional normative view on immigration. I argue that discretionary control over immigration is incompatible with fundamental democratic principles and that justice requires open borders. I then consider what that challenge implies about how the world ought to be organized and also how our understanding of the ethics of immigration might be affected if the world were organized in a different, more egalitarian way.

Many people are puzzled by this way of proceeding. Those who agree with my open borders argument often object that I am conceding too much to the power of the status quo by adopting the conventional view (i.e., that states are entitled to control borders) in the first several chapters. Those who disagree with my open borders argument (the larger group, by far) often object that my initial assumption about the legitimacy of immigration control is some sort of Trojan Horse and that all of the claims in the earlier chapters ultimately rest upon my open borders argument. Neither of these views is correct.

Given that I do not think that states really have a fundamental moral right to control immigration, why assume it for so much of the book? One obvious answer is pragmatic. Most people do think that states are morally entitled to control their borders, and my arguments to the contrary are unlikely to convince them. The conventional moral view is deeply entrenched. So, if I am to have any hope of persuading people of the merits of my views on the other issues that I discuss, such as access to citizenship, the rights of temporary workers, and so on, I must not tie those arguments to the case for open borders. Adopting the conventional view as a presupposition permits me to explore the nature and extent of the limits justice imposes on immigration policies within a more "realistic" framework.[6]

My approach is not merely pragmatic, however. It also reflects a principled commitment to a certain kind of dialogue. The idea of adopting as presuppositions moral views that are widely shared by others has deep roots in the idea of democratic deliberation as a practice in which people who disagree about fundamental matters of principle nevertheless come together to try to find a common ground that is based not only on shared interests but also on a shared view of what is right. We adopt presuppositions that we do not fully accept all the time in ordinary life in conversations with friends and colleagues. We could talk about where we might go for dinner, even if we disagree about whether or not to go out. You may talk about the best way to implement a departmental policy, even though you disagree with the policy, because you know that most of your colleagues support it and aren't likely to change their minds. Adopting the presupposition of the state's right to control immigration is a way of looking at the issue from the perspective of someone who holds that view, as many—indeed most—of our fellow citizens do.

I know from previous reactions to my work that some will see the open borders question as *the* normative question about immigration, the bottom line issue, the only one that really matters, at least philosophically. Readers may suppose that this is the fundamental question on which all the other arguments about immigration ultimately depend. By comparison, the earlier chapters may seem more practical in orientation. Some may think that it is only when we remove the conventional presupposition that we really engage in serious philosophical work.

I understand that reaction. The open borders issue is the one that has attracted the most attention from other philosophers, and it is the one that I discuss at greatest length myself (partly because it has attracted so much attention from others). The claims that I make about open borders are the most controversial ones in the book. Moreover, the last few chapters sound and feel more like a typical philosophical discussion than the earlier ones. They are more abstract, general, and intellectually demanding.

Despite all that, or perhaps because of it, I want to insist that the first ten chapters of the book are just as philosophical as the last ones. They are simply philosophy in a slightly different style. The dialectical approach that I take in these earlier chapters has a respectable philosophical pedigree that stretches back to Socrates. The fact that an argument is more radical or more controversial does not make it more philosophical. Part I is fully as concerned with how we should understand justice, freedom, and political community as Part II. I start from practical problems in the earlier chapters but the whole point is to show that the practical problems raise questions of philosophical principle.

It is also important to remember that removing the presupposition of the conventional view in the last few chapters does not make those chapters free of all presuppositions. For example, I still presuppose a commitment to democratic principles, a presupposition that could be challenged from a number of different perspectives. As I explain more fully in the appendix, it is an illusion that one can conduct an inquiry without presuppositions. The challenge is to become as conscious as possible of the presuppositions used in one's own inquiry and open to alternative choices of presuppositions in other inquiries.

I have reasons beyond a desire for methodological clarity to challenge the idea that the key philosophical issues do not emerge until the last few chapters of the book. I see the philosophical arguments about membership and citizenship that I advance in the first part of the book, as almost entirely independent from the arguments about free movement in those later chapters. In support of this claim, I note that many of those who think that the state has the right to control immigration have an understanding of democracy and citizenship that is similar to mine in most other respects. We often agree about the implications of democratic values for immigrants who are already present, even if we disagree about the principles that should govern admissions. For example, my arguments about naturalization in chapter 3 were originally inspired by Michael Walzer's discussion of this issue in *Spheres of Justice*, even though Walzer is one of the most famous defenders of the state's right to control admissions. I know that the open borders argument is controversial and that many readers will not be persuaded by it. The willingness of those readers to accept my earlier arguments about membership and citizenship may therefore depend upon whether or not they see the earlier arguments as distinct from, or inextricably intertwined with, the later ones. I am claiming that the different parts of the book rest on compatible but separable philosophical arguments (though, of course, critics are free to challenge this claim).

In chapter 13, I will review the discussion of the first ten chapters in the light of the arguments for open borders that I develop in chapters 11 and 12. I will show that most of the arguments about access to citizenship, social inclusion, and the rights of noncitizens that I advanced in the first part of the book would still be relevant and valid if the open borders argument were accepted. This will confirm my claim that the earlier arguments do not ultimately rest upon some problematic concession to the status quo. That is another reason why it makes sense to conduct the earlier analysis within the framework of the conventional view. Thus treating the state's right to control entry as a background assumption in the first part of the book contributes to philosophical analysis and democratic deliberation without misleading anyone about my overall views which include the later critique of this assumption.

In the Appendix I have a fuller discussion of the methodological issues raised by this book and the ways in which I have tried to address them, but this is likely to be of interest only to specialists in the field. As the old saying goes, the proof of the pudding is in the eating. The best justification for my approach will be that readers find my substantive discussion helpful in thinking about immigration. Nevertheless, you are welcome to start with the Appendix if you prefer not to taste anything before seeing how it was made (or even if you are just someone who likes to eat dessert first).

Outline

The book is divided into two main parts. In the first part (chapters 2 through 8), I look at questions about how immigrants who have arrived should be treated by the states where they live; in the second (chapters 9 through 13), I look at questions about who should be admitted. There is much less disagreement about the former than about the latter. That is one reason why I start with questions about how to treat those already present rather than with questions about admissions.

Chapters 2 and 3 together address the question of access to citizenship, the central marker of formal membership in a modern political community. I argue that democratic legitimacy requires the inclusion within the citizenry of all those who live in the state on an ongoing basis.

Chapter 2 explores the moral logic underlying birthright citizenship. I first identify the rationale for granting citizenship at birth to the children of citizens. I then argue that the same rationale explains why the children born to settled immigrants should also receive citizenship at birth. In a section on theory and practice, I consider the relationship between this normative analysis and contemporary rules governing birthright citizenship in democratic states. In the final section, I explain why a desire to avoid dual citizenship provides no justification for refusing to grant birthright citizenship to the children of immigrants.

Chapter 3 addresses the question of naturalization for immigrants and for descendants of immigrants who do not acquire citizenship at birth. I argue that the children who arrive as immigrants but are raised in the society from a young age should get citizenship automatically by the age of majority without passing any tests or meeting any other requirements. I contend that immigrants who arrive as adults should have the option of acquiring citizenship after some years of residence, as a matter of right. If conditions for naturalization are imposed, they should include no more than the satisfaction of a few modest, objective requirements regarding language and knowledge of the country's history and institutions, but I argue that ideally even these conditions would not be required.

In chapter 4 I explain why a commitment to equal citizenship requires the full inclusion of immigrants in ways that go beyond the granting of equal legal rights. I argue that full inclusion requires widespread acceptance of a democratic ethos, including a commitment to mutual adaptation by both citizens of immigrant origin and nonimmigrant citizens. I illustrate the general point with a discussion of five areas where this sort of ethos matters greatly: rules, informal norms, incentives, practices of recognition, and national identity.

Chapter 5 focuses on the question of how the rights of immigrants who are legal permanent residents should resemble or differ from the rights of citizens. Here I challenge the widespread assumption that citizenship is and ought to be special, something that sharply distinguishes insiders from outsiders. Belonging, I argue, depends primarily on where one lives. Residence makes a person a member of society, and that has implications for the legal rights a person should have. I argue that legal residents should enjoy most of the rights of citizenship and that in practice they normally do. I criticize most of the key remaining areas of difference.

The sixth chapter takes up questions about temporary workers. I argue that some limitations on the duration of stay and some limitations on access to redistributive social programs may be defensible, but that temporary workers should normally enjoy the same workplace rights as residents and citizens and should either have access to work-related social programs or be compensated for their exclusion from such programs. I argue that other restrictions on the rights of temporary migrants usually have a morally problematic, exploitative element built into them, and I criticize arguments that seek to justify such restrictions.

Chapter 7 addresses the difficult problem of migrants who settle without authorization, whom I call irregular migrants. (Their critics use the term "illegal immigrants" and their supporters "undocumented workers.") I argue that these irregular migrants are morally entitled to some important legal rights and that democratic states have a duty to build a firewall between the enforcement of their immigration laws and the protection of many of these rights. I also argue that over time irregular migrants acquire a moral right to stay that ought to be recognized through their gaining of legal status on an individual basis rather than through periodic amnesties.

Chapter 8 draws together the implications of the previous several chapters, building them into a theory of social membership. The theory of social membership corrects tendencies in democratic thought to overvalue citizenship, by showing that social membership grounds moral claims to citizenship and moral claims to rights for migrants who are not citizens. It corrects tendencies in cosmopolitan thought to neglect the importance of belonging by showing that membership provides the moral grounds for most claims to legal rights, including even some human rights.

Part II begins with chapter 9. There I turn for the first time to questions about admissions. I argue that states face significant moral constraints on admissions decisions, even under the conventional view that states have considerable discretion to control admissions. First, I show that states are constrained in the criteria that they may use for selection and exclusion. Second, I claim that states have a moral obligation to admit outsiders for purposes of family reunification, an obligation that is widely, if imperfectly, acknowledged in practice.

In chapter 10 I take up the question of refugees. Here I focus for the first time on the possibility that people who have no claim to belong to a political community may nevertheless have a moral right to entry. I first identify three complementary reasons why democratic states have a moral duty to admit refugees. The bulk of the chapter then seeks to clarify that duty by exploring questions about who should qualify as a refugee, what kinds of assistance refugees need, who should provide that assistance and whether there are limits on what could be asked of states in assisting refugees. I argue that, in principle, we should expand the definition of refugee to include anyone fleeing serious threats to basic rights, regardless of the source; that refugees need only a safe haven at first but are entitled to full membership in a new society eventually, if they cannot go home safely; that it is reasonable to expect those nearby to provide the initial shelter but that all states have duties to admit long-term refugees in accordance with their capacities to absorb them and other factors; and that ultimately there is almost no justification for refusing to admit refugees. I also argue, however, that there is such a big gap between the ideal refugee regime identified by these answers and what democratic states are actually willing to do, that there is no realistic chance of the ideal refugee regime being implemented.

In chapter 11 I finally step back from the conventional assumption about the state's right to exercise discretionary control over immigration and consider the possibility that what justice really requires is open borders, the free movement of people across the world. I lay out the prima facie case for open borders, showing that it follows from our commitments to freedom, equality of opportunity, and equality. I deepen the argument first by exploring the relationship between open borders and global equality and then by considering the reasons why we should regard freedom of movement as a human right.

In chapter 12 I consider a range of objections to open borders that focus on the moral claims of the political communities that immigrants might seek to enter. I consider claims about the limits of justice; about the need for closure to protect the distinctive characters of different communities; about the necessary connection between self-determination and control over immigration; about the relationship between sovereignty and immigration; and about the duty to give priority to compatriots. I argue that none of these considerations can justify the conventional view that states are entitled to exercise discretionary control over immigration. I also consider more limited arguments that seek only to qualify open borders in the name of national security, public order, preservation of the welfare state, or protection of a public culture. I acknowledge that these more limited arguments have some merit but contend that they lead only to modest qualifications of the general commitment to open borders.

In chapter 13 I review the conclusions that I have reached in the course of the book, consider how to integrate the argument for open borders with the discussion in the first several chapters, and explore the implications of the whole analysis for questions about how we ought to act in the world.

The book concludes with a methodological appendix that discusses the strategy of inquiry used in the book. As I have already indicated, this is likely to be of interest primarily to academics, especially to political theorists concerned with issues where there is a large gap between what some sort of normative ideal prescribes and what it is feasible to pursue in the present.

PART ONE

WHO BELONGS?

2

Birthright Citizenship

In 1993 the *New York Times* published an article that told the story of Senay Kocadag, a young woman born and raised in Berlin whose parents were immigrants from Turkey. Kocadag was 22 at the time, completing a degree in business administration. She had been educated in Germany and had lived her entire life there, leaving only for vacations. Yet she was not a citizen. "[I]t's frustrating," she was quoted as saying. "I'm completely at home here, and when I visit Turkey, I feel like a foreigner. But this society doesn't want to recognize me or accept me as German."[1]

The *Times* story contrasted Kocadag's situation with that of people born in the United States who automatically receive citizenship at birth. Although the article did not say so explicitly, the implication was clear. The American policy was better. It treated people more fairly.

What should we think of this? Was the *Times* right to suggest that the American policy was morally superior or was that an expression of American cultural imperialism, projecting the view that the American way is always the best way and failing to respect the rights of other democratic states to choose their own policies? If Kocadag had been born after 2000, she would have received German citizenship automatically at birth, because by then Germany had changed its citizenship law.[2] What should we think about this change in German policy? Was this merely a normal policy decision like raising or lowering taxes or spending more or less on various public programs? Was it the sort of policy choice that every democratic state is morally free to decide for itself in accord with its own priorities (at least within wide limits), or was it a decision that involved fundamental principles of morality?

The question I am asking is a normative one, not a legal one. There is no doubt that under international law, Germany, as a sovereign state, had the legal authority to keep its old citizenship law or to adopt the new one and that no other actor had any right to intervene on that matter. The question is whether it was morally free to keep its old law or whether it was morally obliged to change it. Is each democracy morally free to determine for itself the criteria it will use in granting citizenship at birth? Alternatively, are there standards of justice that govern birthright citizenship in contemporary democracies, setting moral limits to state discretion on this issue?

In this chapter I defend the latter view.[3] Justice requires that democratic states grant citizenship at birth to the descendants of settled immigrants.

Preliminaries

This chapter and the next one form a unit, exploring questions about access to legal citizenship for settled immigrants, that is, immigrants who have legal authorization to reside on an ongoing basis in the state where they are living, and for their descendants.[4] In this chapter I focus only on children born to settled immigrants in the new state where the immigrants are living. In the next chapter I explore questions about access to citizenship for those who arrive after birth.

Throughout this chapter and the next one, for reasons given in the introduction, I am simply presupposing that the questions I ask about access to citizenship arise in the context of an international order which divides the world into independent, sovereign states and within a moral framework that includes what I have called the conventional moral view on immigration, that is, that states are morally free to exercise considerable discretionary control over the admission and exclusion of immigrants despite the differences between states.

Finally, my discussion in this chapter and the next focuses on immigrants' access to citizenship as a legal status.[5] As we will see in chapter 5, the importance of citizenship as a legal status is often exaggerated. Indeed, we could imagine other ways of institutionalizing the legal functions of citizenship as a legal status, perhaps eliminating the need for such a formal status altogether.[6] Nevertheless, the legal status of citizenship does matter in some important respects now. For example, the legal status of citizenship is normally a prerequisite for voting in national elections. The status of citizenship also has implications under international law, entailing a right to diplomatic protection and a right to enter and reside in any state where one is a citizen. Above all, it is through the granting of legal status as a citizen that a modern state officially recognizes someone as a member of the political community. These facts about what the legal status of citizenship means today provide the anchor for my reflections in these two chapters. Over the course of the next two chapters, I will argue that there are moral principles that should govern access to the legal status of citizenship and that these principles apply to every contemporary democratic state in Europe and North America.

Birth and Belonging

How do people usually become citizens in democratic states? Most people acquire their citizenship automatically at birth. Birthright citizenship is such a familiar political and legal practice that it is hard even to notice it.[7] Indeed, it seems so natural that when immigrants acquire citizenship after arriving in their new state, we call the process "naturalization." But legal citizenship is not a natural category, and acquiring citizenship is not a natural outcome of being born. People acquire citizenship as a result of some chosen set of legal rules, some political practice that states have established.

Does birthright citizenship make sense morally? In some ways granting citizenship at birth seems like an odd practice from a democratic perspective. After all, contemporary democracies emerged historically as a challenge to social orders based on inherited status.[8] When democratic theorists ask who should be included in the citizenry, they usually emphasize factors like ongoing subjection to the laws or long-term residence in a state and participation in its civil society, and they appeal to norms like consent to authority and participation in decisions that affect one's interests.[9] These sorts of considerations will play an important role in the next chapter when we turn to the issue of naturalization for adult immigrants, but they cannot easily be applied to babies. Newborns have no past (outside the womb) so one cannot appeal to their experience as a justification for granting them citizenship. They cannot be political agents, deliberating among political alternatives and exercising political will through voting and running for office. So, we cannot appeal directly to their right to consent or to participate as a justification for granting them citizenship. So, why do democratic states confer citizenship on newborn infants?

One part of the answer to that question is the modern international system. The world is divided up into states. Everybody is supposed to be assigned to some state, and that state is responsible, in certain respects, for its citizens. Statelessness, not having any formal nationality, is a problem from the perspective of the international system. It is also a problem from the perspective of the individual. Being stateless is a precarious and vulnerable condition in the modern world. That applies to babies as well.

The way the modern world is organized may give us one reason why everyone should be assigned some citizenship at birth, but it does not explain why any particular state ought to grant citizenship to any particular child. Indeed the principle of state sovereignty, which is a key part of the international system, grants each state the authority to decide for itself how to allocate its citizenship. There is an international convention on human rights that prohibits states from arbitrarily depriving an individual of her nationality once she has it and another international convention on statelessness that provides guidelines for granting nationality to individuals who do not automatically get some citizenship at birth, but there are no general guidelines for how states ought to assign citizenship, whether at birth or afterwards.[10] From the perspective of the international system, what matters primarily is that everyone has some citizenship not which citizenship anyone has.

Another answer to the question of why democratic states confer citizenship on babies is that even infants are moral persons. They cannot (yet) exercise political agency but they can be and are bearers of legal rights. So, the state has a duty to recognize them as moral persons and to protect their rights. Someone might say that the state acknowledges this duty by making the babies citizens. This response is more salient from a democratic perspective. It draws appropriate attention to the moral status of babies as persons and to the duty of the state to recognize that moral status by granting babies legal rights, but it does not yet explain why those legal rights should include the status of citizenship. After all, the state has a duty to respect the moral personhood and protect the legal rights of all those within its jurisdiction, even temporary visitors. It does not have to make them citizens to do this. So, we are back at the question of why a democratic state confers its *citizenship* at birth on *particular* infants and why it should do so.

The answer to that question has to lie in our sense of the moral relevance of the connections that are established at birth between a particular baby and a particular political community. Let's look first at the sorts of connections that make it morally obligatory for democratic states to grant citizenship at birth to the children of citizens. This will enable us to see that the children of immigrants have similar sorts of connections and so similar moral claims to birthright citizenship.

The Children of Resident Citizens

Consider first children who are born to parents who are citizens of the state where their children are born and who live in that state as well. In other words, the baby's parents are resident citizens. Every democratic state grants citizenship automatically to such children at birth.[11] Some readers may be inclined to say "Of course!" (or something less polite). It may seem intuitively obvious that this practice makes moral sense, but I want to make the underlying rationale explicit, and that rationale is not self-evident. As I noted above, birthright citizenship is not a natural phenomenon. It is a political practice, even when it concerns the children of resident citizens. What justifies this practice from a democratic perspective?

Some will want to point out that granting citizenship at birth to the children of resident citizens is in the state's interest. That is a highly plausible claim, although anyone with a little imagination could come up with circumstances under which a state might find it in its interest not to grant citizenship to the children of some segment of its resident citizen population. In any event, my question is not why states follow this practice but whether they are morally obliged to do so. The fact that a policy is in the state's interest does not prove that the policy is morally permissible, and I want to know something more than that. I want to know whether the policy is morally required. Would a state act wrongly, from a democratic perspective, if it did not grant citizenship to the children of resident citizens? Is this something that justice requires? My answer to both of these questions is "yes." The challenge is to explain why.

Babies do not appear upon the earth unconnected to other human beings.[12] A baby emerges physically from her mother, of course, but she enters a social world. From the outset, she has various sorts of relationships and belongs to various sorts of human communities. She is connected to people, most intimately to parents and siblings, and through them to friends and more distant family members. Of course, these connections vary enormously. Her family may have one parent or two; the parent(s) may or may not be physically related to her; the extended social network may be large or small, intense or diffuse; it may or may not involve a religious or a cultural community into which she is welcomed as a new member. Unless a child is very unlucky, however, she will, from the moment of her birth, have connections to other human beings who feel an interest in and a responsibility for her well-being (even though the degree of interest and responsibility will vary enormously across individuals and communities). In various ways, these connections will affect not only the child's well-being but also her identity. Who we are depends in large part on how we see ourselves in relation to others, and how they see us.

One important relationship for a new baby is her relationship with a particular political community, namely, the state where she lives. We are embodied creatures. Most of our activities take place within some physical space. In the modern world, the physical spaces in which people live are organized politically primarily as territories governed by states.[13] So, even though a baby cannot exercise any political agency, the state where she lives matters a lot to her life. As I noted above, the state can and should recognize her as a person and a bearer of rights. Beyond that, the state where she lives inevitably structures, secures and promotes her relationships with other human beings, including her family, in various ways. Indeed, the state has a fallback responsibility for the baby's well-being in case of a catastrophic failure of familial relationships (e.g., parental death, violence, or abandonment). In addition, the state has a wide range of responsibilities for the welfare and security of those living within its territory (though particular states interpret and implement these responsibilities in different ways).

When a baby is born to parents who are resident citizens, it is reasonable to expect that she will grow up in that state and receive her social formation there. Her parents will play an important role in that formation, of course, but so will the state through its educational system. Her life chances and choices will also be affected in central ways by the state's laws and policies. Although a child cannot exercise political agency at birth, she will be able to do so as an adult. If she is to play that role properly, she should see herself prospectively in it as she is growing up. She needs to know that she will be entitled to a voice in the community where she lives and that her voice will matter. In addition, political communities are an important source of identity for many, perhaps most, people in the modern world. A baby born to resident citizens is likely to develop a strong sense of identification with the political community in which she lives and in which her parents are citizens. She is likely to see herself and to be seen by others as someone who belongs in that community. All of these circumstances shape her relationship with the state where she is born from the outset. They give her a fundamental interest in being recognized as a member of that particular political community. Granting her citizenship at birth is a way of recognizing that relationship and giving it legal backing.

But why is granting her citizenship the appropriate way of recognizing this relationship? In the modern world, citizenship is the legal status by which we recognize a human being as an official member of the political community. This is not a necessary truth about the meaning of citizenship, but it is a fact about what citizenship means in contemporary democracies. Similarly, it is a fact that legal citizenship is a status that can be held by children as well as adults. Even human beings who are too young to exercise all of the rights or bear all of the duties that adult citizens bear can be citizens.[14]

The legal differences between adults and children should probably lead us to be more careful in deploying the rhetoric of equal citizenship because that rhetoric sometimes obscures children from our view. Nevertheless, the language of equal citizenship does capture an important truth about the relationship between citizen children and their political community. A young citizen will automatically acquire all of the rights and face all of the duties of an adult citizen once she reaches the age of maturity.[15] She does not have to pass any tests or meet any standards to qualify for full citizenship. Thus, the child citizen is recognized as a full member, in important respects, even before she is capable of political agency or in possession of all of the rights of an adult citizen.

Birthright citizenship rests upon expectations that may not be fulfilled. The child's parents may take her abroad to live. If this happens after the child has spent much of her youth in the state, it is irrelevant to her claim to citizenship because the child will have developed her own connections to the political community and will have been profoundly shaped by her upbringing within the state, even if she has not yet reached adulthood. But what if the family leaves while the child is still quite young? She may never develop the anticipated deep connections with the political community, but she will still have its citizenship. And citizenship tends to be sticky. Once granted, it is relatively hard to take back. So, a child of resident citizens who is granted citizenship at birth will probably keep that citizenship even if her parents move elsewhere and she does not grow up in the political community after all. Is that something to be concerned about?

I don't think so, at least in the absence of some plausible story about why this is likely to happen with great frequency and why it would create problems for the political community. If a child of resident citizens gets birthright citizenship and then leaves at a young age with her parents and grows up abroad, this simply means that the state has extended citizenship and the right to return to the political community to someone who was not raised there as had been expected. Relationships are always vulnerable to the possibility of disruption and disconnection. That is not a good enough reason to make only tentative commitments. It would be wrong for a state to hand out citizenship capriciously or randomly, but granting citizenship at birth to the children of resident citizens is neither random nor capricious, even if some of those who get citizenship leave and never return. No great harm is done to the community or to any individual if a state grants citizenship to someone whom it expects to live within its boundaries on an ongoing basis but who turns out, for whatever reason, not to do so. In a democratic state, citizenship policy should err on the side of inclusion. The fact that some children of resident citizens may leave is not a sufficient reason to deny citizenship to all of them.[16] In sum, birthright citizenship for the children of resident citizens makes moral sense as a practice because it acknowledges the realities of the child's relationship to the community and the fundamental interest she has in maintaining that relationship. In a democratic framework, the state is morally obliged to take these sorts of fundamental interests into account in its citizenship policies.[17] Granting citizenship at birth to the children of resident citizens is not just an administrative device that serves the state's interests. In a world in which every child is supposed to be assigned some citizenship at birth, it is a moral imperative. It would be unjust to do otherwise.

In thinking about the moral logic underlying birthright citizenship for the children of resident citizens, we should pay almost as much attention to the things that the state does not take into account as to the ones it does. In the actual practice of contemporary democratic states, all that matters is that the baby's parents are citizens of the state where the baby is born and that they live there. Nothing depends upon the baby's ancestry beyond her parents. The transmission of citizenship to children of resident citizens is not contingent upon what language the child's parents speak at home, what their political, religious, and moral views are, how patriotic they feel, how they live their lives, or what they believe or value in general. These considerations and many others might be relevant if one were thinking about questions of belonging and exclusion from a sociological perspective, but they don't matter when the question is about the transmission of citizenship at birth.

Limiting what is relevant to birthright citizenship for the children of resident citizens is not some radical philosophical proposal. It is the way existing legal regimes treat this question in every contemporary democratic state. And so they should. In the past states restricted birthright citizenship on the basis of race, religion, and ethnicity, but no one defends that sort of policy today. The fundamental democratic principles of equal citizenship and respect for individual rights clearly exclude the idea of limiting access to citizenship on those sorts of grounds. Similarly, at birth, children have no cultural commitments or values or beliefs, so it is not possible to assign citizenship to them on the basis of such factors. The prerequisites for an undisputed right to the acquisition of citizenship at birth may legitimately involve only certain forms of connection to the community—important forms of connection but also ones that are limited in their content. They may involve only questions about the child's birthplace and about the legal status and residence of the child's parents.

The Children of Emigrant Citizens

I have focused so far on children born in a state to citizen parents who live there. That is, statistically, the normal case. But there is another group of citizens to consider—emigrant citizens, i.e., people who have moved abroad but who retain their citizenship in their country of origin. Let's call them emigrants for short. What sort of access should the children of emigrants have to citizenship in their parents' country of origin, at least if that country is a democracy?

Let's start again with actual practice. So far as I have been able to determine, every country in Europe and North America grants some sort of birthright entitlement to citizenship to children born abroad to emigrants.[18] Often the child of emigrants simply becomes a citizen of her parents' country of origin at birth as a matter of law. Sometimes, the child has access to citizenship as an optional right. For example, the parents have to register the child with a consulate or fill out some form in order for her to gain citizenship status. In a few cases this transmission of parental citizenship is made contingent upon the child spending some time living in the country of parental origin before a certain age. Finally, the capacity of the children of emigrants to pass on that citizenship to their own descendants is sometimes limited in significant ways.

Let me illustrate from my own experience. My wife Jenny and I are American citizens. We were both born and raised in the United States and began our working careers there. We moved to Canada to pursue professional opportunities, and our two sons were born in Canada. Because of our American citizenship, our children automatically became American citizens at birth, even though they also obtained Canadian citizenship at birth because Canada grants citizenship to anyone born on Canadian territory. Their American citizenship is not contingent. In other words, they will not lose their American citizenship unless they voluntarily renounce it. But their American citizenship differs from ours in one important way. Their capacity to pass on American citizenship to their own children is limited. If one of our sons has a child who is born outside the United States (and whose other parent is not an American), the child will not become an American citizen at birth—or indeed have any claim to American citizenship—unless our son has lived in the United States for a few years before the child is born. The point of this policy is to limit the indefinite transmission of American citizenship to people who have no real connection to the United States.

What should we make of this practice of granting birthright citizenship to the children of emigrants but limiting its subsequent transmission?[19] I think this sort of policy is not only morally permissible but also morally required, at least within a certain discretionary range.

One possible justification for the practice is that it is a way for states to meet their general obligation to avoid statelessness. That is not entirely implausible, but if that were the only reason for the practice it would seem hard to explain why the children of emigrant citizens acquire their parents' citizenship even if they also obtain citizenship at birth in the state where their family lives.[20] That is often the case, as the story about my children illustrates. So, I think we have to look for a deeper rationale.

Leaving aside questions about the merits of specific rules, I think the general pattern of granting birthright citizenship to the children of emigrant citizens makes moral sense from a democratic perspective. It reflects a normative logic that is similar in some respects to the one that underlies birthright citizenship for the children of resident citizens, namely that moral claims to a particular citizenship at birth derive from the baby's connections to that political community and the ways in which those connections are likely to affect the child's interests and identity. In other words, having parents who are citizens matters morally to a child's claim to citizenship because it means that the child has important social connections to the community.

By definition, a child born abroad to emigrants is not connected to her parents' political community through birthplace and residence. In that respect, her claims to birthright citizenship are weaker than the claims of a child born in the state where her parents are citizens. Nevertheless, her claims are still strong enough to warrant recognizing her as a member of the community. A baby born abroad will have important ties to her parents' original political community through her immediate family, not because of some imagined genetic link to most other citizens but because of her social situation and her existing and potential relationships. She has a reasonable prospect of growing up in the state if her parents decide to return there. In the meantime, she will almost certainly have relatives and family friends there whom her family will visit, and she is likely to acquire cultural and emotional ties to the country through her parents. Her parents' identities are likely to be shaped in powerful ways by the country they have left, and they may well want to pass that identity on to their child.

At the same time, states are, above all, territorial communities. Citizenship status should not become too disconnected from that fact. The emigrants themselves have a direct connection to the state, having lived on its territory. The potential for the children to live there, if their parents take them back, is strong enough to justify their citizenship. But if the children don't live there, it's less plausible to pass on citizenship to a generation twice removed from the one that did live there.

Let me again illustrate these general points from my own experience. As I noted, our sons acquired Canadian citizenship at birth. Nevertheless, it was very important to us that our children also have American citizenship. For one thing, our children were born relatively soon after we moved to Canada. We still saw ourselves then primarily as Americans rather than Canadians, and we wanted our children to have an American identity as well as a Canadian one. We were not certain that we would stay in Canada permanently. Our children's American citizenship guaranteed that we would have the legal right to move the entire family "back" to the United States if we wanted to do so. In fact we loved our jobs, we loved living in Toronto and in Canada, and over time we came to see ourselves as Canadian (as well as American). Things could have turned out differently, however. Moreover, when we moved to Canada, almost all of our close relatives were in the United States, including my parents and siblings and Jenny's parents and siblings. We returned frequently for visits. As a practical matter the fact that we all had American passports made family travel easier. A more fundamental issue was that the children would have had a right to move to the United States to live with relatives there if both of us had died while they were young. So, from our perspective, the fact that our children had acquired American citizenship at birth protected their (and our) vital interests, interests that were rooted in the lives we had led in the United States.[21] On the other hand, having grown up in Canada and having Canadian citizenship, our sons see themselves primarily as Canadians. If they do not move to the United States, their own connections to the United States will be far more limited than the connections that Jenny and I had and have, and their identification with the United States much more attenuated. America was home for both of us for a long time. It has never been home for them. So, their moral claims to pass on American citizenship to their own children are much weaker than our claims to pass on American citizenship to them.

The relative importance of children gaining citizenship in their emigrant parents' country of origin varies from case to case, depending on a wide range of individual and social circumstances, even among children who remain permanently in the state where they were born. Some have such strong connections to their parents' original country that it really is a second home, perhaps even their primary home in their identity and affections (though this is rare for children who are treated decently in the land where they live). For others, it is just a vague point of reference in their parents' past (though this, too, is rare if the parents left voluntarily as adults). Most fall somewhere in between these extremes. In any event, there is no plausible way to construct birthright citizenship rules that respond to these individual variations.

As we have already seen in discussing birthright citizenship for the children of resident citizens, a state cannot avoid adopting rules regarding the transmission of citizenship whose underlying rationale rests in part on generalizations, probabilities, and expectations about human lives and relationships. Given this indeterminacy and the fact that the children of emigrants have weaker moral claims to birthright citizenship than the children of resident citizens, it is reasonable for different states to make somewhat different judgments about the relative importance of their connections with the children of emigrants and to adopt somewhat different policies regarding the transmission of citizenship to them. Like the United States, many states grant the children of emigrants a simple and unqualified citizenship at birth, while setting further conditions on the transmission of that citizenship to their own children. That is clearly a morally permissible policy, given the analysis I have offered, but so would be a policy that was somewhat more restrictive or somewhat more expansive. For example, it would also be morally permissible (in my view) for states to grant only a right to citizenship and to require some form of registration for this right to be activated. This is one way of ensuring that the parents actually want their children to gain citizenship in their land of origin. By the same token, it would not be morally wrong for a state to adopt a somewhat less restrictive policy than the American one, for example, by permitting the children of emigrants to pass on citizenship to their own children automatically.

While there are no precise moral boundaries to the rules regulating the transmission of citizenship to the children of emigrants, the range of morally permissible rules is not unlimited. On the one hand, the children of emigrants normally have sufficient ties to their parents' community of origin to warrant some effective access to citizenship in that country. It would be unjust to exclude them altogether, even in cases where this would not leave them stateless. As we have seen, every democratic state does in fact grant the children of emigrants some

sort of birthright claim to citizenship. On the other hand, states should not be
unduly expansive in granting citizenship to descendants of emigrants who have
no other tie to the political community than their ancestry. Normally the grandchildren of immigrants have much weaker ties to their grandparents' country of
origin than the children do and the great-grandchildren few if any ties. It would
be wrong to regard citizenship in a democracy as a sort of feudal title or property right that could be passed on from one generation to the next regardless of
where the heirs actually lived their lives.[22] As the proximity to an ancestor who
lived in the country decreases, so too does the plausibility of any justification
for automatically granting citizenship.[23] This principle fits with the practices of
many democratic states but it poses a strong challenge to the nationality policies
of others which do permit the indefinite transmission of citizenship to generations born abroad.[24]

Descendants of Immigrants

If the account I have offered of the moral logic underlying birthright citizenship
for the children of citizens is correct, it has important implications for the question of access to citizenship for the children of immigrants: children who are
born in a democratic state in which their parents have settled as legal immigrants
should acquire citizenship automatically at birth because they, too, have sufficient ties to the community to merit recognition as members. Indeed because
they have been born in the state and are likely to be raised there, they normally
have even stronger ties to the political community and so stronger claims to
birthright citizenship than the children of emigrant citizens (who, as we have
seen, enjoy some form of birthright citizenship in every democratic state).

Recall the rationale that I offered for granting citizenship at birth to the children of resident citizens. It emphasized the fact that the baby was likely to grow
up in the state, to receive her social formation there, and to have her life chances
and choices deeply affected by the state's policies. These considerations apply
also to the children of settled immigrants. If they are reasons why the children
of resident citizens should get citizenship at birth, they are also reasons why the
children of immigrants should get citizenship at birth. So, too, with the culti-
vation of political agency. The child of immigrants should be taught from the
beginning that she is entitled to a voice in the community where she lives and
that her voice will matter. And so, too, with political identity. Like the child of
resident citizens, the child of immigrants has a deep interest in seeing herself
and in being seen by others as someone who belongs in the political community
in which she lives. Finally, like resident citizens, settled immigrants may leave,
returning to their country of origin or going elsewhere and taking their children
with them. If the children are old enough, they will have developed their own

connections to the community and so this fact will be irrelevant to their claim to citizenship. But like the children of resident citizens, some children of settled immigrants may leave at a young age and never return. As with the children of resident citizens and for the same sorts of reasons, this possibility does not provide a good enough reason not to grant them citizenship at birth.

In sum, the most important circumstances shaping a child's relationship with the state from the outset are the same for the child of immigrants as they are for the child of resident citizens. So, the child of immigrants has the same sort of fundamental interest in being recognized at birth as a member of the political community.

To be sure, the child of immigrants has a somewhat weaker claim to membership than the child of resident citizens, because, in the latter case, the parents' status as citizens provides another important social connection to the political community. This is not because the political community is constituted by blood ties among the citizens. Parentage is only relevant because it is an indicator of the child's social connections to the community. From that perspective the child of immigrants has a considerably stronger set of social connections and hence a stronger claim to membership than a child born to emigrant parents. The ties that come from actually living in a state are the most powerful basis for a claim to membership. Home is where one lives, and where one lives is the crucial variable for interests and for identity, both empirically and normatively. Senay Kocadag's story illustrates this point. Germany was her home, the place where she was born and brought up. That ought to have been recognized by granting her citizenship at birth (as is indeed the case now for children born in similar circumstances in Germany). Birthright citizenship is the only proper way to recognize the relationship between the newborn child of settled immigrants and the political community in which her family lives and in which she is expected to grow up. It is unjust not to grant citizenship at birth to the children of settled immigrants for the same reasons that make it unjust not to grant citizenship to the children of resident citizens.

Theory and Practice

Do my normative arguments about birthright citizenship for the children of immigrants present an interpretation of existing practices in democratic states or a critique of them? Later in this book I will sometimes defend positions that are radically at odds with the status quo, but on this issue there is no need to do so. Most democratic states now accept, implicitly or explicitly, some version of the principle that I have been defending about birthright citizenship for the descendants of immigrants. Let's consider how democratic states have dealt with the transmission of citizenship in the past and how this has changed in response to immigration.

Understanding Ius Sanguinis

There are two common legal techniques for transmitting citizenship at birth: *ius soli* (literally, right of the soil), which grants citizenship on the basis of birth on the state's territory, and *ius sanguinis* (literally, right of blood), which grants citizenship on the basis of descent from citizen parents. These techniques can be qualified and combined in various ways. Either of these techniques will normally result in the automatic transmission of citizenship to the children of resident citizens, thus satisfying one of the requirements of justice with regard to the transmission of citizenship at birth.

In most states the citizenship laws rely primarily on one technique rather than the other for historical reasons that have nothing to do with immigration. Nevertheless, the choice of techniques does affect immigrants. A policy that transmits citizenship on the basis of birthplace (*ius soli*) will normally grant citizenship to the children of resident immigrants, while a policy that transmits citizenship only on the basis of descent from citizen parents (*ius sanguinis*) will not. In part for that reason and in part because several states that have long had a tradition of admitting immigrants also have long had *ius soli* policies in place (e.g., the United States, Canada, and Australia), people have tended to assume that states that rely primarily on *ius sanguinis* for the transmission of citizenship are hostile to immigrants while those that rely primarily on *ius soli* policies are welcoming. There is an element of truth in this view because it is not possible to extend birthright citizenship to the children of immigrants without introducing some form of *ius soli*, but it is deeply misleading in some respects.

Some people think that a citizenship policy that relies on *ius sanguinis* reflects an understanding of the state as an ethnic community in which citizens are connected to one another by blood, at least in the public imagination. That is not the only possible meaning of *ius sanguinis*, however. French reformers introduced the practice of *ius sanguinis* into modern Europe after the French Revolution on the grounds that it reflected a more republican conception of citizenship and community than *ius soli*, which was tied historically to the relation between subject and sovereign.[25] This change was not rooted in an ethnic conception of the nation. Most of the other states on the Continent followed the French example. Ironically, France itself supplemented its *ius sanguinis* rule with a (qualified) *ius soli* rule in the late nineteenth century, but few other continental states did likewise.[26]

In the contemporary world, even countries like Canada and the United States that rely primarily on *ius soli* employ a version of *ius sanguinis* in granting citizenship at birth to the children of their emigrant citizens (as my own children's case illustrates). These are states that have been built through immigration. Their populations are composed of many different ethnic backgrounds. Clearly, it does not make sense to interpret the use of *ius sanguinis* for the transmission of citizenship by states like Canada and the United States as a reflection of their ethnic conception of nationality. Being American or Canadian can certainly be an important identity but to think of it as an "ethnic" identity would be to stretch the meaning of that term considerably beyond its normal use. The use of *ius sanguinis* for the transmission of citizenship by these states is simply a way to meet the legitimate moral claims that children of emigrants have to be recognized as members of their parents' political community of origin.

In sum, it would be a mistake to throw the baby who gets her citizenship through *ius sanguinis* out with the soiled ethnic bathwater. It is not plausible to interpret every policy employing *ius sanguinis* as an expression of an ethnic conception of political community. *Ius sanguinis* is a perfectly legitimate mechanism for the transmission of citizenship so long as it is limited in extent.

Although *ius sanguinis* policies may be morally justifiable as a technique for citizenship transmission, it does not follow that there is no basis for criticizing particular uses of *ius sanguinis*. It is plausible to suppose that those who do think of the political community in ethnic terms would find *ius sanguinis* congenial and would want to resist the introduction of any form of *ius soli*. Such policies deserve criticism not because they use the technique of *ius sanguinis* but because they are ultimately based on a conception of political community that is incompatible with democratic principles.

Transforming Birthright Citizenship in Europe

If we look at contemporary developments in Western Europe over the past few decades we can see these different tendencies playing themselves out. Most of the states that had traditionally relied exclusively on *ius sanguinis* for the transmission of citizenship have introduced some version of *ius soli*. The few that have not are the ones most resistant to the inclusion of immigrants in the citizenry.

In general terms, and with occasional exceptions, the pattern is this.[27] In the 1950s and 1960s, many people entered Western European states as "guestworkers" who were expected to go home after a few years. Many did in fact return but many others stayed permanently and had children. In states that transmitted citizenship at birth only through *ius sanguinis*—and that was the case for most of the states on the Continent—the children of the guestworkers (the "second generation") were legally defined as foreigners even though they had been born in the "host" country and subsequently lived their entire lives there. This was the situation of Senay Kocadag, the woman in my opening anecdote about

German citizenship. Some of these children became citizens through naturalization, but most did not, in part because the process of naturalization was often
demanding and discretionary, in part because they were not encouraged to do
so by the "host" society, in part because they did not want to do so given their
own attachments to their "home country" (i.e., their parents' country of origin),
even though it was a place most of them had never lived. They in turn stayed
and had children (the "third generation") who were also classified as foreigners.
It became clear that unless the rules about the acquisition of citizenship were
changed, there would be a "fourth generation" of "foreigners" and then a fifth—
people whose families would have been living in the country since the time of
their great-great grandparents but who would still be excluded from citizenship.
Over time, most states came to recognize that there was no way to reconcile the
ongoing exclusion of an entire segment of the settled population with democratic norms.[28]

In the first instance, states saw that the third generation and beyond had to
be included in the citizenry. It was not reasonable to pretend that the children of
people who had lived their entire lives in the society would eventually go "home"
to the country their grandparents or great-grandparents had left. Once the need
to include the third generation was accepted, it became clear to many that they
ought to be considered citizens from birth, just like the children of citizens, so
that they could be socialized into the norms and practices of the society as they
grew up. Most states now grant the third generation citizenship or at least a right
to citizenship. In some cases, the third generation acquires citizenship automatically at birth (like the children of citizens) through what is called a double *ius soli*
rule which grants birthright citizenship to any child born in the state to parents
who were also born in the state.

Most democratic states have also recognized that this principle of inclusion
applies, at least to some extent, to the second generation—children born to
immigrant parents who have settled in a new state. The second generation generally enjoys at least a legal entitlement to citizenship and in many cases acquires
citizenship automatically either at birth or at some later age. For example, some
states (like Germany) grant citizenship at birth to any child born on the territory
whose parents have been legal residents for a certain period of time. That was the
reform introduced in 2000.

In sum, most Western European states have accepted the view that excluding the descendants of immigrants from citizenship generation after generation
is incompatible with any plausible account of democratic principles and that
this means that some form of birthright citizenship must be extended to the
descendants of immigrants. The transformation of Germany's citizenship laws
is the case that has been most widely discussed, but several other states have
also moved away from limiting citizenship transmission to *ius sanguinis* and have

recognized that birth in the country to settled immigrants gives rise to some sort of legal right to citizenship.[29]

I do not mean to suggest that everyone in Europe accepts this view of citizenship and immigration. A few states in Western Europe (e.g., Austria, Denmark) have no provisions to recognize the claims of the descendants of immigrants to birthright citizenship, although even these states usually facilitate access to citizenship for these children as adults which is a partial concession to the principles I am advancing. The states from Eastern Europe that have recently joined the EU base their birthright citizenship policies exclusively on *ius sanguinis* and permit indefinite transmission of citizenship to generations born abroad (although these states have only recently begun to deal with significant immigration and have not yet had to deal with the challenges that generational exclusion poses for democracy). Finally, it is probably fair to say that the acceptance of the rationale for birthright citizenship for the descendants of immigrants is more firmly established among the elites in many states than among the general population. Nevertheless, the most noteworthy fact is that many states with traditions of relying exclusively on *ius sanguinis* have changed their laws regarding birthright citizenship to add some version of a *ius soli* rule in order to include the descendants of immigrants in the citizenry. I do not think it is possible to explain these changes without appealing to ideas like the ones I have presented in this chapter about who should be regarded as a member of the political community at birth.[30]

Limiting Ius Soli

None of the states that have adopted new *ius soli* laws has extended birthright citizenship to every person born on the state's territory. In most cases they grant birthright citizenship only if the child's parents are legal residents, sometimes requiring them to have had that status for an extended period of time, and sometimes only granting birthright citizenship to the third generation. So, the new *ius soli* policies are restricted in various ways. Moreover, some states that previously had unqualified or universal *ius soli* rules in place have made their rules more restrictive. The United Kingdom, Ireland, and Australia all had a long tradition of *ius soli* rules that granted citizenship to everyone born on the state's territory, but they have now adopted reforms that grant birthright citizenship to children who are born on the state's territory only if at least one of the parents is a citizen or a legal resident. A few states with long-standing universal *ius soli* laws, notably the United States and Canada, have not changed their policies (despite some public demands that they do so).

What should we make of this from a normative perspective? Should the states that have only recently introduced *ius soli* laws have extended birthright citizenship further to include everyone born on the territory? Were the states that have changed their universal *ius soli* laws wrong to do so? Alternatively, were the states that have kept their universal *ius soli* laws wrong not to change them? Or is this an area where states are morally free to exercise their own preferences in how expansive or restrictive they will be?

For the reasons laid out in my earlier arguments, I think that states have an obligation to grant birthright citizenship to the children of settled immigrants. I would therefore argue that policies that only grant birthright citizenship to the third generation (as is the case with some of the states that have reformed their laws) do not go quite far enough. They do not grant citizenship at birth to everyone who ought to receive it. Nevertheless, I don't want to overstate this point. The most important consideration from a moral perspective is that, by adopting some sort of *ius soli* law, these states have recognized the principle that the descendants of immigrants deserve birthright citizenship when there is good reason to believe that they will grow up in the state where they were born. That is an important development, and it is much more important than the details of how a particular state determines the threshold for the assumption that a child is likely to grow up in the political community. By contrast, it seems to me that states that make no provisions to grant citizenship at birth to the descendants of immigrants are failing to meet basic democratic standards of justice.

The principle that I have been defending does not entail the view that anyone born in a state deserves birthright citizenship, however. My argument emphasizes the central importance of the expectation that a child will be raised in the state. It is not plausible to expect that everyone born in a state will grow up there, regardless of why the mother happens to be present in the state at the moment of her child's birth. Suppose that a child is born to parents who are present as tourists or temporary visitors. It seems reasonable to expect that the child will be raised elsewhere, presumably in her parents' home state, not in the place where she happened to be born. By itself, birthplace creates no compelling claim to membership. It is only when birthplace is linked to future expectations of living in the society that it gives rise to such a claim. For that reason, states adopting new *ius soli* laws do nothing wrong when they limit the reach of these laws to the children of settled immigrants.[31]

Of course, things can always turn out differently from what we expect. A temporary stay can become a permanent one. It is not necessary to address this contingency by extending birthright citizenship to everyone born on the territory, however. If the child does stay on, she will indeed establish the sorts of connections that generate a moral claim to citizenship, but this claim can be met by policies that grant citizenship automatically to any child who resides within the state for an extended period as a minor. Indeed, I will argue in the next chapter that justice requires states to adopt such policies.

If it is morally permissible for states introducing new *ius soli* laws to adopt rules that grant birthright citizenship only to children whose parents have ongoing residence permits, isn't it also acceptable, or perhaps even obligatory, for states with universal *ius soli* laws in place to modify their rules so as to impose the same sorts of restrictions? As I noted above, the United Kingdom, Ireland, and Australia have already changed their laws. Some argue that Canada and the United States should do so as well. Some of the public arguments that have been and still are advanced in these cases echo the analysis I have offered, namely, that the mere fact of being born in a country does not normally give rise to a strong moral claim to citizenship.[32]

If the analysis I have offered so far is correct, it is morally permissible in principle for states with universal *ius soli* laws to modify them so as to restrict *ius soli* birthright citizenship to the children of citizens and settled immigrants. The reforms that have taken place in the *ius soli* states are sometimes described as moves in an illiberal or undemocratic direction. But the first and most important point to make about these changes is that they have respected the moral constraints imposed by democratic principles. As I explain below, there may be other grounds for criticizing these changes, but the changes themselves do not violate the state's obligations with regard to birthright citizenship, at least as I have interpreted those obligations. All of these states continue to grant citizenship at birth to the children of settled immigrants. In some ways, this is surprising, given the presence of strong anti-immigrant movements in all of these states. So, rather than simply seeing the changes that have taken place as illiberal or undemocratic, we can view the continued respect for this principle of granting birthright citizenship to the children of settled immigrants as a sign of how deeply rooted this understanding of democratic norms really is.

If policies restricting birthright citizenship to the children of citizens and residents are morally permissible in principle, why should anyone object to the fact that states with universal *ius soli* laws have changed them so as not to grant automatic citizenship to children born to tourists or temporary workers or irregular migrants? The answer is that laws and policies sometimes involve more than rules and rights. The reforms in the United Kingdom, Ireland, and Australia are troubling not because of the content of the policies but because of the symbolic meaning of the changes. At the time that the new policies were introduced, each of these states was faced with popular anti-immigrant movements that demonized and denigrated immigrants, often in racial terms. Critics have charged that the changes in the citizenship laws were introduced as a way of placating these anti-immigrant forces and that the reforms served to legitimate their anti-immigrant rhetoric. To the extent that these charges are true, the changes deserve criticism. I phrase my claim in this cautious way simply because I do not know the circumstances of each case well enough to make an informed judgment about the criticisms. This requires a detailed contextual interpretation that is beyond the scope of this book. But the motives behind the changes and the symbolic effects of the changes are relevant moral considerations in assessing these cases. Even though there is nothing morally objectionable in principle in laws restricting *ius soli* to the children of citizens and residents, we should be concerned if the changes to the citizenship laws grew out of and contributed to racist or anti-immigrant currents in a society.

Should Canada and the United States follow in the wake of these other states and revise their universal birthright citizenship rules? There is no compelling moral reason to do so. The fact that it is morally permissible for a democratic state to adopt a more restrictive *ius soli* law does not mean that every democratic state is obliged to take this approach. A universal *ius soli* law runs a greater risk of granting birthright citizenship to some children who will not grow up within the state, but every birthright citizenship law runs that risk to some degree. To extend birthright citizenship to everyone born in the territory is not to give implicit endorsement to a morally objectionable conception of the political community as an unqualified *ius sanguinis* law does. The latter implicitly endorses an ethnic conception of the state; the former merely extends citizenship to some who have no strong moral claim to it. So, there is nothing morally unjust in the existing universal *ius soli* rules in Canada and the United States.

But wouldn't it be good public policy for them to bring their birthright citizenship laws into closer alignment with the underlying moral principle that gives rise to moral claims to birthright citizenship? Not necessarily. There are good contextual reasons for both Canada and the United States not to modify their universal *ius soli* policy.

Both Canada and the United States see themselves as countries of immigration. In various ways, welcoming immigrants is a central element in the national ideals of both states. Needless to say, this ideal has not always been realized in practice, but one important area where the inclusion of immigrants has never been in doubt has been the acceptance of the children of immigrants as citizens. The certainty that everyone born in the country would be included in the citizenry has played an important role in both states in sustaining their self-understandings as countries open to immigration. Any change in the universal reach of the citizenship laws, even one that continued to grant birthright citizenship to the children of settled immigrants, would probably be seen as a repudiation of that basic openness to immigration. I do not claim that it would be unjust to change these laws, but I do think that a restrictive change in either country would be a betrayal of a fundamental national ideal.

Changing the universal *ius soli* rule in the United States would be particularly damaging. The rule is part of the Fourteenth Amendment to the Constitution.[33] It is very difficult to change the Constitution. It requires the approval of two-thirds of both houses of Congress and three-quarters of the state legislatures. So, it would only be feasible politically to amend this rule if a massive and power-ful anti-immigrant movement swept the country. The Fourteenth Amendment overturned the notorious *Dred Scott* decision. It represents the deepest articu-lation of America's commitment to equality. To modify that amendment in response to an anti-immigrant movement would be a national tragedy.

Most of my discussion in this chapter, and indeed in the book as a whole, focuses on general principles that apply to all democratic states in Europe and North America. General principles are not the only normative considerations that count in assessing public policies, however. In this section, especially in the last few paragraphs, I have drawn attention to the importance of what a policy means in a given context and why that should matter to a normative evaluation of that policy. I cannot go into the detail required to consider these complica-tions with respect to most of the issues I take up in this book. I emphasize them here in order to strike a cautionary note. Discussion of moral principles is not the only form of normative discourse. It is important not to move too quickly from an analysis of moral principles to conclusions about how we should act in the world.

Dual Citizenship at Birth

The issue of dual citizenship has played an important role in public debates about access to citizenship for immigrants and their descendants.[34] The refusal to grant birthright citizenship to the children of immigrants is often justified on the grounds that these children will gain another citizenship at birth—citizen-ship in their parents' country of origin.[35] Some states say that they regard dual citizenship as a problem and present their desire to avoid it as a justification for citizenship policies that restrict birthright citizenship for the second generation. Does the fact that the children of immigrants get their parents' citizenship at birth provide a democratic state any grounds for denying the children citizen-ship in the state where they are born and where their parents live?

No, for three interrelated reasons. First, citizenship in one's parents' coun-try of origin is not an adequate substitute for citizenship in the country where one lives. Second, dual citizenship itself does not pose serious problems. Finally, acquiring dual citizenship at birth is widespread, unavoidable, and accepted for the children of citizens, and so it should be for the children of immigrants as well.

The first objection to using the prevention of dual citizenship as a justification for denying birthright citizenship to the children of immigrants is simple. The strongest moral claim that a child of immigrants has to citizenship at birth is her claim to be treated as a full member of the political community in the society in which she was born and will be raised. Her claims to citizenship in her parents' country of origin are real but weaker. It is wrong for the state where she has the strongest claim to fail to recognize this claim. The fact that another state has recognized her as a member is no excuse for excluding her from membership in her actual home community.

Why does dual citizenship seem problematic to some people? Some compare the relationship between the citizen and the state to marriage, seeing dual citizenship as a form of bigamy. On this view, the state is entitled to the citizen's loyalty, allegiance, commitment, and emotional attachment. It is feared that dual citizenship will create divisions, even conflicts, in all these areas. Some worry about issues of political equality and fairness. They think that dual citizens will be able to vote in two different national elections which they see as a violation of the principle of one person, one vote. They also argue that having the additional options that a second citizenship provides conflicts with norms of fairness and equality of opportunity among citizens. Finally, people sometimes worry about the effects of dual citizenship on international order or on the dual citizens themselves. Who will be responsible for diplomatic protection if the dual citizen is in a third country? The dual citizen might owe similar legal duties to both states with respect to things like taxes and military service, but it would seem unfair to have to fulfill both. And what if the two states were in conflict with one another? Where would the dual citizen's loyalty and duty lie?

Few people who have studied the way dual citizenship works in practice share these worries. There is now a substantial scholarly literature that shows that alleged problems created by dual citizenship are exaggerated or misguided.[36] Even scholars who continue to express concerns about dual citizenship usually seek only to regulate or constrain it in some way rather than to eliminate it. These proposed regulations and constraints normally have no bearing on the acquisition of citizenship at birth.[37]

The growing acceptance of dual citizenship is in part a response to two social developments of the late twentieth century that have changed the way we think about citizenship: the decline of compulsory military service for young men and the rise of feminism. Historically, military service was seen as one of the most important duties of a citizen. The citizen was expected to risk his life for his country if called upon to do so, and in an era of universal compulsory military service, almost every young man was asked to prepare to serve in that way even if he did not actually have to engage in armed conflict. Military service, even if compulsory, was seen as a very concrete manifestation of a citizen's loyalty and commitment to his political community. At the same time, the demand for exclusivity, for attachment to a single state, could readily be linked to a military role in which matters of life and death could depend upon whether one could count upon the loyalty and commitment of one's fellow soldiers. Many people found it difficult to imagine that someone might serve in two different armies or might be free to choose between them, even if they were not in conflict with one another. Many took it as self-evident that the citizen soldier should be committed to a single state.

I have deliberately used the masculine pronoun in the previous paragraph (in contrast to my usual habit of using the feminine as the generic) because this conception of the citizen as soldier only applied to men. With very rare exceptions, women were never compelled to perform military service and often were permitted to do so only at the margins (say, as nurses and secretaries) if at all. Thus the view that military service was at the core of citizenship implicitly presupposed that the "real" citizen was a man.[38]

In practice, the problems posed by someone having dual citizenship and thus military obligations to two states were never as great as some supposed. States often entered into bilateral treaties which stipulated that service in either state fulfilled the individual's obligation or that he should do his military service in his place of habitual residence (reflecting the moral importance of residence). In the relatively rare case that a dual citizen was serving in the army of a state that was at war with the state of his other citizenship, it was possible to construe the decision to fight in one army as a renunciation of the opposing state's citizenship so that the person could be seen just as an enemy soldier and not as a traitor. But these cases were rare. Over the past few decades most states in Europe and North America have abolished universal conscription for technological, economic, and political reasons. With the elimination of compulsory military service for men, it has become harder to maintain the picture that citizenship has to be exclusive because the citizen's loyalty and commitment to the political community involve matters of life and death.

The decline of compulsory military service coincided in time with the rise of the feminist movement. This brought women more into the public realm and led to demands in many different areas that women be treated as equal citizens. One such area was the legal status of citizenship itself, and specifically the right to pass on one's citizenship to one's children. One of the earliest and easiest targets of feminist critiques was the common practice of giving priority to the male line of descent in the transmission of citizenship.

Step back for a moment and consider the question of citizenship acquisition in a "mixed" marriage (i.e., a marriage in which the spouses hold different citizenships).[39] In my previous discussion I observed that every democratic state grants birthright citizenship to the children of citizens, whether residents or emigrants. In that earlier discussion I implicitly assumed (for simplicity of exposition) that both parents had the same citizenship. But what if they don't? What if it is a mixed marriage? Should the child get only one parent's citizenship at birth or should she receive both?

The normative rationale for birthright citizenship that I have been presenting implies that a child should be entitled to some form of birthright citizenship in a democratic state, even if only one of her parents is a citizen and an emigrant at that. In my view, that single line of connection to the community generates strong enough links of interest and identity to justify recognition of the child as a member from the outset.

What about the actual practice of liberal democratic states in this regard? It fits with this rationale now, although it did not do so in the past. For much of the twentieth century, many states dealt with the question of mixed marriages by saying that children should receive only the father's citizenship.[40] In mixed marriages, the children often did not inherit the mother's citizenship even if the entire family was living in the mother's home country. These rules were defended in part as necessary to avoid dual citizenship and in part as ways to promote the unity of the family.[41] I trust that it is unnecessary to spell out to contemporary readers how these citizenship practices disadvantaged women, denied the relevance of their political identities, and created serious practical difficulties in cases of marital breakups. I will assume that I do not need to explain why feminist critics regarded such rules as morally objectionable and unfair. In response to political and legal challenges, democratic states that still had such patriarchal rules in place changed their laws in the 1970s and 1980s. All democratic states now grant birthright citizenship of some sort to a child if either parent is a citizen. Since at least one spouse in a mixed marriage must be an emigrant (if the family is living together), this means that children are in fact entitled to some form of birthright citizenship on the basis of a single emigrant parent, as I have argued ought to be the case.

As a result of these changes designed to meet the requirements of gender equality, the number of children who have acquired two citizenships at birth has grown enormously over the past few decades, especially since the incidence of mixed marriages has also increased as a result of greater mobility and human contact across borders. There is no reliable data about how many people have acquired dual citizenship at birth because their parents have different citizenships, but all of the scholarly observers agree both that the number is large and growing and that this development has led to relatively few serious practical problems with respect to diplomacy or taxes or other overlapping obligations.

What about the other worries about dual citizenship? The concern that dual citizenship creates unfair advantages is hard to take very seriously. It does not create any advantages for a person within the state where she is living. It simply gives her an opportunity to live elsewhere that others do not enjoy, and that is an advantage only in relation to any of her fellow citizens who might want to live in the other state. Often most of them would not.

The idea that dual citizenship conflicts with a commitment to political equality is more contested. Some deny that it is a problem if someone votes in two different national elections on the grounds that the person is still only exercising a single vote within a given electorate. Others contend that even this violates democratic norms and worry further about dual citizens taking up high public office. I won't try to resolve these normative disputes here. The main point for my purposes is that even those most worried about the issue of political equality do not claim that this justifies a general opposition to dual citizenship as opposed to either restrictions on the voting rights of citizens living outside the country or expectations about the renunciation of a second citizenship by someone who takes up high public office.[42]

The biggest concern about dual citizenship is the issue of divided loyalties. So, let's reconsider the image of citizenship as marriage and dual citizenship as bigamy. It's a curious choice of family analogies. One of the most common ways of describing one's home country is to call it a motherland or a fatherland. From this perspective, the appropriate family analogy for the relationship between citizen and state, especially a relationship that is established at birth, would not be the voluntary relationship of a marriage but the unchosen relationship of child to parent. Most children have two parents. We don't usually insist that they choose between them or even give priority to one over the other. The loyalty, commitment, allegiance, and emotional attachment that a child has to one parent need not conflict with the same sorts of connections to the other. Indeed, in a healthy family, the parents try to minimize such conflicts, even if they are at odds with each other through separation or divorce. It is rarely necessary to force the child to choose between the parents and important to avoid doing so in order to enable the child to maintain a loving relationship with both parents.

It is the same with a child who acquires two citizenships at birth. In fact in the vast majority of cases there is never any conflict that makes it necessary to choose between the two states, much less to make a definitive commitment to one over the other. Indeed, to require such a choice where the child has inherited one citizenship from one parent and another from the other would be, at least symbolically, to ask her to choose between her parents, to prefer her mother over her father or vice versa. This would be not only unnecessary but cruel. So far as I know, no democratic state requires its citizens to make such a choice. In any event, none should.

We are now in a position to see why denying birthright citizenship to the children of immigrants out of a desire to prevent their acquisition of more than one citizenship would be hypocritical and arbitrary. It would be hypocritical because all democratic states now accept dual citizenship at birth when it results from the child's parents' holding different citizenships. There is no plausible reason for treating dual citizenship at birth differently because one of the claims to citizenship arises from birthplace and residence rather than from parentage.[43] It would be arbitrary because it is no longer plausible (if it ever was) to argue that there is a deep public interest in preventing dual citizenship. By contrast, it is clear why individuals have a deep interest in acquiring citizenship in the place where they are born and raised as well as in the state(s) where their parents hold citizenship. Democratic states are not morally free to do whatever they want to the populations they govern. For a public policy to be justifiable, there must be some genuine public interest at stake and there must be some proportionality between whatever burden a policy imposes on individuals and the public good that the policy achieves. That is not the case if the children of immigrants are denied birthright citizenship to prevent their acquiring dual citizenship. The legitimate interest that the children of immigrants have in being able to possess dual citizenship clearly outweighs whatever interest the state may have in trying to restrict it.

3

Naturalization

Milikije Arifi is in her fifties. She was born in Macedonia, but she has lived in Switzerland since she was 18 and she raised a family there. Arifi applied for Swiss citizenship three times. Each time the town council of Adliswil, the Zurich suburb where Arifi lives, rejected her application, most recently in the spring of 2008, despite the fact that Arifi is fluent in German and had passed an exam on the history and government of Switzerland (and the local area, as well) at the time of her first application. The town council offered no public explanation for its decision not to approve Arifi's application for citizenship, but one member told a reporter: "It is not a matter of insufficient language ability or that they are a public threat. It is that their environment is not so good.... We are hearing people in the vicinity of the Arifis who don't want us to do it."[1]

In the previous chapter I explored the moral claims of the descendants of immigrants to gain citizenship automatically in the country in which they are born. Now I turn to questions about access to citizenship for those who arrive after birth. Was the Swiss decision to deny citizenship to Arifi morally justifiable? The term for the acquisition of a new citizenship after birth is naturalization. What moral principles govern naturalization in liberal democratic states? Do immigrants like Arifi have any moral claims to naturalization or is this something that is entirely at the discretion of the states where they live? Are democratic states entitled to require immigrants seeking access to citizenship to meet certain conditions before gaining citizenship, and, if so, what sorts of conditions may they require?

In this chapter, I will build on arguments advanced in the previous chapter to defend the view that democratic principles severely limit the conditions which a democratic state may impose as prerequisites for citizenship. While states may exercise some discretion in the rules they establish for naturalization, they are obliged to respect the claims of belonging that arise from living in a political community on an ongoing basis. Policies that permit the exclusion of long-term legal immigrants like Milikije Arifi from citizenship are unjust. Keep in mind that in this chapter I am only talking about immigrants who have official permission to reside in the state on an ongoing basis.

Young Immigrants

Let's begin by considering immigrants who arrive as young children. From both a sociological and a moral perspective, these children are very much like the children born in the state to immigrant parents. They belong, and that belonging should be recognized by making them citizens.

Children who arrive in a state after they are born had no moral claim to gain citizenship in that state at birth because there was no reason at the time of their birth to expect that they would grow up there. They do have a moral claim to acquire citizenship after they have settled in the state with their parents, however. All of the reasons why children should get citizenship as a birthright if they are born in a state after their parents have settled there are also reasons why children who settle in a state at a young age should acquire that state's citizenship. The state where an immigrant child lives profoundly shapes her socialization, her education, her life chances, her identity, and her opportunities for political agency. Her possession of citizenship in another state is not a good reason for denying her citizenship in the state where she lives, and for reasons we have just seen in the discussion of dual citizenship there is no good reason to require her to give up any other citizenship as a condition of gaining citizenship in the place where she lives. The state where she lives is her home. She has a profound interest in seeing herself and in being seen by others as a member of that political community, and the state has a duty to respect that interest because it has admitted her.

The state's grant of citizenship to immigrants who arrive as young children should be unconditional and automatic, just as birthright citizenship for the children of resident citizens and settled immigrants is unconditional and automatic. By unconditional, I mean that an immigrant who arrives as a young child should not be subjected to any tests of knowledge or culture or values or any standards of behavior as a condition for her acquisition of citizenship. The state is responsible for those aspects of her social formation that are relevant to citizenship. It is morally wrong to make an immigrant child's acquisition of the legal status of citizenship contingent on what she learns or how she behaves for the same reasons that it would be wrong to make the citizenship of children born in the country (whether to immigrant or citizen parents) contingent upon what they know or do.

Let me emphasize this point about unconditionality by taking up the hardest case: those who become criminals. Many states make the absence of a criminal record a condition of access to citizenship. That has some plausibility when it concerns immigrants who have arrived as adults, though even there it should be less absolute than people sometimes assume as we will see below. But when it concerns immigrants who have arrived as young children, their behavior, criminal or otherwise, should be treated as irrelevant to their acquisition of citizenship. Some children of citizens become criminals but we do not strip them of their citizenship for doing so (even if they have another citizenship and would not be rendered stateless as a result). However popular such an idea might be in some quarters, it is incompatible with our basic understanding of citizenship in contemporary democracies to make the continued possession of citizenship status contingent on good behavior.[2] For the same reason, the acquisition of citizenship by immigrants who arrive as young children and grow up in the society should not be contingent on their good behavior.

In saying that the grant of citizenship should be automatic, I mean that it is not sufficient merely to give these children a right to citizenship, leaving it optional as to whether they take up that right or not. Citizenship is not optional for the children of resident citizens, and it would be wrong to make it so. It is simply conferred upon them at birth, officially recognizing the reality of a relationship. I argued in the previous chapter that the same principle applies to children born to resident immigrants. For the same reasons, the state should simply confer citizenship automatically upon an immigrant who arrives as a young child and grows up in the state.

In saying that citizenship for children should not be optional, I am not denying the right of expatriation. The right to leave any state, including one's own, and the right to change nationalities are basic human rights. The point is that there is no reason of principle to treat either the acquisition or the renunciation of citizenship as more optional for the children of resident immigrants than it is for the children of resident citizens.

While I think that there are good reasons in principle not to make citizenship for children optional, the extent to which the acquisition of citizenship is something optional admits of degrees and sometimes the degrees matter much more than the question of whether citizenship is (technically) optional. France has a policy that grants citizenship automatically at age 18 to immigrant children born and raised in France, unless the children explicitly choose not to accept French citizenship. Conservatives have accepted the principle that these children have a right to French citizenship, thus implicitly endorsing a version of my social membership account, but they have argued that the children should receive citizenship only if they actually ask for it, thereby demonstrating that they want to be French. The conservatives managed to implement this policy of requiring an affirmative declaration for a few years in the 1990s. It dramatically reduced the number of these children who acquired French citizenship. The Mitterrand government restored the old rule in the late 1990s, making automatic acquisition the default rule but allowing for an opt out.[3]

Both sides in the French debate agree that it is important to allow the children of immigrants the freedom to choose whether or not to be French. So, from a theoretical perspective, there is a disagreement in principle between the shared French view (i.e., that the children should have an option) and my own view (i.e., that citizenship acquisition should not be optional for these children). I note in support of my position that no one in the French debate seems to think it is important to grant the same freedom to choose whether or not to be French to the children of French citizens, even if the children have inherited another citizenship from one of their parents. Nevertheless, I think that the debate over how the default rule is constructed is much more important than this disagreement over the principle. Under the current rule, very few children of immigrants opt out of French citizenship. From my perspective, the traditional rule that grants citizenship automatically unless someone explicitly rejects it is a satisfactory arrangement, despite its theoretical defects. It is so close in practice to the ideal of simple automatic acquisition that it is not worth fighting about. As in many areas of public policy, the key question is not whether there is a formal option but whether there is a default position and how the default is constructed. Here and elsewhere, we should temper the desire for theoretical clarity about principles with attention to the question of what issues really matter morally. Sometimes, as is the case here, the design of a policy may be more important morally than its underlying principle.

When should the state confer citizenship on children who immigrate at a young age? I feel uncertain about how to answer this question. On the one hand, there is a case for bestowing citizenship as soon as the child is settled in the state under terms that permit her to reside there on an ongoing basis (even if this involves renewable permits rather than formal permanent residence). That fits well with the logic of expectations that governs birthright citizenship. Remember that expectations are the basis for the claims of the children of citizens as well as for the children of settled immigrants. On the other hand, one could argue that once the moment of birth has passed, immediate recognition is less crucial and it is permissible for the state to wait until the child has actually become firmly rooted in the community before granting citizenship. I favor the former view, but I don't think this is an issue of vital importance if people accept the principle that a child who grows up in a state is morally entitled to automatic and unconditional citizenship in that state.

I have been speaking of immigrants who arrive at a young age, without specifying how young that age was. Clearly, the children who are most like those born in the country are those who arrive as infants and who undergo their entire social formation within the state where their parents have settled. So, one might say the earlier their arrival, the stronger their claim to citizenship.

However, in many ways, the strongest claim to membership in a political community derives from the fact of having undergone one's social formation within that community. From this perspective, the time spent between the ages of six and eighteen, when children are in school, is the most crucial period. It is possible to develop policies that recognize the relevance of these sorts of variables, specifying the number of years of residence or the number of years of schooling in the country required to establish a right to naturalization. I won't pretend that there is some philosophical basis for choosing a specific number of years. There is no way to eliminate the gray areas, but that does not mean that one cannot make confident judgments about the extremes. There is a big difference between someone who arrives as an infant and someone who arrives as an adult, both with respect to time spent and with respect to social formation.

Adult Immigrants

Let's turn now to the question of naturalization for adult immigrants. What conditions may a democratic state require adult immigrants to meet before granting them citizenship?[4] Let's first consider the reasons why adult immigrants have strong moral claims to citizenship and then see whether there are countervailing moral considerations that make it justifiable for states to require immigrants to meet certain standards before gaining citizenship.

In elaborating my answer, I mean to focus only on conditions that are constructed as formal, legal requirements in the naturalization process. It is important to distinguish between such formal requirements and other ways of influencing immigrants and integrating them into the political community. Formal requirements are legally enforceable standards like length of residence, demonstration of a certain level of language proficiency, passing a test in the country's history and institutions, and so on. Every political community also uses social expectations and incentives to affect the way immigrants engage with the political community. Social expectations and incentives have effects on people but they do not rely upon the force of law.

Many of the things that people sometimes say should be conditions of naturalization might be acceptable if they were encouraged through incentives or even pressed as social expectations but are not morally permissible if they are imposed as requirements. In the next chapter, I will consider questions about the extent to which it is legitimate for states to try to shape immigrants' behavior, values, and identities. In this chapter, I focus exclusively on formal, legal requirements for the acquisition of citizenship.

Social Membership and Democratic Legitimacy

The moral claims that adult immigrants have to citizenship rest on two distinct but related foundations: social membership and democratic legitimacy.[5] Consider their social membership claims first. Immigrants who arrive in a state as adults have received their social formation elsewhere. For that reason, they do not have quite as obvious a claim to be members of the community as their children who grow up within the state and may even be born there. Nevertheless, undergoing one's original social formation in a community is not the only path to social membership. Living in a community also makes people members. As adult immigrants settle into their new home, they become involved in a network of relationships that multiply and deepen over time. They acquire interests and identities that are tied up with other members of the society. Their choices and life chances, like those of their children, become shaped by the state's laws and policies. The longer they live there, the stronger their claims to social membership become. At some point, a threshold is passed. They have been there long enough that they simply are members of the community with a strong moral claim to have that membership officially recognized by the state by its granting of citizenship, or at least a right to citizenship if they want it.

The principles of democratic legitimacy give rise to a second basis for adult immigrants to assert a moral claim to citizenship. It is a fundamental democratic principle that everyone should be able to participate in shaping the laws by which she is to be governed and in choosing the representatives who actually make the laws, once she has reached an age where she is able to exercise independent agency. Full voting rights and the right to seek high public office are normally reserved for citizens, and I will simply assume that practice in this chapter.[6] Therefore, to meet the requirements of democratic legitimacy, every adult who lives in a democratic political community on an ongoing basis should be a citizen, or, at the least, should have the right to become a citizen if she chooses to do so. Prior to this point, I have not emphasized the democratic legitimacy argument because I have been talking about the citizenship claims of young children who are not old enough to vote or to participate formally in politics, though they have the same sort of claim prospectively, as it were, and the claim would have force if they reached adulthood without receiving citizenship.

The Limits of Discretion

These arguments about the moral claims that immigrants have to citizenship enable us to see what was so problematic about the decision to deny Swiss citizenship to Milikije Arifi, the woman of Macedonian origin whose story opened this chapter. Arifi had lived in Switzerland for over thirty years when she applied for citizenship. She had passed tests of her linguistic competence and civic knowledge. By any reasonable standard of social membership, she was clearly more a member of Swiss society than of any other and she was entitled to participate in the democratic process that generated the laws that she was expected to obey. The local town council seemed to think that it had no obligation to justify its decision to exclude Arifi from citizenship on the basis of reasons that might make sense to a wider public. Indeed, the local authorities explicitly acknowledged that the sorts of considerations that some people might find persuasive— a threat to public order or a failure to learn the language—did not apply to Arifi. The reasons given ("their environment is not so good.... We are hearing people in the vicinity of the Arifis who don't want us to do it") were highly subjective. To defend the exclusion of Arifi from citizenship, you would probably have to think that a state is morally free to do whatever it wants in granting or withholding citizenship.[7] That position essentially gives no weight to the moral claims that immigrants have to citizenship. I do not see how it is possible to reconcile that position with a commitment to democratic principles.

Arifi's story may seem like an extreme case, because she was so clearly integrated into Swiss society by any reasonable measure of integration. Would the social membership and democratic legitimacy arguments seem as strong if we were dealing with immigrants who did not fit in quite so well? Are there standards of social integration that are less subjective and arbitrary and that it is reasonable to impose as requirements for naturalization? For example, the state clearly has a responsibility to maintain the democratic regime that is the framework within which citizens are able to exercise their rights. Many people would argue that the state cannot and should not be indifferent to questions about whether those seeking citizenship accept the state's commitment to a democratic order.

Consider in this context the case of Faiza Silmi, the niqab-wearing Moroccan woman whose story appeared at the beginning of chapter 1. To recall, Silmi had a French husband and four French children, had lived in France for several years, and spoke French. She was denied French citizenship because, in the words of France's highest legal authority, "She has adopted a radical practice of her religion, incompatible with essential values of the French community, particularly the principle of equality of the sexes."[8] Although the decision was not based exclusively on the fact that Silmi wears a niqab, it seems clear from the public discussions about the case that this was a major consideration.

This is a harder case than Arifi's because the French authorities who denied citizenship to Silmi offered explicit reasons for their refusal and appealed to a principle (namely, gender equality) that is a fundamental part of the public normative framework of all contemporary democratic states. So, the decision about Silmi does not seem as capricious or subjective as the decision about Arifi. In addition, many people who are not at all troubled by most forms of religious dress are disturbed by the niqab (and other versions of dress that cover most or all of the face). In all honesty, I must admit that I find myself among them. Nevertheless, I think that the decision to deny Silmi French citizenship was unjust.

It would be possible to object to the decision to exclude Silmi from citizenship from many perspectives. For example, one could ask whether the evidence, including her wearing of the niqab, really proves that she is not an autonomous agent as the government alleged. The *New York Times* interview with her seems to reveal a person of strong convictions and one should not underestimate the courage it takes to wear a form of dress that the vast majority of people find objectionable. One could also argue that the French state is being discriminatory in excluding a Muslim woman from citizenship for views about gender relations that are quite similar to ones held by conservative Catholics, fundamentalist Protestants, orthodox Jews, and others who would never be subjected to this sort of scrutiny in a citizenship application. And one could argue that the state's policy is hypocritical in focusing on this particular manifestation of gender inequality while tolerating and even supporting the many other, much more pervasive forms that gender inequality takes in France and in other democratic states, from social norms regarding women's responsibilities for child-rearing and housekeeping to practices in advertising, fashion, and commerce that rely upon the presentation of the female body in ways that are pleasing to the male gaze.

I will leave these criticisms aside, however. I will focus on the issue that is most relevant to my central argument about access to citizenship. In my view, it is not morally permissible for a democratic state to make access to citizenship contingent upon what a person thinks or believes. The normal freedoms of a democratic society—the right to freedom of religion and conscience, the right to freedom of speech and association, the right to privacy and the general right to live one's life as one chooses so long as one does not violate the laws— set severe limits to what the state may demand of those subject to its control, whatever the state's goals. A democratic state may not use its coercive power against people simply because of what is in their hearts and minds.[9] That is true even when what is in their hearts and minds is antagonistic to democracy. Thus, for example, a democratic state may not take away someone's citizenship status because she professes ideas hostile to democracy, even if she has another citizenship and would not be rendered stateless by this deprivation.

The same principle applies to the naturalization process. To deny citizenship to someone who seeks it is an exercise of the state's coercive power. Of course, if the person seeking citizenship had no strong moral claim to it, the exercise of the coercive power could be easily justified, but that was not the case with Silmi. She had lived in France for several years. She spoke French. She had French children and a French husband. She was clearly a member of French society in many important respects. So, she had a claim to citizenship on the grounds of her social membership and she had a right to participate in shaping the laws to which she was subject. Just as the state should not take away a citizenship acquired at birth because of what that person thinks or feels, the state should not refuse to grant citizenship to someone who has a strong moral claim to it because of what that person thinks or feels.

Remember that we are speaking here of legal residents and legal require-ments. I am not saying that the state may not use its coercive power to restrict behavior (including, perhaps, some forms of speech) nor am I saying that the state must be indifferent to what settled immigrants think or that it may not promote certain values, attitudes, and commitments.[10] On the contrary, as we will see in the next chapter, a democratic state has a duty to create a cer-tain kind of political culture and to foster certain attitudes and dispositions. However, the state may not use coercion against people who do not adopt the attitudes and dispositions it is seeking to foster, and it may not punish people for behavior that is legally permitted. For the same reasons, the state may not exclude a settled immigrant from full membership in the political community because her views and her legally permitted behavior do not conform to the community's normative standards.[11] Denial of citizenship on that basis is mor-ally unacceptable.

If a democratic state should not refuse to grant citizenship to an adult immi-grant either on the basis of some official's purely subjective assessment of the immigrant's integration or on the basis of information about what the immigrant thinks and feels, what about more objective measures of civic integration? There are three other sorts of conditions besides an extended period of residence that some democratic states commonly require applicants for naturalization to meet: the renunciation of other citizenships, evidence of good behavior, and passing tests of linguistic and civic competence. Let's consider each of these in turn.

Dual Citizenship (Again)

Some states insist that applicants for citizenship renounce any other citizenship as a condition of their naturalization. Many states do not require this, and even more do not enforce the requirement. In the United States, for example, immi-grants are required to swear an oath to "absolutely and entirely renounce and abjure all allegiance and fidelity to any foreign prince, potentate, state, or sov-ereignty."[12] As a matter of law, however, it is clearly established that the United States permits dual citizenship for naturalized citizens. So, this rather imposing, old-fashioned oath has no actual legal consequences in the United States (though it probably does deter some immigrants from naturalizing).

In practice, the prohibition on dual citizenship is probably the biggest formal obstacle to naturalization for immigrants in the states that do require effective renunciation of a previous citizenship. Immigrants often have good reasons to want to leave open the possibility of returning to live in their country of origin at some point in the future, and keeping their original citizenship is the only way to guarantee that this will be possible. They may want to pursue economic opportunities there at some later stage in their careers. They may want to be able to return if they have to care for elderly parents. They may want to go back to retire. (Many more immigrants imagine they will return to their country of origin than actually do so in the end, because most immigrants establish families in the state where they settle, and their children and grandchildren tie them to that place.) Sometimes keeping the citizenship of origin protects important economic interests in states that limit the rights of noncitizens to inherit property or to operate businesses. And sometimes immigrants still feel a strong identification with and attachment to the country they left, and they associate that identity and attachment with their continued possession of the country's citizenship. For all these reasons, immigrants are often reluctant to naturalize if this requires them to give up their original citizenship.

Too bad, some will say. They have to make a choice. They have to decide where their primary loyalty lies. But why? Why should the state be able to force immigrants to choose? What interest does the state have in insisting on such a decision? Of course, the state wants its citizens to be loyal, but as we have already seen in the discussion of dual citizenship at birth, people can be loyal to two states just as they can love both of their parents. Indeed, almost all of the arguments that I presented in favor of permitting dual citizenship at birth for the children of immigrants are also arguments for permitting adult immigrants to retain their original citizenship in the course of naturalization. The state has no serious interest at stake in getting those seeking naturalization to give up a previous citizenship. The fact that almost all democratic states permit dual citizenship for the children of citizens when the children acquire both citizenships at birth confirms this. By contrast, immigrants often do have a vital interest in keeping their citizenship of origin, for the reasons laid out above. Remember, too, that we are talking about immigrants who have a strong moral claim to their new citizenship on the basis of their social membership and their right to participate in democratic decision making in the political community where they live. Under these circumstances, to require immigrants to renounce their original citizenship as a condition of naturalization is unjust. Sovereign states may have the power to enact prohibitions on dual nationality for naturalized citizens, but democratic states are morally obliged not to use that power.

Good Behavior

Sometimes states want evidence that immigrants have behaved well during their period of residence prior to naturalization. This takes various forms.

Many states impose a requirement that the person being naturalized not have a criminal record. Given the background assumption that states are morally entitled to control admissions, it seems reasonable to say that states should be able to deny entry to those with serious criminal records and to expel recently arrived immigrants who are convicted of serious crimes, although as we will see in later chapters, this principle is subject to some qualifications. If the immigrant's criminal record is not significant enough to warrant deportation, however, it should not warrant permanent exclusion from citizenship either. It might justify a delay in naturalization but not an absolute barrier.

Some states have a good character requirement in addition to the absence of a criminal record. This is an invitation to discretionary abuse.

Some states require proof of a certain level of income or the absence of reliance upon social assistance. This is a form of discrimination against the poor. If people are entitled to some form of social assistance, they should not then be penalized politically for taking advantage of it. The status of citizenship should not be contingent upon money.

Tests of Civic Competence

As part of the naturalization process, democratic states often require immigrants to pass some sort of test of their knowledge of the dominant language (or at least of some official language) and of the state's history and institutional arrangements and perhaps its culture. I will call these combined requirements "tests of civic competence" because the justification for such tests is that immigrants must acquire certain kinds of knowledge in order to perform their roles as citizens. The tests assess whether they have the requisite knowledge. Many people think that such requirements are perfectly reasonable.[13]

I disagree, but I do not want to overstate the importance of that disagreement. The crucial claim that I am making in this chapter is that citizenship should be easily accessible as a matter of right to immigrants who want it after they have been in the country for a few years. That is largely compatible with tests of linguistic and civic knowledge, if the requirements for passing the tests are set at appropriately modest levels so that most immigrants can pass the tests without difficulty. Reasonable tests of civic competence do not pose a substantial barrier to naturalization for most people.

Even though reasonable tests are generally compatible with my main claim in this chapter, they are objectionable in principle. I think it is worth explaining why.

The first and most important point to note is that we are talking about a *requirement* for naturalization. The question is not whether it is desirable for immigrants to be able to use the local language and to learn about the state's history and institutions and culture. Of course, this is desirable. States should give immigrants opportunities, support, and encouragement to acquire this sort of knowledge. Understanding the local language and learning about the country where they have settled is good for the immigrants and it is good for the community as a whole. The question is whether it is morally permissible to pursue this desirable objective by requiring immigrants to pass certain tests as a condition of naturalization.

The fact that a goal is worthy and legitimate does not automatically make the means used to pursue that goal morally acceptable. Recall the distinction that I drew at the beginning of this section between requirements, on the one hand, and social expectations and incentives, on the other. It would be fine to create incentives for immigrants to learn the dominant language and to learn about the society (though there are strong incentives for them to do so even without state policies creating additional ones). To establish something as a formal requirement for naturalization is another matter. It entails the consequence that those who do not meet that requirement will not become citizens. That is what I want to challenge. Even if tests of civic competence improve the civic capacities of those who prepare for them and so enhance the overall quality of democratic participation, they are not justifiable because they inevitably deny citizenship to some people who have a moral right to be citizens.

When I was first asked to reflect about these tests fifteen years ago, I asked my son Michael (who was then 10 years old) what he thought about the issue. He responded almost incredulously, "You mean someone wouldn't be allowed to be a citizen because he didn't pass a test? That sucks! People who do not have a good education or who are just not good at taking tests have the right to be citizens too." I think that Michael's reaction was entirely right. It is unjust to make access to citizenship contingent on whether or not someone passes a test.

Let me unpack that claim a bit. Even those who defend using tests as part of the naturalization process acknowledge that some European states like the Netherlands have developed tests that are far too difficult.[14] These tests are a lot like the literacy tests that African Americans were required to take in some southern states in the United States in the first half of the twentieth century. Their goal is not really to test knowledge but to exclude. Everyone agrees that tests that are designed to exclude are unjust (even if people sometimes disagree about whether or not a given test belongs in that category).

Let's leave this sort of problem to one side, however. Let's focus instead on tests that most people would regard as reasonable (if they accepted the idea of tests at all). These are tests that only require a modest level of linguistic ability and the sort of civic knowledge that ordinary people can acquire without too much effort. The information to be tested is readily accessible so that it is easy to prepare for the tests, and applicants can take the tests over as often as they want if they fail. There is no cost to take the test, or, at most, a modest one. These are the sorts of tests that have long been used in countries of immigration like the United States and Canada.[15] Most immigrants who take such tests pass them. Similar tests have recently been introduced in some European states. Immigrants who take these tests often say that they find the experience of preparing for them to be very valuable. Some feel that they have earned their citizenship by studying for the test and passing it. What's wrong with that sort of test?

In my view even reasonable and apparently beneficial tests rely implicitly on a morally problematic conception of citizenship that was widely embraced in earlier times but that has now generally been rejected. In that earlier approach, democratic states divided the citizenry into two groups: those capable of participating in politics and those not capable of participating. In the immediate aftermath of the French Revolution, for example, the French Republic distinguished between active citizens and passive citizens. Other democratic states drew similar distinctions, excluding some segment of the citizen population from the political participation on grounds of competence. Sometimes the assessment of competence was based on unchanging, ascriptive characteristics like gender and race, but sometimes it was based on contingent and changeable features of individuals like economic resources and education.

The criterion of education, in particular, was often defended in the late nineteenth and early twentieth century in terms that are remarkably similar to the ones used today as justifications for the tests imposed on immigrants. Doesn't it make sense to require voters to pass a literacy test (or perhaps something more demanding) for the same kinds of reasons that we require drivers to pass a driving test? They are engaged in an activity with important consequences for others and they should be obliged to demonstrate that they have the basic knowledge required to carry out this activity responsibly.

Then, as now, those defending such tests were, for the most part, not using these requirements as pretexts for exclusion. They were genuinely concerned with the quality of democratic politics. Nevertheless, almost no one today would defend the idea of requiring citizens to pass a test to vote. That is not merely because we now have compulsory schooling and can safely assume that people have learned what they need to know in school. As an empirical matter, we know that some students don't learn much, that some even emerge from the educational process as functional illiterates. But we don't deny them the right to vote.

We have come to see that, for adult citizens, making the right to participate in the democratic process contingent on any test or measure of competence is unjust, in part because such screening will always reflect class and other biases, whatever the intention of those designing the screens, and in part because we have come to recognize that the right to have a say in how one is governed should be regarded as something fundamental, not easily subject to qualification. However desirable it may be to have an educated electorate—and I think that it is very desirable—we cannot pursue that goal by excluding a subset of the citizenry from participation.

The most important qualification to this general principle that we no longer accept competency restrictions on political participation is the age requirement for voting. Everyone recognizes that very young children are not capable of exercising political agency. So, children are not allowed to vote, even though they are citizens, on the grounds that they are not competent to participate. But note that, as part of our commitment to the ideal of equal citizenship, we treat every citizen in exactly the same way in imposing and then removing this competency requirement. We establish an age requirement for voting. As an empirical matter, we know that individuals mature at different rates. If we were only concerned with the individual's capacity to participate, it might make sense to design tests that could reveal whether or not a young person was sufficiently mature and knowledgeable to vote. Of course, it is completely predictable that the capacity to pass such tests would correlate with class, and perhaps with other socioeconomic variables as well. To permit formal access to voting to depend on tests that correlated with such socioeconomic characteristics would violate our understanding of democratic equality. That is why no democratic state would seriously consider such a measure.

The same democratic logic should preclude us from subjecting adult immigrants to competence tests as a requirement for citizenship. Someone will object that the immigrants are not yet citizens and so this bar on using competence tests does not apply to them. The objection depends on a circular argument. The immigrants are not yet citizens only because we require them to pass these competence tests. Remember that we are talking here about adult immigrants who are settled members of society. They have been present long enough to have established claims of social membership and they are subject to the laws on an ongoing basis. In other words, they possess the very sorts of claims to belong that are the basis upon which the democratic state where they live granted citizenship to all of its current citizens. I am assuming here that they want to become citizens, and that they would be citizens if they did not have to pass these tests. The justification for the tests is that they need to prove their competence to participate. But, as I have been arguing, we no longer think it is morally appropriate to require people who would otherwise be entitled to participate to prove their competence to do so. Citizenship is not something that normally is earned or that ought to be earned. People acquire a moral right to citizenship from their social membership and the fact of their ongoing subjection to the laws.

I suspect that many people will resist this line of argument, so let me offer another angle of vision on the case I am making. Suppose we have some adult immigrants who are otherwise qualified for citizenship but who have not passed these civic competence tests. Why don't we grant them citizenship but not let them vote until they pass their tests? What would be the point of that? Well, they would be officially recognized as members of the political community. They would enjoy the greater security and protection that comes with the status of citizenship. Even if gaining citizenship did not affect many of their legal rights within the state, it would be a tremendous practical advantage for many immigrants to have the passport of the state where they live and it might matter a great deal to them emotionally.

In practice, this kind of change would be unthinkable (or, at least, I hope it would). We can no longer seriously entertain the possibility of severing the legal status of citizenship in a state where you live from the right to participate in that state's political process, once you are an adult.[16] But what it would be unthinkable to do openly, we do covertly. Instead of denying the right to vote on grounds of competence to people who are citizens, we deny citizenship on grounds of competence to people who qualify for and deserve citizenship in every other respect. That is why I say that the test requirement relies upon a (disguised) version of an outmoded conception of democratic citizenship.

Let me add one final point. Tests of civic competence never actually test civic competence. The tests that assess a person's knowledge of various facts about the history and institutions of the country tell us nothing about a person's civic capacities. Citizens have to make political judgments. The knowledge required for wise political judgment is complex, multifaceted, and often intuitive. It's not something that can be captured on a test. Think realistically about the kinds of questions that voters have to ask themselves about parties and candidates. Do I share their values? Do I trust them to take the country in the right direction? These are the crucial sorts of questions that citizens have to ask themselves in deciding how to vote, and knowing when the constitution was written or how parliament is organized is won't help.

But isn't it at least reasonable to insist that immigrants have some knowledge of the language of public life before they become citizens? I readily grant that competence in the language of public life is the most plausible requirement for naturalization. Knowledge of the language facilitates interactions with others in civil society and makes it easier to engage in public discussions. So, it is directly relevant to the political competence that citizens need in a democracy.

Even if we accept the relevance of this consideration, however, it is important not to use a romanticised conception of public deliberation as a justification for depriving people of access to citizenship. One may wish and hope that citizens will be well informed, but it is unreasonable to insist on knowledge of the dominant language for the sake of an idealized form of political information that typical native citizens do not possess.

Even the legitimacy of any linguistic requirement fades over time. It is hard to learn a language as an adult and harder as one grows older. Some states, like Canada and the United States, recognize this by granting exemptions to the language requirements for naturalization to people over 60. It's highly desirable that immigrants learn the language of public life, but people do sometimes get by without it. People who have functioned in civil society for several years without knowing the dominant language should be presumed to be capable of participating in the political process as well. They will have many forms of information available from friends and neighbors and media in their native language, and that should be enough. In fact, many of those who pass the modest language requirements of reasonable competence tests actually rely on sources in their native language for most of their political information, since their knowledge of the dominant language is limited. In this respect, they are not greatly different from citizens who grow up in the society. The political knowledge of most citizens is always heavily filtered through friends and neighbors and other trusted local sources, regardless of the language they speak.

Perhaps it is reasonable to offer accelerated naturalization to those who can pass tests of civic competence as an incentive to immigrants to acquire this sort of knowledge. But the linguistic barrier to citizenship should not be absolute. After several years of residence, ten at the most in my view, any language requirement should be set aside. *Requiring* immigrants to pass tests of linguistic capacity and civic knowledge as a condition of naturalization is ultimately unjust.

Does it follow that we should criticize such requirements wherever we find them and seek to abolish them? Not necessarily. As I noted in the previous chapter, the meaning of particular policies depends in part on context. Some European states are moving away from the idea that citizenship is a privilege, not a right, and away from the idea that the state is entitled to exercise complete discretion in deciding whether to grant an immigrant citizenship. As part of that transformation of the conception of citizenship, these states have sometimes replaced a subjective and intrusive assessment of whether an immigrant seeking naturalization is sufficiently integrated with an objective measure of integration as measured by tests of linguistic capacity and civic knowledge that are set at reasonable levels and ask reasonable questions. In that sort of context, the new test requirement may actually represent a reduction in the demands being made of immigrants in the naturalization process. The test can be a significant step in the right direction, and it is important to recognize that. Furthermore, as I noted earlier in this chapter in my discussion of the French policy of optional natural-ization for children who grow up in France, sometimes the crucial moral ques-tion is how a policy is designed rather than whether it satisfies a formal principle. If tests of civic competence are inexpensive and easy to pass, they may not con-stitute a significant barrier to naturalization. That is more important in practice than the question of whether such tests are morally permissible in principle. As I observed in the previous chapter in my discussion of the reform of *ius soli* laws, we cannot leap directly from analysis of principles to prescriptions for policy.

Beyond Legal Citizenship to Inclusion

A couple of years ago when I was travelling by train in Britain, I was sitting opposite an elderly Pakistani couple and next to their adolescent daughter. When the crowded train pulled out of the station, the parents began to talk in Urdu. The girl felt restless and nervous and started making strange signals to them. As they carried on their conversation for a few more minutes, she angrily leaned over the table and asked them to shut up. When the confused mother asked why, the girl shot back 'just as you do not expose your private parts in public, you should not speak in *that language* in public'.[1]

This poignant story told by the political theorist Bhikhu Parekh illustrates one of the ways in which immigrants or their children can feel as though they don't really belong in the society where they live or, at least, that they will only fit in if they keep some aspects of their culture and identity, including their native tongue, behind closed doors. We don't know anything about the citizenship status of the parents in the story, but it is plausible to suppose that they were British citizens. In any event, they clearly were not violating any law in speaking Urdu to one another. Their daughter apparently believed, however, that they were violating a British social norm in doing so. Given the analogy that she drew between speaking Urdu in public and public exposure of one's genitalia, she must have internalized this norm herself, experiencing her parents' use of Urdu on the train as deeply embarrassing.

Of course, we don't have to take the girl's perceptions at face value. Adolescents in Europe and North America often feel mortified by their parents' behavior in public spaces for reasons that seem utterly mysterious to the parents themselves. Perhaps no one else on the train would have been affronted to hear her parents speaking Urdu. (Their fellow traveler Parekh certainly was not.) Her parents themselves apparently felt free to speak Urdu to one another, and her mother was puzzled by her daughter's request. So, the girl may have been mistaken about British social norms. On the other hand, one has to wonder how a child would ever develop on her own such a strong view about the shamefulness of speaking

Urdu in public. The children of immigrants are often much more attuned to the informal social norms of the wider society than the immigrants themselves.

Whether the girl was right or not about this particular social norm, the story alerts us to the fact that belonging to a political community involves much more than legal status and legal rights. In the previous two chapters, I looked at questions about the acquisition of citizenship. In this chapter I want to consider issues that go beyond legal status and the legal rights that accompany that status. I will focus therefore on immigrants and their descendants who have the legal status of citizenship. I will call them citizens of immigrant origin. My goal is to explore some of the factors that affect the extent to which citizens of immigrant origin are included in the political community where they live.

It is certainly possible for people to be citizens, to have equal legal rights, and to be marginalized nevertheless. If immigrants or their descendants possess citizenship status but are excluded from the economic and educational opportunities that others enjoy, if they are expected to conceal things related to their immigrant origins in order to fit in, if they are viewed with suspicion and hostility by others, if their concerns are ignored and their voices not heard in political life, then they are not really included in the political community, even though they are citizens in a formal, legal sense. They are not likely to see themselves or to be seen by others as genuine members of the community. In many important ways, they will not belong.

From a democratic perspective, that would clearly be wrong. No one thinks that citizens must be the same in every respect, but the democratic ideal of equal citizenship entails much more than formal legal equality. It requires that citizens should feel free to live their lives as they choose to a considerable extent, that they should enjoy at least rough equality of opportunity in education and economic life, that they should be able to help shape the rules to which they are subject, and that they should interact with their fellow citizens on a basis of mutual respect and fairness. This democratic ideal of equal citizenship applies to citizens of immigrant origin as much as to other citizens.

In democracies, majorities carry a lot of weight, and so they should. But democratic theorists have long worried about the abuse of that power, the tyranny of majorities over minorities. Citizens of immigrant origin are one important kind of vulnerable minority. At the very least, they differ from the majority of their fellow citizens in virtue of their immigrant origins. Often they differ in other ways as well: physical appearance, religion, language, cultural patterns, and values. Is it morally acceptable if any of these differences affect their ability to be equal citizens in the fuller sense that I have just outlined? What (if anything) may citizens of immigrant origin reasonably be expected to do or to change in order to be fully included in the political communities where they live? And what can they reasonably expect of the democratic states where they live and of the nonimmigrant majorities in those states to make their full inclusion possible?[2]

I use the language of "reasonable expectations" deliberately. Most of the issues that I explore in this chapter do not lend themselves to codification in terms of formal rights and duties. It is a familiar point that democratic states cannot rest entirely on rules, procedures, and formal institutions. Democracies work well only if most of the citizens accept democratic values and principles and if they reflect these commitments in their attitudes and dispositions. In short, democracies require a democratic ethos.

The challenge for this chapter is to say something about the sort of democratic ethos that is needed in a political community if citizens of immigrant origin are to be fully included. Here a caution is in order. In public discussions of immigration, it is a recurring theme that immigrants and their descendants should accept democratic values and practice democratic virtues. Suitably qualified, that is a reasonable expectation, as we shall see. But an equally reasonable and perhaps more important expectation is that other citizens also accept democratic values and practice democratic virtues. All too often, the assumption seems to be that the majority of citizens already possess the values and virtues that are needed for a democracy to function properly. But that is frequently not the case. Democratic principles require the inclusion of immigrants, and the inclusion of immigrants requires the majority of citizens to embrace the implications of the principles and values that they profess. This will often entail developing attitudes and dispositions that many citizens do not yet exhibit, at least in the requisite degree. I will say more about these requirements as the chapter proceeds. People sometimes speak of the need for democratic states to engage in a more "muscular" assertion of their values and to demand adherence to those values from people living in their societies. If that is indeed what is called for, a lot more of the muscle should be applied to the nonimmigrant majority of citizens than is commonly acknowledged.

In the rest of this chapter I will offer a number of illustrations of the sorts of reasonable expectations that flow from a democratic ethos of inclusion. I organize my discussion around five categories: rules, informal norms, incentives, practices of recognition, and national identity. I use these categories simply as an expositional device. Nothing hinges on the categories themselves. They are disparate in nature, and the lines between different categories are sometimes blurred. It would be possible to move the discussion of some of the examples from one category to another without changing anything significant. Some of the topics involve state action or public policies and some do not. Some focus more on demands made of citizens of immigrant origin, others more on demands made of public officials or citizens from the nonimmigrant majority. I make no pretence of offering a comprehensive account. My goal is simply to present some evocative examples which draw attention to the many different ways in which the full inclusion of citizens of immigrant origin requires the mutual adaptation of citizens of immigrant origin and nonimmigrant citizens and can be promoted by a democratic ethos of inclusion or discouraged by its absence.[3] If there is anything distinctive about this chapter—I do not say that it is original—it is the emphasis that I place here both on the importance of informal mechanisms (as distinct from formal rights and duties) for issues of inclusion and exclusion and on the challenges that the idea of a democratic ethos poses to the majority population as well as to immigrants.

Rules

Formal rules often affect the inclusion of immigrants. A rule is a formal requirement, imposed by some authority and backed with some explicit sanction. A law passed by a legislature is obviously a rule of this sort, but rules include a much wider array of phenomena. Almost any policy or regulation to which some formal sanction is attached is a rule in the sense in which I am using the term. For example, if a business requires its employees to wear a uniform, that is a rule. Rules impose duties but also often create corresponding rights or formal entitlements.

It may seem puzzling that I start with a discussion of rules, given that I am emphasizing the need to go beyond the formally equal rights and duties of citizenship in order to include immigrants. My primary concern, however, is not with the content of particular rules but with the attitude that citizens take towards constructing and modifying rules. In other words, my concern is with the way a democratic ethos that aims to include citizens of immigrant origin will affect the rules that govern economic, social, and political life. I start with a type of rule whose content is directly related to inclusion.

Rules against Discrimination

One obvious way to promote the inclusion of immigrants is to establish rules that prohibit discrimination on the basis of characteristics that tend to distinguish citizens of immigrant origin from other citizens. For example, many democratic states have adopted rules against discrimination on the basis of race, ethnicity, or religion. Of course, some nonimmigrant citizens may also differ from the majority of citizens in these ways, and some immigrants may not. There may also be other bases of discrimination (e.g., gender, sexual orientation) that are not linked to immigrant origins and that should be prohibited.

My focus on immigration is not intended to deny the importance of these other concerns. I simply want to pay attention to the issues that are most salient to immigration.

The general democratic commitment to equal citizenship and especially to equality of opportunity requires that no one be subjected to social disadvantage on the basis of arbitrary criteria. Citizens of immigrant origin who are as well qualified as other applicants should have an equal chance of getting a job or gaining admission to a school. If someone is buying a house or renting an apartment or starting a business or taking out a loan, the fact that she is an immigrant or the child or grandchild of immigrants should be irrelevant.

These days no one committed to democratic principles openly challenges this general principle of nondiscrimination. I mention it, however, because, as I said in the introduction, in discussing the ethics of immigration, it is sometimes important to state the obvious. We have to pay attention to what is agreed upon as well as to what is in dispute. Also, we should not forget that this consensus on nondiscrimination is a relatively recent development in democratic states. It emerged only in the second half of the twentieth century. Prior to that, the rules in many democratic states permitted or even required discrimination against immigrants (and other minorities).

The fact that almost no one openly defends discrimination today does not mean that discrimination has disappeared. Much of it has simply gone underground. It still operates to create social disadvantages, but it is not usually openly acknowledged. Often discrimination is both indirect and unintended, the unconscious byproduct of criteria that are ostensibly measures of qualifications but that turn out, upon critical scrutiny, to incorporate biases unrelated to performance or other relevant considerations. Simply having a rule against discrimination is clearly insufficient to address this sort of problem. It's a necessary step, but nowhere near sufficient. Usually, additional rules of one kind or another are necessary. There is a vast literature on this topic, and I cannot begin to address it here. This is an area where the specifics of the history, institutions, and practices of particular political communities matter a great deal in determining what will work once one moves past a general rule prohibiting discrimination. What I can say, as a general matter, is that developing effective policies to combat discrimination is one of the key prerequisites for the inclusion of citizens of immigrant origin.

In this chapter I am asking what citizens of immigrant origin and other citizens can reasonably expect of one another and of the state. One thing that it is clearly reasonable for citizens of immigrant origin to expect is that the democratic states where they live will develop effective rules to protect them against discrimination.

Rules, Exemptions, and Reasonable Mutual Adjustment

As a general matter, all citizens in a democratic community are subject to the same rules. We don't normally find one rule for citizens of immigrant origin and a different rule for other citizens, whether as general laws or in other settings like workplaces. But rules that treat everyone equally in a formal sense may have a disparate impact on citizens of immigrant origin because of the ways in which citizens of immigrant origin typically differ from other citizens. Sometimes the rules may require citizens of immigrant origin to make adaptations that the majority of citizens do not have to make because of their different backgrounds. Sometimes there may be a conflict between the cultural and religious practices of citizens of immigrant origin and the behavior required or prohibited by the existing rules. In such cases, it is not enough to say that citizens of immigrant origin should obey whatever rules are in place so long as they were duly passed in accordance with democratic procedures. As I noted before, we have to worry about majority tyranny. We have to ask whether it is reasonable for citizens of immigrant origin to expect the existing rules to be modified in some way to take account of their differences.

The general principle that I would put forward for dealing with such cases is that all parties (i.e., citizens of immigrant origin, other citizens, and the political authorities responsible for constructing and applying the existing rules) should be willing to adjust their demands or expectations when the burdens of such adjustments are reasonable. All parties have an obligation to consider how important the issue is to them and whether their concerns can be met in some other way. Not every cultural and religious concern carries the same weight. So, citizens of immigrant origin should object to rules that serve some legitimate general purpose only when the rules impose a significant burden that cannot be easily avoided by some acceptable shift in their own practice or behavior. On the other hand, when they feel that a rule is interfering with some important religious or cultural commitment of theirs (and, in practice, they rarely challenge rules otherwise), the state and the other citizens have an obligation to consider whether the objectives of the rule might be met in some other, less burdensome way. This might involve either rewriting the rule in a way that achieves the basic objective without imposing the same limitation on citizens of immigrant origin or carefully crafting an exemption from the rule for the minority of people whose important religious and cultural concerns will otherwise be negatively affected. There may be cases where it will be appropriate to insist on maintaining established rules without changes or exemptions, but the state and other citizens ought to at least consider carefully the alternatives.

Some people argue that we should only consider maintaining or changing rules but not the possibility of creating exemptions to rules.[4] On this view, it is a basic democratic principle that the rules should be the same for everyone, unlike feudalism which had different rules for nobles and commoners. In democracies there is not supposed to be any privileged class. Laws and rules should be the same for all.

There is something to this approach but it is easily overstated. There are often good reasons for having a general rule but recognizing exceptions.[5] It is easy to think of examples of this that have nothing to do with immigration and that don't involve the creation of a privileged class. Rules against allowing animals into certain places often make exceptions for dogs that are assisting the blind. We want everyone to observe the speed limit but we make an exception for police and emergency vehicles (when they need to go fast). Perhaps the most striking example is the common practice in democratic states of providing an exemption from compulsory military service, even in time of war, to those who have a conscientious objection to such service. In that case, the state permits exceptions to the general rule even though it has (what it regards as) a compelling interest (national security) in requiring people to comply with the rule and the advantages of noncompliance for the individual (not having to risk one's life) are huge, thus presumably creating strong incentives to make opportunistic and unjustified use of the exception. The fact that many democratic states still permit exemptions from the rule requiring military service under these circumstances shows how far democratic states think they ought to go to avoid requiring people to violate their conscience. Many of the cases where citizens of immigrant origin seek exemptions from existing rules also involve issues of conscience or religious conviction. Respecting such claims does not make citizens of immigrant origin into a privileged class.

Overall then, if the goal is the inclusion of immigrants, sometimes it will make sense to keep existing rules as they are, sometimes it will make sense to adopt a new rule that achieves the same goal without imposing a differential burden, and sometimes it will make sense to keep the existing rule but to provide an exemption for those unduly burdened by it.

Language and Education

Let's explore what this general approach might mean concretely. I start with a rule that imposes a greater burden on citizens of immigrant origin than on other citizens, but that also achieves an important goal that could not be achieved in any other way. This is the requirement that all children receive an education in the public language of the place where the children are receiving the education.[6] Getting an education in a language other than the one that is spoken at home is burdensome for both children and parents, but economic, social, and political inclusion depend upon children acquiring the capacity to function effectively in the language of public life. Opportunities for people who do not have this capacity are severely limited. So, it is reasonable to expect citizens of immigrant origin to send their children to schools where they will be educated in the language of public life rather than in the parents' native tongue. This rule places heavier demands on citizens of immigrant origin than on citizens for whom the language of public life is the language spoken at home, but it does so for the sake of inclusion and there is no feasible, less burdensome alternative. Citizens of immigrant origin normally recognize this. That is why this basic requirement is rarely controversial, even though there are sometimes significant disputes about the best way to achieve this goal, as in some of the American debates over bilingual education.[7]

Diet, Dress, Holidays, and Places of Worship

Consider now some examples of cases in which it is reasonable for citizens of immigrant origin to expect that existing rules will be modified to accommodate them. Most of these cases concern things like diet, dress, and religious holidays. Let me say a few brief things about each.

Dietary restrictions are normally the easiest to accommodate. Indeed, accommodating dietary concerns, whether prompted by health, ethics, or religion, is now entirely commonplace in many contexts. Reasonable accommodation means that it is appropriate to take into account the costs of various dietary alternatives, the numbers involved and so on.

There are often rules about what people should wear in an organizational context like a school or a firm or a public organization. When some citizen of immigrant origin seeks a modification of the uniform to permit her to respect a religious commitment (e.g., Islamic hijab or Sikh headgear), it is almost always possible to accommodate such requests with little inconvenience to the organization. In such cases, the democratic ethos requires that the uniform be modified or an exemption be granted so that the person can participate without violating her conscience. In rare cases there may be health or safety concerns that make compromises with respect to the religiously mandated clothing difficult or that even preclude it.

All democratic states in Europe and North America have calendars and weekly schedules shaped by Christian traditions with the work week built around the idea of Sunday as a day off for most people and Christmas an official state holiday (and sometimes other Christian holidays as well). This permits devout Christians to worship on Sundays, as is the Christian tradition, and to celebrate their most important religious holidays without having to work. It is a less convenient schedule for Jews whose Sabbath is on Saturday (and begins Friday at sundown) or for Muslims who place special emphasis on Friday afternoon services. If the state had to be completely neutral between different religions, perhaps it would be necessary to switch the weekend to Tuesday and Wednesday and abolish all holidays with religious significance, replacing them with purely civic holidays on different dates. No one seriously proposes that sort of approach. But to be fair to Muslims, Jews, and others, democratic states should try to find ways to enable them to get time off from work or school in order to be able to celebrate their important religious holidays and to attend services on the days that are customary for them. It is often possible to make these arrangements with modest adjustments that involve only minor inconveniences or costs to the organization. Again, a democratic ethos of inclusion requires this sort of accommodation. At the same time, the underlying commitment is to accommodation that is reasonable and mutual. The cost of accommodating these sorts of religious concerns varies from one situation to another, and the importance of being able to attend services or celebrate particular religious holidays varies among religious traditions and among different individuals within a given religious tradition. These factors matter in determining what sort of accommodation is reasonable.

For historical reasons, every state in Europe and North America has an abundance of Christian churches, but relatively few places of worship for Muslims and adherents of other religions. It is often difficult to build mosques or other places of worship in the places where citizens of immigrant origin live because of zoning issues, parking requirements, and other constraints. Most of these constraints were introduced in response to sensible concerns about the regulation of construction and traffic, and not to prevent citizens of immigrant origin from having public places for religious gatherings. Nevertheless, that is often the effect of these regulations if they are not modified or adjusted in some way. It matters substantively and symbolically whether citizens of immigrant origin have access to public places for their religious practices. So, this is another area where it is particularly important for authorities to show some flexibility and creativity with respect to the established rules.[8]

These four issues (diet, dress, holidays, and places of worship) provide just a few ordinary examples of the many different ways in which it is appropriate to respond to the presence of citizens of immigrant origins by modifying rules or creating exemptions. In some political and legal cultures it may be possible to pursue reasonable mutual adjustment without a formal legal or administrative process. An official commission studying the challenges of this sort of approach in Quebec found that, in the vast majority of cases where some conflict emerged between an existing rule or practice and the cultural or religious concerns of minorities, it was possible to reach a solution informally by having discussions between those immediately responsible for carrying out the rules and the individuals who were negatively affected by it.[9] Through these discussions, each party was normally able to understand the other's concerns, and it was usually possible to negotiate a solution that maintained whatever important principles lay behind the rule while permitting the minorities to live up to their most important cultural or religious commitments. The commission argued, and I agree, that it is preferable to rely upon this sort of informal mode of resolving conflicts whenever possible because it encourages ordinary citizens and grass-roots officials to exercise their own agency and manage their relationships with one another rather than relying upon an authoritative solution from above. I would acknowledge, however, that the idea of informal adjustments relies on a particular understanding of law and administration that may not fit well with the traditions of some democratic states.[10] In any event, the habits of mutual understanding, respect, good will, and compromise that make such informal arrangements possible are precisely the sorts of virtues that are required of most citizens, whether of immigrant origin or not, if a democracy is to function effectively. For citizens of immigrant origin to feel that they belong, they have to see that other citizens regard them as equals, take their concerns and interests seriously, and want to find ways of living together that are satisfactory to all. And the other citizens can reasonably expect to see the same attitudes and dispositions in the citizens of immigrant origin. But the power lies with the majority and the weight of the existing rules reflects that. So, in many respects, it is incumbent on the majority to signal first its willingness to take an approach that is open to reasonable accommodation.

In sum, the idea that all parties should approach conflicts over rules with a commitment to reasonable mutual adjustment is an essential element of a democratic ethos in any democratic state that is concerned with the inclusion of citizens of immigrant origin. The duty to take this approach applies to all citizens, whether of immigrant origin or not, and has special relevance for those in positions of authority.

Informal Norms

Informal norms also play a crucial role in promoting or discouraging the inclusion of immigrants. Most social interactions are shaped in part by informal norms about roles and relationships—what it is to be a good parent or friend, how to behave responsibly as a colleague or supervisor, and so on. Like rules, informal norms have a coercive dimension. They make demands on those subject to them. The key difference between rules and informal norms is the degree of explicitness about what is being demanded and what consequences will greet a failure to meet the demand. The girl in the story that opened this chapter was responding to what she perceived to be an informal norm in the sense in which

I am using the term. She was probably aware that there was no explicit rule forbidding her parents from speaking Urdu, but she felt that their doing so violated a strong social norm and one that she accepted. Her reaction to their behavior is an example of the ways in which informal norms are often enforced: through personal and social disapproval.

Informal norms can play a crucial role in supporting rules. Few rules work effectively if people are constrained only by the consequences they will face if caught breaking the rule. The rules work better if those subject to them feel the rules ought to be obeyed. At the same time, the creation of rules can affect what people think. They can generate informal norms. For example, rules against discrimination may be difficult to enforce unless most people accept the idea that the prohibited discrimination is actually wrong. If they think that, they may disapprove of people who engage in discrimination even in cases when that does not violate any formal rule. At the same time, rules can help to establish norms. Having a rule against discrimination may contribute to people seeing it as wrong. So, rules and informal norms can interact and can reinforce one another.

Sometimes informal norms do not reinforce rules but substitute for them. It may be impractical to use formal rules to regulate social interactions in some contexts but possible to rely on informal norms instead. The norms of polite behavior are a good example. It may also be against our principles to use a rule for something but acceptable to construct a social norm about it. For example, it is difficult and often morally problematic to construct rules about values, attitudes, dispositions, and feelings, but it may be both possible and acceptable to have social expectations about such matters. As we will see below, even a political community that places great weight on freedom from social pressure will have to make use of informal norms to make freedom from social pressure possible.

Many of the conflicts related to immigration are concerned not with what people do but with what they think and feel, things that are normally not subject to rules. That is one reason why it is so important to pay attention to informal norms as well as rules in this chapter. Some of the most crucial questions relating to inclusion are about the reasonableness and defensibility of informal social norms. Political authorities and the nonimmigrant majority may say that they want citizens of immigrant origin not just to obey the law but to accept the fundamental democratic values underlying legal rules. They may also assert that citizens of immigrant origin ought to adapt to the way the majority does things in the society and not insist on doing things their own way, even if there are no rules requiring them to conform. Citizens of immigrant origin may want to live their lives in many respects in the way they did when in their country of origin and want the nonimmigrant majority to accept their choice to do so and to see them as full members of the community regardless of that.

What should we say about these different informal demands about values and behavior? When is it reasonable to expect citizens of immigrant origin to conform to the majority's way of thinking and its way of doing things (even in the absence of formal rules requiring anyone to do this), and when is it reasonable to expect the majority to respect whatever desires citizens of immigrant origin have to think and act differently from the majority?

When in Rome

In my discussion of rules, I focused on the ways in which rules may need to be modified to include citizens of immigrant origin. This can give a misleading impression about the overall dynamics of inclusion. In the vast majority of cases, the rules that have been established in democratic states will not have to be changed in order to include citizens of immigrant origin. On the contrary, citizens of immigrant origin will have to adjust to existing rules in order to include themselves, and it is reasonable to expect them to do so.

The same thing is true of informal norms. Those who think that citizens of immigrant origin should simply conform to the pre-existing informal norms in the states in which they live like to cite the old proverb "When in Rome, do as the Romans do."[11] There are dangers in relying too heavily on this maxim, as we shall see, but it is right in some respects. Citizens of immigrant origin, especially those in the first generation, always do much more changing and adapting than other citizens and it is not unreasonable that they be expected to do so.

The institutions, practices, and social life of any complex modern society rest in part upon informal norms which make it possible for people to coordinate their activities without direct supervision or instruction. Those in the receiving society have a legitimate interest in maintaining the institutions, practices, and patterns of social life that they have established. Immigrants usually have to learn about and adapt to these established institutions, practices, and patterns. Getting a job, finding a place to live, sending children to school—all these ordinary human activities are enmeshed in a social environment that immigrants must inevitably take largely as given and to which they have to adjust in order to get what they want.

Many of these informal norms and social patterns have no deep moral foundation in themselves. A norm about how to stand in line is quite different in this respect from a norm about nondiscrimination. Many informal norms are really just coordination points that make it easier for people to interact effectively. But once such coordination points are established, they are of great social value because of the ways in which they facilitate social interaction. So, it is reasonable in many areas of daily life for the nonimmigrant majority to expect immigrants not to try to replace the existing patterns and norms with their own, but instead to learn what the established patterns and norms are and to conform to them.

Anyone who has ever lived in another country for an extended period has had this experience. For example, every modern state relies on bureaucracies that are structurally alike in the main respects but different from one another in important ways. Italian public bureaucracies do not function in quite the same way as German ones which differ in turn from those in France and those in the United States. When in Rome, you just have to learn how the Italian bureaucracy works. You cannot expect it to change for you (whatever you think of the merits of how it works).

Think of the issue of names as another everyday example. If an immigrant comes to the United States from Russia or China or Saudi Arabia or Israel, all places with alphabets different from the one used in English, she will have to adjust and write her name using the English alphabet. No one would suggest that that is an unreasonable expectation. If she comes from China where family names normally come first, she will have to take into account the American practice of listing family names last in deciding how to communicate when asked her name. Some people may be aware of Chinese practices and ask for clarification, but many will not and she cannot reasonably expect them to do so. If she comes from Spain, where people have two family names with the first normally taking precedence, she will have to be aware that what she regards as her primary family name is likely to be treated as a middle name. The burden will be on her to adjust to this communication issue, and again this is normally not unreasonable. For many social practices and patterns of interaction, it really is sufficient to say "That's just the way we do things around here" and to expect newcomers to adjust to that reality, so long as their adjustment does not require them to violate any principled commitments of their own.

On the other hand, some demands for conformity are unreasonable, even when the reasons for not conforming have nothing to do with conscience. One common complaint about immigrants is that they stick together and don't mix with the majority population. But it is precisely because immigrants are (reasonably) expected to adjust in so many ways that many of them want to live in neighborhoods with others of similar backgrounds. They will not have to change quite so much all at once, and those who have been present longer can serve as interpreters, not just linguistically but socially. They can explain about the myriad norms and expectations that are not written down, how they should interpret the behavior and communications of the nonimmigrant majority, what are likely to be points of conflict or misunderstanding, and so on. They can anticipate difficulties, offer analogies, and, in short, help the newcomers to learn the ropes. So, expecting immigrants to scatter themselves among the general population would be unreasonable, although, of course, any immigrants who want to live among the nonimmigrant majority should be free to do so.

The kinds of changes and adjustments that I am describing here apply to the greatest extent to the first generation. The children of the original immigrants normally learn most of these things just by growing up in the society to which their parents moved. They don't usually experience the informal norms and established social patterns as alien in the way that their parents often do. I don't mean to say that younger citizens of immigrant origin accept all of the informal norms of other citizens, however, or that they ought to do so. Informal social norms and patterns of interaction are not static. Think about the ways in which social norms govern things like modes of greeting, gestures, tones of voice, body language, physical distance, forms of respect, humor, politeness, acceptable displays of sexuality, and countless other aspects of daily life. On the one hand, it is easier to navigate social interactions if one understands the dominant norms of the society in all these areas. On the other hand, immigrants often stick to their established patterns in such matters, and their children can and often do challenge some of the wider society's norms, holding on to the patterns and practices of their parents and of families of similar backgrounds rather than simply accepting the prevailing norms. Often they blend both in ways that may influence others in society, a pattern that is evident in the areas of food, fashion, and art as well. Citizens of immigrant origin are not obliged simply to accept the practices they find in place.

A Norm against Norms

There is one particularly important democratic principle that sets severe limits to the informal norms and social expectations that citizens of immigrant origin should face, namely the principle that people should be able to live their lives as they choose so long as they are not harming others. This idea was given its classic formulation in Mill's *On Liberty*. As is well known, it is an idea with many internal tensions and contradictions, and I won't attempt to sort those out here. Nevertheless, Mill was certainly right to argue that human freedom will be very limited, especially for minorities, if the majority feels free to impose the informal sanctions of public disapproval on any behavior that does not conform to the majority's view of what is appropriate or even their view of what is moral. To put the point another way, the respect that citizens owe one another requires a sense of what is not anyone else's business except that of the person directly involved. This applies not only to what people do behind closed doors but also to how they conduct themselves in the public sphere, at least within very broad limits. Citizens in a democratic state have what is sometimes called in France a "right to indifference," a right to present themselves in public and to interact with others on a voluntary basis without having to submit to the judgment of others. For example, they have a right to ride the subway and to be ignored like everyone else. That is why the Pakistani parents in my opening story should have felt free to speak Urdu on a train without embarrassment. It is why a gay couple should be free to appear in public displaying affection for one another to the same extent as a heterosexual couple without evoking any reaction. And it is why Muslims should be free to appear in public in hijab without drawing attention, much less harassment. The principle applies to all three cases in the same way.

The irony is that for this democratic principle to function effectively it must be part of a democratic ethos that is internalized by most of the citizenry. In other words, the right not to be subject to informal social norms in many areas of one's life must itself be a widely accepted, informal social norm—a norm against norms. That's a bit of a paradox, but one that people can and usually do learn to live with. Applying this norm against norms to the issue of immigration, we can say that it is reasonable for all citizens, whether of immigrant origin or not, to expect that other citizens will leave them alone and let them live as they choose to a very considerable degree.

That's So Gay!

The respect that citizens owe one another goes deeper than the right to be left alone. It also entails a duty not to denigrate the identities of one's fellow citizens. Let me cite an example that has nothing directly to do with immigration. A common schoolyard taunt in Toronto some years ago—and I gather that it has not entirely disappeared—was "That's so gay!" This taunt as it was normally used had nothing to do with stereotyping of behavior as gay. Rather the word "gay" was used as a general term of derision and mockery. The phrase depended for its rhetorical power on the assumption that no one would want to be identified as gay.

What would it feel like to be a young gay person in the school, hearing this phrase, used publicly, not even in anger and not even directed at gay people or people actually thought to be gay? Even if one were not gay oneself, what would it feel like to hear the phrase if one's parents were gay or a sibling or a cousin? The phrase sends a message that gay people don't really belong. In my view, that message is incompatible with the civic equality to which democracies are committed.

Some may object that my criticism of "That's so gay!" is a form of "political correctness." Well, in one sense it is. Every political order has norms and standards, and that includes democracies. That is the whole point of my discussion of informal norms. On the one hand, democracies create great freedom for people to live as they choose, but, as I have just argued, they can do so only if there is a widely accepted norm about that sort of freedom. At the same time, democracies also contain positive norms about how people interact and what they say to and about each other. For example, there is clearly a norm against the use of racial and ethnic slurs in democracies. I don't mean that no one uses them. All norms are sometimes broken. The issue is rather whether most people see their use as acceptable in public discourse. And the answer in contemporary democracies is clearly no. In my view, "That's so gay!" belongs in the same category as a racial or ethnic slur.[12]

I set off on this brief discussion of the phrase "That's so gay!" for two reasons. First, I wanted to establish the general point that democratic principles entail a norm against the denigration of the particular identities of citizens. My sense is that this norm is partially reflected in practice (as in the criticism that would greet any public use of ethnic and racial slurs) but not yet fully developed. I do not have a pithy phrase to illustrate the point, but given the nature of the public debate, I feel confident that in some places, citizens of immigrant origin, especially but not only Muslims, are subjected to comparable or worse forms of denigration of their identities as gays are in the phrase "That's so gay!"

The second reason for the digression was that I wanted to use this discussion to highlight the similarities between the structural position of gays and the structural position of Muslim immigrants. The two groups are sometimes at odds politically. Muslims are often critical of homosexuality, seeing it as immoral. In some contexts, notably in the Netherlands, some openly gay activists have supported policies hostile to Muslim immigrants on the grounds that they represent a threat to hard won sexual freedoms. I want to bring the two groups together in our minds because from one important perspective they face the same sort of threat—they are vulnerable minorities whose identities are often denigrated by members of the majority. And against this threat, both groups have recourse to the same normative principle, a principle that majorities committed to democracy ought to endorse, namely that the democratic commitment to equal citizenship entails as a corollary that citizens should treat one another respectfully and no citizen's identity should be subject to denigration. And that principle of non-denigration entails not only that members of the majority should grant members of each of these minority groups the civic respect they deserve but also that members of each of these minority groups should show the same civic respect to members of the other minority. In sum, a democratic ethos requires all citizens not just to allow others to live their lives as they choose but also to show respect for the identities of fellow citizens.

Democratic Values

It is common to hear people say that if immigrants and their descendants want to be accepted as full members of a democratic political community, they should accept democratic values. Sometimes this sort of demand is expressed in ways that are deeply problematic from a democratic perspective. Thus, for example, leading figures in the Christian Democratic Party in Germany have asserted that immigrants ought to "accept the value order of our Christian-occidental culture in Germany."[13] Advocates of this view usually hasten to add that this Christian-occidental culture includes Judaism. Even so, they have difficulty in explaining how this sort of demand is to be reconciled with the freedom of religion that is part of Germany's constitutional order and that is also supposed to be accepted by immigrants. It is clear enough that the purpose of this sort of demand is to exclude Muslims who take their faith seriously or perhaps just those who identify themselves as Muslim regardless of their beliefs and practices.

One hears comparable demands for cultural and religious assimilation even in countries with a long history of immigration. In a recent book, Samuel Huntington argued that immigrants to the United States should be expected to accept the Anglo-Protestant culture that has made America what it is today, including as one of its key components the explicit recognition that the United States is a Christian country. Huntington observes that Irish and Italian Catholics, and for that matter European Jews, "were in various ways compelled, induced, and persuaded to adhere to the central elements of the Anglo-Protestant culture" during most of the nineteenth and twentieth centuries and he applauds this history, saying, "[t]his benefitted them and the country."[14] He is worried, however, that Mexican Catholic immigrants pose a real threat to this pattern of assimilation. Again, Huntington does not say how this recognition of America as a Christian country and the normative expectation that immigrants accept its Anglo-Protestant culture are to be reconciled with American commitments to freedom of religion and freedom of conscience or what sorts of compulsion, inducement, and persuasion would be morally acceptable in the twenty-first century.

As these examples illustrate, some people would like to impose expectations on immigrants and their descendants that are difficult to reconcile with fundamental democratic commitments. It is not reasonable to expect citizens of immigrant origin to adopt new religious commitments or to conform to the existing culture in these sorts of ways. These efforts to promote democratic values violate those values in the attempt to promote them.

Are all efforts to promote democratic values as objectionable as these? No. As should be clear by now, I do not think that every expectation that citizens of immigrant origin conform to informal social norms is an illegitimate demand for assimilation. In what sense then is it reasonable to expect citizens of immigrant origin to accept democratic values?

As I observed at the outset of this chapter, democratic states need more than rules and citizens' willingness to obey rules in order to function effectively. They require a democratic ethos. The whole point of this chapter is to explore aspects of that ethos that are especially relevant to the full inclusion of immigrants. If one accepts the moral legitimacy of democratic principles as a basis for regulating public life, then citizens are morally entitled to expect each other, individually and collectively, to act in accordance with a democratic ethos. That applies both to citizens of immigrant origin and to other citizens. As I have said before, I am simply working within the framework of these democratic principles in this book. In this chapter and in the book as a whole, I am working out the implications of democratic values rather than trying to justify them. From that perspective, then, I am presupposing that it is reasonable to expect citizens of immigrant origin to accept democratic values. At the same time, I am presupposing just as much that it is reasonable to expect the nonimmigrant majority to accept democratic values, and it is a recurring theme of the chapter that this is an important caveat. As I have been trying to show, the reasonable expectation that citizens act in accordance with a democratic ethos places significant demands not only on citizens of immigrant origin but also on other citizens and on public officials.

To maintain democratic norms over time, it is essential that children learn to act in accordance with them as they are growing up. Others have written about the requirements of civic education and the formation of democratic citizens.[15] I won't try to pursue those issues here. In terms of the categories of this chapter, this sort of education clearly has much less to do with formal rules than it does with the creation and inculcation of informal social norms. The key point, however, is that whatever the appropriate practices of civic education in a democracy, the same principles should apply to children who are citizens of immigrant origin as apply to other citizen children.

I need to add a caveat to this discussion of the legitimacy of democratic expectations and the role they play in the inclusion of citizens of immigrant origin. One central democratic principle is a commitment to freedom of thought and opinion. So, democracies cannot impose a normative expectation that citizens believe certain things without contradicting a fundamental democratic principle. Democratic citizens must be permitted to read, and to be persuaded by, Plato or Nietzsche, though neither is a democrat. They do not forfeit their formal citizenship status or even their right to full membership if they adopt intellectual views at odds with democracy. Similarly citizens can accept religious views at odds with democracy without forfeiting their claims to be included fully. It is a complex question how this commitment to freedom of thought and belief is to be reconciled with the need to promote a democratic ethos and especially to inculcate democratic habits of mind and heart in children. I do not have the space to explore these issues here but I can say again that whatever principles we use to address these issues, they will apply just as much to citizens of immigrant origin as to other citizens and vice versa. Democracies ought to leave space even for positions that challenge the basic presuppositions of democracy. That is a long-standing internal tension within democratic principles that is simply unavoidable.

Incentives

In the broadest sense of the term an incentive is something that a person finds advantageous (a positive incentive) or disadvantageous (a negative incentive). One could think of the sanctions that are used to enforce rules and informal norms as negative incentives, but in the sense in which I want to use the term the key difference between incentives, on the one hand, and rules and informal norms, on the other, is that incentives are purely about interests. Rules and informal norms tell people how they ought to behave. Sanctions enforce rules and informal norms but the "ought" is primary, not the sanctions. Incentives, by contrast, are contingent. No one insists that you respond to an incentive (in my sense of the term) or criticizes you for failing to do so (unless there is an informal norm in addition to the incentive). People respond to incentives because they see it as in their interest to do so. Different people may respond to a given incentive differently because they have different interests. In a modern market society economic incentives are usually relatively effective for most people, but not always and not for everyone. Some people care much more about money than others. To say that people *ought* to respond to economic incentives would be to add a normative expectation to the incentive itself.

Most citizens of immigrant origin see themselves as having interests that are similar to the interests of other citizens, at least to a considerable degree, and especially in the economic domain. As a result, social life is filled with incentives for them to accept the way things are usually done in the state where they live, even when there are no rules or informal norms demanding conformity. These incentives often emerge spontaneously, as it were, from the interactive effects of people simply pursuing their own interests without much conscious concern for the interests of others (as in the invisible hand of the market). For example, if the vast majority of people in a state speak one language and do not understand yours, your social options will be very limited if you don't learn to speak that language. In the absence of any norm about speaking English, the girl's parents in my opening story will be free to speak Urdu to one another, but if they want to buy something to eat on the train or get information from a fellow passenger, they will probably have to speak English, simply because that is the language most other people in the United Kingdom speak. More generally, anyone who wants to have a reasonable range of economic opportunities will have to learn the language that most people speak and use in economic life. This social reality creates powerful incentives for citizens of immigrant origin to learn the majority language.

The same social reality leads in a different direction, however. It creates incentives for citizens of immigrant origin to live in neighborhoods with others of a similar background. They will then be able to use their native language more in daily life. Most people find it easier to use their native language even when they have learned a new one (as was presumably the case with the parents in the opening story). People who share the same immigrant background often eat similar foods, interact with one another in familiar ways, and so on. There are great advantages to sticking with what is familiar and comfortable. If the education system is working properly, those incentives will be much reduced for subsequent generations who will have learned the dominant language very well and will have acquired a lot of other informal social knowledge as well.

For the purposes of this book, the crucial question is how to evaluate general patterns of incentives from a normative perspective. Even though incentives themselves (in my sense of the term) carry no normative weight, some patterns of incentives are morally problematic. It matters whether the incentives for citizens of immigrant origin to live in the same neighborhoods are primarily the advantages of shared social patterns as I described above or the disadvantages of living elsewhere because of the hostility and discrimination that they would encounter in other neighborhoods. The former pattern of incentives is completely compatible with democratic principles, but the latter is not. It is one that democratic states have an obligation to try to change.

Immigrants often face incentives to change, as is illustrated by the incentives for immigrants to learn the majority's language, an important form of cultural adaptation. There is nothing morally wrong with incentives to learn the dominant language of the society if they are of the sort that I described above. Most of the existing population has no moral duty to learn the native language of immigrants. So, the incentives that flow from their failure to do so are not unjust.

Other incentives to change are more problematic. Let's return to the issue of names. In the late nineteenth and early twentieth century it was common for immigrants to the United States to change their names to ones that sounded more "American."[16] There was certainly no rule and arguably not even an informal norm demanding that immigrants change their names, and many did not do so, but many others made the calculation that it would be advantageous to disguise their immigrant origins in this way, that it would make them less likely to be subject to discrimination and more likely to be accepted by the rest of society. This incentive for immigrants to change their names was an indication that the immigrants were not adequately included in society, not being treated equally. By the early twenty-first century, this practice of immigrants to America changing their names had virtually disappeared, again because the incentives had shifted. Immigrants no longer thought that it would be a great advantage in social life to change their names. On the whole, this transformation should be seen as a positive development.[17]

Although most incentives emerge spontaneously, public policies can affect the incentives that people face. Sometimes policies are explicitly designed to change incentives. For example, if a school offers courses in the language of origin of some group of immigrants, that makes it easier for the descendants of the original immigrants to learn their parents' or grandparents' native language and to pass it on to their own children. Hence, it increases the incentives for them to do so. Notice that it is possible to offer this on a purely optional basis without either a rule requiring children to take the courses or an informal norm pressuring them to do so. The key question for my purposes is how the creation of such incentives fits with democratic principles. Democratic states have considerable latitude to create or not create incentives of this sort (e.g., to offer or not offer such language of origin courses) but that the latitude is not unlimited.

Some people argue that "multiculturalism" has created incentives for citizens of immigrant origin to live separate lives from the majority population.[18] This is unpersuasive. As I explained above, there are powerful spontaneous incentives for the first generation of immigrants to cluster together with people from a similar background. These incentives have nothing to do with public policies, multicultural or otherwise.

I am not suggesting that democratic states should be entirely indifferent to patterns of social interaction. There is certainly a responsibility to eliminate discrimination, as I have said, and also a legitimate public interest in overcoming social barriers between citizens of immigrant origin and other citizens even when these are not the product of discrimination. It is important to find ways to bring citizens together to promote social ties and a sense of common belonging. It matters how states pursue this goal, however. Apart from prohibiting discrimination, it can be wrong to force people together through rules or even through informal norms, although it may be morally permissible and desirable to create incentives for people to come together. Indeed, many public policies that have been adopted under the rubric of "multiculturalism" are designed to do just that.[19] Contrary to what the critics say, these policies often create incentives for citizens of immigrant origin to participate in mainstream institutions and to engage with other citizens.

Practices of Recognition

A practice of recognition is any action that takes account of or makes visible those aspects of culture, religion, and identity that differentiate citizens of immigrant origin (or some subset of these citizens) from the nonimmigrant majority of other citizens. Both the state and ordinary citizens can engage in practices of recognition, and there are both positive and negative forms of recognition.

Practices of negative recognition often involve stereotyping and prejudice. They define identities in ways that denigrate the holders of these identities and contribute to the exclusion of citizens of immigrant origin. The clearest recent example is the negative ways in which Islam and Muslim immigrants have been treated in the media and in political discourse, especially over the past decade or so.[20] Sometimes a practice of negative recognition takes the form of a public, symbolic act of exclusion. A recent Swiss law that prohibits the building of new minarets is perhaps the clearest example in recent memory.[21] There is no pretence that the law is serving some general neutral purpose, like restricting the heights of buildings in certain areas. Its sole goal is to limit the visibility of Muslims within the Swiss community, to restrict their access to public space. It would be hard to imagine a more direct way of communicating the message that Muslim citizens of immigrant origin are not welcome or that Islam is not part of the Swiss national identity. It should be obvious that practices of negative recognition are incompatible with a democratic ethos that seeks to include citizens of immigrant origin as full members of the political community.

Practices of positive recognition involve acknowledgment and acceptance of the broad ways in which citizens of immigrant origin differ from the majority. This does not entail an endorsement of particular practices or beliefs, but rather an affirmation that some practice or identity connected to being of immigrant origins is not incompatible with the political community. If citizens of immigrant origin are to be included, they cannot be expected to conceal or disguise important aspects of their identities. A democratic state and its citizens have to communicate clearly that citizens with these cultural and religious identities are regarded as full members of the political community.

This does not mean that the state has to impose identities on individual citizens or require them to reveal their identities if they prefer not to do so. What will be publicly visible about any particular individual will depend on the nature of her identity and the character of her commitments. But cultural and religious identities have a collective as well an individual dimension. It is the collective identity that must be acknowledged and affirmed. For example, it is important when leading public officials say that Islam is part of Germany or the United States (as some have done) because this sends the message that the national

identity does not exclude Muslims. Whether any individual wears clothing that
identifies her as a Muslim will vary, depending on her own understanding of her
religious duties, but practices of positive recognition make it more likely that
others will regard Muslims as normal citizens and that Muslim citizens will see
themselves that way, whether others are aware of their identity or not.

Practices of positive recognition can take a number of forms. For example,
school curricula can contain information about the histories and background
cultures of citizens of immigrant origins, perhaps taking particular account of the
composition of the school's population if there are too many sources to include
all in a general curriculum. Information can be provided in schools and in the
media about the major holidays that citizens of immigrant origin celebrate.

The practices of adjustment described in the section on informal norms
could also be seen as practices of recognition. Recall what I said about accommodating the dietary requirements of citizens of immigrant origin, for example.
This can also be seen as a practice of recognition, and one that can be carried out
by ordinary citizens from the majority in their everyday interactions with their
fellow citizens. Indeed, the failure to make these accommodations amounts to a
form of negative recognition. When I was a boy, the Catholic Church still had a
prohibition on eating meat on Fridays. If Irish Catholics went somewhere on a
Friday where lunch was served and there was no fish option, we felt that this was
a place that either did not like Catholics or did not expect to have any present.
Either way, it did not feel welcoming. Paying attention to the dietary restrictions
of citizens of immigrant origin is a small but significant way of recognizing their
presence and their right to equal treatment.

Another practice of recognition involves the use of languages of origin in
various forms of communication, not as a substitute for the official language,
especially in school, but as a supplement in contexts where it can help those
with particular needs. For example, in most cases public services are delivered
in the official language(s), and reasonably so. However, if some area contains
many immigrants who speak a particular language, it is reasonable for them to
expect that some public employees will learn their language and also that the
public services will hire some native speakers of their language (ones who also
speak the dominant language) to serve as linguistic (and cultural) mediators.
After all, immigrants are members of the public, and as such, they are entitled
to have their needs taken into account when public services are delivered. This
obviously applies to any agencies whose responsibility it is to help immigrants
adjust to the new society, but it applies as well to agencies supplying basic public
services: police, fire departments, hospitals, and front line public bureaucracies
generally. There is no way to specify with precision how many of those providing public services should be able to communicate in the immigrants' language
since that depends on many factors including the numbers and concentration of

immigrants speaking a given language, the availability of suitable personnel, and so on. It is not a matter of establishing an individual right to receive communications in one's preferred language.[22] But it would be wrong for a state to ignore altogether the need for effective communication on the grounds that the immigrants should learn the language of the society to which they have moved, and it sends a positive signal about the fact that the immigrants are seen as members of the community when officials reach out to them in their original language. Of course, this also contributes to the effective delivery of services.

Still another practice of recognition is the provision of models. When citizens of immigrant origin occupy positions of authority in public life, especially in symbolically important fields like law and politics, and when they are visible in positions of responsibility in the media, that also sends a message about the acceptance of identities. I am not suggesting here that this is best achieved through particular targeted programs like affirmative action, but I am saying that it matters for a sense of inclusion whether citizens of immigrant origin see people like themselves in positions of responsibility.[23]

Practices of positive recognition contribute to the inclusion of citizens of immigrant origin. However, what practices of positive recognition any particular state should pursue depends a great deal on circumstances. The important point is to be aware that the cultural and religious identities of the majority will already be publicly recognized to a very considerable degree. That is simply inevitable in a democracy. There is nothing wrong with that, and I am not suggesting that citizens of immigrant origin should aspire to comparable levels of recognition. That is impossible. Rather my suggestion is that some recognition is appropriate, enough to make it clear that the differences of culture and identity connected with immigrant origins are compatible with full and equal membership in the political community.

National Identity

Finally, let's consider the way in which understandings of national identity can affect the inclusion of immigrants. Every political community constructs a national identity in a variety of ways, from symbols like the flag and national anthem to school curricula (especially in areas like history and literature) to public communications (verbal and nonverbal) by officials and others.[24] This always involves more cultural and historical specificity than simply having common institutions based on democratic principles and a common language.

What does it mean to be Danish or Dutch, German or Greek, Canadian or American? The answers to such questions are always contested internally even among the nonimmigrant majority. For the purposes of this book the key point is that a conception of the national identity that excludes citizens of immigrant origin is incompatible with the democratic ethos of full inclusion that is required by democratic principles. The national identity of a state may be open to contestation, but the only morally acceptable alternatives from a democratic perspective are ones that permit citizens of immigrant origin to see themselves and to be seen by others as members of the nation. A democratic "people" must include all citizens, or at least all those who want to be included.

What does this entail? Well, in the first instance, it means that it is not morally acceptable if citizens from the nonimmigrant majority think that "real" members of the nation must have several generations of ancestors who were also members of the nation. Equal citizenship is incompatible with that sort of hierarchy. More broadly, morally defensible national identities cannot be tied to ascribed characteristics like race and ethnicity that people cannot change or to things like religion that it is unreasonable to ask people to change. The history of the nation has to be imagined and recounted in a way that enables citizens of immigrant origin to identify with it. Citizens of immigrant origin have to be visible as representatives of the nation.

This requirement of an inclusive national identity is probably more of a challenge for states (like most of those in Europe) in which most current citizens are the descendants of many previous generations of citizens than in states (like the United States and Canada) in which most of the population is of immigrant origin, at least in the not too distant past, although the latter also have deep traditions of excluding some immigrants from the national identity.[25] Nevertheless, if democratic states and their citizens are to respect the requirements of the principles they espouse, they have to find ways to reconstruct both the official images of the nation and the pictures that people carry around in their heads about what it means to be a member of the nation, so that these identities are just as open to citizens of immigrant origin as to citizens of ancient ancestry. This is just one more way in which we can see that demands for the acceptance of democratic values pose challenges to the nonimmigrant majority that are as great as or greater than those posed to citizens of immigrant origin.

Conclusion

In this chapter I have tried to point to a few of the many ways in which the full inclusion of immigrants and their descendants depends on more than granting them formal citizenship and the legal rights that go with it. The ideal of inclusion that underlies all of these particular examples is one in which citizens of immigrant origin are free to maintain particular religious, cultural, and collective identities that distinguish them from the majority of other citizens without suffering marginalization or subordination and equally free to abandon these identities if they choose to do so. In either case, under this ideal, they would see themselves and be seen by others as full members of the community.

5

Permanent Residents

I was a permanent resident (or "landed immigrant") in Canada for about ten years before I became a citizen. During this period, I enjoyed the same legal rights and was subject to the same legal duties as Canadian citizens, for almost all practical purposes. I bought a house, I sent my children to the local public schools, I had access to the government's health insurance program and I became a member of the national pension plan. I was able to apply for various national programs, including grants for research. I was free to apply on equal terms for most jobs in the Canadian economy (though I was in fact extremely happy with the one I had). I also paid taxes and was subject to Canadian law generally. There were a few differences that I was aware of. I could not vote in Canadian elections. I was subject to deportation if I committed a major crime. I would have had lower priority in relation to citizens if I had applied for a position in the federal civil service (though I was legally entitled to equal consideration for jobs in the provincial civil service and in the private sector). I was not subject to jury duty. There were probably a few other minor differences, of which I was not aware. When I became a citizen, my life did not change in any material way. I applied for citizenship because I wanted to vote in Canadian elections and gain a legal status that officially recognized the identity that I had acquired—my sense of myself as a Canadian.

I was a privileged immigrant in many ways, but not with respect to the legal rights and duties I had as a permanent resident. Other Canadian permanent residents had the same legal rights and duties. Indeed the legal position of permanent residents in Canada is pretty typical of permanent residents throughout Europe and North America.

This poses an interesting puzzle. We tend to think of citizenship as something special, the status that marks off those who belong from those who do not. That was even the implicit message of my own analysis in the previous three chapters which focused on access to citizenship and on the inclusion of citizens of immigrant origin. Yet every state in Western Europe and North America has a significant number of people who are settled there but are not citizens. These residents tend to have most of the same rights and duties as citizens. So, as a matter of fact, citizenship is not so special, at least in legal terms. Is that a good thing or a bad thing? Turning our attention to resident noncitizens may complicate our understanding of democracy and citizenship in fruitful ways.

How should immigrants who are legal residents be treated before they become citizens or if they choose not to do so? Even if the principles governing access to citizenship that I defended in chapters 2 and 3 were fully accepted, there would still be residents who were not citizens. Under current practices, there are even more. Is the existing pattern of drawing relatively few legal distinctions between citizens and residents required by justice or is it merely a policy that most states have adopted for contingent reasons and that they are morally free to change?[1] If a democratic state wants to emphasize that citizenship is special, that it is an important and meaningful status, may it do so by differentiating the legal status of citizen more sharply from that of (mere) resident? What about the legal distinctions between citizens and residents that persist in current practice? Should those be maintained or abolished? Finally, what is the range of morally permissible policies? Must all democratic states treat residents in the same way or are there many morally acceptable options, depending upon the historical traditions and political choices of particular democratic communities?

In broad outline my answer is this. Democratic justice, properly understood, greatly constrains the legal distinctions that can be drawn between citizens and residents. Once people have been settled for an extended period, they are morally entitled to the same civil, economic, and social rights as citizens and they should be subject to most of the same legal duties. During the early stages of settlement it is permissible to limit a few rights (e.g., to redistributive benefits or protection against deportation) but not most of them. The longer people stay in a society, the stronger their moral claims become. After a while they pass a threshold that entitles them to virtually the same legal status as citizens, whether they acquire formal citizenship status or not.

These principles apply to all democratic states. While one can never rule out in advance the possibility that general principles of this sort may need to be qualified in the light of particular circumstances, no such qualification is warranted for states in Western Europe and North America. With regard to these issues, the many differences among European states or between the Old World and the New, especially with regard to immigration, are not morally significant enough to modify the principles.

In the opening paragraphs of this chapter, I repeatedly mentioned legal duties as well as legal rights, but in the rest of the chapter I will focus almost exclusively on legal rights. I do this only for simplicity of exposition. To the extent that there is a debate about this topic—and it is not very controversial—the issue is whether residents should have the same rights as citizens. Legal duties are not much in dispute. Everyone has a legal duty to obey the law. Apart from the laws governing immigration (which sometimes impose ongoing duties on residents that do not apply to citizens), the law's commands rarely distinguish between citizens and residents.[2]

In framing my discussion here in terms of a comparison between the rights of residents and the rights of citizens, I am implicitly setting to one side many normative questions about what rights citizens should have. A full theory of justice would have to consider such questions. For example, does democratic justice require that citizens have certain kinds of economic and social rights, and, if so, which ones? We know that in practice there is considerable variation in the economic and social rights that citizens enjoy in different democratic states. It is important to ask whether all of these existing arrangements are compatible with justice. In this book, however, I want to keep the focus on the ethics of immigration. So, I ask only what justice requires with respect to the similarities and differences between the rights of citizens and the rights of residents, thus leaving open the broader questions about what justice requires with respect to the rights of citizens.

I limit my discussion in this chapter to noncitizens who have the state's permission to reside in the country on an ongoing basis. They either have a right of permanent residence or are on a path to obtain such a right within a few years in the normal course of events.[3] I take up questions about temporary workers and those present without authorization in later chapters.

The fact that the presence of immigrants is officially authorized and that they have a legal right to stay does not mean that they are wanted in a sociological sense, that is, that most of the citizens welcome or even accept their presence. The processes of state decision making are complex, and any democratic constitutional order includes constraints on the popular will and majority rule. For that reason, my arguments about what rights residents ought to have do not rest too heavily on the claim that "we" have chosen to admit them and to let them stay. On the one hand, the fact that their presence is legally authorized by the state is an important fact that distinguishes their situation from that of people present without authorization. On the other hand, political leaders and the wider public may only grudgingly acknowledge the residents' right to stay and may want to accord them the minimum possible rights. Part of my enterprise in this chapter is to try to identify the minimum package of legal rights to which settled noncitizens are morally entitled. Of course, this moral minimum may still turn out to be a lot higher than some would like.

The Historical Context

In thinking about what we ought to do in a given area, it is often helpful to begin with what we are doing and to ask whether we think that is justifiable. For one thing, an analysis of existing practice may draw our attention to relevant moral considerations that we would overlook if we began from a purely theoretical position. For another, it may be helpful to know to what extent a particular normative position is an endorsement of existing practice and to what extent a critique of it.[4]

If there is one point that contemporary scholars of immigration seem to agree upon, it is that the legal position of resident noncitizens in Europe and North America improved significantly during the course of the twentieth century, especially the decades of the 1970s and the 1980s. The general pattern was to extend first civil and economic rights to immigrants and then social rights. Political rights were the last and least extensively provided.[5] In earlier periods, as these scholars have documented, noncitizens were much more vulnerable to deportation (sometimes en masse); their economic activities were subject to severe limitations, including extensive restrictions on property ownership and on entry into the professions and other occupations; they were denied basic civil rights such as freedom of assembly, association, movement, and expression and the right of family unification; they were excluded from a wide variety of public programs, not only redistributive programs but even regulatory ones (e.g., health and safety regulations at work) and recreational activities.[6]

Today, all this has changed. One of the striking developments in the area of immigration during the late twentieth century was the extent to which the legal distinctions between citizens and resident noncitizens were reduced. Scholars disagree to some extent about the source of this change. Some emphasize the convergence among democratic states on a new status for immigrants and attribute this to the emergence of new international human rights norms.[7] Others say that attention to the details of particular cases will show that the changes were due to local causes, the political and legal factors at play within particular national traditions.[8] Whatever explanatory account one accepts, the facts of the matter are not in dispute. A pattern of systematic and widespread legal differentiation between immigrants and citizens has been replaced by a pattern in which settled immigrants generally enjoy the same civil, economic, and social rights as citizens. Many of these changes were brought about by courts acting in the name of legal norms that reflect deep democratic principles. In other words, they were seen not merely as prudent changes in policy but rather as transformations required by justice.

I do not want to overstate this point. Some legal differences between citizens and residents persist. For example, the right to vote in national elections and the right to hold public office are almost always reserved for citizens. In some countries, there are significant legal differences between citizens and residents with regard to important matters like security of residence, public employment, and access to redistributive social programs, and there are many minor differences as well. Moreover, we cannot simply assume that the trend toward equalization of rights is irreversible. Legislation passed by the United States in 1996 deprived permanent residents of some rights they had previously enjoyed.[9] In Europe, the gap between the rights of citizens and residents widened for a time as a result of developments in the European Union that granted a number of rights on the basis of citizenship in a member state. As a result, so-called third country nationals (that is, residents who were citizens of a state outside the EU) enjoyed fewer rights than residents who held citizenship in another EU state. This gap has narrowed considerably in recent years, however, as a result of subsequent EU policy developments.[10] In the wake of the attack on the United States on September 11, 2001, noncitizens of all kinds, including residents, became subject to greater scrutiny, especially in the United States. Finally, there is some variation among democratic states regarding the extent to which the legal status of residents resembles that of citizens.

Despite these qualifications, the basic picture of movement in the direction of legal equality between residents and citizens remains valid. Throughout Europe and North America, the distinction between citizens and residents simply matters much less in legal terms than it once did. Overall, many permanent residents spend their entire lives in states in Europe or North America without becoming legal citizens and without that fact affecting their lives in any significant way apart from their not being able to vote (which many citizens, especially in North America, choose not to do anyway) and their not being able to get an EU or North American passport.

What should we make of this trend toward legal equality between citizens and residents? Should we celebrate this development as a triumph for justice or deplore it as a devaluation of citizenship? Should we criticize the remaining distinctions or defend them as appropriate markers of the distinctive status of citizenship?

General Human Rights and the Obligations of the State

Let us start by considering cases in which the allocation of equal legal rights to noncitizens is generally uncontested.[11] In that way we can bring to consciousness normative principles that are implicit in practices we already accept. Sometimes what is most important is taken for granted. We have to be reminded of the underlying justification of arrangements that seem obvious or self-evident in order to be able to reflect more clearly about ones that are disputed.

There are some legal rights that people possess simply in virtue of the fact that they are within the territory of a given state. With regard to these sorts of rights, we normally do not distinguish between citizens and noncitizens or even between resident noncitizens and nonresidents. All that matters is physical presence.

Let's call the rights that everyone possesses general human rights. I don't want to attempt to provide a precise list of these rights but merely to establish that there are some rights that everyone acknowledges ought to be granted by the state to any person within its jurisdiction. The most obvious example of this is the right to personal security. People have a right to protection against murder, assault, and robbery. Of course, such protection is never perfect, but no state deliberately provides less protection against crime to noncitizens than to citizens (or at least no state would admit to doing so).

General human rights include rights that are designed not only to protect people from others within the state but also to give them claims against the state itself. For example, familiar rights like the right to freedom of thought, freedom of religion, freedom of speech, and so on are legal rights that all people possess against the state within whose jurisdiction they find themselves. The fact that people have come as tourists is not an adequate reason for prohibiting them from praying. Again, these basic liberties are rights to which everyone is equally entitled, noncitizens as well as citizens, visitors as well as residents. Within a democratic context, no one, not even the most fervent chauvinist, argues that it would be proper to deny such rights to noncitizens.

Critics of the idea of human rights sometimes like to say that citizenship is a necessary presupposition of all other effective legal rights. It is "the right to have rights," they say, quoting Arendt out of context.[12] But this is not plausible as an account of either principle or practice. Simply as an empirical matter, the suggestion that citizenship (somewhere) is what makes it possible for people to enjoy effective legal rights in another country is clearly wrong. Whether a noncitizen actually enjoys any effective legal rights is much more a function of the way the legal system works in the state in which the noncitizen is located than it is of the fact that he or she has citizenship in some other country. Whatever effective legal rights people from, say, Ghana or Sri Lanka enjoy in France or the United States has little or nothing to do with their possession of citizenship in their country of origin and everything to do with the norms and practices of the legal system in the country in which they find themselves. I emphasize this point because some people see citizenship and legal rights as inextricably intertwined. This is simply wrong conceptually, normatively, and empirically.

I do not mean to deny that noncitizens are vulnerable to state authorities in ways that citizens are not, because their right to be present is normally much less secure than that of citizens, even when they are present with authorization, and this affects their ability to enjoy the formal legal rights to which they are entitled.[13] (I criticize that vulnerability below.) But the ability to exercise formal legal rights is also deeply affected by class, gender, and race. In many situations, a rich noncitizen is less legally vulnerable in practice than a poor citizen. The key point for my purposes is that every democratic state makes a formal commitment to grant certain legal rights to noncitizens—what I have called general human rights—and, under normal circumstances, democratic states respect those rights.

Why is it that even noncitizens who are only temporary visitors enjoy some of the same legal rights as citizens? How can we make moral sense of this phenomenon? The practice of granting legal rights to noncitizens presupposes that governments have some responsibility toward all those who are subject to their jurisdiction, even if only on a temporary basis. This is a necessary (normative) corollary of the state's claim to exclusive control over the legitimate use of violence within a given territory. For that kind of power to be legitimate, it must not be exercised arbitrarily. People have legitimate interests and moral claims that governments must respect whether the people in question are citizens or not.

Does the obligation of democratic governments to respect the legitimate interests and moral claims of noncitizens entail that noncitizens have the *same* legal rights as citizens? It is not simply a choice between granting the same rights or no rights. Noncitizens could be given a lesser bundle of legal rights. Indeed, in some areas they are given lesser bundles, as we shall see. When it comes to general human rights, however, they get the same legal rights as citizens. Why?

We can see the force of this question more clearly if we pay attention to the fact that the concrete legal entitlements provided for the protection of general human rights *do* vary between states. All democratic states are committed to protecting basic rights and freedoms like personal security, freedom of religion, freedom of speech, and so on, but different legal regimes interpret and institutionalize these commitments in different ways. Citizens of the United Kingdom do not enjoy exactly the same specific legal rights with regard to basic protections and liberties as citizens of the United States. Citizens of France have still different rights and so on. Yet within each of these states, the specific legal rights granted to noncitizens to protect their basic rights and liberties are normally exactly the same as the ones granted to citizens.

Take a concrete example: the right to a fair trial. Different states have different interpretations of what the right to a fair trial entails, but no state has one interpretation that applies to citizens and another that applies to noncitizens, at least for ordinary criminal cases.[14] The construction of criminal procedures is shaped in part by political, legal, and cultural traditions that vary from one place to another. This inevitably leads to differences in procedures and in the legal rights associated with them. For example, different states have different rules of evidence. Moreover, there is at least some tension between the goals of apprehending criminals and protecting people from criminal activity, on the one hand, and the goals of protecting innocent accused people and securing the freedom of all against overly intrusive law enforcement, on the other. Different political communities may weigh these competing considerations differently or assess the risks and benefits of a given approach differently. This does not mean that states have the moral equivalent of carte blanche, but it is simply not plausible to suppose that there is only one correct balance to be struck among the many competing considerations.

So, why don't states differentiate between citizens and noncitizens when it comes to such criminal procedures?[15] One can see why it might be politically attractive to do so. After all, noncitizens don't vote. We have just acknowledged that there is no universally valid set of criminal procedures and that one state may tilt the balance differently from another. So, why not tilt the balance differently between citizens and noncitizens (within whatever range we take to be the permissible variations between states)? For example, a state might require noncitizens to respond to accusations while granting citizens the right to remain silent or a state might allow authorities to use illegally gathered evidence against noncitizens but not against citizens. The incentives for a differentiated approach are even stronger when financial costs are directly involved. Why not adopt a rule that citizens are entitled to a lawyer at public expense if they cannot afford to pay for one, but noncitizens are not? In short, why not make greater protections in the criminal process one of the benefits of citizenship?

The proper response to these questions, I hasten to say, is to recoil in horror (rather than to regard them as promising ideas for legal reform). Citizenship status is entirely irrelevant to the question of whether a person is innocent or guilty of a crime. States cannot avoid adopting procedures that affect the relative likelihood of the innocent being convicted or the guilty being set free, but a commitment to justice requires them to adopt those procedures that reflect their best judgments about the appropriate balance between these competing risks. I do not mean to suggest that this is directly subject to conscious calculation. The judgments are mediated by complex legal traditions and institutional processes. But in adopting a particular set of procedures for their citizens, a state is, in effect, announcing what its political community, with its particular history and traditions, regards as the requirements of a fair trial in its legal system. For a state to adopt different procedures for noncitizens from the ones it uses for citizens would be incompatible with the idea that its goal was to set the standards for a fair trial. It would make a mockery of the aspiration to pursue justice.[16]

Let me add that this normative argument applies just as much in cases involving national security and terrorism as it does in other areas. Even if the threat of terrorism required a rebalancing of the trade-off between the protection of the rights of the accused and protection of the public in judicial procedures (something I am inclined to doubt), it would not follow that this balance should be struck differently for citizens and noncitizens. Terrorists may be citizens rather than foreigners, as recent cases of terrorism and attempted terrorism in the United States, Canada, the United Kingdom, Norway, and elsewhere reveal. It is the nature of the threat that putatively justifies the shift in procedural practices. So, why should the nationality of the sources of the threat be relevant to the question of what procedures are used?

What is true of the criminal justice arena is true also of other areas where states have a responsibility to protect the human rights of all those who are subject, even temporarily, to their jurisdiction. Different states will pursue these responsibilities in different ways in their legal systems, but in doing so they cannot distinguish between citizens and noncitizens without contradicting the claim that they are adequately protecting general human rights. To favor citizens in these sorts of matters would be to act unjustly.

Belonging, Reciprocity, and the Rights of Membership

The state's obligation to provide equal protection for general human rights provides a partial normative explanation of why noncitizens should have some of the same legal rights as citizens, but it does not help us to understand the sharp differences between different categories of noncitizens. Residents have many rights that visitors do not possess. An appeal to general human rights cannot explain or justify that. Indeed if we were to place visitors, residents, and citizens as three categories along a continuum as holders of legal rights, the biggest gap would not be between citizens and residents but between residents and visitors, that is, not between citizens and noncitizens but between two different kinds of noncitizens.[17] Most of the legal rights created by modern democratic states are neither rights granted to everyone present nor rights possessed only by citizens. Instead, they are rights possessed by both citizens and permanent residents. Let's see why that makes moral sense.[18]

What is it that residents and citizens have in common that is morally significant and makes it justifiable to give them rights that are not given to visitors? The answer is obvious. Unlike visitors, both residents and citizens live within the state and participate in its civil society on an ongoing basis. Like citizens, residents are members of society. This fact gives them interests that visitors do not have, interests that deserve legal recognition and protection. Of course, someone might object that this is circular, that it begs the question of why the visitors are only visitors. Perhaps they would like to become residents too and are not being allowed to do so. But that is an issue I will consider later in the book. For the moment I am just assuming the legitimacy of the state's right to decide which noncitizens will become residents and asking how states should treat those to whom it has granted resident status.

Some of the rights enjoyed by citizens and residents (but not visitors) can appropriately be described as human rights in the sense that they appeal to standards of justice that we think ought to constrain all regimes, and they appear on familiar lists of human rights. The right to seek employment is an example. It is widely accepted as fundamentally unjust and a violation of human rights if a regime makes it impossible for someone who lives in its society on an ongoing basis to find work or if it arbitrarily restricts her employment opportunities. The reasons are obvious. In any society in which acquiring the means to live depends upon gainful employment, denying access to work to people who live there is like denying access to life itself. Even if life itself is not threatened, employment provides so many other instrumental and intrinsic goods that denying or even limiting access to it is a serious harm and something that requires a substantial justification.

These arguments apply to residents as much as they do to citizens. Remember that in this chapter we are concerned only with noncitizens who are living in the society on an ongoing basis with the state's permission. It would be contradictory to allow people to live in a society while denying them the means to do so. Even restricting residents' access to employment (as opposed to denying them the right to work altogether) is something that requires substantial justification once one sees the right to seek work as a human right.

On the other hand, the right to seek work is a different kind of human right from the ones we were considering above. Visitors are not normally allowed to seek employment, but it is not a violation of human rights, on any conventional understanding of that term, to deny a tourist the right to work.[19] To call the right to seek employment a human right then is to use the term in a somewhat different sense from the way it is used when speaking of human rights (like the right to a fair trial) that the state is obliged to provide to all within its jurisdiction, even temporarily. This second type of human right is derived not from one's general humanity but from one's social location (that is, from the kinds of ties one has to the society). To distinguish these rights from the general human rights discussed earlier, I propose that we call them "membership-specific human rights." This is a departure from the usual terminology in the human rights field, but I think that it draws attention more effectively than the conventional language to the fact that certain human rights depend upon a person's connection to a particular community.

Not every legal right deserves to be called a human right. Human rights are moral claims that states are obliged to respect in their legal systems (even though, as we have seen, the interpretation and implementation of these rights may vary among states).States also create many legal rights that do not have this kind of moral status. They are entitlements that states are not obliged to establish in the first place and could abolish without acting unjustly (at least within

certain procedural constraints). Let's call them "discretionary rights." For example, the Canadian government set up a program a few years ago that provides
grants to people who set aside money for their children's university education.
Even supporters of the program would probably not claim that the grant should
be regarded as a basic human right. Yet it does create a legal right (an entitlement
to a grant provided certain conditions are met), and this right is allocated not
on the basis of citizenship but on the basis of where people live. Non-Canadians
who live outside Canada are obviously not eligible for the grant, but neither are
Canadian citizens who live outside Canada. By contrast, the right to a grant is
given not only to Canadian citizens who live in Canada but also to noncitizens
who live there as officially authorized residents. It is, in short, a right of residen-
tial membership.

This Canadian program is a typical government program in many ways (not
least in that it has the effect of redistributing money to the better off because
their children are more apt to go to university). Every state in Europe and North
America has hundreds or even thousands of programs that create legal rights
of one kind or another, rights that are intended to achieve some public policy
goal but that could not be described as human rights without stretching the
meaning of that term beyond useful confines. In the vast majority of cases, these
legal rights are granted to permanent residents and citizens, but not to temporary visitors. (They may or may not be granted to citizens who live abroad.) To
draw attention to this pattern of allocation while distinguishing these rights from
membership-specific human rights, we might call them membership-specific
discretionary rights.[20]

I will not try to mark out the precise contours of the dividing line between
these two kinds of membership-specific rights (or, what I will call, for the sake of
felicity of expression, the rights of membership). For my purposes what matters
most is the contrast between rights of membership and general human rights,
because this contrast reveals that what matters most for the distribution of many
legal rights is neither physical presence nor full citizenship but rather social
membership.

Some people think that democratic states have gone too far in extending
rights of membership to noncitizen residents. For example, recent initiatives
in the United States have reduced the social benefits available to immigrants,
and there are comparable proposals, if not yet comparable policies, in some
European states. Other people think that democratic states have still not gone far
enough in extending the rights of membership to residents despite the developments of the past half century. So, there is a real debate here, and one that I will
address. Nevertheless, it is important not to exaggerate the area of disagreement.

Most of the membership rights enjoyed by noncitizen residents are not seriously contested. There is widespread acceptance of most of the changes of the

past century that removed legal restrictions on residents and granted them rights that had previously been possessed only by citizens. Even among critics of immigration, the challenges to the overall pattern of development come only at the margins. Almost no one advocates a return to policies that would exclude residents from access to the professions or deny them basic health and safety protections provided to citizen workers. Of course, this does not settle the matter from a normative perspective, but it does shift the burden of proof. People are free to argue for a much more radical differentiation between the rights of citizens and the rights of residents, but they must acknowledge that in doing so they are opposing a trend that is both deep and widespread in modern democracies. For my own part, I want to defend these trends and to argue for their extension.

Let's start with some of the areas where residents do generally enjoy the same rights as citizens and see why this arrangement makes moral sense. We have already seen why states should provide a general right of access to the labor market to noncitizen residents. By the same token, to deny them the kinds of labor rights that other workers enjoy (e.g., the protections provided by health and safety legislation, the right to join unions, and so on) would be to place them at an unfair disadvantage. I know of no one advocating such a course.

If we consider social insurance programs financed by compulsory deductions from workers' pay (old age pensions, income support for the unemployed, compensation for workplace accidents), we can see that it would hardly be reasonable to require people to pay into these programs and then to deny them access to the benefits they provide. The principle of reciprocity on which such programs are based requires that those who pay should be eligible. (Some programs of this sort have minimum periods of employment that must be fulfilled before one can collect, and, of course, it is appropriate to impose the same limits on noncitizens—but not longer ones.) Again, I don't think this principle is seriously contested even if it is sometimes breached in practice.

Finally, consider access to general social programs, such as publicly funded education and health care, provided to the general population. Of course, different states provide different levels of benefits, but one rarely hears arguments for treating legal permanent residents differently from citizens with regard to these programs. The reason why seems obvious. Residents also pay the taxes that fund these programs. Again, an elementary sense of reciprocity makes it clear that excluding residents from the benefits of such general public expenditures would be unjust.

So, for the vast majority of the rights of membership, there is no plausible case to be made for distinguishing between residents and citizens. The debates come at the margins. Despite the changes of the last half century, a few important differences between the rights of residents and the rights of citizens persist, apart from political rights. Some people support the changes that have eliminated the worst forms of discrimination against residents but think that the current distinctions between citizens and residents are morally justifiable and even desirable. Some would even extend such distinctions a bit, as was done with the welfare reforms in the United States in the mid-1990s. Others, including me, think these remaining distinctions are unjustifiable relics of past discrimination and should also be eliminated.

In the next sections, I discuss three of the most important areas where legal distinctions between citizens and permanent residents endure: security of residence, access to public employment, and access to redistributive social programs. In each case I argue for a reduction, though not complete elimination, of the remaining distinctions.[21]

Security of Residence

Freedom of exit is widely recognized as a general human right, enjoyed by everyone regardless of whether one is a citizen of the country one wishes to leave, though like all rights, this one is subject to limitations (e.g., one cannot leave while charged with a crime) and is sometimes violated.[22] But the right to remain in a country if one does not want to leave and the right to return to a country after one has left are not rights enjoyed in principle by everyone. These are also widely recognized as human rights, but they are membership-specific human rights. These rights are held most securely by citizens. In principle, citizens may not be refused entry and may not be deported, even if there is someplace else willing to take them. Residents also have some legal rights regarding re-entry and protection against deportation, but their rights in these areas are normally not as strong as the rights of citizens. Should they be? I will argue that they should, though with some qualifications.

Let's start with the question of why citizens should have a right not to be deported or excluded from re-entry. This is sometimes treated as if it were self-evident, but it's not. In ancient Greece, for example, it was widely considered acceptable to send citizens into exile, sometimes as a punishment for crimes, but sometimes simply because their presence was perceived to be contrary to the public interest or dangerous to the security of the regime, without any evidence of wrongdoing on their part. As recently as a couple of centuries ago, states like Britain sent criminals across the ocean to distant colonies, exiling them from British society. Exile and exclusion could be useful weapons in the arsenal of sovereignty, so why don't modern states claim a right to use them?

Of course, there are no longer any colonies that imperial states can use as dumping grounds for their undesirables, but why hasn't the option formerly provided by colonies been replaced by a negotiated arrangement between states? It could be mutually advantageous for states to agree upon rules permitting exile and exclusion, on the condition that some other state was willing to take the exile. One state might agree to take in another's unwanted citizens for political or economic or other reasons. What is wrong with that?

We cannot find a satisfactory answer to that question from the perspective of the state system alone. We must appeal instead to the fundamental values that human rights are supposed to protect. From that perspective, the problem with the arrangement I have just outlined is that it does not pay enough attention to the claims of the exiles and the excluded. To deprive people involuntarily of their home society is (normally) to harm them in a fundamental way, so fundamental that it is no longer considered an acceptable form of punishment for citizens, even heinous criminals, and certainly not something that one can impose upon someone who has not been convicted of any wrongdoing. That is why forced exile of citizens is regarded as a violation of human rights.

What about residents? Their interests in not being forced to leave the place where they live (and in being able to return there if they leave on a trip) are often just as strong as the interests of citizens. In fact, in democratic states, noncitizens who have been admitted for an indefinite period normally do enjoy considerable security of residence. Democratic states cannot deport long-term residents because they have become unemployed or ill, for example, even though they may represent a drain on the treasury. Nevertheless, residents are often subject to deportation if convicted of a serious criminal offense or a series of offenses. The deportation of noncitizens convicted of crimes is usually presented not as a punishment but simply as a routine exercise of a state's power to exclude unwanted immigrants. Of course, from the perspective of the resident, deportation is often a much harsher sanction than whatever penalty is imposed by the criminal justice system.

In some cases, especially in North America, the amount of time the noncitizen has been present is treated as legally irrelevant, or at most, as something that authorities have the discretion to take into account if they wish in deciding whether to seek deportation. (European human rights legislation provides better protection for residents in this regard.)

Consider the case of Victor Castillo as reported by Susan Coutin who interviewed him.[23] He came to the United States as a legal resident in 1967 at the age of 4. He was adopted at the age of 8 by his stepfather who was an American citizen. He received his education in American schools, married an American woman, had American children, voted in American elections, and worked as a carpenter in the United States. He also joined a gang, became addicted to drugs, and acquired several drug-related criminal convictions. In 2004, at the age of 40, he was deported to El Salvador, a country whose formal citizenship he held but one where he had not lived since his early childhood.

Castillo's case is typical. It is not uncommon for people who have spent all but the first few years of their lives in, say, Canada or the United States to be deported to their "home" state which may be a place where they know no one and whose local language they do not speak.

I regard this practice as a scandal, the most blatant and severe injustice against noncitizens of any of the practices I shall criticize. Nevertheless, it is likely to be one of the most difficult to change because convicted criminals are unpopular and courts tend to be highly deferential to political authorities on this issue.

There are three interrelated reasons why the deportation of long-term residents convicted of serious criminal offenses is morally wrong: membership, fairness to other societies, and the rights of family members.

The first and most important argument is one that we have seen before and will see again: an argument about the implications of social membership. Long-term residents are members of society, and, for that reason, ought to be entitled to stay regardless of their conduct. Of course, by definition, the residents in question are not citizens, not formal members of the political community. But they are members of civil society. They participate in labor and housing markets, hey pay taxes, they have families that connect them to others in the society in myriad ways, they send children to schools, they participate in neighborhood and other associations, and they are involved in cultural and recreational activities. In short, they belong. And that belonging matters morally.

To elaborate this argument I will begin with the easiest case and then show why the principles for that sort of case should be extended to less obvious ones. So, consider first noncitizens like Victor Castillo who come to the society at a very young age, perhaps even are born there if the country has no rule that grants citizenship on the basis of birthplace (ius soli). They grow up speaking the local language, using their parents' native tongue only at home if at all. Their schooling, their friendships, their cultural experiences (television, music, etc.), their formal and informal socialization are very similar to those of the children of the citizens in the land where they live and very different from those of the children in the land their parents came from. To suggest that such children are not integrated into society would be ludicrous. To classify them as aliens denies a social reality.

On what grounds might someone say that such children are not members of the society where they have always lived and so entitled to live there all their lives whatever their conduct and behavior? Two possible answers occur to me. First, they are not entitled to stay because they possess citizenship in another country. Second, their failure to naturalize when they had the opportunity to do so implies a tacit consent to the conditions that distinguish permanent residents from citizens. Neither is persuasive.

Their right to remain in the land where they live is not lessened if their parents' country of origin happens to grant them citizenship because that citizenship does not secure their place in the society to which they most clearly belong. If they are members of any society, they are members of the society where they have lived their entire lives, the society whose language they speak and whose culture they share. Surely they are much more members of that society than of the one from which their parents came, in a land where they have never lived and have no friends, whose culture and customs are unfamiliar at best. Perhaps they have some claim to membership in both societies. But to refuse them the right to stay in the land where they live, and thus formal legal recognition and protection of their status as members of society, is to treat them unjustly.

What about their failure to naturalize? Even for adults, consent counts as a justification only when it reflects a genuine choice or at least a free affirmation. In many cases, children do not become citizens because of their parents' choices (or inaction), and by the time they are old enough to choose for themselves, they have already become embroiled in the legal system in ways that preclude naturalization. Even if these obstacles do not exist, it is unreasonable to infer from inaction the deliberate forfeiture of such a vital interest as the right to stay in one's homeland (even if it is not the place of one's birth). In Castillo's case, for example, Coutin reports that Castillo believed that he had acquired citizenship when he was adopted by his citizen stepfather. That is why he had voted in elections.

If people are to give up a fundamental right, like the right to live in the society in which they are most deeply rooted, it must be done as a deliberate and conscious choice in circumstances that are not coercive. Even those who do choose freely and consciously not to naturalize are entitled to protection against deportation, because the right to remain in a society of which one is a member, even if not a citizen, is a fundamental human interest that ought to be respected.

To recall, the general principle I am defending is that the longer the presence, the stronger the claims to membership. The shorter the presence, the weaker the claims. As I argued in chapter 3, a child who comes to a country as an infant is virtually indistinguishable, in moral terms, from one who was born there. People who spend all or most of their formative years as children in a country have powerful ties and a powerful moral claim to remain there.

How long must children spend in a country before they have become members with a moral claim to remain? I can't answer that question precisely, but I would think that several years (especially ones between the ages of 6 and 18) should be enough. Castillo clearly qualified on multiple grounds.

The argument I have advanced about why people raised in a society should not be deported closely parallels the arguments presented in chapters 2 and 3 about why people raised in a society should become citizens automatically. In both cases, the fundamental claim is about the moral relevance of social membership. Cases like Castillo's would disappear if democratic states implemented the principles that I advocated in chapters 2 and 3 regarding access to citizenship. Castillo would have become a citizen automatically at some point, and his crimes would have been dealt with in the normal way that the crimes of any citizen are addressed. Nevertheless, I thought it was worth laying out the arguments against deportation of people like Castillo because not everyone will accept my earlier arguments that social membership gives rise to a claim to legal citizenship. In fact the most potent political argument against that idea would probably be that it would entail granting citizenship to criminals or potential criminals. So, it is important for readers to see why a history of criminality should be regarded as irrelevant to the question of why someone raised in a society should be allowed to remain there. Moreover, even if some people are not persuaded that social membership entitles people to citizenship, as I argued in the earlier chapters, they may nevertheless accept the claim that social membership entitles someone not to be deported. One might argue that this is precisely the view reflected in European legislation, where the protections against deportation for long-term residents are stronger, on the whole, than rights of access to citizenship. In North America, it is the reverse.

So far I have focused on people who have spent virtually their whole lives in the country. If we turn now to the question of what claims people who come as adults have to remain, we find that the same principle applies. The longer one stays, the more one becomes a member. The shorter the stay, the weaker the claim. If a person arrives as an immigrant and commits a serious crime within six months or a year, it would not be wrong to deport her.[24] She will not have built up the kinds of social ties that make expulsion so inhuman. But if she has been there for ten years, then the case is entirely different.

How long must adults spend before they have the kind of claim to membership that should bar deportation? Again, I won't try to answer this question precisely. But it is important to recognize that in assessing the claims that come from living in a society, there is a threshold after which the length of time does not matter because the claim should be regarded as absolute. Five years seems to me a reasonable length of time for such a threshold, though I don't pretend that the question can be precisely settled on the basis of a theoretical principle.

"But these are criminals," someone will object. "They cause social problems. They are destructive to the rest of society. Isn't it in our interest to send them away?" Let us assume that this is true, as it appears to be in Castillo's case.[25] This takes us to the fairness argument. To deport someone like Victor Castillo is to take advantage of a legal technicality that ought not to exist. It is not fair to dump criminals like Castillo on another society, a place where they have a legal membership but no real social connection. Every political community has people who are involved in criminal activity and who create social problems. It seems only fair that a state should deal with its own problems, not try to foist them off on someplace else. The argument is especially powerful again with regard to people who have grown up in the state that seeks to expel them. It is that political community, not the one of their nominal citizenship, that is responsible for their social formation, for successes and failures in the inculcation of social norms and values, for the creation of opportunities and obstacles in social life. In short, one important response to the imagined objection is to say, "These people may be problems, but they are *our* problems, not someone else's, and we should be the ones to cope with them as we do with criminals who are citizens." To the extent that any state is responsible for Victor Castillo's life path, it is clearly the United States not El Salvador. Even if you take a highly individualist approach to issues of criminality and say that the wider society has no responsibility for Castillo's criminal career, the question remains: why should it be El Salvador rather than the United States that is expected to cope with him now?

The final argument against deportation of noncitizens concerns the effect of such deportations upon family members who may themselves be citizens or who, in any event, have done no wrong themselves. Castillo, for example, was forced to leave behind his wife and children. I regard this argument as somewhat weaker than the preceding two, because the same objection can be posed against any sanction (that is, that it affects not only the person against whom it is directed but also those to whom he or she is connected). Nevertheless, it appropriately draws attention to the particular nature of deportation as a harm, and a harm additional to what citizen criminals have to suffer. Ironically, it is this sort of argument, constructed on the basis of guarantees to family life, that has proven the most effective barrier to deportation in a number of European court cases.

So far, I have been focusing on involuntary deportations. The case is more complicated when it comes to the question of whether residents have a right to be readmitted after a sustained period of voluntary absence. Temporary absences of a few weeks or a few months raise no serious problems in principle or, for the most part, in practice. Such absences clearly do not affect residents' connection to the place where they live. So, they should—and normally do—enjoy a legal right to return home, where home is defined as the place where they actually live not the place where they hold legal citizenship. But what if a resident moves abroad on a long-term basis, setting up residence either in her country of citizenship or in a third country? Should residents who have left enjoy an indefinite right to return, no matter how long they stay away and no matter how little time they lived in the country where they hold resident status? Or is there perhaps some correlation between the length of residence and the right to return, so that

the longer one has resided in a country, the longer one can be away without forfeiting the right to return?

I will confess that, in contrast to my views on involuntary deportation, I do
not have strong or clear views on this issue. The principle that I have been
defending—the longer the stay, the stronger the claim to remain—would
seem to have, as a logical corollary, the principle that the longer the absence,
the weaker the claim to return. That certainly seems plausible if the resident has
only been present for a short period, but what if she has passed the (somewhat
indeterminate) threshold that I said should establish a permanent bar to deportation? Should this also establish a permanent right of return? The cases do not
seem entirely parallel, since the bar to deportation secures one's right to continue living where one been residing for a long time. On the other hand, citizens
do have a permanent right to return no matter how long they have lived abroad,
or even if they have never lived in the land of their citizenship. That principle of
international law is thought to protect a vital human interest, and perhaps one
could argue that a permanent right of return for long-term residents would do so
also, while recognizing that it may be overbroad in particular cases (perhaps like
the right to citizenship in certain cases of dual citizenship). Another possibility
would be to establish the right of residents to return to their place of residence
as a proportional right rather than a permanent one. So, for example, someone
who had lived in a country for ten years might have a right to return after an
absence of up to ten years but would need permission after that. I am inclined
to think that even when we are dealing with the right to return rather than with
the bar to deportation, some sort of threshold should be established after which
the right to return would be permanent, but the threshold could reasonably be
quite a bit higher than the one established as a bar to deportation. On the whole,
I think this question raises less urgent moral issues so long as residents have a
completely secure right to return after temporary absences and some reasonable
protection for a right of return after more extended absences.

Public Employment

As we have seen, in democratic states, residents normally have access to the general labor market. As I have argued, this is a logical corollary of granting them
a right of permanent residence. When it comes to public sector employment,
however, the situation is different. At least in the national civil service, and sometimes in local or regional public employment as well, citizens are often given
preferential access in relation to noncitizens, and sometimes noncitizen residents are excluded altogether. There is rarely any attempt to justify this practice,
and it is difficult to justify, if one reflects upon it at all.

Let me first distinguish, as many jurisdictions have done, between public sector jobs that involve national security or major policy making responsibilities and other public sector jobs. It is reasonable to restrict the former categories to citizens (provided that the categories are not interpreted so expansively as to eviscerate the distinction) because in those cases being a full member of the political community is arguably relevant to the responsibilities of the position. But for the vast majority of public sector jobs, there is no functional connection between citizenship and the tasks that the employee must perform. Even if we assume that citizenship is a reasonable proxy (or at least a preliminary screen) for loyalty to the state, an assumption that is deeply problematic, most civil service jobs do not require that sort of loyalty. They merely require that one carry out one's assigned responsibilities competently, something that is entirely unrelated to one's citizenship status.

In a recent Canadian legal case, defenders of preferential treatment for citizens in the federal civil service argued that this policy enhanced the meaning of citizenship and created an incentive for noncitizens to naturalize.[26] But as the dissenting judges powerfully argued, we do not enhance the meaning of citizenship in any positive sense when we make citizenship the basis for a form of discrimination against people who are otherwise entitled to be treated as equals. As for incentives to naturalize—an argument that only applies in states that are encouraging immigrants to naturalize—one must always consider whether the incentives are effective and appropriate. Privileging citizenship is an ineffective incentive because it has an impact only on that small subset of the immigrant population that wants public sector jobs and it is inappropriate because it links the incentive to discrimination. Moreover, this sort of incentive sends the wrong message about why people should naturalize. It encourages immigrants to take the attitude "What's in it for me?" in thinking about whether to become citizens whereas we ought to encourage them to become citizens not primarily for narrow, instrumental reasons but out of a sense of identity and attachment and out of a desire to participate in a shared public life. Attaching special (nonpolitical) privileges to citizenship sends the wrong message about citizenship and the nature of our community not only to immigrants but also to citizens. It emphasizes divisions among people who live together, and it encourages citizens to think of lawfully resident noncitizens as "others" not as fellow members of the community. Encouraging people to naturalize is a good thing, but it should be done in the right way.

In short, the continued exclusion of permanent residents from much of the public sector is a form of discrimination that has little plausible justification beyond the discrimination itself (that is, favoring citizens over residents with regard to a class of economic opportunities). This sort of overt discrimination was once widespread in the private sector and the professions but has now been largely eliminated. The opening of the public sector in Europe to all EU citizens establishes the irrelevance of citizenship to most public sector jobs and confirms the point that restricting or favoring citizens in public employment is an unreflective vestige of past patterns of discrimination that serves no defensible public purpose.

Redistributive Rights

As I have argued above, residents enjoy most of the same economic and social rights as citizens, and no one seriously contests this at the level of principle when it comes to contributory social programs or general public expenditures. The real debates, and the recent policy changes, have focused on one small sector of social programs: means-tested social welfare benefits. In other words, what is at issue is whether immigrants should have access to redistributive programs that provide income and other benefits that are contingent upon one's income falling below a certain level.

Now let me distinguish here between what justice requires and what would be a wise or even a morally desirable policy. Justice sets a minimum standard (even if one we often fail to reach). It does not exhaust the moral universe. In my view, *as a matter of justice*, immigrants who have been settled in a society for a number of years are morally entitled to all of the social rights that citizens enjoy. The argument here is the same one advanced above in my discussion of deportation. The longer one stays in a society, the stronger one's moral claims and after a certain point one is entitled to be treated simply as a full member. (Again, I recognize that it is impossible to say on theoretical grounds precisely how many years, but I think five is about the right number.) So, in my view, it is unjust to exclude permanent residents from any social programs, means-tested or not, for a much more extended period such as ten years (or even permanently as some have proposed in the United States).

But is it unjust to insist that immigrants not be immediately eligible for such programs? On that issue, I am much less certain. I think that such a policy is unwise and mean-spirited, and that it scapegoats immigrants for fiscal problems they have not caused. As a citizen I would want my political community to welcome the immigrants who have been admitted and to make them immediately eligible for the same programs as everyone else. But that is not the same as saying that such a course is morally required. My general argument—the longer one stays, the stronger one's moral claims—implies that the claims of immigrants when they first arrive are not as strong as when they have been there for some time. I suggested above that that was true with regard to security of residence, and it seems to me that it is true also with regard to redistributive social programs whose goal is to compensate for economic disparities among members.

Conclusion

While most of the persisting legal distinctions between citizens and long settled residents deserve criticism, we should not lose sight of the fact that the distinctions actually affect only a small minority of resident noncitizens and pale in comparison to the systematic and widespread differentiation between citizens and residents that was common a few decades ago in both Europe and North America. To restate the main point, current practice in democratic states draws very few distinctions between citizens and permanent residents apart from the right to vote and the right to hold public office, and that is how it should be. The idea that citizenship is the special status that distinguishes insiders from outsiders is so deeply rooted in our traditions of thought and expression that it is hard sometimes to recognize how poorly this fits with our actual practices, how rare it is to reserve rights exclusively for citizens, and how difficult it would be to justify doing so.

Finally, to avoid any misunderstanding, let me distinguish the position I am defending here from what is sometimes described as a cosmopolitan view. Nothing in my argument rests on the proposition that we have to treat all human beings alike, that we cannot distinguish between members and strangers. My argument does not depend in any way on a claim that democratic states are obliged to admit any immigrants who want to come. It does not depend, for the most part, on an appeal to general human rights. On the contrary, it rests primarily on the distinction between members and others, and on a claim about the moral significance of social membership. Once democratic states have admitted immigrants as permanent residents, they are obliged not to marginalize them, not to exclude them from the security and opportunities that the rights of membership bring. In sum, long-term residence in society creates a moral entitlement to the legal rights of membership.

6

Temporary Workers

In the previous chapter I drew a sharp distinction between the moral claims of permanent residents and those of tourists or visitors, but noncitizens do not always fall neatly into these categories. Some people are admitted to democratic states for work but with restrictions on how long they can remain and what they can do while they are present.[1] Unlike visitors or tourists, these are people who have permission to set up residence in the territory and to participate in the paid workforce, but unlike permanent residents, they do not enjoy a right to stay on indefinitely and they may be subject to other restrictive conditions as well. I will call these people "temporary workers."

There are lots of temporary workers in democratic states in Europe and North America. Even countries that have traditionally accepted most immigrants as permanent residents now admit many on a temporary basis. The United States, for example, has dozens of lawful immigration statuses besides that of permanent resident or tourist. Most of these statuses provide an authorization to work, but one that is limited in various ways. Canada now admits more economic immigrants under programs that require workers to leave after a relatively short, fixed period than in its traditional landed immigrant stream. European states also have temporary worker programs. Ireland has a program (in which my own son participated) that permits young people (from certain countries) to come and work for a year, with the clear expectation that they will leave at the end of that period, and other states have similar arrangements. Many democratic states admit seasonal workers for the agricultural harvest but require them to work only at that task and to leave at the end of the season.

Where should we locate temporary workers on a normative map of democracy? Is it morally permissible for democratic states to admit people to work only on a temporary basis, and, if so, under what conditions?

I am interested here only in what democratic justice requires with respect to temporary workers, not whether a state gains by admitting them. There are many policies that are morally permissible but foolish, and others that might be economically advantageous but unjust. In this book, I aim only to sketch the contours of justice, not those of wisdom.

The Case for Limited Rights for Temporary Workers

Some people think that we should draw a fundamental distinction between people admitted as permanent residents and those admitted as temporary workers.[2] Permanent residents should be seen as prospective citizens and for that reason should be granted most of the rights that citizens enjoy.[3] Temporary workers are in a very different position, however. As David Miller puts it:

> …their human rights must be protected, of course. But beyond that, their position is better understood in contractual terms: what rights they get should depend on what agreements they have made (or are in place) before they enter.[4]

From this perspective, any terms of admission for temporary workers are morally acceptable so long as they are based on informed consent and do not violate human rights.[5]

If consent is the only criterion besides respect for human rights that is used to determine what legal rights temporary workers get, they may wind up with very few. Hong Kong and Singapore, for example, both grant temporary admission permits to large numbers of foreign women to work as domestics. The women have no opportunity to gain a right of permanent residence, much less citizenship, no matter how long they stay. It is not unusual to find workers who have been present for fifteen years or more in a "temporary" status. In Hong Kong, workers must exit the territory within two weeks if they leave their employers and do not find another job, and in Singapore they have to return home if they quit or are fired. They are not allowed to bring their families to live with them. In Singapore, they are prohibited from marrying or cohabiting with a Singaporean citizen or resident and are expelled if they do so or if they become pregnant. Workers in Hong Kong have better legal protections than those in Singapore, but in both cases the protections for these temporary workers are much more limited than the ones extended to citizens and residents. The normal working hours are extremely long. Many foreign domestic workers in Hong Kong work 14 to16 hours a day, 6 days a week. The hours are even longer on average in Singapore. The Persian Gulf states such as Kuwait and Qatar admit proportionally even more foreigners on temporary permits than Hong Kong and Singapore, often under even more restrictive conditions.

Democratic states in Europe and North America have been reluctant to follow this approach. When they do admit temporary workers, they normally provide them much more extensive rights than places like Singapore and Kuwait do. On the other hand, they also admit proportionally far fewer temporary workers. And some people think that is the fundamental problem from a moral perspective.

Critics of current policies in democratic states argue that there is a tradeoff between rights and numbers. So long as temporary workers get most of the rights of membership, many potential temporary workers will never be able to gain legal admission at all. To be sure, some temporary workers will get in and they will benefit from having such substantial rights. Overall, however, democratic states will bring in many fewer temporary workers than they would if they did not grant the workers so many rights.

As the critics see it, this creates moral problems. Some migrants will come anyway and work without legal authorization, finding themselves worse off than they would be with legal status and limited rights. Others will remain at home, facing conditions of work that are far worse in every respect than those they would face in a rich democratic country even if their rights there were much more restricted than the rights of members. Indeed, those who stay at home may well perform the same sort of work that they would undertake in rich states and produce goods that the people in these rich states will consume. A Mexican farmworker who picks tomatoes in Mexico for export to the United States is paid much less and faces much worse working conditions than a Mexican farmworker who picks tomatoes in the United States, even if the latter is not given the benefits and protections that American workers normally enjoy. In other words, the workers who are unable to migrate will still be working for people in rich states, just indirectly and for less pay and under worse conditions.

To the critics, this is a perverse outcome. They argue that it is not only morally permissible, but morally superior, perhaps even morally required, for rich democratic states to admit more temporary workers with fewer legal rights. This would contribute to a reduction of global poverty because the increase in the number of temporary workers would increase the overall level of remittances sent home to their countries of origin, thus transferring resources from rich countries to poor ones. It would also enable people who would otherwise come without authorization to enter and work legally. That would be better both for the workers and for the country where they work. Above all, it would respect the agency of the workers. No one forces temporary workers to come (or no one should). But if they are willing to accept a limited bundle of rights, they should be free to do so. Of course, they may agree to these terms only because their alternatives at home are worse, but all choices are made in the context of alternatives. Granting more rights to temporary workers reduces the number who will be admitted and does not do anything to improve the conditions at home for those left behind.

This is a powerful challenge, but I think that it is profoundly misguided. I propose to defend the current practice of granting extensive rights to temporary workers in democratic states. Indeed, I will argue that temporary workers should get even more rights.

Temporary Admissions

Let's start with the question of whether democratic states may admit people to work only for a limited period. Given the general background assumption of the state's right to exercise discretionary control over immigration, I think that admitting workers on a temporary basis is morally permissible, but only if the duration of their stay is truly limited. If we accept the principle that I defended in the previous chapter that the longer one stays in a society, the stronger one's claim to remain, it follows that the shorter one's stay, the weaker one's claim to remain (other things being equal). So, if people are admitted to work on a temporary visa and have no other moral claim to residence than their presence in the state, it is normally reasonable to expect them to leave when their visa expires, if they have only been present for a year or two.[6] On the other hand, if a temporary visa of this sort is renewed, it ought at some point to be converted into a right of permanent residence. That is also the implication of the principle that the longer the stay, the stronger the claim to remain.

Democratic states cannot keep people indefinitely in a "temporary" status. That is the clear lesson of the European experience with guestworkers in the mid-twentieth century. States that are not committed to democratic principles behave differently. Kuwait and Singapore are able to keep foreign workers in a temporary status for decades precisely because they are not committed to democratic norms. That way of treating people who are living and working within a state is incompatible with contemporary understandings of democracy. It does not give sufficient weight to the way membership claims grow over time from living in a society. All of the temporary worker programs in democratic states that I mentioned at the outset of the chapter recognize this principle. All of them set strict limits to renewals of work permits. The programs are consciously designed to send the immigrants back home before they have acquired the sort of deep social roots that give rise to a right to remain in a democratic state.[7]

When do workers admitted on a temporary basis acquire a moral right to remain permanently? As we have seen before, philosophical reflection cannot provide precise answers to such questions. Identifying a specific moment when immigrants should acquire a firm moral right to remain inevitably involves both a contestable interpretation of the rate at which the claim to remain grows over time and an element of arbitrariness in setting a particular demarcation point for recognizing the growing moral claim as a legal right. The European Union has recently issued a directive recommending that third country nationals (that is, people from outside the EU) be granted a right of permanent residence if they have been legally residing in an EU state for five years.[8] This is clearly an attempt to recognize and implement the (somewhat indeterminate) moral principle that the moral claim to remain grows over time, along with a recognition that some threshold must be established beyond which the right to stay is firm.

Why five years rather than four or six? No one can pretend that the answer to this question entails any fundamental principle. It is more a matter of the social psychology of coordination, given the need to settle on one point within a range. But if one asks why five years rather than one or ten, it is easier to make the case that one is too short and ten too long, given common European understandings of the ways in which people normally settle into the societies where they live.

The Rights of Temporary Workers

Let's turn now to the question of what rights temporary workers should have. I propose to pursue this issue by asking how the rights of temporary workers should resemble or differ from the rights of citizens and residents. As in the previous chapter, I frame the inquiry in a comparative way in order to set aside broader questions about what rights are required by democratic justice and to keep the focus on questions about how immigration status affects claims to rights.

Temporary workers clearly differ from tourists and visitors in being entitled to participate in the workforce and to set up residence in the state, if only for a limited period. That fact makes them members in certain important respects from the outset. On the other hand, their temporary status makes them members of a different sort from citizens and permanent residents. So, we can't just assume that they have a moral claim to all of the rights of membership that citizens and residents enjoy. How, if at all, does the limited character of their stay affect the membership rights that temporary workers should enjoy while they are present?

In reflecting on this question, we may find it helpful to distinguish among three kinds of membership rights: rights with respect to working conditions (which include things like health and safety regulations and laws regarding minimum wages, overtime pay, and paid holidays and vacations), rights to participation in social programs directly tied to workforce participation (which include things like unemployment compensation and compulsory pension plans), and rights to participation in other social programs (which include income support programs, health care, education, recreation, and anything else the state spends money on for the benefit of the domestic population).

Working Conditions

Consider first the conditions of work. While the development of the global economy has made it more difficult for individual states to control economic activity, every democratic state regulates working conditions in some respects. Is it morally acceptable for a democratic state to have one set of rules regarding working conditions for citizens and permanent residents and a different set of rules for workers who are present on a temporary basis?

I think not. The purpose of these regulations is to establish *minimum* standards for economic activity, thus limiting the terms to which workers can agree and the risks to which they can be exposed within a given jurisdiction. Of course, the rules regulating working conditions vary between states, but that does not make it justifiable for a state to grant temporary workers weaker or fewer rights in this area than citizens and residents enjoy. As we saw in the last chapter, the fact that the rights of criminal defendants vary from one democratic state to another does not make it justifiable for a state to provide a lesser bundle of rights to foreign defendants than to domestic ones.

Every state is responsible for what goes on inside its own jurisdiction. A state has to make a judgment about acceptable health and safety standards and other minimum working conditions within its own territory. Temporary workers are people working within the state's jurisdiction. It makes no sense to say that conditions that are deemed to be unsafe or unhealthy for citizens and residents are fine for temporary workers. Therefore, the policies that regulate working conditions for citizens and residents should apply to temporary workers as well.

Some might object that temporary workers would be willing to work under worse conditions than citizens and residents. That might be true, but it is beside the point. After all, the rules are preventing citizens and residents from working under terms that they might otherwise accept. So, the fact that temporary workers might be willing to accept even worse conditions is irrelevant. The whole purpose of the rules governing working conditions is to prevent workers (citizens and residents, as well as temporary workers) from accepting certain terms of employment. Democratic states regulate working conditions and set limits to the terms that workers can accept for a number of reasons: protecting human dignity, solving collective active problems, ensuring that people will not make decisions under duress or out of ignorance, preventing workers from acting unwisely or without sufficient foresight, and for other reasons as well. For the most part, these reasons apply just as much to temporary workers as they do to citizens and residents.

Of course, some may argue that it is wrong to place restrictions on the choices that workers can make. But others will say that the restrictions do not go far enough. As I have said before, I am trying to avoid these wider debates in order to keep the focus on the ethics of immigration. For my purposes, the crucial question is not what regulations, if any, a democratic state should place on working conditions but whether there is any reason to think that the regulation of working conditions for temporary workers should be different from the regulation of working conditions for citizens and residents. As I have just shown, the mere fact that regulations restrict choice does not provide such a reason. In the absence of some more specific reason to think that the considerations that underlie restrictions on the choices of citizens and residents do not apply to temporary workers, whatever regulations of working conditions apply to citizens and residents should apply also to temporary workers.

There are two other reasons for thinking that the rules governing working conditions for temporary workers should be the same as the ones governing working conditions for citizens and residents, although these two reasons are concerned with the interests of citizens and residents rather than with the interests of the temporary workers themselves.

First, if temporary workers are competing for jobs with citizens and residents, the same minimum standards regarding wages, working conditions, and other employment related costs will have to apply to them or the standards will be ineffective for citizens and residents because employers will have an incentive to prefer foreign workers. This is a concern that frequently motivates opposition to programs for temporary migrant workers.

The second reason is that deliberately permitting temporary workers to labor under conditions inferior to those established as the minimum standards set for citizens and residents would undermine the ethos that is necessary for a democratic state to maintain itself over time. As we saw in chapter 4, democratic institutions and practices require a democratic culture. Part of that democratic culture must be that people in the society can see themselves as equal in some fundamental sense. To establish a legally differentiated and subordinate status for temporary workers would erode that culture by creating a category of people who live and work within the state under conditions that render them less than equal.[9] The negative effects of having a class of legally subordinated people within the state are only somewhat reduced by the fact that the occupants of that category keep changing.

By and large, the policies of democratic states fit with the arguments outlined in this section. There are some special programs in which temporary workers are restricted to particular jobs and in which they are subject to conditions not imposed upon other workers. I discuss such programs briefly later in the chapter. Apart from these special cases, temporary workers generally are subject to the same legal standards regarding working conditions as citizens and residents.

What about the farmworker in Mexico objection? If we insist that conditions for farmworkers in California meet normal American standards, California farms won't be able to compete with those in Mexico where pay and other conditions are much worse. Workers who might have come as temporary workers to California farms will wind up doing the same job under worse conditions in Mexico.

This objection ignores the moral relevance of the state system for the assignment of moral responsibility. The division of the world into separate states matters for the extent of our moral responsibilities. We have a different kind of responsibility for what goes on in our own jurisdiction than we do for what goes on elsewhere. Normally, we should not try to impose our collective will on other states, and we will not be as responsible for what goes on there as we are for what goes on in our own state. Of course, one can object that a powerful state like the United States does impose its will elsewhere and so is responsible for what happens there. But this argument is usually advanced as a critique of American control over other states, not an invitation for it to wield still more power. One can also object that the inequalities generated by the current state system are unjust, and so we should not simply accept the pattern of responsibilities that grows out of current arrangements. I agree with this objection and will take it up in chapters 11 and 12. For the moment, however, as I explained in chapter 1, I am accepting existing international arrangements as a given. In that context, states are much more responsible for what goes on in their own jurisdictions than they are for what goes on elsewhere.

Our relationships with people who live in another state are normally very different from our relationships with people living in our own state and subject to our laws. The contractual model does not provide a good way for regulating our interactions with temporary workers but it does provide a reasonable basis for regulating most of our interactions with people living elsewhere with whom we engage in economic relations through trade and exchange because they are not subject to our laws. We can perhaps insist on certain minimum background conditions of work for those with whom we engage in trading relationships (e.g., no child labor, no penal labor, some health and safety standards), but we cannot impose our own standards regarding working conditions and should not try to do so.

In sum, we are morally responsible for the conditions under which people work in our own state, whether they are here on a temporary or a permanent basis, and we are not nearly as morally responsible for the conditions under which people work elsewhere. These arguments about the scope of our responsibilities apply to the next two sections as well.

Work-Related Social Programs

Now consider social programs directly tied to workforce participation. These programs are intended to provide a form of insurance protection, often against hardships that will predictably fall upon some subset of workers. Typical examples are programs to provide income if workers become unemployed, programs to provide compensation for industrial accidents, and compulsory pension plans. Often these programs are based directly on the principle of reciprocity and are designed as contributory programs in which the state imposes a tax on workers and/or their employers for a specific purpose. You pay in and you receive a benefit if you need it.[10] Even citizens are normally not entitled to the benefits of such programs unless they have participated in the workforce, paid the appropriate tax (where that is required), and, sometimes, passed a designated waiting period.

Temporary workers should either be included in such programs or compensated for their exclusion. In many cases, simple inclusion is the better solution, but as I will show below, there is sometimes an acceptable alternative.

When programs are designed as contributory schemes, the injustice of excluding temporary workers from them is especially obvious. It is blatantly unfair to require people to pay into an insurance scheme if they are not eligible for the benefits. This violates an elementary principle of reciprocity. But the basic principle of including temporary workers in the programs or compensating them for their exclusion does not rest solely on the method by which the program is financed. So long as the rationale of the program is intimately linked to workforce participation, it should include all workers, temporary or not.

In this area, practice varies from one state to another, but in some states practice diverges much more sharply from the principle of equal treatment than it normally does with respect to working conditions. Temporary workers are often required to pay into pension plans with no reasonable expectation of actually collecting a pension. They are often required to pay unemployment insurance but are not eligible to collect benefits. Those policies are unfair.

Sometimes there are alternative arrangements that would be more defensible. States may have legitimate reasons for wanting to exclude temporary workers from some contributory programs. In such cases, it might be acceptable to exclude temporary workers from the programs, if they are not expected to make the relevant contributions, but not otherwise.

Take the question of pensions. Historically, most state pension programs have included an element of redistribution from those of working age to the elderly. In that sense, state pension plans are not pure insurance schemes and not exclusively based on the principle of reciprocity (although this practice has become less viable with demographic changes and the aging of the populations in Europe and North America). For reasons I will explore below, temporary workers do not have the same claims on redistributive social programs as on other programs. It might be justifiable therefore for a state to exclude temporary workers from the benefits of the normal pension plan, but only if the state does not collect money from the worker and the employer for the state pension plan. On the other hand, simply failing to collect this money at all would mean that temporary workers would be getting a higher net pay at a lower cost to the employer than citizens and residents doing the same work. That might not be unjust, but it is politically unattractive and does nothing to address the need temporary workers will eventually have for pensions in their home states. So, it would clearly be preferable to collect the same level of taxes from all workers and employers and to put the taxes collected from temporary workers in a separate fund to be disbursed to them either upon their return home or upon their retirement. The temporary workers would then receive less pension income than they would have if they had been participants in the general pension plan with its redistributive component, but they would not have been deprived of the benefits of the monies collected for their pensions. This presupposes, however, that the pension plan is funded from a specific tax rather than from general revenues. If pensions are funded from general revenues, the temporary workers should simply be included in the plan, and the conditions of eligibility should not require such an extended period of workforce participation that most temporary workers would be excluded.

Now consider unemployment compensation. These programs are designed in different ways in different states, but the underlying principle of all of them is to provide working members of society with some income security in the face of the changes generated by the market. Temporary workers are workers but not full members of society. If they lose their jobs, should they be entitled to the same level of income support as citizens and residents would receive under similar conditions? I have already established the principle that it is unreasonable to expect people to pay into a program for which they are not eligible. That leaves three potentially defensible options: (1) making temporary workers pay the tax and including them in the normal program, subject to normal constraints on eligibility; (2) excluding them from eligibility for the program, while not collecting the tax at all; or (3) collecting the tax (so that the cost of hiring a temporary worker is the same as hiring a citizen or resident) and putting the money in a special fund to be paid out upon the temporary worker's return home.

In addressing this question, I confess to more ambivalence than I feel with respect to the preceding one and the one that follows. On the one hand, if a temporary worker loses her job, she needs some alternative source of support for the same reasons that workers who are citizens and residents do. That argues for allowing temporary workers to be eligible for the normal unemployment compensation programs. On the other hand, temporary workers are only permitted to be present in the state for a limited time. Presumably they will not be eligible for unemployment compensation once they have left the country. (Otherwise, it would be economically advantageous for them to become unemployed shortly before they were due to return home.) So, if they were simply included in the normal program, as their exit date approached they would be paying into a program for which they were no longer fully eligible. Moreover, from the state's perspective, the whole point of admitting immigrants with temporary work visas is to gain the advantage of their contribution to the economy. Temporary workers who have lost their jobs and cannot readily find new ones will have stronger incentives to return home early if they are not receiving unemployment compensation. It is arguable that they are not being unfairly treated, even though they are treated differently from workers who are citizens and residents, so long as they have not had to pay taxes to support an unemployment compensation program for which they are not eligible and so long as they are permitted to stay and try to find a new job while living on their savings.[11]

Pensions and unemployment compensation provide examples of cases where it would be justifiable to exclude temporary workers from social programs linked to workforce participation so long as they were not bearing the costs of the programs. Not all contributory social programs fit this model, however. Some compulsory contributory social programs are more akin to health and safety regulations in the sense that they simply establish minimum standards for morally acceptable working conditions in a particular democratic state.

Consider social programs that compensate workers who suffer a work-related accident or illness. The structure of such programs is often quite similar to that of pensions and unemployment compensation programs. Workers and/or employers pay a tax, the monies go into a common fund, and workers who suffer a work-related harm receive benefits from the fund. These programs are designed to address some of the inevitable risks that economic activities pose to workers. Even with good health and safety regulations in place, work often entails risks of injury or illness for the workers. Sometimes this harm is due to negligence on the part of the employer or the worker or both; sometimes it is an unavoidable occasional outcome of the activity.[12] Democratic states have typically found it advantageous to limit litigation over responsibility for workplace accidents and illnesses and to establish instead programs to provide compensation for workers who suffer a work-related injury or illness, often using standard formulas to determine appropriate levels of compensation. The general justification for this is that some level of work-related injury and illness is unavoidable, and it makes more sense for both employers and employees to have a social insurance scheme of finance and compensation for this harm than to leave compensation to the vagaries of the legal process. The goal is to compensate for any health-related costs and lost income, and, in the case of permanent injuries, to provide an appropriate level of compensation for the harm suffered. (There are many debates about the adequacy of these arrangements in various states, but, as usual, I leave such issues aside here.) The rationale for workers' compensation programs are thus closely linked to the rationales for the health and safety regulations that they closely complement. Just as it would be wrong to permit temporary workers to labor under substandard working conditions with respect to health and safety, even if they were compensated financially for doing so, it would also be wrong to permit them to opt out of workers' compensation programs.

Other Social Programs

Every state provides a wide range of services to those within its territory. Some of these (police protection, emergency medical care) are, in principle, available to any person who needs it. For others, one must be a resident but any resident status will do, including residence as a temporary worker. For example, to borrow books from the local library, one must normally show only that one lives in the local area, not establish one's citizenship or one's immigration status. Similarly, one must sometimes prove that one is a resident to use local recreational facilities, but it would be hard to imagine the justification for excluding temporary workers from such facilities. At a more serious level, any state that treats health care as a basic right is obliged to provide health care to temporary workers, and their families, too, if they are present. Every democratic state has a system of free and compulsory public education, and again, temporary workers have a right to this education for their children if their children are present.

So far, I have been arguing that temporary workers should have access to the same social programs as citizens and permanent residents. Are there any exceptions to this principle?

The most obvious candidate is redistributive social programs. I argued in the previous chapter that permanent residents only acquire a strong moral right to participate in such programs after they have been present for a period of time, even though states may choose to be generous and include them before they have a strong moral entitlement. The same argument applies to temporary workers. Their moral claim to participate in a program based on redistributive taxation—taking from better off members of the community to benefit the less well off—is not as powerful as their claim to participate in a program whose benefits are directly tied to the worker's contributions. The moral claims of temporary workers to be able to participate in redistributive programs do grow over time, but, as we have seen, so does their claim to permanent, full membership if they are permitted to stay on.

Even if one accepts my argument about the permissibility of excluding temporary workers from redistributive programs, the overall picture remains unchanged. For the most part, temporary workers should receive most of the economic and social rights that citizens and residents enjoy.

Restrictive Programs

So far, I have been discussing temporary worker programs in which the primary restriction placed on participants was the length of time they could stay in the country. What if we add further restrictions to this picture? How does that affect our evaluation? The most common sort of restriction is one that limits temporary workers to a particular sector of the economy or a particular occupation or even a particular employer.

Limiting a temporary worker to a single employer is the most severe sort of restriction because it renders temporary workers highly vulnerable to abuses of power by their employers. Normally, the possibility of leaving one's employer and finding another job (often, but not always, one in the same field) limits the power that any given employer can exercise over employees.[13]

There is one possible justification for requiring a temporary worker to work only for a particular employer. If an immigrant is admitted under a program that requires her to have a job before entry, and if there is some cost to the employer in arranging for her entry, one can argue that the employer should be able to count on not losing the prospective employee upon arrival, even, or perhaps especially, to another employer in the same field. There are things to be said for and against this argument, but even if we accept it at full value, it would only justify a limited period during which a migrant could legitimately be tied to a particular employer. With all the usual caveats about philosophical analysis and specific time limits, I would suggest that something like three months would be a maximum, perhaps less, depending on how much the employer actually has to invest in the recruitment process (which can vary from one program to another). Even then, there ought to be an escape clause for abusive behavior by the employer.

What about the common practice of limiting temporary workers to a particular occupation or sector? Here it is worth distinguishing between temporary worker programs for highly skilled workers and ones for less skilled workers. The former (which are becoming more and more common in rich countries) involve the recruitment of highly trained professionals (e.g., computer programmers, engineers, doctors, even academics). Highly skilled people have little incentive to look for work outside their field of expertise. So, there is not much point in restricting them to a given field. In addition, there is such competition for these migrants that states have to offer them bundles of rights comparable to the ones enjoyed by citizens and residents in order to have much hope of inducing them to come.[14]

The real issue is with temporary worker programs for the less skilled. In my view, restricting migrant workers to a particular sector or occupation is morally problematic. The usual justification for temporary worker programs for less skilled migrants is that employers cannot find enough workers within the domestic labor market because citizens and permanent residents are unwilling to do some particular kind of work at the wages that employers are offering. In a market economy, however, the normal response to labor shortages is to allow supply and demand to adjust to one another. As the wage offered for a given sort of work rises, more workers will be willing to undertake it and fewer employers will find it worth their while to hire. In that sense, shortages should always be temporary, a matter of normal market adjustment, especially for less skilled jobs which, by definition, do not require long periods of training before a person can do the work.

People sometimes say that in affluent states with strong welfare provisions, citizens and residents will not take up jobs that are dirty, dangerous, demeaning, and demanding. That is misleading, however. There are no jobs for which workers cannot be found if the pay is high enough, even in rich states. What is really meant is that citizens and residents will not take up such jobs for the minimum wage or for a relatively low rate of pay, especially when the state ensures that they will not starve or be homeless if they decline the work. But raising the rate at which dirty, dangerous, demeaning, and demanding jobs must be paid is a perfectly normal function of social programs in a democratic society. The point of many social welfare provisions is precisely to create background conditions that shift the relative bargaining power of workers and employers. Even in conventional economic analysis, it is perfectly appropriate for workers to take into account the nonpecuniary costs and benefits of a job in deciding whether to take it. Other things being equal, jobs that are unpleasant in one way or another should pay more than jobs that are pleasant. If they don't, it is because people have no effective alternative to working at an unpleasant job. So, when people speak of a persistent shortage of less skilled labor, what they really mean is that some employers would like to have less skilled work done at a price that is below the market price for that sort of labor in a particular state, given the characteristics of the work, so long as we accept social welfare provisions simply as background conditions affecting labor supply, rather than seeing them as intrusions into the working of the market.[15]

The whole point of a temporary workers program that restricts people to a given sector or occupation is to find workers who will do the job at below the market rate (that is, the price that would be required to attract people from the domestic workforce into this sort of activity), because the conditions under which these temporary workers are admitted leave them with no effective alternative within the receiving state to taking these jobs at the pay that is offered. So, restrictions on the economic activities that a temporary worker can undertake involve a deliberate element of unfairness. The restrictions force temporary workers to perform tasks for wages that are lower than the wages they could command if they were free to compete on the entire labor market.[16]

Revisiting the Case for Limited Rights

So far in this chapter I have tried to show that, for the most part, democratic states ought to grant temporary workers either the same legal rights that permanent residents enjoy or, in some cases, a comparable set of rights. They are temporary members of society and the legal rights that they possess should reflect that membership. Any attempt to create a fundamental difference between temporary workers and other workers, apart from the temporary character of their presence, violates democratic principles. In this final section of the chapter, I want to return to two of the arguments for limiting the rights of temporary workers that I mentioned at the outset: the global poverty reduction argument and the inevitability argument.

The Global Poverty Reduction Argument

Let's start with the argument that limiting the rights of temporary workers would lead to rich democratic states admitting more of them and that the increased remittances from these workers would lead to a reduction in global poverty. To simplify the discussion, I won't challenge any of the empirical presuppositions in the argument about the potential consequences of reduced rights and increased remittances.

Should we think of global poverty reduction as a moral duty for rich democratic states or as something that is morally admirable but not obligatory?

Let's assume the latter first, that is, that reducing global poverty is something that is morally admirable but not, strictly speaking, obligatory for rich democratic states. What follows?

Given this assumption together with the conventional assumption that states are morally free to exercise discretionary control over immigration, it follows that democratic states have no obligation to admit temporary workers at all. If they do admit temporary workers, however, they must treat them in accordance with their own standards of democratic justice. If my earlier arguments in this chapter are correct, democratic states are required, as a matter of justice, to provide a considerable bundle of rights to temporary workers. They are not morally free to reduce that bundle in order to make it more economically attractive to admit and hire temporary workers, even if doing so would help to reduce global poverty. To put it tendentiously, it is not morally acceptable to rob from the poor even if the goal is to help those who are even poorer. Some potential temporary workers may not be admitted as a result of states respecting the requirements of democratic justice. That is morally irrelevant, however, precisely because the potential workers have no moral claim to admission.

In the domestic economy, there is a clear analogy. Employers normally have no obligation to hire any workers, even in times of high unemployment, but if they do hire workers, they must respect their legal (and moral) obligations to those workers. They are not entitled to set aside these obligations in order to hire more workers, however desirable it might be to reduce unemployment.

I do not mean to be an absolutist about this line of argument. There are degrees of injustice. It might make sense to put up with a small, temporary injustice for the sake of a substantial positive consequence overall for those subject to the injustice. But this sort of compromise would not justify significant departures from standards of treatment required by democratic justice.

Now let's adopt the assumption that rich democratic states *do* have an obligation to reduce global poverty and see where that leads. Even if we combine this assumption with the premise that increased remittances from temporary migrant workers would contribute to global poverty reduction, we cannot just leap to the conclusion that rich states should restrict the rights of temporary migrant workers in order to admit more of them.

The obligation to reduce global poverty does not eliminate the duty to treat temporary workers fairly. If rich democratic states have a duty to contribute to global poverty reduction and if admitting temporary workers is an effective way to do this, these states may no longer be morally free (as they were under the first assumption) simply to limit their intake of temporary workers. Of course, merely admitting temporary workers will not help if the workers cannot get jobs, so in order to fulfill their obligation to reduce global poverty, states might also have to create incentives for employers to hire these temporary workers.

If we pursue this line of analysis, it quickly becomes apparent that adopting the assumption that rich states have an obligation to contribute to global poverty reduction raises many other moral questions that go far beyond the scope of this chapter and, indeed, this book. Once one assumes that rich states have a moral obligation to reduce global poverty, it makes no sense to think that one can say anything about the implications of this obligation for a narrowly confined set of immigration policies. Questions about programs for temporary workers would have to be explored in a much broader context. I will discuss that broader context to some extent in the final part of the book when I consider the relationship between global justice and open borders.

Perhaps someone will object that I am misconstruing the global poverty reduction argument by focusing on questions about moral principles. The real point of the argument is to draw attention to feasible options and political realities.[17] The political reality is that rich democratic states will not act in accordance with their obligations to reduce global poverty, however those obligations are interpreted, if they entail any serious costs. Like all states, rich democratic states will only act in accordance with their interests. From this perspective, the challenge for those who care about moral principles is to find a way to align the interests of states with what justice requires. That is precisely what the proposal to limit the rights of temporary workers does. It offers a concrete opportunity to advance the cause of global poverty reduction by drawing attention to the interests that rich states have in recruiting temporary migrant workers with limited rights.

I am not unsympathetic to the view that human action always takes place within constraints or, for that matter, to the view that it is important for political theorists to think about how to align interests and morality. Nevertheless, there are dangers in leaping too quickly to the question "What is to be done?" That impulse can make it harder to see the difference between what we should embrace and what we should only endure. Moreover, realistic approaches sometimes obscure reality. If we really thought that principles never mattered to states, we would not have to worry about democratic states granting too many rights to temporary workers. They would all act like Singapore and Kuwait.

I have already acknowledged at many points in this book that we should not assume that there is a straight line from principle to policy. Nevertheless, principles do matter. We have to think about what our principles entail, even, or perhaps especially, if we decide to depart from them.

The Inevitability Argument

The other argument for limiting the rights of temporary workers that I want to revisit asserts that the presence of large numbers of foreign workers with fewer rights is inevitable in rich states. The only question is whether these workers will be present legally as temporary workers with limited rights or illegally with no rights. This argument rests on two empirical claims. First, rich democratic states will not agree to grant legal entry to substantial numbers of temporary workers on terms that give them most of the rights that citizens and residents possess. Second, the gap between what people from poor states can earn at home and what they can earn in rich states makes an influx of migrants looking for work inevitable. They will find ways to evade the state's restrictions on entry, and they will work without the authorization of the state. These migrants will be especially disadvantaged and vulnerable. So, from this perspective, insisting on equal rights for temporary workers sounds admirable but is unrealistic and counterproductive in practice. It harms those it is intended to help. It is morally preferable to provide temporary workers with a modest set of rights that gives them legal status and protection against the worst forms of abuse. The real alternative for many migrants is not a full set of legal rights but none at all and life in the shadows.

I agree that it is morally problematic to adopt policies that meet the formal requirements of justice but in practice harm the people they are supposed to protect. As I noted in previous chapters, the way a policy works is sometimes more important morally than whether it formally satisfies some principle. Nevertheless, we should not leap too quickly to the conclusion that we face an inevitable choice between legal migration with very limited rights and unauthorized migration with no rights. Even more importantly, we need to distinguish between the question of what course of action is the best one available to us in a given set of circumstances and the question of whether that policy is morally legitimate at a deeper level.

The inevitability argument depends in part on contestable assumptions. One such assumption is the assertion that expanding programs for temporary workers will reduce the number of those working without authorization. That might be true but it might have the opposite effect. The social networks created by those who enter legally under temporary worker programs may make it easier for others to enter and stay without authorization. Those who are allowed to enter as temporary workers may want to stay longer than the state wishes to permit and may stay on after their visas expire. So, creating legal channels for temporary workers with limited rights may increase rather than reduce the number of those working without authorization.

Another issue has to do with the degree of control that is possible if states really want to exercise it. We should not simply assume that all states are incapable of preventing unauthorized immigration for work or that all states are similarly situated in the challenges they face in trying to do so. The possibilities of control depend on a wide range of circumstances.

A more fundamental objection to this line of argument is that it fails to distinguish between inevitabilities due to external factors beyond the power of a state to control and inevitabilities that arise from political realities internal to the state. Some versions of the inevitability argument sound like the old joke about the man who killed his parents and then threw himself upon the mercy of the court on the grounds that he was an orphan. They ignore the fact that the dilemma with which we are presented flows from the fact that states are not willing to adopt appropriate policies.

The inevitability argument insists that the only alternative to the admission of temporary workers with limited rights is an influx of irregular migrants with no effective rights at all. But why assume that irregular migrants will have no effective legal rights? In the next chapter I will argue that irregular migrants are morally entitled to a range of legal rights, many of which are not now respected primarily because any attempt by irregular migrants to claim their rights exposes them to the authorities and to deportation. That fact is not a natural necessity, however. It is a social choice. There are alternatives.

Claims about inevitability tend to obscure the range of choices open to us and the principles that should govern those choices. This book is an attempt to identify the moral considerations that bear upon questions of immigration rather than to tell policymakers and activists what to do in a set of politically constrained circumstances. If the inevitability of a given outcome flows from the fact that the state is not willing to do what justice requires (perhaps because it is a democratic state and the democratic majority want the state to pursue a course that serves their interests but conflicts with justice), then it is essential that we recognize and criticize this outcome as a collective choice, even if we have no realistic hope of changing the outcome. It is always easier to get individuals and states to act morally when what morality requires coincides with self-interest. Often enough it does. But we should not redefine justice and morality to fit the requirements of self-interest. The fact that democratic states behave in a certain way does not establish that this way of behaving is compatible with democratic principles of justice.

Irregular Migrants

A woman came into our office. She was visibly physically assaulted and reporting also sexual abuse by a man she knew but was not partnered with. She had no status and was obviously in crisis. Our worker called around. There was not a single rape crisis place that would take her and, so, our worker accompanied her to the hospital where the nurse gave her three options. One was to involve the police, one was to not involve the police and one was to have the forensic testing done but just keep it on file in case she decides to report it to the police at another time. And they had the conversation about what it means to involve the police if you have no status. She decided to take the risk in hopes that the police would not get to the immigration question, but they did. And after the forensic testing was done at the hospital she was taken to the police station, she was incarcerated. Our worker accompanied her there and was not allowed in when they questioned her. She was questioned for quite a long time. They called immigration and then she was questioned by immigration officers several hours later and now she has a deportation that is pending the trial against the man who raped her. (Service provider)[1]

What should we think about how this irregular migrant in Toronto was treated? Was it appropriate for the rape crisis centers not to accept her? Was the hospital right to treat her? Should the police have reported her to immigration authorities, as they did, or should she have been able to report the crime against her without fear of being made subject to deportation?

What about Miguel Sanchez, the irregular migrant from Mexico whose story opened this book? He has been in the United States for over ten years, has married an American citizen, and has a son. Should he be deported if the immigration authorities learn about his presence or should he be permitted to stay?

In the contemporary politics of immigration, few issues are more contentious than the question of how democratic states should respond to the presence of those who have settled without official authorization. Indeed, even the terminology of this issue is hotly disputed. Critics of the migrants and most of the popular press use the term "illegal" to characterize these migrants. Their supporters often use the term "undocumented." I will use instead the terms "irregular" and "unauthorized" in an effort to find words that are less tied to established positions in the debate. Of course, in this case, like many, there are no neutral terms. Every choice of terminology has implications and can be seen as objectionable from one perspective or another. Nevertheless, some words are more laden than others. "Illegal" and "undocumented" are both terms that are very heavy with associations.[2]

I divide the chapter into two main parts. The first considers what legal rights (if any) irregular migrants should have. The second explores the conditions under which irregular migrants should gain a legal residence status.

Although I am concerned with legal rights and legal status, this is a moral and philosophical inquiry, not a legal one.[3] I am concerned with what legal rights irregular migrants ought to have and why their legal status should eventually change as a matter of democratic morality. States create and modify legal rights for a variety of reasons. Not all legal rights have the same moral underpinning. As we shall see, the strength of the moral case for granting a particular legal right to irregular migrants depends in part on the nature of the right.

In discussing this topic, I will simply assume that normally the state is morally entitled to apprehend and deport migrants who settle without authorization. That is a corollary of the conventional view of the state's right to control immigration that I have adopted as a background assumption for the first several chapters of this book. However, this assumption does not preclude the possibility that there are moral constraints upon the ways in which a democratic state may exercise its authority in dealing with irregular migrants. That is the issue I will explore here. As we shall see, the moral claims of irregular migrants are surprisingly strong, even within the limits of this assumption.

The Rights of Irregular Migrants

The first part of this chapter asks one basic question: In what ways should the legal rights of irregular migrants resemble or differ from the legal rights of migrants who are present and working with the permission of the state? As in the two previous chapters, I frame the question in terms of a comparison that allows me to ignore variations among states in the kinds of legal rights they establish in order to keep the focus on the ethics of immigration.

Human Rights

At first blush, asking about the legal rights of irregular migrants may appear puzzling. Since irregular migrants are violating the state's law by settling and working without authorization, why should the state be obliged to grant them any legal rights at all? A moment's reflection, however, makes us aware that irregular migrants are entitled to at least some legal rights.[4] Unlike medieval regimes, modern democratic states do not make criminals into outlaws—people entirely outside the pale of the law's protection.[5] Moreover, as we will see in a moment, democratic states themselves often do not even regard irregular migrants as criminals.

As we saw in chapter 5, there are many legal rights that people ought to possess (and normally do possess) simply in virtue of the fact that they are within the jurisdiction of the state. I labeled such rights, *general human rights*. People should possess general human rights, and technically do possess them under the law, whether they have permission to be present in the state or not. The police are supposed to protect even irregular migrants from being robbed or killed. Human beings do not forfeit their right to be secure in their persons and their possessions simply in virtue of being present without authorization. The right to a fair trial is another example. If irregular migrants are accused of a crime, they have the same rights as any other criminal defendant.

This last fact has important implications for the way we view irregular migrants. In popular political rhetoric, irregular migrants are routinely described as lawbreakers and criminals because of their violation of immigration laws. For the most part, however, democratic states treat violations of immigration laws quite differently from violations of criminal laws. One can see this by comparing the procedural protections afforded irregular migrants when they are accused of a criminal offense and the procedural protections provided them with respect to a violation of immigration laws. Most democratic states treat their own immigration rules as administrative matters. As a result, they usually provide much weaker procedural safeguards for those accused of violating immigration rules than they do for defendants in criminal trials.

Why are the procedural protections in immigration law weaker than the procedural protections in criminal law? It is not because being an irregular migrant entitles a person to fewer protections in a legal process than being a citizen or a legal resident. When irregular migrants are accused of an ordinary crime, they receive the same panoply of protections as anyone else (access to legal counsel, at state expense if necessary; rights of appeal; rules of evidence, etc.). As I observed in chapter 5, different democratic states have somewhat different procedural practices but each state has one set of practices for all criminal defendants, regardless of immigration status. To act otherwise, to establish a different set of rules for citizens and irregular migrants in criminal trials, would violate our most basic notions of the rule of law, due process, and a fair trial. When violations of immigration laws are treated as crimes with criminal penalties attached, those accused normally acquire the usual set of rights provided to criminal defendants. Again, that is simply required by our understanding of the rule of law.

The justification for providing fewer protections to those accused of immigration violations than for those accused of crimes is precisely that immigration violations are not criminal offenses, and that detention and deportation are not criminal penalties. While this distinction can be abused (and clearly was in the United States in the wake of 9/11), it makes sense in principle. However, it entails the corresponding notion that the violators of immigration laws are not criminals. So, this fact provides one reason (among many) for rejecting attempts to label irregular migrants as criminals.

In addition to the right to personal security and the right to a fair trial, democratic states are morally obliged to provide everyone within their jurisdiction, including irregular migrants, with a number of other general human rights. Emergency medical care is one familiar example. If a tourist or other temporary visitor is struck by a car or has a heart attack, she has a right to receive lifesaving medical treatment. So does an irregular migrant. The Toronto woman who was raped had a moral right to get emergency medical care in the hospital (and she did). Similarly, irregular migrants are entitled to such basic general human rights as freedom of religion and freedom of speech. So far as I know, even the harshest critics of unauthorized immigration do not openly challenge this principle.

The fact that irregular migrants are entitled to general human rights shows that democratic norms and standards limit the means that may be used to achieve immigration control, even though these limitations make it more difficult to pursue the goal of immigration control. From the perspective of control, every legal right granted to irregular migrants, including protection of their most fundamental human rights, increases the incentives for them to come and to stay. Nevertheless, that incentive effect is not a sufficient justification to deny them general human rights.

The Firewall Argument

The fact that people are legally entitled to certain rights does not mean that they are actually able to make use of those rights. It is a familiar point that irregular migrants are so worried about coming to the attention of the authorities that they are often reluctant to pursue legal protections and remedies to which they are entitled, even when their most basic human rights are at stake. Here is a typical story:

> I would not call them for anything. One day he almost kill me, choked me with construction boot ties, and I would not call them. One time when I was pregnant with my son, he took me and fling me on the ground, and I was scared of calling them. What will they do with my kids, what will they do with me, you know?[6]

This fear creates a serious normative problem for democratic states. It makes no moral sense to provide people with purely formal legal rights under conditions that make it impossible for them to exercise those rights effectively.

What is to be done? There is at least a partial solution to this problem. Democratic states can and should build a firewall between the enforcement of immigration law, on the one hand, and the protection of general human rights, on the other. We ought to establish as a firm legal principle that no information gathered by those responsible for protecting general human rights can be used for immigration enforcement purposes. We ought to guarantee that people will be able to pursue their human rights without exposing themselves to arrest and expulsion. For example, if irregular migrants are victims of a crime or witnesses to one, they should be able to go to the police, report the crime, and serve as witnesses without fear that this will increase the chances of their being apprehended and deported. If they need emergency health care, they should be able to seek help without worrying that the hospital will disclose their identity to those responsible for enforcing immigration laws.

Some people are skeptical that such a firewall could ever work. Is it realistic to expect one part of the state's administrative apparatus to keep information from another, given modern means of communication and the increased integration of state functions?

I think that it is, for two reasons. First, we already have functional equivalents of firewalls in areas that have nothing to do with immigration, and they work reasonably well. Think, for example, of the American rule that says that police cannot use evidence in a criminal case if the evidence has been obtained in violation of someone's constitutional rights. This rule restricts the ways in which police gather evidence. It doesn't work perfectly, to be sure, but it is a significant constraint, and it makes various constitutional protections much more secure. We could imagine a similar rule in the immigration context. Suppose, for example, that the immigration authorities were required to show how they had acquired knowledge of an irregular migrant's presence and status. If they obtained this information through sources connected to the protections of the human rights of the irregular migrants, the migrant would then be entitled to stay. This is the functional equivalent of not prosecuting a criminal on the basis of tainted evidence even when the evidence shows that the criminal is guilty.

Another practical example of a firewall that works quite effectively is the rule that says that the information that the Internal Revenue Service gathers for purposes of taxation cannot be used for other governmental purposes. That's a serious and generally effective constraint. It's true that controlling and restricting information is more difficult in the digital era, but there are lots of privacy mechanisms in place that work reasonably well. We know how to devise and implement such rules.

The second reason for thinking that firewalls are feasible is that the modern state is highly segmented. Different state actors operate under different rules, have different professional norms, and face different incentives. Even in a legal context, there is a big difference between judges and police officers, although both are agents of the state and concerned with law enforcement. In the immigration context, there are even sharper differences. Many of those whose job it is to protect the basic human rights of irregular migrants have little desire to enforce immigration laws. Most teachers, doctors, and other professionals want to treat the people they are dealing with in accordance with their professional norms and not to serve as agents of law enforcement. A firewall rule enables them to do what they want to do in withholding information from those charged with enforcing immigration laws. Even police officers often prefer not to be dealing with immigration issues. They also want to be able to get the cooperation of immigrants as witnesses, and they know that will be easier if the immigrants know that the police will not have links to the immigration authorities even in cases where the immigrants are present without authorization. Of course, some police are hostile to immigrants. So, in those cases, a firewall rule would be forcing them to behave contrary to their own inclinations. However, that is also true of laws restricting the ways in which evidence can be gathered.

In sum, reasonably effective firewalls are feasible if there is the will to create them and implement them. A firewall approach would make a big difference to the lives of those protected by it, dramatically reducing their vulnerability and exploitation, even if it did not work perfectly.

In North America and Europe, some cities where large numbers of irregular migrants are present have actually adopted policies of this sort, sometimes formally, but more often informally. Some jurisdictions, like Arizona in the United States, have moved in the opposite direction. Instead of building a firewall between immigration enforcement and other state activities, they seek to establish a policy of administrative linkage, requiring ordinary police officers or hospital officials to report any contacts with irregular migrants to immigration authorities. This has the effect of taking away with one hand what was granted with the other. It reduces the legal protections of the human rights of irregular migrants to a nominal entitlement stripped of any substantive effect. This seems an especially pernicious approach when used in connection with general human rights because the interests at stake are so fundamental.

There are tensions between pursuing deportation and protecting the rights of irregular migrants, but there are always tensions between enforcing rules and protecting the rights of people suspected of violating those rules. Without a firewall, irregular migrants enjoy the protection of their general human rights in name only.

The arguments for a firewall and against linkage are especially strong when general human rights are at stake. Are there other legal rights that immigrants should enjoy? If so, which of these, if any, should be protected by a firewall and why?

Children's Rights

Within the general category of "irregular migrants," children constitute a group with special claims. For one thing, they are a particularly vulnerable subcategory of human beings, one standing in need of special protection, as is reflected, for example, in the existence of a special international convention on *The Rights of the Child*.[7] For another, they are not responsible for their unauthorized presence within the state, since it is their parents who have brought them in. This means that the state is even more morally constrained in dealing with irregular migrants who are children than it is in dealing with irregular migrants who are adults.

Irregular migrant children are morally entitled to certain legal rights that are not granted to adults, the most important of which is the right to a free public education. The US Supreme Court recognized this right in the famous case of *Plyler v. Doe* in 1982, and many other democratic states have established some comparable right. Indeed, the language of rights understates the importance of education because, unlike most rights, education is not optional. In every democratic state, primary education (and often secondary education as well) is compulsory for all legally resident children. This legal requirement simply recognizes the vital importance that education plays in shaping the future of the children and of the society in which they live. The state's duty to educate children extends to irregular migrants as well.

Not everyone would agree that children who are irregular migrants should have a legal right to a free public education and that a democratic state has a moral duty to ensure that such children are educated. Consider the following interrelated objections. According to the immigration laws, these children are not supposed to become part of the future of the society in which they are currently living. If apprehended, they can be deported. Providing such children with a free public education does more than anything else to enable irregular migrants to sink deep roots into the society to which they have moved, and it makes their subsequent expulsion that much harder, in part because of the negative effects of deportation on the children. Granting irregular migrant children a right to a free public education creates strong incentives for irregular migrants to try to arrange for their children to join them. In the absence of such an option, more irregular migrants might leave their children at home, and more of the migrants themselves might eventually return to their countries of origin. It also matters that granting irregular migrant children a right to a free public education imposes a substantial financial cost on the receiving society against its expressed will (as reflected in the immigration laws). Some might argue that it makes no sense to see access to a free public education as a general human right owed to everyone within the jurisdiction of the state. People who come as tourists or temporary visitors are not automatically entitled to put their children into a free public school. Why should irregular migrants have that right? Finally, some might say, the innocence of the children is not decisive. While the children are not morally responsible for their presence, their parents are, and children often suffer from the bad decisions of their parents. That is a regrettable but inevitable consequence of the institution of the family itself. Parents should not bring their children into a state where they are not legally entitled to reside. If they do, it is their fault, not the state's, if the children do not receive an education.

I have tried to articulate the strongest objections I could find to my view that children who are irregular migrants should receive a free public education in the state in which they find themselves. These objections have some force, but in my view they are clearly outweighed by the moral reasons for granting irregular migrant children a legal right to a free public education. The decisive factor here is the well-being of the children.[8] The effects on the receiving society also weigh in favor of educating the children of irregular migrants, but I regard this as only a supplementary consideration.

Access to a free public education should be regarded as a human right because the interest at stake is so fundamental. It is normally regarded as a human right for citizens and those legally resident, even on a temporary basis. However, it is a human right that is usually seen, at least implicitly, as a membership-specific human right rather than a general human right. So, why should irregular migrant children possess a right to a free education in a state in which they have no legal membership status?

In my view, it is accurate to say that the right to a free public education is best understood as a membership-specific human right, but it is residence, not immigration status, that gives rise to the form of membership that grounds this human right. The state is morally obliged to provide a free public education to all children residing within its jurisdiction, regardless of their immigration status.

In the modern world, it is simply not possible for most children to flourish (or even to function) without receiving a basic education. A basic education is therefore a fundamental need, and it is a need that must be met by the society in which the child lives. Where the child lives is a matter of fact. If she is living inside a state's territory, that state must provide her with an education that will enable her to function later in life, regardless of whether she is legally entitled to live there.

Educating irregular migrant children does create problems for the state. In educating the child in its own school system, a state is preparing the child to live in the society that it governs, not in the society that the child's parents came from. Indeed, that is one reason why children should have a right to live in the society in which they are raised, regardless of the legal status of their parents. The state may see this as an undesirable development, but that is not a reason for refusing to educate children at all. Nor is the possibility that irregular migrant children will be forced to leave with their parents if the family is apprehended and deported a good reason for not educating them. For one thing, this may not happen. Even if they do leave, voluntarily or otherwise, the basic education they receive while present will stand them in much better stead than no education at all.

To refuse to educate a child in the modern world is to condemn that child to a life of very limited possibilities. Even if it is the parents who are responsible for the child's presence, the state has a responsibility to see that the actions of parents cause no extreme harm (physical or otherwise) to children within its jurisdiction. That responsibility flows from the state's claim to be entitled to exercise such enormous powers over those within its jurisdiction. The state cannot escape this responsibility by blaming the parents and saying the child would not have suffered this harm if they had not come in the first place. That excuse would not justify a state's failure to protect the children of irregular migrants from physical abuse (whether by the children's parents or by others). It cannot justify the state in failing to meet the children's basic need for an education. The state controls access to the school system. It has the power to admit or exclude the child, and it has a moral duty to admit her.

It is true, as one line of objection indicated, that the right to education differs in certain ways from the general human rights that I discussed in the first section of this chapter. Tourists and short-term visitors are not normally entitled to put their children in public schools. So, why should irregular migrants be able to do so? The answer is that the passage of time matters with respect to the right to education, and that makes it different from the general human rights that I discussed earlier. No great harm is done to a child if she misses school for a week or even, perhaps, a month. But if she misses school for six months or a year, that is another matter. Tourists do not put their children in the local school, but parents who are visiting abroad for six months or a year normally do.

Children of irregular migrants belong in school, not merely because they are physically present in the territory, but because they are living in the society. In this respect, they are like the children of temporary workers. They may not be present indefinitely, but while they are, they should receive an education. The fact that they can be deported if discovered by immigration authorities is not a good reason for failing to provide that education. The place where they live currently, with or without authorization, is the place where they must be educated.

The duty to provide a free public education to irregular migrant children certainly does impose an unwanted cost upon the state and the availability of such an education does increases the incentives for irregular migrants to have their families join them. On the other hand, we should not exaggerate the significance of these points. Estimates of the net costs of public schooling for the children of irregular migrants vary widely when one takes into account the taxes paid by the migrants. Moreover, calculating only the costs of providing such an education ignores the predictable and much more substantial costs to society of creating a group of uneducated, marginalized children who will grow to adulthood in the society. Even the Supreme Court minority in *Plyler* recognized the folly of failing to provide such children with an education as a matter of social policy, despite the minority's view that there was no duty to provide this education, as a matter of constitutional law.

The arguments about costs point to the fact that there are prudential reasons for providing the children of irregular migrants with a free public education. It is more in the state's interest to provide the education than to fail to do so. The most important point, however, is the one made earlier. This is a matter of fundamental justice. That is much more important than the question of whether educating the children of irregular migrants is a wise or unwise public investment. Every human right that is recognized as a legal right to which irregular migrants are entitled can be seen as a cost to the receiving state and as an incentive to more irregular migration. If the costs and incentives are indeed substantial, this might provide reasons for the state to be more diligent in pursuing morally permissible policies for reducing unauthorized migration. It is not a sufficient reason for denying a fundamental human right, however.

As with the general human rights discussed earlier, the right to a free public education can be effective only if there is a firewall between the provision of educational services and the enforcement of immigration laws. If school officials are required or even permitted to pass information about the irregular status of students (or their parents) to immigration officials, or if immigration officials can visit schools to examine records, to interrogate students, or to look for parents suspected of immigration violations, irregular migrant parents will be very reluctant to send their children to school and the children will not really have access to the right to which they are ostensibly entitled. Those who would say that irregular migrant children should have a legal right to education but that state authorities should be able to use information from schools in connection with immigration enforcement efforts are not really serious about their acknowledgment of the children's right to education. That sort of position uses the formal legal right as a veneer to disguise a de facto policy of denying education to irregular migrant children, a policy that it would be embarrassing to defend openly.

Work-Related Rights

Irregular migrants normally come in order to work. As we have seen, migrants who are legally admitted to work, even those admitted only for a limited period, normally enjoy a wide range of legal rights in relation to their participation in the economy. In the first instance, except for those admitted under some restrictive program like the ones discussed in the previous chapter, they are usually entitled to look for employment on the general labor market. Once they find a job, they have a right to be paid for the work that they perform at whatever rate was agreed upon. In addition, as I argued in the previous chapter, even temporary workers are morally entitled to the protections provided by the state's regulation of working conditions and to the benefits of work-related social programs to which they are expected to contribute. Should irregular migrants enjoy any of these legal rights, and if so, which ones and why?

Some argue that irregular migrants are not morally entitled to work-related rights because granting them such rights undermines the state's ability to control immigration. From this perspective, it would be inconsistent to say that states have a right to control entry and settlement, and then to deny states the means to exercise that control effectively. This objection parallels my own earlier argument that it would be inconsistent to guarantee the general human rights of irregular migrants while adopting enforcement policies that made it very difficult for them to exercise those rights effectively, but it takes the state rather than the irregular migrant as the one demanding consistency. Granting work-related rights to irregular migrants would increase the incentives for them to come in the first place and would thus undercut the state's ability to exercise its right to control immigration effectively. Furthermore, it would increase the benefits of working without authorization much more directly than merely protecting the basic human rights of irregular migrants. This is a powerful line of argument, but I think that it is ultimately outweighed in most respects by other considerations.

Finding Employment

Let me start with one issue where I think the previous argument wins. One work-related legal right that irregular migrants cannot enjoy without fundamentally challenging the conventional assumption about state control over immigration is the legal right to seek employment.[9] I said in chapter 5 that the right to seek employment should be seen as a human right, but I argued there that, under the conventional assumption, it had to be seen as a membership-specific human right, not a general human right. Irregular migrants are not members of society, in the sense required to ground this sort of membership-specific human right, at least during the early stages of their presence. I argue in the second part of this chapter that they become members over time and acquire moral claims to the rights of membership as a result, but I don't want to confuse the two issues. So, let's assume here that we are talking about irregular migrants who have not been present long enough to establish the moral claims of membership that I discuss in the second part of the chapter.

I know that advocates for irregular migrants will be troubled by my statement (and that opponents of irregular migrants will cite it—often out of context). But this is one of those points at which political considerations conflict with the requirements of intellectual clarity, and in this book I am trying to give priority to the latter. I do not see how one could reconcile the conventional assumption that states have a right to exercise discretionary control over immigration with the claim that irregular migrants are morally entitled to a legal right to seek employment. Of course, one can object to the conventional assumption, but, as I have said before, I will consider that challenge in the final part of the book. For now I want to work within its constraints.

The fact that irregular migrants are not entitled to a legal right to seek employment does not mean that they have no moral claims to other work-related legal rights, if they do find work. Consider some of the other issues.

Earnings

The first, and in some ways most fundamental, question is whether irregular migrants should have a legal right to be paid for the work they perform. This is obviously a right that all those working with official authorization normally enjoy. Some would argue that irregular migrants should not have this right. One long-standing principle in some jurisdictions is that the state will not enforce contracts that are against public policy—for example, a contract that includes a provision requiring discrimination on the basis of race or religion. Similarly, the state will not enforce a contract emerging from legally prohibited activities, such as drug dealing or killing someone for pay. No one imagines that the absence of this legal right makes drug dealing and contract killing less likely. The rule is adopted not for its consequences but to express a principle.

On this analogy, some think that the state should refuse to enforce contracts between irregular migrants and their employers as a matter of principle, because the migrants are not authorized to work in the first place. What is against public policy is their employment itself, not the specific tasks they perform. And indeed, in some jurisdictions, irregular migrants are not legally entitled to their pay, presumably for just this reason, although in other jurisdictions, including the United States, irregular migrants do have a legal right to be paid for work performed, regardless of whether they were authorized to undertake the work.

In my view, denying irregular migrants a legal right to be paid for their work is fundamentally wrong. No one thinks that the work that irregular migrants normally do is morally wrong in itself in the way that criminal activities and acts of racial or religious discrimination are morally wrong in themselves. The vast majority of irregular migrants are engaged in productive work. It is only the workers' immigration status that is problematic. Of course, some irregular migrants, like some citizens, engage in criminal activities, but ordinary criminal laws already cover them. Indeed, one of the things that is most objectionable about denying irregular migrants a legal right to their pay is precisely the way in which it links unauthorized migration for employment with criminal activity, conceptually and legally. This ignores the social reality. The work that irregular migrants do is often dirty, difficult, and dangerous, but it is almost always honest work. The money that they receive in compensation is not a form of ill-gotten gain; they have earned it with the sweat of their brows.

It is morally wrong for the state to announce that employers are legally free to withhold promised pay from irregular migrants after extracting work from them. In practice, unscrupulous employers often do deny irregular migrants payment for their work, knowing that the workers have no effective legal recourse and sometimes not even any formal entitlement to their pay. However, this is not a practice that a democratic state should endorse, even implicitly. As I noted above in the discussion of general human rights, the state's right to apprehend and deport migrants does not affect its obligation to protect them against being robbed while within its jurisdiction. If a democratic state refuses to grant irregular migrants a legal right to their pay, it effectively abandons its responsibility to prevent them from being robbed.

The right to be paid for one's work should be more than a formal right. The firewall argument should apply to it, as it does to general human rights. Indeed, it is plausible to regard the right to receive pay for work performed as a human right, and it is identified as such in some human rights documents, though I do not claim that it is as firmly established a human right as the general human rights that I discussed previously. Whether it qualifies technically as a human right or not, however, it would be fundamentally unfair to allow employers to get away with extracting labor without remuneration, and a firewall arrangement is the only effective legal way to prevent this. If an employer seeks to deny workers pay that they have earned, the workers should be able to pursue legal remedies to recover that pay without exposing themselves to the immigration authorities.

Working Conditions

What about the array of rights associated with the state's regulation of the conditions of work? It is well known that irregular migrants often work under conditions that do not meet the state's standards, whatever those standards are. That is one reason why irregular migrants are so often described as marginalized and exploited. But before considering the question of whether something *can* be done to change this, we have to consider the question of whether something *ought* to be done. Again, I want to focus first on the question of principle. Are irregular migrants morally entitled to the protections that public policies regulating working conditions are supposed to provide?

In my view, the answer is clearly "yes." The arguments advanced in the previous chapter about why we should use the same standards to govern working conditions for temporary workers that we use for citizens and residents apply to irregular migrants as well. Whatever rules a state has established with respect to working conditions for citizens and residents reflect a particular democracy's conception of the minimum standards under which economic activity should be conducted within its borders. It is one thing to enforce immigration rules; it would be quite another to authorize the subjection of irregular migrants to substandard conditions of work by limiting the applicability of workplace standards to those with the proper immigration status. However the state regulates working conditions for those working with authorization, it should regulate them in the same way for those working without authorization.

Note that this argument is a bit different from the previous ones. The previous arguments focused on the moral claims of irregular migrants to protection of their general human rights, which should include children's right to a free public education and workers' rights to receive pay for work performed, regardless of immigration status. I am not claiming that all laws regulating working conditions should be regarded as implementing human rights claims (though some can be seen that way). My argument about working conditions focuses more on the moral responsibilities of the state to enforce whatever standards it has established than on the fundamental moral claims of irregular migrants themselves.

So far I have been focusing on principled reasons why state regulations governing working conditions should apply to irregular migrants. There is another, more pragmatic consideration in favor of granting irregular migrants the same legal entitlements as others. The state's capacity to secure these minimum standards for its own citizens and for immigrants legally authorized to work is contingent in part upon its capacity to secure the same standards for irregular migrants. This pragmatic argument parallels one of the arguments advanced in the previous chapters for granting temporary workers the same rights as citizens and residents with respect to working conditions. I would add here that the same pragmatic considerations support the idea of establishing a firewall separating the enforcement of workplace protections from the enforcement of immigration law. I have developed these arguments more fully elsewhere and for reasons of space will not pursue them here.[10]

Work-Related Social Programs

Now consider social programs directly connected to employment. In practice, irregular migrants often work in the informal economy, where they are paid in cash and do not contribute to such programs. But some irregular migrants are part of the formal economy, especially in states where the linkage between the enforcement of immigration rules and other governmental activities is not very tight and where the supervision of documents for work is not strictly controlled. For example, many irregular migrants in the United States manage to obtain a Social Security number and pay Social Security taxes.

Should irregular migrants who participate in the formal economy be included in work-related social programs? Again, there are arguments on both sides. I think that the arguments for providing irregular migrants with the benefits of these programs vary from one program to another, but that they are weaker overall than the arguments for providing irregular migrants with other work-related rights. The arguments for including them, sometimes with modifications, broadly parallel the arguments for including temporary workers, but there are arguments for the exclusion of irregular migrants from these programs that are stronger than in the case of temporary workers. Again, I have developed these arguments elsewhere and won't pursue them here for reasons of space.[11]

Social and Administrative Rights

Many of the legal rights that modern democratic states provide are not basic human rights, or children's rights, or work-related rights. Some of these legal rights are administrative permissions connected to the state's regulatory functions. A license to drive a car or a boat is a typical example. Others are rights of access to public facilities, such as libraries and swimming pools. Still others provide some benefit or meet some need that the political community has decided should not be left entirely to the market, such as subsidized tuition or loan programs to make it easier to obtain a higher education, or publicly funded health care, or social housing and income support programs. Although these rights are disparate in many respects, I will lump them together here under the general heading of administrative and social rights.

As a general matter, tourists and temporary visitors are not entitled to administrative and social rights. This distinguishes them from general human rights of the sort that I discussed in the first section. So far as I know, no one regards the exclusion of tourists and temporary visitors from these rights as morally problematic. It is normally reasonable to tie administrative and social rights to membership in the society that provides them. On the other hand, they are rights of membership, not rights of citizenship. Every democratic state provides these rights not only to citizens but also to permanent residents, at least for the most part. I have argued in chapter 5 that granting such rights to residents is more than a common pattern: it is something morally required as a matter of democratic justice. As I pointed out in chapter 6, when it comes to temporary residents, the picture is a little blurrier. They normally receive most social and administrative rights, but often not ones whose goal is redistribution, and the strength of their moral claims depends in part on how long they have been resident and why they are present.

Where do irregular migrants fit on this moral map? Should their unauthorized immigration status affect their access to administrative and social rights, or should their access to such rights simply follow the principles that apply to migrants whose presence is authorized, at least temporarily?

One position, by now familiar, is that irregular migrants should not have access to any of these rights. An even stronger view is that officials charged with providing such rights should be required to report any efforts by irregular migrants to obtain these rights or to make use of them. The underlying principle is that the state should do nothing to facilitate the presence of irregular migrants within its territory or to reward those who have violated immigration laws. Indeed some think that the government should actively make life more difficult for irregular migrants where it can do so in order to encourage those present to go home and to discourage new ones from coming. On the stronger view, the state should affirmatively coordinate the actions of all its administrative officials with an eye to enhancing the enforcement of immigration laws. This general line of argument provides the public justification for initiatives to deny drivers' licenses and in-state tuition at public universities to irregular migrants, for example.

As readers will have anticipated, I reject this view. Given the presupposition of this chapter that the state is entitled to control its borders and to enforce immigration laws, the state must be able to employ some methods to pursue these goals, and I will indicate in the next section what some permissible methods might be. Nevertheless, as I have argued throughout, the right to enforce immigration laws is not a moral carte blanche. The state is still constrained by norms of proportionality and rationality, norms that are violated by punitive policies that drive irregular migrants further underground without significantly advancing the goals of immigration control. Moreover, the state's assignment of administrative responsibility for law enforcement is constrained by norms of competence and fairness, norms that are violated when people with no special training in immigration matters are given responsibility for carrying out immigration laws.

Take, for example, the policy of denying drivers' licenses to irregular migrants. Such a policy makes it more likely that irregular migrants will drive without licenses and without insurance, thereby increasing risks that these general regulations are designed to reduce. Of course, the issue is not just about driving. A driver's license serves as an important source of identification that can be used (in some states) to open bank accounts. But why should the state seek to deny irregular migrants the opportunity to open bank accounts? To do so makes their lives a little more difficult, but not so much so that they are likely to leave the country or not come in the first place. On the other hand, such a denial increases incentives to expand the informal economy (including the informal banking sector), which reduces overall societal control over activities that the state wishes in principle to regulate.

When it comes to programs that involve a significant element of redistribution or financial support (as in income support programs or reduced-tuition programs), I think the crucial issue is the length of residency. As I argued in the previous chapter, it is not unjust (though it is ungenerous) to deny access to such programs, even to authorized migrants who have only recently arrived or who are staying only for a short time. The same principle should apply to recently arrived irregular migrants. As time passes, the justification for excluding authorized migrants from such programs diminishes. As we will see in the second part of this chapter, however, the passage of time also generates membership claims for irregular migrants and with those membership claims come claims for access to these sorts of programs. Time is the crucial variable.

In sum, irregular migrants should normally have access to administrative and social rights on the same basis as authorized migrants. On the other hand, the arguments supporting equal rights for irregular migrants in this area are not as fundamental and powerful as they are in the areas previously discussed, because the rights in question are (often) less clearly grounded in the fundamental moral claims of individuals or the fundamental moral standards of the society. They are (often) legal rights created to advance some legitimate, but less-than-vital, social or political goal. Moreover, while there is still a good case for a firewall between immigration enforcement and other state activities, the case for such a firewall is less tied to the fundamental rights of the irregular migrants or to the need to maintain the basic standards of the community than to general concerns for such values as proportionality, rationality, consistency, and competence.

Immigration Enforcement and Employer Sanctions

Although this chapter focuses on the rights of irregular migrants, the mechanisms for enforcement of immigration laws are not limited to restrictions on the legal rights of the migrants themselves. As we have seen, one of the strongest arguments against granting work-related legal rights to irregular migrants is that such rights increase the incentives for the migrants to come. Making things harder for the migrants by restricting their rights is not the only way to reduce their incentives to come and stay, however. Employer sanctions constitute an alternative (and often underutilized) mechanism of enforcement.

Irregular migrants normally want to work. If they could not find jobs, they would be much less likely to come in the first place. From an economic perspective, a reduction in demand seems far more likely to be effective in reducing supply than any effort to reduce supply directly (e.g., by increased border control) or indirectly (e.g., by worsening the conditions of work). In a context of extreme economic inequality between states, the potential economic gains for irregular migrants are so great that, even in the face of severely restricted rights, the supply is likely to be reduced only if the overall level of demand declines sharply. From a democratic perspective, one of the clear advantages of employer sanctions over policies aimed at irregular migrants themselves is that employer sanctions impose duties on people who are already legally recognized members of the community. From this perspective, the employers' moral duty to obey laws prohibiting them from hiring irregular migrants is arguably clearer and stronger than any duty of irregular migrants not to seek jobs without the state's authorization.[12]

The real debate over employer sanctions is about design and implementation. Given the initial assumptions of this chapter, there would be no objection in principle if a state were to deploy an effective system of controls that required employers to check all workers for work authorization status at the time of hire, that provided a reliable form of documentation about that status, and that made it easy for employers to satisfy a requirement to verify the identity of the individual possessing the document, provided that these measures did not infringe too much on the liberty and privacy of individuals.

Whether such desiderata can actually be combined in any real-world system is another question. The stronger the documentation requirements, the more likely it is that they will violate civil libertarian concerns. The easier it is for employers to meet the verification requirements, the more likely it is that they will be ineffective, since the employers can avoid sanctions simply by meeting the requirements, even if they may suspect that the workers are irregular migrants. The harder it is for employers to meet the verification requirements, the more unwilling they will be to hire workers who share the socioeconomic and ethnic characteristics of the groups from which most irregular migrants in a particular state come, thus discriminating in morally objectionable ways against people who are authorized to work. If the sanctions are severe and rigorously enforced, employers will have strong incentives not to hire workers whom they otherwise would hire. If the sanctions are modest and only occasionally enforced, they will be treated by employers simply as a cost of doing business. Indeed, some ways of implementing employer sanctions actually increase the power of employers with respect to irregular migrants, perhaps increasing the incentives to hire such migrants in the first place. For example, if employers are able to examine the work authorization papers of their workers subsequent to the initial hiring, or are able to report their own workers to immigration authorities, they may be able to threaten irregular migrants with exposure of their unauthorized status if the workers are not sufficiently quiescent with respect to pay and working conditions. That appears to have been the result of recent employer sanction policies in the United States.[13]

It may sometimes be the case that the ineffectiveness of employer sanctions is deliberate. Some of those designing or implementing the policy may want rules that look good on paper but are ineffective in practice, because the presence of the restrictive policy on the books satisfies one political constituency, while the weak implementation satisfies another. For the purposes of this chapter, however, the important point is that employer sanctions provide a more legitimate option for restricting irregular migration than most restrictions on the legal rights of the irregular migrants themselves. The fact that a state may be unable to use this mechanism effectively because of the political power of other forces within the state does not affect this normative argument.

The Case for Regularization

So far, I have focused on the question of what legal rights irregular migrants should have despite their not being authorized to live and work within the state. Now I want to consider whether their irregular status should change over time, and, if so, why.

Under what circumstances (if any), should irregular migrants acquire legal residence status? In my view, irregular migrants should be given legal status as residents once they have been settled for a long time.[14] Some circumstances— arriving as children or marrying citizens or permanent residents—may accelerate or strengthen their moral claims to stay, but the most important consideration is the passage of time.

Some think that the passage of time is irrelevant. Some might even say that the longer the stay, the greater the blame and the more the irregular migrant deserves to be deported. In my view, the opposite is true. I argued in previous chapters that for legal migrants, moral claims to membership grow stronger over time. The same principle applies to irregular migrants: the longer the stay, the stronger the moral claim to remain.

Why the Passage of Time Matters Morally

Consider the case of Marguerite Grimmond.[15] Grimmond was born in the United States but moved to Scotland with her mother as a young child. In 2007, at the age of 80, she left to go on a family vacation to Australia, her first excursion outside the United Kingdom since her arrival there as a child. On her trip, she used a newly acquired American passport. When she returned, immigration officials told Grimmond that she was not legally entitled to stay and had four weeks to leave the country. In effect, the officials saw her as an irregular migrant because she had never established a legal right to reside in the United Kingdom during all her years there. And Grimmond clearly knew that she was not a British citizen because she had acquired an American passport for her trip.

Once the story appeared in the newspapers—and it received international attention—Grimmond was allowed to remain. Whatever the legal technicalities of the case, the moral absurdity of forcing Grimmond to leave a place where she had lived so long was evident to all (apart from a few bureaucrats in the immigration department). Even if she had been an irregular migrant, that clearly no longer mattered.

Grimmond had a moral right to stay for at least two reasons: she had arrived at a very young age and she had stayed a very long time. Because Grimmond had arrived as a child, she was not responsible for the decision to settle in the United Kingdom. Being raised there made her a member of UK society, regardless of her legal status.

As I observed in chapter 3, growing up in a society makes one a member of that society. That is true regardless of one's immigration status. The years of childhood during which a child is educated and socialized more broadly are the most important ones in terms of one's development, identity, and connections. It is morally wrong to force someone to leave the place where she was raised, where she has received her social formation, and where she has her most important human connections just because her parents brought her there without official authorization. Yet current legal rules in North America and Europe threaten many young people in just this way.

The principle that irregular status becomes irrelevant over time is clearest for those who arrive as young children. But the second element in Grimmond's case—the sheer length of time she had lived in the United Kingdom—is also powerful. What if Grimmond had arrived in the United Kingdom at 20 rather than 2? Would anyone really think that this difference would make it acceptable to deport her, 60 years later? Grimmond's case clearly illustrates that there is some period of time beyond which it is unreasonable to deport people who have settled without authorization.

How long is too long? What if Grimmond had been 60 rather than 80? Would that have diminished her claim to stay? I assume not. What if she had been 40? The poignancy of the case certainly diminishes, but the underlying principle remains: there is something deeply wrong in forcing people to leave a place where they have lived for a long time. Most people form their deepest human connections where they live. It becomes home. Even if someone has arrived only as an adult, it seems cruel and inhumane to uproot a person who has spent fifteen or twenty years as a contributing member of society in the name of enforcing immigration restrictions. The harm done to her is entirely out of proportion to the wrong of unauthorized entry and settlement.

When her ordeal was over, Grimmond said she was "overjoyed and relieved." "I was trying to put a brave face on things," she said, "but I was a bit churned up inside at the thought that I might have to move to America because I don't know anyone there."[16] Normally we do not think of moving to America as a terrible prospect. But think about the fear and anxiety Grimmond must have felt, and then about the reality of irregular migrants, who can be and are deported even after very long periods of residence. Grimmond was lucky because her case attracted such public attention. Had it not, the immigration bureaucracy might well have sent her "home."

Grimmond poses a particularly difficult challenge for those who would uphold at all costs the state's right to deport irregular migrants, but her claims are not unique. Recall the story of Miguel Sanchez with which I opened this book. Sanchez arrived as an adult, not a young child, so his early social formation did not take place in the United States, but he has been in America for over ten years. As in Grimmond's case, the passage of time matters. Sanchez is also married to an American citizen. That is another important consideration.[17]

Family Ties

Marriage creates deep ties, not only with the person one marries but also with the communities to which that person belongs. Living with one's family is a fundamental human interest. The right to family life is recognized as a basic human right in various European laws, and concern for family values has played a central role in American political rhetoric in recent decades. As I will discuss in chapter 9, all democratic states recognize the principle of family reunification (that is, that citizens and legal residents should normally be able to have their foreign spouses and minor children join them and that this takes priority over the normal discretionary power that the state exercises over immigration). Once Sanchez was married to an American citizen, his ties to the United States, his interest in living here, and his spouse's interest in having him live here all assumed a new importance and greatly outweighed any interest the state had in deporting him in order to enforce its immigration laws. Even if the state is generally entitled to enforce its immigration laws (as I assume in this chapter), it is not right to do so without regard for the harm done in such a case. If an irregular migrant marries a citizen or a legal permanent resident, he or she should no longer be subject to deportation.[18]

In addition to his moral claim to remain in the United States because of his marriage to an American citizen, Sanchez had a powerful claim to stay simply because he had already been here so long and thus had become a member of society. Unlike Grimmond, he had not been present for over seven decades, but he had lived peacefully in the United States for over ten years, working, building social connections, creating a life. Ten years is a long time in a human life. In ten years, connections grow: to spouses and partners, sons and daughters, friends and neighbors and fellow-workers, people we love and people we hate. Experiences accumulate: birthdays and braces, tones of voice and senses of humor, public parks and corner stores, the shape of the streets and the way the sun shines through the leaves, the smell of flowers and the sounds of local accents, the look of the stars and the taste of the air—all that gives life its purpose and texture. We sink deep roots over ten years, and these roots matter even if we were not authorized to plant ourselves in the first place. On a moral scale, the significance of Sanchez's social membership outweighs the importance of enforcing immigration restrictions.

The moral right of states to apprehend and deport irregular migrants erodes with the passage of time. As irregular migrants become more and more settled, their membership in society grows in moral importance, and the fact that they have settled without authorization becomes correspondingly less relevant. At some point a threshold is crossed, and they acquire a moral claim to have their actual social membership legally recognized. They should acquire a legal right of permanent residence and all the rights that go with that, including eventual access to citizenship.

Can migrants become members of society without legal authorization? Yes, they can, because social membership does not depend upon official permission. That is the central point. People who live and work and raise their families in a society become members, whatever their legal status. That is why we find it hard to expel them when they are discovered. Their presence may be against the law, but they are not criminals like thieves and murderers. It would be wrong to deport them once they have become members, even if we have good reasons for wanting to make them leave and trying to prevent others like them from coming.

Over time, the circumstances of entry grow less important. Eventually, they become altogether irrelevant. As we saw in chapter 5, that was recognized in Europe in the 1970s when people who had originally been admitted as guest-workers, with explicit expectations that they would leave after a limited period, nevertheless were granted resident status. Of course, the guestworkers' claim to stay was somewhat stronger than that of irregular migrants, because the guestworkers were invited. But this difference is not decisive: after all, the guestworkers' permanent settlement contradicted the terms of their initial admission.

What was morally important was that they had established themselves firmly as members of society.

My argument that time matters cuts in both directions. If there is a threshold of time after which it is wrong to expel settled irregular migrants, then there is also some period of time before this threshold is crossed. How much time must pass before irregular migrants acquire a strong moral claim to stay? Or from the opposite perspective, how long does the state have to apprehend and expel irregular migrants?

Identifying a specific moment after which irregular migrants should have a legal right to remain inevitably involves an element of arbitrariness for reasons we have seen in previous chapters, but the principle that time matters sets some limits to the range of reasonable alternatives. If someone says that twenty years is not long enough to establish a claim to stay or that one year is sufficient, that is a person who does not take the principle that time matters very seriously.

Legalization Policies

The implication of this analysis is that states should move away from the practice of granting occasional large-scale amnesties or providing a right to stay on a case-by-case basis through appeal to humanitarian considerations. Instead, states should establish an individual right for migrants to transform their status from irregular to legal after a fixed period of time of residence, such as five to seven years.

Proving length of residence can be a problem, but past practice shows that this difficulty is not insuperable. For example, France had for many years a policy that granted an entitlement to legal resident status to anyone who could show that she had lived there for at least ten years. (When a right wing government came to power in 2003, the policy was made much more discretionary and restrictive, but the change was spurred by ideological hostility to immigration, not by evidence that the previous policy increased the level of irregular migration or created other problems.) In 2000 Spain adopted a law that goes even further. It permits individuals to legalize their status if they can show from work records or other means that they have been settled in the country without a criminal record for a few years. Almost 80,000 people had gained legal status in 2009 under this policy.[19]

For a long time, the United States also had a policy that went some way in this direction. It permitted the Attorney General to grant permanent resident status to migrants (including irregular migrants) who could establish that they had lived here continuously for ten years and met certain other requirements regarding employment, the lack of a criminal record, and so on. The same rule gave positive weight to family ties to American citizens and residents. Unlike the French and Spanish policies, the American one did not give migrants a legal entitlement to the regularization of their status, and the discretion that it gave to officials was often used in a racially discriminatory way.[20] Despite these serious limitations, this form of legalization was granted fairly often. Like the French and Spanish policies, it recognized the moral logic I defend here: that people become members of our community over time, even if they settle without authorization, and that this membership should be recognized by law. In recent years, opponents of immigration in the United States placed legislative restrictions on the exercise of this discretionary authority, and political dynamics have further limited its use. It is much more difficult for irregular migrants to gain legal status under this provision today than it was once, although some recent administrative decisions by the Obama administration reflect a move back in this direction. In any event, the principle remains on the books: the passage of time creates a moral claim to stay.

Time versus Other Social Ties: The Limits of Discretion

Some people are puzzled by the weight in my approach given to the passage of time, rather than the actual range and intensity of the migrant's social ties in the new society. Is it really right to pay attention only to the passage of time?

There is some merit in this concern. Individuals form attachments and become members of a community at different rates. And the harm done to someone in forcing her to leave will vary too. It is not the passage of time per se that matters but what that normally signifies about the development of a human life. For that reason, it does seem appropriate to give special weight to certain factors: social formation in the country, marriage to a citizen or legal resident, a clean record, and a history of employment. Nevertheless, it would be a mistake to try to establish a much wider range of criteria of belonging and an especially big mistake to grant more discretion to officials in judging whether individual migrants have passed the threshold of belonging that should entitle them to stay. I explore this point more fully in the next chapter.

The State Complicity Argument

So far, I have been focusing on the ways in which irregular migrants become members of society over time and hence acquire moral claims to legal status. There is another line of argument that we should also consider, namely that states are complicit in the processes that generate irregular migration and that this creates a moral claim to regularization.

Some argue that rich democratic states do not actually want to exclude irregular migrants, despite loud public pronouncements to that effect. The critics say that, from the state's perspective, keeping workers in an irregular status is attractive because the workers' vulnerability makes them tractable and easy to exploit. If this is true, then it undermines the argument that irregular migrants are present without the consent of the political community and so not entitled to the same rights as legally authorized migrants. If a state covertly encourage migrants to enter, it arguably owes them the same status and legal rights to which they would be entitled if they were recruited openly. And even if it is not a question of the state explicitly recruiting irregular migrants, but only of failing to enforce immigration laws and controls when it could do so, the state bears considerable responsibility for the results of its inaction.

State complicity in irregular migration certainly does reinforce the moral case for regularization. And this is not just a point of principle. In Spain, Italy, and even the United States, recognition of the state's past complicity in irregular migration movements has helped to generate public support for regularization policies. We should be careful not to overuse the state complicity argument, however, for the following three reasons.

First, the argument that the state is complicit in irregular migration only makes sense when there is scope for state action (or inaction) to make some difference in the number of irregular migrants. To the extent that irregular migration flows are determined by structural factors beyond the state's control, as some analysts argue, the state cannot be held responsible for failing to prevent the entry and settlement of irregular migrants.[21] If structural factors make irregular migration inevitable, we can criticize state policies for being ineffective or counterproductive but not for complicity.

Second, we cannot simply infer the state's complicity from the fact that some employers within the receiving society want to hire irregular migrants. No state can be held responsible for the desires or actions of every citizen or corporation within its jurisdiction. To establish complicity, it is necessary to show that the state is facilitating or permitting irregular migration, despite its formal policies—for example, by relaxing enforcement efforts against migrant workers during the hiring season. This is sometimes the case, but not always.

Third, we cannot charge a state with complicity simply because of its failure to deter unauthorized immigration. Every enforcement effort has some failure rate. In some cases, a state's effort to prevent unauthorized immigration and to expel those who are discovered may legitimately be hampered by other considerations. For example, some argue that efforts in the United States and Southern Europe to keep people out already go too far because they cost too many lives.[22] If border officials were to cut back on some of these measures to save lives, we should not turn around and accuse them of complicity in letting the migrants in.

For similar reasons, the mere presence of visa overstayers does not by itself show that a state is encouraging unauthorized immigration. Visitors from poor states to rich ones already face restrictions on entry that are severe and discriminatory. Tightening those restrictions further because some of the visitors do not leave before their visas expire would impose too high a cost to be a defensible way of restricting irregular migration.

Various moral considerations will always limit the ways in which states may try to control irregular migration, even if one accepts the legitimacy of the goal itself. But these limits and the presence of irregular migrants generated by them do not represent evidence of a state's complicity in irregular migration or undercut its right to try to restrict unauthorized settlement. Actual complicity, in the form of deliberately lax or fluctuating enforcement, is another matter. It does undercut the state's right to deport irregular migrants.

Objections to Regularization

Up to this point, I have concentrated primarily on the positive case for regularization. But the moral arguments against the idea of granting legal status to long-settled irregular migrants also deserve a hearing.

One such argument is that a self-governing political community has a moral right to determine its own membership.[23] I have already explained in chapter 1 why the question of membership cannot be treated as purely a matter of discretionary choice by the state even when that reflects the will of a democratic majority. In the past, people of African and Asian and indigenous descent with strong moral claims to membership were excluded from full legal membership in the United States, often with the support of democratic majorities.[24] We all recognize the injustice of such exclusions today. My claim is that our collective refusal to recognize long-settled irregular migrants as members is another example of a failure of democratic majorities to include people who belong. Like earlier exclusions supported by democratic majorities, it is an injustice.

Another moral objection to regularization is that allowing irregular migrants to stay is unfair to foreigners who have played by the rules and waited in line for admission. Stated abstractly, this argument seems to have force, but when one considers the reality, it is much less persuasive. In many democratic states, there is no effective line for admissions for those without family ties or special credentials. Even in countries like the United States and Canada that encourage legal immigration, there are almost no immigration lines for less skilled workers without close family ties to current citizens or residents. (Recall the story of Miguel Sanchez who tried to get authorization to immigrate for years without success.) Most of those who settle as irregular migrants would have no possibility of getting in through any authorized channel. To say that they should stand in a line that does not exist or does not move is disingenuous.

Perhaps the strongest moral objection to amnesty is that it rewards lawbreaking. Again, the force of the argument depends upon our not noticing the stance toward what we might call "ordinary" lawbreaking in other contexts. It is true that the rules governing immigration are laws but so are the rules governing automobile traffic. We don't describe drivers who exceed the speed limit as illegal drivers or criminals. It's a rare person who has never driven above the speed limit.

We all recognize that laws vary enormously in the harms they seek to prevent and the order they seek to maintain. Laws against murder are more important than laws against theft, laws against theft more important than laws regulating automobile traffic. The laws restricting immigration are a lot more like traffic regulations than like laws prohibiting murder and theft. The laws serve a useful social function, but that function can be served reasonably well even if there is a fair amount of deviance and most of those violating the rules never get caught. For enforcement purposes, it makes sense to focus on the really dangerous violators—those driving drunk or so recklessly as to endanger lives in the case of traffic laws, those who engage in terrorism or crime in the case of immigration laws. For run of the mill violations (ordinary speeding, irregular migration for work), just having the rules in place and occasional enforcement will maintain order at a sufficient level.

Settling without authorization violates immigration laws, but that does not mean that we should punish people many years after the fact. There is a parallel here between statutes of limitations for criminal offenses and a policy of not deporting long settled irregular migrants.[25] Most states recognize that the passage of time matters morally, at least for less serious criminal violations. If a person has not been arrested and charged with a crime within a specified period after the crime took place (often three to five years), legal authorities may no longer pursue her for that offense.

Why do states establish statutes of limitations?[26] Because it is not right to make people live indefinitely with a threat of serious legal consequences hanging over their heads for some long-past action, except for the most serious sorts of offenses. Keeping the threat in place for a long period does not enhance deterrence and causes great harm to the individual—more than is warranted by the original offense. If we are prepared to let time erode the state's power to pursue actual crimes, it makes even more sense to let time erode the power of the state to pursue immigration violations, which are not normally treated as crimes and should not be viewed as crimes.

In a related vein, we should be wary of efforts to criminalize actions that irregular migrants take simply to live ordinary lives. Most jurisdictions have criminal laws prohibiting identity theft and the use of false documentation. These are usually sensible laws intended to prevent fraud. Irregular migrants often provide false information to satisfy administrative or legal requirements. For example, they may provide a social security number that is not their own to an employer who uses this to deduct taxes from their pay. In most such cases, the irregular migrants are only trying to conceal their presence and are not engaged in deception designed to harm others. They pay their taxes, even when they are not entitled to the benefits that taxpayers normally receive (such as Social Security or unemployment compensation). Their actions may be technical violations of laws against identity theft and the use of false documents, but they are not normally the kinds of actions those laws were intended to prevent. Treating irregular migrants as criminals under these laws, as some authorities in the United States have been doing, is an abuse of the legal process. Of course, the state does have the power to make irregular migrants the targets of those laws, just as it has the power to make violations of immigration laws a criminal offence. But if we weigh the harm criminalization aims to prevent against the social costs it incurs, criminalization makes no sense.

Another challenge to the case for regularization is the claim that we have to choose between granting legal status to irregular migrants and providing assistance to disadvantaged citizens and that we should choose the latter.[27] In my view, this way of looking at the issue is a mistake whether we look at it from the perspective of morality or of public policy or even of politics.

It is a moral mistake because, if one accepts the claim that irregular migrants are (at some point) members who are entitled to legal status, then it is simply wrong to deny them that status for the sake of some other disadvantaged group. This sort of reprehensible rationale was used to justify the legal subordination of African Americans for generations. Their exclusion was necessary, it was said, to improve the lot of poor whites. Excluding members from a legal status to which they are morally entitled is not a morally permissible policy option.

Opposing regularization for the sake of poor citizens is not only immoral but also unwise. Trying to deport settled irregular migrants is a policy mistake. It is not an effective way to improve the situation of the least skilled among current citizens and legal residents. Ironically, the firewall that I have proposed would probably do more to improve the lot of disadvantaged citizens and residents by reducing the conflict between them and irregular migrants. Enabling irregular migrants to join unions and to receive the minimum wage and other job-related protections without fear of deportation would make them less vulnerable to employers and would thus reduce employers' incentives to seek out irregular migrants in preference to citizens and legal residents.

Finally, it is a political mistake to divide disadvantaged groups and to set them against one another instead of building alliances to promote their common interests.

The last objection is that regularization for long-term irregular migrants would encourage others to come without authorization. We should not dismiss this claim but neither should we accept at face value every claim about incentive effects. The actual effect of a rolling regularization such as I have proposed is an empirical question dependent on a variety of factors. It is worth recalling that the French had such a policy in effect for years, and it did not open the flood-gates. The more important point, however, is that a regularization policy by itself is not a solution to all of the problems raised by irregular migration. Any satisfactory approach will be contextually specific and will have many components from trade policy to visa allocations. In this chapter I am just trying to draw attention to moral principles that should govern the treatment of long-settled irregular migrants. That is only one aspect of the wider problem.

Even if we accept the state's right to control immigration as a basic premise, that right is not absolute and unqualified. Over time an irregular migration status becomes morally less relevant while the harm suffered by the person in that status grows. The state's right to deport irregular migrants weakens as the migrants become members of society. Democratic states should recognize that fact by institutionalizing an automatic transition to legal status for irregular migrants who have settled in a state for an extended period.

The argument that I have been developing in this chapter is a constraint on the state's right to control immigration, not a repudiation of it. Nothing in my argument in this chapter denies a government's moral and legal right to prevent entry in the first place and to deport those who settle without authorization, so long as these expulsions take place at a relatively early state of residence.

At the same time, the case I have advanced is only a minimalist one (though doubtless it will not appear so to many). I have identified only general moral constraints upon acceptable policies for the exclusion of irregular migrants from legal rights and legal status in democratic states, not all of the moral considerations that might generate responsibilities to irregular migrants or limit a state's right to deport them.

8

The Theory of Social Membership

I said in the introduction to this book that I would be doing political theory from the ground up, constructing a general account of the ethics of immigration from the building blocks provided by answers to specific questions. Now is a good moment to see how well that is working so far. In the past several chapters I have discussed a number of different issues raised by the presence of immigrants and their descendants in contemporary democratic states. Let's consider how the various arguments fit together.

There is one general idea that plays an important role in almost all of the chapters. It is that living within the territorial boundaries of a state makes one a member of society, that this social membership gives rise to moral claims in relation to the political community, and that these claims deepen over time. To put this idea in a four-word slogan: social membership matters morally.

Let me recall briefly what this idea of social membership contributed in each of the preceding chapters.

Chapter 2 addressed the issue of whether the descendants of immigrants should get citizenship at birth. I began with the fact that children of resident citizens normally acquire citizenship at birth. I argued that granting birthright citizenship to the children of resident citizens makes moral sense only if we see it primarily as a way of recognizing the child's social membership. The child of resident citizens is living in the society at the moment of birth and is expected to grow up there. That is the primary reason why it is appropriate to grant her citizenship at birth. The child of permanent resident immigrants, I argued, has similar social membership claims to birthright citizenship.

Chapter 3 considered the question of access to citizenship for people who arrive as immigrants, whether as children or as adults. Again, my central claim was that social membership gives rise over time to a moral claim to citizenship. The argument is clearest for a child who grows up and is educated in the political community to which she has immigrated because that state has such an important role in the child's social formation. The social membership of such a child can hardly be denied. But, I argued, even adults become members of society over time as they sink roots in the place where they have settled. For that reason, I said, naturalization should be tied primarily to facts about the length of a person's residence rather than to other aspects of social life.

Chapter 4 is the outlier. I was concerned in that chapter with forms of economic, social, and political inclusion (or exclusion) that go beyond the allocation of legal status and formal legal rights. As a result, the idea that social membership generates moral claims to status and rights does not play an important role in the chapter. However, chapter 4 provides an important complementary perspective on the issue of belonging to a society in ways I will explain later in this chapter.

Chapter 5 focused on the question of what legal rights permanent residents should have. I started with the fact that residents enjoy most of the rights that citizens possess, but that tourists or other visitors do not. The best way to make moral sense of this practice, I suggested, is through the idea that it is not citizenship but social membership that provides the basis for moral claims to most legal rights because social membership is what citizens and residents have in common and what distinguishes them from visitors. The idea of social membership also makes it possible to understand why the moral claims of residents to some rights (like security of residence and redistributive rights) grow over time.

Chapter 6 was concerned with temporary workers. It might seem that the idea of social membership would be less relevant to a chapter on temporary workers, but in fact it played a crucial role in two respects. First, I noted that democratic states normally set strict limits to the time that people can stay as temporary workers. A democratic state can only make temporary workers leave if it has not permitted them to sink deep roots. The reason for this constraint is that democratic states have come to accept the principle that the longer workers stay in a society, the stronger their claim to remain. That principle is part of the idea of social membership. Second, with respect to the rights that temporary workers enjoy while they are present, I argued that democratic states should and generally do regard these workers as temporary members, granting them most of the rights that residents and citizens enjoy. It is morally preferable, I contended, to see temporary workers as temporary members of society than to regard them simply as individual agents whose willingness to accept a lesser bundle of rights would provide an adequate justification for limiting their rights.

Finally, in chapter 7, I argued that even those present without the state's authorization become members of society by living there over time and that eventually this social membership gives rise to a moral claim to regularization of their legal status. I also argued that the children of irregular migrants are entitled to a free public education because their ongoing presence makes them members in the sense relevant to claims to a right to education.

In sum, many of the central arguments in five of the previous six chapters draw upon the idea that living in a society over time makes one a member and being a member generates moral claims to legal rights and to legal status. What matters most morally with respect to a person's legal status and legal rights in a democratic political community is not ancestry or birthplace or culture or identity or values or actions or even the choices that individuals and political communities make but simply the social membership that comes from residence over time.

The Importance of the Theory of Social Membership

If we draw the arguments of the different chapters together, we can see that they constitute a theory of social membership. This theory of social membership brings into view some normative underpinnings of democratic practices that are often not noticed.

Discussions of justice and democracy often simply presuppose a context in which all the relevant actors are fellow citizens. Questions about why people are morally entitled to citizenship do not arise because the possession of citizenship is simply a background presupposition of the discussion. That is perfectly reasonable for many purposes. But once we bring immigrants and their descendants into the picture, we cannot avoid questions about the basis of moral claims to citizenship. These questions arise not only for immigrants but for everyone who is or might become a citizen. The theory of social membership offers an answer to these questions. It says that almost every moral claim to citizenship rests upon facts and expectations about social membership. This is as true for the children of citizens as it is for the children of immigrants. If this claim is correct, it follows that social membership is normatively prior to citizenship. Social membership (actual or anticipated, authorized or unauthorized) provides the foundation upon which moral claims to citizenship normally rest.

Just as questions about access to citizenship do not arise when it is assumed that everyone is a citizen, so too, some questions about who deserves legal rights do not arise when it is assumed both that everyone is a citizen and that all citizens are morally entitled to equal rights. (Of course, there can still be disputes about what equal rights entail, about the rights of minority citizens, and so on.) Again, once we bring immigrants into the picture, we cannot escape questions about the similarities and differences between the legal rights of immigrants and the legal rights of citizens. These questions cannot be answered adequately from the perspective of citizenship itself. Being a citizen is not a prerequisite for moral entitlements to legal rights. The theory of social membership asserts that people can be members of a society even when they are not citizens and that their membership gives them moral claims to legal rights. The theory of social membership thus provides a foundation for moral claims to many legal rights. This foundation is an alternative to citizenship and is more fundamental than citizenship because it is actually the basis for the moral claims of citizens themselves to many legal rights. In this way, too, social membership is normatively prior to citizenship. By drawing attention to the presence of people who are members but not citizens, the theory of social membership disrupts the conventional understanding of citizenship in democratic theory and brings the normative underpinnings of democratic practices more clearly into view.

The theory of social membership also serves as an important corrective to certain tendencies in cosmopolitan thought. If some democratic theorists focus too much on citizenship, some cosmopolitan thinkers go too far in denigrating the significance of belonging. Some cosmopolitans think that the only thing that really matters is the protection of human rights and that everyone within a state ought to enjoy the same legal rights. That is not my view, and the theory of social membership explains why. The general human rights to which everyone is morally entitled (like the right to freedom of religion or the right to a fair trial) constitute only a small fraction of the legal rights possessed by people who live in a democratic state. Most of these other legal rights (like the right to work or the right to have access to social programs) are membership-specific rights. In other words, only members are entitled to these rights, both legally and morally. The simple fact of one's humanity is not sufficient to create a moral claim to these rights, and the status of citizenship is not necessary for a moral claim to most of them. Moral claims to these other legal rights depend primarily upon where one lives and how long one has lived there because that is what makes one a member of society in the sense that is relevant to these membership-specific rights.

The theory of social membership poses an even more specific challenge to certain ways of thinking about human rights. It is a commonplace in human rights discourse to speak of human rights as rights that all human beings enjoy against all states simply in virtue of their humanity. Some people think that is what it means to speak of human rights as universal. The theory of social membership draws attention to the fact that some familiar human rights, like the rights of citizens to security of entry and residence, are rights that people hold only in relation to their own country. That is, they are membership-specific human rights, not rights (like freedom of speech or religion) which everyone enjoys in relation to any country, regardless of their legal status in that country. These membership-specific human rights are still universal human rights in the sense that every human being possesses them in relation to a political community in which she is a member, but membership-specific human rights protect particular connections to particular communities rather than generic human interests. By shining a light on the conjuncture between two ideas often assumed to be at odds—the specific claims of membership and the universal claims of human rights—the theory of social membership disrupts the conventional understanding of human rights in cosmopolitan theory and invites reconsideration of familiar categories of cosmopolitan thought.

In sum, the theory of social membership contributes not only to our understanding of the ethics of immigration but also to our understanding of democracy and rights more generally.

The Limits of the Theory of Social Membership

At the same time, it is a theory with limited aspirations. It does not purport to be a comprehensive political theory. It does not even provide a comprehensive account of the ethics of immigration. The theory of social membership draws together some common elements in the way we address questions about the ethics of immigration, but it is limited in a number of ways.

First, the theory of social membership is mainly concerned with people who are already present. It is not very helpful in thinking about admissions. As we will see in the next chapter, it has a little—but only a little—to contribute to the question of who should get in, under the conventional assumption of the state's right to exercise discretionary control over entry and settlement. As we will see in subsequent chapters, it has nothing to contribute to the discussion of refugees or to the arguments in favor of freedom of movement, although I will contend in chapter 13 that it is compatible with those arguments.

Second, the theory of social membership is only concerned with questions about access to the legal status of citizenship and access to the legal rights that citizens normally enjoy. As chapter 4 makes clear, belonging involves much more than that. Formal citizenship and equal legal rights are necessary but not sufficient bases for full inclusion in the political community. Moreover, the focus on access to status and rights says little about what the political community can reasonably expect of citizens, new and old.

Third, the moral claims that flow from social membership need to be supplemented by at least two other considerations. First, a democratic state has a moral responsibility to protect the general human rights of every person within its jurisdiction regardless of her membership claims. This is a point that I emphasize in chapters 5 through 7. Second, a democratic state is morally constrained by norms like reciprocity, proportionality, rationality, and fairness. These norms are not derived from the idea of social membership, but they play an important role in a number of the arguments about membership and what it entails. For example, the norm of proportionality plays a key role in the arguments in chapters 2 and 3 about why democratic states should permit dual citizenship. Similarly, the norm of reciprocity plays a key supplementary role in some of the arguments for extending legal rights to temporary workers and irregular migrants.

Finally, the theory of social membership is a theory about the bases for moral claims that democratic states ought to respect. It sets minimum moral requirements for democratic states when allocating legal rights and citizenship. But for the most part, the theory does not prohibit additional allocations of legal rights and citizenship on other grounds. It is a theory of floors not ceilings. It leaves room for other considerations to affect policies regarding the allocation of citizenship and legal rights so long as they do not contradict the underlying principle of respect for claims of social membership.

Let me illustrate this last point with the example of birthright citizenship for the children of emigrants. As I noted in chapter 2, these children have weaker claims to birthright citizenship than the children of settled immigrants because it is much less likely that the children of the emigrants will grow up and live in their parents' country of origin than that the children of immigrants will grow up and live in the place where their parents have settled. I assume that everyone will agree that minor children should be able to accompany their emigrant parents, if the parents return to their country of origin, and that it is appropriate to see this as a kind of membership claim. But still, one may ask, why is that a sufficient membership claim to ground a policy of birthright citizenship for the children of emigrants? Why grant citizenship to children who have been born and raised abroad rather than simply giving them a secure right to enter and settle with their parents, if the parents decide to return while the children are still minors?

In fact, the latter, more limited approach is all that is required by justice in my view. As I noted in chapter 2, some democratic states do take that sort of approach. They do not grant citizenship to children born to emigrant parents, but only a right to citizenship, and they make the activation of that right contingent upon the children actually living in the country for a certain length of time before maturity. I said explicitly that this was a morally permissible policy, one that meets the membership claims of the children of emigrants. But that is not the same as saying that this is the only morally acceptable policy.

The children of emigrants don't have a compelling moral claim to birthright citizenship, but granting them citizenship at birth addresses a number of practical problems for their families and for the state. As I noted in chapter 2, granting birthright citizenship to the children of emigrants makes it easier for the family to function as a unit. In a previous era, promoting the unity of the family was seen as an important consideration in citizenship policy. Indeed, this was one of the primary justifications for insisting that children and even wives take on only the citizenship of the father/husband, the "head" of the family. That was a bad reason for restricting the transmission of a mother's citizenship to her children or for taking it away from a wife, but it is a good reason for extending the citizenship of (both) parents to their children. Indeed, if people knew that children born abroad would not get their parents' citizenship at birth, it could create major incentives not to live abroad. As a general matter democratic states should not create unnecessary obstacles to exit, temporary or permanent, out of respect for human freedom. People need passports and, occasionally, consular protection. If family members have the same citizenship, it can solve a lot of practical problems. In sum, there are a number of good, practical reasons connected to the nature of the way the modern world is organized for granting birthright citizenship to the children of emigrants. They have sufficient connections to the political community that is granting them citizenship that such a policy does not seem arbitrary or discriminatory (in an objectionable sense). The theory of social membership does not generate a moral entitlement to citizenship for such children but it does not prohibit it either, and, as we have just seen, there are other reasons for regarding this as a practice which makes moral sense.

Why Residence and Time Are the Keys to Social Membership

The deepest puzzle about the theory of social membership may be that it relies on two rather limited criteria of membership: residence and the passage of time. In explaining why social membership is morally important, I have appealed to the relationships, interests, and identities that connect people to the place where they live. In these contexts the term "social membership" evokes the sense that being a member of a society involves a dense network of relationships and associations. What is at stake is a person's ability to maintain and develop a rich and highly particular set of human ties. The stories about Miguel Sanchez, Faiza Silmi, Senay Kodacag, Milikije Arifi, Victor Castillo, and Margaret Grimmond are able to move us because we can see even from a brief vignette the many ways in which these people are connected to the societies in which they live. The stories mention values, lifestyles, language, occupation, family, and so on. These specifics are part of what make us feel that these individuals deserve certain kinds of recognition and rights from the states in which they live.

In contrast to these accounts, the theory of social membership mentions only two considerations: residence and length of stay. Those are the only factors that play a role in the formal arguments about who should count as a member and how strong particular membership claims are. Why? Residence and length of stay are clearly factors in all of these stories but by themselves they do not evoke a sense of belonging. Are they just proxies for a richer set of indicators of social membership? If so, why rely on these proxies? If what really matters are a person's connections to the society in which she lives, why not try to measure those connections directly? If not, why evoke all the specific details in the stories? Might it not be possible for some people to live a long time on the state's territory without really establishing any deep connections to the society? Would their stories evoke the same sense of belonging? Can residence and the passage of time really carry such moral weight by themselves?

In responding to these questions, I will try to draw together some of the specific points made in the preceding chapters, while raising the overall argument to a new level of generality. My basic answer to the questions is that residence and time are proxies for richer, deeper forms of connection but that we have both practical and principled reasons not to try to go beyond these proxies, at least under most circumstances. If we want to institutionalize a principle that gives weight to the degree to which a person has become a member of society and if we expect to have to deal with a large number of cases, we will want to use indicators of social membership that are relevant, objective, and easy to measure. Residence and time clearly meet these requirements. Other ways of assessing social membership do not.

Let me explain this with an analogy. To understand why it is morally appropriate to rely so much upon residence and time as indicators of social membership when what we care about with regard to social membership goes much deeper, it may be helpful to consider a comparable but quite different case: the way democratic states determine when children should be given the rights and responsibilities of adults. This issue has nothing directly to do with immigration but it poses some of the same structural problems of requiring the state to determine when someone has passed a threshold that should give rise to a legal entitlement.

Everyone recognizes that children should not have all of the legal rights and responsibilities of adults because the exercise of many legal rights and responsibilities depends upon the development of capacities that children do not possess when they are very young. We also recognize, as a social fact, that individual children mature at different rates and so acquire these capacities at different ages. Some children are highly responsible at 12, others still not at 30. When it comes to assigning legal rights and responsibilities, however, a state does not normally inquire into the subjective capacities of each individual person or assign officials to determine whether a particular child is able to bear the rights and responsibilities of an adult. Rather, for most purposes, it establishes rules that tie the possession of legal rights and responsibilities to an objective measure of the passage of time. We set an age at which a person normally acquires the right to vote or to marry or to enter into economic contracts or at which a person can be held responsible for a crime (although the latter is sometimes subject to some degree of individual assessment). Different democratic states may set different age limits for one or another of these rights and responsibilities, but the range is not limitless.

Why do states rely on age as a proxy for the development of the capacity to exercise rights and responsibilities? In part, of course, it is a simple recognition of the way things generally go in human lives. As people get older they normally become more capable of taking responsibility for their actions, though, as I just noted, there is variation in the rate at which this happens for particular individuals. There is a direct analogy here to the use of the passage of time as a measure of the depth of one's social membership. People's roots in a society normally deepen over time. The connections grow stronger. There is variation in the rate at which this happens for particular individuals, to be sure, but the general pattern is clear.

Another reason why states rely on age as a proxy for capacity is that it would be very expensive to test every individual to see if she had reached the desired threshold of responsibility before granting her legal authorization to vote or marry or sign contracts. It is not that it is impossible to imagine how to construct such tests. After all, as I just mentioned, in the highly specialized context of a criminal trial, psychological assessments are used by some states to determine whether a person should be tried as a juvenile (and hence as someone less responsible for her actions) or as an adult. And normally people are required not only to reach a certain age but also to pass a test before they are allowed to drive a car. That is a requirement imposed on everyone who wants to drive, even though it does entail significant expenditures of public and private money. But few suppose that it would be worth the cost to have testing for the other activities I have mentioned (voting, marriage, economic contracts) despite their central importance in human lives. Similarly, it seems doubtful that it would be worth the cost of trying to assess the social membership of immigrants on an individualized basis, although again in the highly specialized context of a judicial proceeding, European courts do undertake related individualized assessments in determining whether the expulsion of a foreign resident would violate the person's right to a family life which is guaranteed under the European Convention on Human Rights.

Finally, and most importantly, there are principled reasons for relying on age as a proxy for capacity. We want to avoid discrimination on the basis of gender, race, class, and other categories that reflect unfair bias. We know from past experience that these factors have often played a role in assessments of capacity for responsible agency. They have been used to justify excluding people from a range of rights. We have good reason to be wary of letting unconscious biases influence the outcomes of assessments of capacity. A criterion like age that applies in the same way to all human beings is a shield against this sort of problem.

Again, the same concern lies behind reliance upon residence and time as criteria of social membership. We know that it is much easier for immigrants to be seen as members of society when the immigrants resemble most of the existing population with respect to race, ethnicity, religion, lifestyles, values, and so on. But these are not morally acceptable criteria of social membership. Leave the issue of immigration aside for a moment. Every society contains minorities who differ from the majority in significant ways, even though these minorities may be able to trace their ancestry in the country back several generations. From the perspective of democratic principles, it is not acceptable to call the social membership of these minorities into question. It is the same for immigrants and their descendants. The fact that they are often different from the existing population in various ways is no justification for refusing to see them as members of society. If the state attempts to use criteria of membership beyond residence and length of stay, that is almost inevitably what happens. If states wish to avoid morally objectionable forms of discrimination, they must rely only on residence and length of time in allocating rights and ultimately citizenship itself.

Even if readers accept these arguments for relying only on residence and time as criteria of social membership, some readers will undoubtedly want to know whether residence and time are really sufficient as a matter of principle. I have been asked on more than one occasion to imagine an immigrant who establishes no relationships with others. Does she become a member of society as time passes? Is it really just physical presence over time on the state's territory that makes one a member of society?

I am tempted to resist this sort of hypothetical question which bears so little relation to the actual experience of most immigrants. One concern that I have is that this kind of question may evoke the idea that the only social connections that make an immigrant a member of society are connections that link immigrants to people who are not immigrants. Sometimes people think that immigrants who associate primarily with fellow immigrants have no social membership claims in the state to which they have moved if they continue to speak the language of their country of origin and continue to eat the same food, wear the same clothes, follow the same patterns of social interaction and maintain the same values as they did in their country of origin. That is a view that I want to challenge. As an empirical matter, this sort of view reflects a distortion of the social reality. Being a Pakistani in London or a Moroccan in Paris or a Somali in Toronto is not the same as being a Pakistani in Pakistan or a Moroccan in Morocco or a Somali in Somalia. The air people breathe, the streets they walk, the buildings in which they live and work, the money they use, the taxes they pay, the laws they must obey, the language in which most social institutions function—all these are concrete realities linking the lives of immigrants to the new society where they live. As I pointed out in chapter 4, most immigrants must and do adjust to their new social environment in a wide variety of ways even when they seek to maintain as many elements of their previous ways of living as they can. There is also an issue of principle at stake here. Treating relationships with fellow immigrants as irrelevant to social membership denigrates the immigrants and denies that they belong. Relationships with fellow immigrants should be seen as just as important as relationships with nonimmigrants in establishing claims to social membership.

The point of the hypothetical example, however, is to clarify the principle at stake, and the principle involves not a lack of connections to nonimmigrants but a lack of social connections altogether. So, let's just keep this caution about the rhetorical effect of such a hypothetical in view and consider the underlying issue. Imagine an immigrant who really does not establish relationships with other people in the society, immigrants or not. She is a recluse. She has been physically present on the state's territory for several years but has built no real social connections. Should we regard her as a member of society with a claim to legal rights and citizenship?

My answer is "Certainly. Why not?" Imagine another recluse who is not an immigrant. Why should she have any legal rights? Why should she be a citizen? No one would suggest that we take away legal rights and legal status from someone just because she does not have many connections to other people in the community in which she lives. Why would a similar pattern of social disconnection provide grounds for denying legal rights and legal status to an immigrant? One of the central themes in the idea of social membership is that it is something that applies to everyone living in a society, whether they can trace their ancestry back several generations or not. The recluse who is the descendant of several generations of citizens is still a member of society, not because of her ancestry but because of where she lives. The immigrant recluse has the same claims to social membership.

In reality, there are not many people who live in a society over an extended period but have no real connections there, and fewer still for whom social isolation is a chosen path rather than the outcome of unhappy circumstances. In most cases, both for immigrants and for nonimmigrants, social disconnection should be seen as a reason for concern rather than a justification of exclusion. But this hypothetical testing of principles does remind us of one key feature of the theory of social membership, namely that social membership is what ultimately undergirds almost all claims to citizenship and legal rights, not just the claims of immigrants and their descendants but those of citizens with deep ancestral roots as well. Most people do develop deep and rich networks of relationships in the place where they live, and this normal pattern of human life is what makes sense of the idea of social membership. Nevertheless, in the end, simply living in a state over time is sufficient to make one a member of society and to ground claims to legal rights and ultimately to citizenship.

Theory and Practice

The theory of social membership that emerges from the previous chapters and that I have briefly summarized in this one is not a seamless web that must be accepted or rejected in its entirety. Readers can accept the general thrust of the account while rejecting some of the specifics. For example, someone could accept my general view of the moral importance of social membership while thinking that the political community has an interest in ensuring the competence of its citizens and that this justifies requiring candidates for naturalization to pass reasonable tests of linguistic and civic knowledge. Or someone could accept the basic outlines of the theory but think that it is reasonable for a state to reserve civil service jobs for citizens so long as immigrants have good access to naturalization. And one could make a similar point about many of the other specific claims that I make. In other words, it is possible to accept the core claim of the theory of social membership that living in a society over time generates moral claims to legal rights and eventually to citizenship while disagreeing with my arguments about particular issues.

On the other hand, it would be difficult to accept the theory while disagreeing with my views on all or even most of the issues I discuss because the theory itself grows out of my answers to questions about particular issues. I did not begin with a general theory of social membership which I then applied to the ethical questions raised by immigration. The theory has emerged from my attempt to make sense of existing practices in the area of immigration in light of our democratic commitments. The theory is simply an attempt to make the implicit rationale of policies explicit and to connect the rationales of different policies together. Similarly, my criticisms of current policies come from the interplay between my understanding of our practices and my understanding of our democratic commitments. I criticize policies or practices when they seem at odds with those commitments, not because they do not fit well with an independent theory of social membership.

I have been trying to make sense of our practices and to make our practices more sensible. This requires examining the practices for consistency with one another and seeking general principles that identify the values underlying the practices. I think the concept of social membership helps to do this. It is not a master concept, however. It does not tell us everything that we need to know about who deserves citizenship or why immigrants deserve various sorts of rights, and I do not think that we should look for a single concept that does. With all of its limitations, I think that the theory of social membership makes better sense of our practices than any alternative currently on offer. In my view, there is no plausible account of democracy that rejects the core principle of the theory of social membership, that is, that living in a state gives rise to moral claims to a range of legal rights, including, ultimately, the status of citizenship.

PART TWO

WHO SHOULD GET IN?

9

Ordinary Admissions

Up to this point I have focused on immigrants who are already present, and I have discussed how democratic states should respond to these immigrants. I turn now to questions about the decision to admit immigrants in the first place. In this chapter and the next, I propose to explore questions about admissions in the context of the now familiar conventional assumption that states have a moral right to exercise considerable discretionary control over entry and settlement. As we shall see, democratic states are not morally unfettered with regard to admissions even under the conventional assumption. Many options that might seem attractive from the state's perspective are ruled out of bounds on moral grounds.[1] My goal in these two chapters is to draw attention to this phenomenon and to try to make sense of it.

In the next chapter, I will consider questions about the admission of refugees to democratic states. In this chapter, I discuss other issues relating to admissions. The chapter has two main sections. The first discusses the question of what criteria are permissible for selecting or excluding immigrants. The second shows that the moral obligation to permit family reunification constrains state discretion with respect to immigration.

Discretionary Admissions

Why would states ever choose to admit immigrants? Leave aside for a moment immediate family members and refugees, both of whom states may be morally obliged to admit. I will discuss those issues in the second part of this chapter and in the next chapter. Why would states take in other sorts of immigrants?

Some states like Canada, Australia, and the United States see ongoing immigration as serving their long-term interests.[2] They want to admit new immigrants every year, and they have policies and administrative arrangements in place designed to regulate this flow. Other states, including many in Europe, have a different view of their interests. They try not to take in any immigrants whom they are not obliged to admit. Still other states fall somewhere in between, admitting a limited number (beyond their obligations) for specific purposes. Given the conventional assumption, all of these approaches are morally permissible.

Even if we assume that states are morally free to take in as many or as few immigrants as they choose, it does not follow that they are morally free to use whatever criteria they want in deciding which immigrants to admit. What may states take into account in choosing among potential immigrants? We may distinguish between criteria of exclusion and criteria of selection. The former are used to identify people who will not be admitted, the latter to choose which ones among those eligible for admission will actually be taken in. Some people would object to this distinction. They see the categories as mirrors: every criterion of exclusion is an implicit criterion of selection (of those who are not excluded) and every criterion of selection is an implicit criterion of exclusion (of those who are not selected). There is a logic of sorts to that identification, but I think it distorts the social reality. Normally, those who are formally excluded on the basis of some explicit criterion are a small subset of those who are not selected. Treating the categories as mirror images obscures this important fact. In this section on discretionary admissions, my examples will largely be drawn from countries like the United States and Canada that choose to admit large numbers.

Criteria of Exclusion

Consider criteria of exclusion first. Some criteria of exclusion are clearly morally impermissible. No state may legitimately exclude potential immigrants on the basis of race, ethnicity, or religion. It is important to remember that countries like Canada, the United States, and Australia have all used explicitly racial criteria to exclude potential immigrants in the past.[3] These criteria were not officially abandoned until the 1960s. Nevertheless, the moral impermissibility of this sort of overt discrimination is one of the clearest points of consensus today among those who accept democratic principles. As I have indicated before, I won't try to defend that consensus in this book. As always, I am reminding readers of the obvious so that we can put disagreements into perspective. Virtually all democrats agree that the discretionary authority of states with respect to admissions is limited by the duty not to exclude potential immigrants on the basis of race, ethnicity, or religion. I want to use that agreement as a starting point for reflection about more contested issues.[4]

At first glance, it might seem odd to say that states are morally free to exclude immigrants altogether but not free to exclude immigrants on the basis of race, ethnicity, or religion. In fact, this sort of moral constraint is common. One familiar analogy in the domestic context comes from the area of employment. A potential employer is under no obligation to hire anyone, but if the employer does hire, she must not exclude applicants on the basis of race, ethnicity, or religion.

To the previous list of morally impermissible criteria of exclusion, I would add the category of sexual orientation. For many years, homosexuality was grounds for declaring potential immigrants inadmissible to the United States. This is incompatible with respect for human freedom and human dignity. As with the case of race, ethnicity, and religion, the use of sexual orientation as a criterion of exclusion in immigration policy reflects deeply rooted prejudices that cannot any longer be defended publicly. I do not claim that this position has the same consensus behind it as the prohibition of exclusions based on race, ethnicity, and religion, but I claim that it should.

Let's turn now to criteria of exclusion that may be justifiable. All states use some sort of security screen, denying admission to people perceived to be threats to national security. Is that morally permissible? To some people this question will seem absurd. In their view, protection of national security is the fundamental responsibility of every state, so, of course, the state can prevent people from immigrating if they pose a threat to national security.

At one level this is a reasonable view, but a blanket endorsement of exclusion for reasons of national security covers over some important problems. There is nothing intrinsically problematic about the principle that states may exclude potential immigrants who pose a threat to national security. It clearly reflects an important public interest. No state is obliged to admit terrorists or enemy agents. The problem is that the category is so easily abused.

The concept of national security can be and has been interpreted in such an expansive manner that it can be used to justify excluding anyone whom state authorities choose to keep out for any reason whatsoever. In the wake of 9/11, Muslims found it much harder to gain entry to states in Europe and North America, especially the United States. During much of the twentieth century, the United States used national security as a justification for excluding people identified as gays or lesbians, as well as all sorts of people whose views did not conform to the reigning American ideology. To the extent that the national security rationale has been limited in practice, it is largely due to the efforts of NGOs and other actors in civil society who have scrutinized and challenged the practices of exclusion. It is all too easy to construct any category of immigrants as dangerous, thus smuggling back in under the national security banner forms of discriminatory exclusion that would be morally impermissible if used openly.

Despite the abuses of the national security rationale for exclusion, we should not allow the failures of practice to muddle our thinking about principle. Every category is subject to interpretation, expansion, and abuse. That does not mean that we can do without categories. Rather we should insist upon sensible standards and criteria. Even if one accepts the idea that each state must be the final judge of what threatens its own security, it does not follow that states are free to do whatever they want. The vast majority of immigrants (actual and potential) cannot be construed as threats to national security under any plausible definition of that term. A principled use of national security as a criterion of exclusion is morally permissible, but it would affect very few of those trying to move.

Some people think that democratic states should exclude potential immigrants who do not accept democratic norms and values. To distinguish this issue from the preceding one, I want to make it clear that we are not talking now about individuals whom we have reason to believe pose an actual danger to national security.[5] The mere fact that someone has views critical of democracy is not a threat, on any reasonable understanding of the concept of threat. The concern is rather with the maintenance of the underlying conditions that enable democracies to function effectively over time. As I observed in chapter 4 and elsewhere, democracies cannot sustain themselves on the basis of rules alone. They require democratic virtues and dispositions to be widely shared within the population. So, the worry is that admitting immigrants who are not committed to the principles of democracy will, over time, erode the public culture that makes democracy work. The problem is not with any single immigrant's views but with the collective effect of ideas hostile to democracy.[6]

I don't think that we can dismiss this idea out of hand, but I do think that we have empirical and principled reasons to resist it. The empirical reasons have to do with our actual experience of attempts to identify those with ideas hostile to democracy. In the current environment, an abstractly stated fear of the illiberal other is often a code for fear of Muslims who are assumed to hold views that are fundamentally incompatible with liberal democracy. Anyone who reads the anti-immigrant literature from the nineteenth and early twentieth century in the United States is bound to be struck by the similarity between the doubts and fears expressed then with respect to Catholics and Jews from Europe and all immigrants from Asia and the doubts and fears expressed now with respect to Muslims. One finds the same rhetoric about alien invasions, with Asians, Catholics, and Jews portrayed as threatening and unassimilable because of their illiberal and undemocratic values.[7] One finds the same dissection of religious doctrines and proofs that the real loyalties of adherents of this religion lie elsewhere, that they aspire to become a majority and replace democracy with religious authoritarianism, and so on. Nobody today would defend those earlier views (or at least nobody should). We should apply the same skepticism to contemporary prejudices. Like immigrants to North America in earlier centuries, the overwhelming majority of Muslim immigrants to Europe and North America have embraced democracy and have no desire to replace it with any alternative regime. It is worth noting as well that most of the potential migrants to Europe and North America from Asia, Africa, and Latin America are not Muslims, and that many potential migrants, Muslim and non-Muslim, want to come precisely because they want to live in democratic regimes (and rightly object, on democratic grounds, to the discrimination and exclusion to which they are often subjected after they arrive).

I have been discussing the historical reasons why we should be very skeptical of the idea that an ideological screen of potential immigrants is warranted or would be conducted without bias. There is also a deep principled objection to the use of an ideological screen, namely that it conflicts with the democratic commitment to freedom of thought, freedom of religion, and freedom of conscience. In chapter 3, I argued that democratic states should not exclude established residents from citizenship because of their ideological commitments, and in chapter 4, I argued that democratic states could not use rules or even social expectations to coerce citizens into internal acceptance of democratic principles, even though the viability of democracy over the long run would depend on those principles being accepted by most people. I do not say that the situation of immigrants seeking admission is exactly the same as the ones discussed earlier. In chapters 3 and 4, I was talking about people who were already permanent members of society and who had moral claims to have their freedoms respected within the state where they lived. Here I am talking about people not yet subject to the jurisdiction of the state (except with respect to the question of admission itself), and, by hypothesis, people without any individual moral claim to admission. So, it is arguable that their claims to have their ideological views ignored in the admissions decision out of respect for their rights to freedom of thought, freedom of religion, and freedom of conscience are somewhat weaker than the claims of those I was discussing in chapters 3 and 4. Nevertheless, it remains the case that the use of ideological screens to exclude potential immigrants would be deeply at odds with democratic ideals of human freedom.

Are there other morally permissible criteria of exclusion? States also often prohibit people with significant criminal records from entering as immigrants. There is obviously a public interest here, although the concern is public safety and the maintenance of law and order rather than national security. The use of this criterion is not unreasonable, so long as some attention is paid to context. For example, some states may use the criminal law to repress political dissent, and democratic states should be very wary about reinforcing that practice by refusing admission to those so convicted.

Another criterion of exclusion with deep historical roots is financial need.[8] States that admit immigrants often require them to provide evidence that they will be able to be self-sustaining economically and will not seek to rely upon the political community for support, at least for some extended period. Of course, the fact that a criterion of exclusion has deep historical roots does not prove that it is morally acceptable, as we have seen with respect to the use of racial criteria of exclusion. The exclusion of potential immigrants who are unable to support themselves seems more defensible, however. Remember that we are concerned for the moment with potential immigrants who have no moral claim to admission. Excluding people who seem likely to need public support gives decisive weight to the risks and burdens created for those in the receiving society by particular admissions decisions, in a context in which we are assuming that the state is not obliged to admit any immigrants from this pool. It is not a generous approach to the admission of immigrants, but the use of this criterion of exclusion seems to me to be morally permissible because there is an important public interest at stake and paying attention to this interest violates no moral claims that the applicants have.

The argument that it is morally permissible to exclude financially needy immigrants clearly rests upon the conventional assumption about the state's right to exercise discretionary control over immigration. It would be possible to construct a theory of global justice that obliged democratic states to give priority in admissions to those in need, and I consider one way of doing so in chapters 11 and 12, but I don't think that it is possible to reconcile that sort of argument with the conventional assumption about discretionary control. The argument here also depends on the further implicit assumption that the need of the excluded does not qualify them for refugee status. I consider the latter issue in the next chapter.

Even if democratic states are morally entitled to exclude people who are unable to support themselves, it does not follow that these states are entitled to deny public support to immigrants who have been admitted if they come to need that support as a result of contingencies that were not foreseeable at the time of admission. In addition, as I argued in chapter 5, it would be unreasonable for democratic states to bar access to public support indefinitely.

Another commonly used criterion of exclusion is health risk. States often screen potential immigrants to determine whether they suffer from illnesses (e.g., contagious diseases like TB or communicable ones like AIDS) that might harm the health of the existing population or whether they have medical conditions (e.g., kidney diseases requiring dialysis or a transplant) that might put unusually high demands upon the health-care system.

Is health risk a morally permissible basis for exclusion? Let us distinguish first between objections to particular applications of this criterion and objections to the criterion itself. Sometimes people object that the criterion of health risk is applied inappropriately or arbitrarily. For example, AIDS activists have rightly objected that the risks of contracting HIV from someone who has AIDS are much smaller than the risks of contracting other equally dangerous diseases that are not treated as grounds for exclusion. Making AIDS a reason for exclusion, they argue, reflects prejudices against gays. Or people may object that the authorities are wrong to assume that a particular medical condition (e.g., a physical or mental disability) is more likely to generate unusually high medical costs than other conditions that are not treated as grounds for exclusion. Again, the objection is that the use of this condition as grounds for exclusion reflects prejudice.

Recall that we are concerned here only with potential immigrants who have no specific moral claim to admittance. Even so, they still have a right to be treated fairly and not to be subject to a stigmatizing form of discrimination. That is why race, religion, and ethnicity cannot be used as criteria of exclusion. So, to the extent that the choice of these medical conditions as grounds for exclusion reflects popular prejudice and uninformed fear rather than a reasonable calculation of the risks or burdens they entail, those excluded on this basis have good grounds to complain that they are not being treated fairly. Democratic states have a moral duty not to apply the criterion of exclusion on the basis of health risk in an arbitrary or prejudicial manner.

What about the general moral permissibility of the criterion, as opposed to its application to particular conditions? Like the criterion of financial dependency, the criterion of health risk is intended to protect those in the receiving society against costs that might flow from particular admissions decisions. Like inadmissibility because of financial need, inadmissibility because of health risk seems to me to be a policy that is ungenerous but not unjust, in the context of the presuppositions governing this chapter.

Criteria of Selection

Let me turn now to criteria of selection. Many seek to enter but few are chosen. What criteria do states use and what may they use in selecting these relative few? If we look at practice we see that states often use secondary family ties, ethnic ties, linguistic competence, and economic potential in selecting among potential immigrants.

Consider secondary family ties first. In the next section I will argue that there are some family relationships that give rise to a moral right to admission. I won't try to say yet what those relationships are, but by "secondary family ties" I mean family relationships that are not strong enough to justify a moral right to admission but ones that are not negligible either. Typical examples of secondary family ties that are sometimes used in admission decisions are adult siblings, grandparents, cousins, aunts and uncles, and nieces and nephews. Some states give no weight to these relationships in their admission policies, while others (like Canada) give them a little consideration, and still others (like the United States) give them quite a bit of emphasis.

In my view, all of these approaches are morally permissible. This is an area in which states are morally free to exercise their discretion. Current members of society do not have a vital enough interest in these secondary family ties for us to conclude that states have a moral obligation to admit such family members. On the other hand, a state may decide to allow these less intimate family connections to play a positive role in its admissions decisions perhaps on the grounds that it is easier for those with such connections to adjust to living in a new society or perhaps because the connections matter to people who are already members of the community or for some combination of these and other factors. The point is that states are morally free to take these relationships into account in the selection process if they choose to do so. They violate no norm of justice and no obligation to the pool of potential immigrants in doing so.

Let me pursue this a bit with a specific example. American immigration policy gives unusually heavy weight to secondary family ties. This has been criticized on a number of grounds. First, it has been objected that the emphasis on secondary family ties leads to a selection of immigrants who are less likely to succeed economically than would be the case if the selection process focused more directly on factors relevant to economic success, as in the Canadian system which gives only a little weight to such family ties and emphasizes instead factors like education, training, and knowledge of the official languages.[9] Whether Canada's selection process actually generates a pool of immigrants who are more likely to adapt successfully is a contested point in the empirical literature, and I have no views on this issue. It does not raise any issues of justice, however. Even if the American policy were inefficient or unwise from certain perspectives, that would not make it unjust.

A second objection is that the American use of secondary family ties as a criterion of selection disadvantages those who do not have relatives in the United States. It is analytically true that giving positive weight to any criterion disadvantages those who do not meet that criterion, at least in a context of scarcity. The question is whether that way of allocating advantages and disadvantages is unjust. In my earlier discussion of the use of health risk as a criterion of exclusion, I noted that it would be arbitrary, and thus unfair, to select certain health conditions for exclusion but not others with comparable risks. But the use of secondary family ties is not arbitrary. There are reasons for using this criterion. It rests on an understanding of what immigration admissions are best for the existing community and its members, and that understanding does not draw upon anything intrinsically objectionable like claims of racial superiority but rather on reasonable, if contestable, views of what sorts of immigrants are likely to fit in best with the existing community.

A third objection is a variant of the previous one. The objection is that the secondary family ties criterion is intended to reproduce the existing racial, ethnic,

and religious makeup of the population. It is disguised form of unjust discrimination. I do not find this criticism persuasive in the end, although it has more
merit than the previous two.

From the 1920s to the 1960s American immigration policy had a "national
origins" quota, which tied the number of spaces available for immigrants from
other countries to the proportion of people from those countries already in the
United States.[10] This was explicitly intended to restrict the flow of immigrants
from outside Europe and to maintain the ethnic, racial, and religious composition of the United States as it was. This was indeed an unjust policy. It is also true
that the replacement of this policy in the mid-1960s with one that abolished
overt forms of discrimination and introduced the system of secondary family
preferences was defended by its proponents on the grounds that it would per-
petuate the patterns of the old policy without employing their explicitly invidi-
ous categories. So, it may be right to condemn the intentions behind the policy
as unjust. The policy itself, however, did not work as intended because relatively
few people from Europe wanted to immigrate. So, the policy of secondary family
preferences gave rise to a pattern of chain migration in which the overwhelming
proportion of new immigrants to the United States during the past three decades
have come from Asia and Latin America. Indeed, this is precisely what those
who are opposed to the increasing ethnic and cultural diversity in the United
States object to in the current policy.[11] In this context, it is hard to maintain that
the policy should be seen as unjustly discriminating on the basis of race, ethnicity, and religion.

Some states actually use ethnicity as a criterion of selection for immigrants.[12]
It is important to distinguish here between ethnicity and secondary family ties.
Secondary family ties involve actual personal relationships by descent or marriage: aunts and uncles, nieces and nephews, cousins, and so on. By contrast, an
ethnic connection is something more distant, stretching back over generations
and involving no close link to any particular individual in the receiving country.
Potential immigrants with ethnic ties to the dominant group(s) in the receiving
society are given preference in selection, in part on the grounds that the existing population will find it easier to accept the arrival of this sort of immigrant,
in part on the assumption that immigrants from this sort of ethnic background
will have more in common culturally with most of the population of the receiving country than other immigrants would and will find it easier to adapt as a
result. Sometimes fellow ethnics are favored not only in the initial admission
decision but also in forms of social support and in access to citizenship.[13] In the
past, the United States and Canada had immigration policies favoring those with
ethnic ties, and Germany, Italy, Japan, and a number of other states still do today.
Indeed, it may be denied that fellow ethnics are really immigrants at all, as was
the case with Germany's *Aussiedler* policy for a long time.

In my view, the use of ethnicity as a basis for immigrant selection is deeply problematic. To give preferential treatment to people with a certain ethnic background is to establish that ethnic group as having a privileged position in relation to the political community as a whole. It implicitly calls into question the status of members of the society who come from other ethnic groups, all the more so when it is ethnicity alone that is the crucial factor. In Germany, for example, for many years people whose ancestors had left Germany hundreds of years before and who sometimes spoke no German themselves were accepted into Germany, given extensive social support and easy access to citizenship, while other people who had lived in Germany their entire lives (the descendants of Turkish "guestworkers") were effectively excluded from citizenship.[14] These policies were widely criticized both inside and outside Germany as being incompatible with democratic commitments, because they effectively identified the political community with an ethnic group.[15] As I argued in earlier chapters, any satisfactory conception of national identity in a contemporary democracy has to include all of those who are subject to the state's political authority over the long term and cannot create special access for those who share only an ethnic link but no substantive social ties to members of the dominant ethnic group.

The only possible justification for using ethnicity as a criterion for the selection of immigrants is that a particular ethnic identity may sometimes lead people to be subjected to bad treatment elsewhere in the world. In that respect, Germany's *Aussiedler* policy had a more plausible justification in decades past than it does today. In the period following World War II, people of German descent in Eastern Europe and the Soviet Union were the subject of discrimination and worse because of their German ethnicity. In that context, it may have been reasonable to give special preference to people of German descent seeking to immigrate to Germany from these areas. By the early 1990s, if not before, that had ceased to be a plausible rationale. German policy has now recognized this fact and has phased out this special admission track.

Another criterion that is sometimes used in the selection of immigrants is knowledge of the official language of a society. For example, Canada's system of selecting immigrants gives weight to knowledge of Canada's official languages, English and French.[16] The rationale behind this practice is that knowledge of the language used in the society will facilitate economic and social inclusion. This is a reasonable assumption, well supported by empirical evidence. Moreover, knowledge of English or French is something that anyone can acquire and is not a covert marker of racial or ethnic or religious identity. Of course, this criterion is an advantage for those who know the official language of the state into which they are trying to immigrate and a disadvantage for those who do not, but as we have seen before, there is no basis within conventional understandings of the state's moral responsibility for asserting that the state may not favor immigrants who will fit in more easily, so long as this is not based on prohibited grounds like race, ethnicity, or religion. So, I can see no reason for objecting to the use of linguistic competence as one factor in the selection of immigrants, at least within the normative framework of the conventional assumption.

Finally, another commonly used criterion of selection is the immigrant's potential economic contribution. For example, the Canadian immigration process assesses potential immigrants in a complex calculation that gives weight to a number of factors, many of which (e.g., age, education, work experience) are assumed to be indicators of the immigrant's potential for economic success in Canada. The United States also relies upon an assessment of economic potential in its selection of immigrants who do not have secondary family ties. A number of European countries that have traditionally not had any formal programs for recruiting immigrants have begun to consider recruitment of immigrants on this basis.

Like linguistic competence, economic potential is another criterion that seems morally permissible, at least as a general matter. To be sure, the receiving country is not acting altruistically in adopting this sort of immigration policy. It is selecting immigrants on the basis of its perception of the national interest. But since the country is morally free not to take any immigrants at all (from the pool we are considering here), the fact that it is guided by its own interest in its selection of some for admission cannot be a decisive objection. States are equally free to adopt a more generous policy, taking in those whom they judge to be in greatest need. That is an admirable course, but it is not morally obligatory.

One important objection to economic potential as a criterion of selection is that it is harmful to poor states when rich democratic states admit immigrants on the basis of what they can contribute economically. This is the familiar "brain drain" argument. The claim is that immigration to rich countries from poor ones involves a transfer of human resources to the detriment of people living in poor countries. This often involves the loss of actual economic investments in the form of scarce and costly expenditures on education and training, but the greatest cost is the loss of people with the capacity to contribute to the transformation of their country's condition.

In some sectors, the statistics on the brain drain are startling. In the late twentieth century, only fifty of the 600 doctors trained in Zambia since independence remained in the country. In 2001, 500 nurses left Ghana, more than twice those who graduated from nursing school in Ghana that year.[17]

I expect most readers to be troubled, as I am, by this picture of medical personnel who are desperately needed in their home countries leaving to serve people who live in rich countries and who are much better off. And the statistics on medical personnel are only the tip of the iceberg. Scientists, engineers, and other trained professionals often leave poor countries to settle in rich ones where the personal and professional opportunities are much better.[18] Do rich states have a responsibility not to contribute to this outflow of human capital? Is it wrong to use economic contribution as a criterion of admission?[19]

In thinking about this question, we should note first that there is a debate among economists about the actual consequences of the current migration patterns. Some scholars say that the movement of people with talents and skills from poor states to rich ones is much less harmful than often asserted, even in areas like medical care. Some even argue that it is beneficial, all things considered.[20]

This is an empirical question in an area where I can claim no expertise. Rather than rest my argument on one set of claims rather than another in a field that I am not equipped to judge, I suggest tracing the moral logic of the different claims.

If the more optimistic view of the consequences of migration is true, the brain drain objection loses its steam. It would be morally permissible to use economic contribution as a criterion of selection.

What if the problem is real and people in poor states are harmed by the outflow of their most talented and skilled? Assume further that the use of economic contribution as a criterion of selection in admissions policy contributes to this problem. Would it still be morally permissible for rich states to use that criterion in their admissions policies? Remember that rich states have no obligation to use this criterion, just as they have no obligation to admit immigrants at all (in the discretionary category we are considering).

One complication is that a fair amount of the migration of highly skilled professionals involves movement from one rich state to another (e.g., from Canada to the United States or vice versa) rather than from a poor state to a rich one. That sort of migration normally does not raise the same concerns about justice, but it would not be easy to permit that flow to continue while limiting the movement from poor states to rich ones. Using economic contribution as a criterion of selection for admission only in relation to people from other rich states would look a lot like a disguised form of prohibited discrimination, whatever its intent. Moreover, there are some people in rich states who would welcome that discriminatory effect.

Let's set that complication aside, however, and just ask whether the criterion of economic contribution is morally permissible, despite the fact that it has bad effects on poor states. One puzzle we face in thinking about this question is what the background views are against which we are to answer it. It seems a little odd to focus only on the question of immigration admissions in abstraction from everything else that affects poor states in their dealings with rich ones. Surely, the answer to the question of whether or not it is morally permissible to use economic contribution as a criterion of admission ultimately depends upon the nature and extent of the obligations of rich states to poor ones, and how immigration fits with other policies in an overall context.[21]

There are accounts of global justice that contend that rich states have extensive obligations to poor ones, and, above all, obligations to change policies that harm poor states.[22] These harmful policies involve many different areas besides immigration: environmental policies, monetary policies, and trade policies, to name just a few. I am quite sympathetic to these arguments about global justice, as will become clear in later chapters, but they are highly controversial views. As I said at the outset of the book, I want to conduct the analysis of the ethics of immigration in the first several chapters within the constraints of the conventional assumption about discretionary control over immigration and the related background assumption about the moral legitimacy of the state system, despite the vast economic inequalities between states. That conventional framework is the one that most people in democratic states accept, and it is important to see what principles we can (and cannot) derive from within it.

Within the constraints of the conventional assumption, I see no basis for asserting an obligation on rich states to adopt immigration policies that do not harm poor ones. As with other topics we have discussed in this chapter, the criterion of economic contribution may be ungenerous but it is not unjust, given the background assumptions. Remember that I am concerned here only with the requirements of justice. Rich states might recognize that their usual approach to the selection of immigrants has a negative effect on poor states and could voluntarily modify that approach in a number of ways, without being compelled to do so as a matter of justice.

If the conclusion that I have just drawn leaves readers frustrated with the constraints of the background assumptions, that is all to the good from my perspective. We are approaching the point when it will be possible to challenge those assumptions, and I would like readers to be motivated to do so. Still, we are not there yet. In the final section of this chapter, I want to show that there are some important moral claims that limit the discretion of the state over admissions, even within the confining constraints of the conventional assumption.

Obligatory Admissions

It is common to hear people say that states are (morally) free to exclude whomever they choose. In fact, however, all democratic states, even states that do not see themselves as countries of immigration, recognize moral obligations to admit noncitizens who are immediate members of the family of a current citizen or resident. Most democratic states even admit the immediate family members of noncitizens who do not have permanent resident status, so long as they are legally present for an extended period (e.g., as students, visiting professionals, or visiting workers).This is the principle of family reunification.[23]

Family reunification has created ongoing substantial flows of immigration even in states that would prefer not to receive immigrants. For example, while many states in Europe ceased recruiting guestworkers in the early 1970s and attempted to restrict other avenues of immigration, they continued to admit the spouses and minor children of those who were already there. Why? After all, the families could have been reunited if the guestworkers had gone home (as they were being encouraged to do). Moreover, the guestworkers (as the name implies) had been admitted only on a temporary basis. The expectation was that they would eventually go back. For the most part the policies permitting these new admissions were not perceived as economically advantageous to the receiving societies and the policies were not politically popular. States, which had demonstrated in their policy choices that they did not want more immigration, took in new immigrants, nevertheless, often in large numbers. Again, why? The answer is that the states felt a moral obligation to do so, an obligation that was sometimes acknowledged by government officials and sometimes pressed by court rulings about the implications of deep constitutional commitments.

So far I have just been making a descriptive point, namely that democratic states often act as though they have a moral obligation to permit family reunification, even when they do not think it is in their interest to do so. Consider now the evaluative question. What should we make of this self-imposed requirement to permit immediate family members to live together?[24] Does it make sense morally?

In responding to this question, we must keep in mind that family reunification is primarily about the moral claims of membership. The state's obligation to admit family members living elsewhere is derived not so much from the claims of those seeking to enter as the claims of those they seek to join: citizens or residents or others who have been admitted for an extended period.

In a world of vast inequalities, many people would like access to rich democratic states but relatively few obtain it. If we were simply comparing the relative moral urgency of claims put forward by outsiders seeking to join family members already inside with outsiders seeking to enter for other reasons (e.g., needy people seeking a chance at a better life), it is not obvious that the claims for family reunification would always be stronger. But I have deliberately set aside that line of inquiry in this chapter in assuming the basic right of the state to control entry. So, it is not a question here of a cosmopolitan challenge to the state's control over admissions but rather of the responsibilities of democratic states toward those whom they govern. Even if we assume that democratic states have very limited obligations toward outsiders, they do have an obligation to take the vital interests of their own members into account. The whole notion that individual rights set limits to what may be done in the name of the collective rests upon this supposition.

People have a deep and vital interest in being able to live with their immediate family members.[25] This is widely recognized in human rights documents and in the laws of democratic states. Why must this interest in family life be met by admitting the family members? Could it not be satisfied just as well by the departure of the family member(s) present to join those abroad (if the state where the other family members reside would permit this)? Why is the state obliged to shape its admissions policies to suit the locational preferences of individuals?

The answer to this question is that people also have a deep and vital interest in being able to continue living in a society where they settled and sunk roots. Of course, people sometimes have good reasons of their own to leave and sometimes face circumstances that require them to make painful choices. If two people from different countries fall in love, they cannot both live in their home countries and live together. So, people must be free to leave. But no one should be forced by the state to choose between home and family. Whatever the state's general interest in controlling immigration, that interest cannot plausibly be construed to require a complete ban on the admission of noncitizens and cannot normally be sufficient to justify restrictions on family reunification.

I add the qualifier "normally" because even basic rights are rarely absolute, and the right to family reunification cannot be conceived as absolute. Earlier in the chapter, I discussed the criteria that states could use to exclude potential immigrants. I argued that states could use evidence that someone was a threat to national security or had a past criminal record indicating a threat to social order as justifiable bases for excluding potential immigrants. Both of these concerns can also be serious enough to justify even the exclusion of an immediate family member from admission, although I think that the threshold for excludability should be raised in both cases. When it comes to financial need and health risks, however, I do not think that these provide sufficient reasons to prevent an immediate family member from immigrating, even though they are justifiable criteria of exclusion for most potential immigrants.

The case against excluding immediate family members because they do not possess criteria of selection is even stronger. Some states like the Netherlands have begun to require applicants for family reunification to pass tests of their knowledge of the official language and of the history and culture of the state they are seeking to enter as a condition for admission. These requirements are unjust. An immediate family member stands in a different relationship to the state from other potential immigrants. She has a specific and strong moral claim to admission that can only be overridden in extreme cases.

I am not claiming that knowledge of the state's official language and familiarity with its history and public culture are irrelevant to the successful inclusion of immigrants. On the contrary, as I said in chapter 4, immigrants have to adapt to the prevailing culture in many ways in order to meet their own needs. Both the immigrants and the wider community will be much better off if the immigrants learn the official language. But these considerations do not justify the creation of barriers to the entry of immediate family members. The right of human beings to live with their immediate family members imposes a moral limit on the state's right simply to set its admissions policy as it chooses. Some special justification is needed to override the claim to family reunification, not merely the usual calculation of state interests.

So far I have been treating the term *family* as though it were an unproblematic category, but the question of who should count as an immediate family member for purposes of family reunification varies in practice and can be contested at the level of principle. From a minimalist perspective, we can say that no matter how narrowly states define the category of family for admissions purposes, it clearly must include a spouse and minor children.

Why might we want to expand the definition of family beyond this highly conventional account? Perhaps because the conventional view of the family is too narrow. In my view, the issue of family reunification provides one more reason, among many others, why democratic states have a moral duty to provide the same opportunities for marriage between same sex partners as between heterosexual partners. Same sex partners have the same sorts of vital interest in being able to live together as heterosexual partners.[26] If the moral claims of heterosexual partners to live together should trump the normal claims of the state to control admissions, so should the claims of same sex partners.

More broadly, the issue of family reunification shows why it is impossible for the state not to be involved in the construction of the family.[27] Some people say that they do not understand why the state should have any role in regulating consensual intimate adult relationships. (Everyone recognizes that the state has to set rules regarding rights and responsibilities with regard to children.) The consensual view has its attractions, but the issue of family reunification reveals one of its limits. If we think that the state generally has the right to control admissions, but that this right of discretionary control is constrained by the moral right that members of society have to be able to live with their immediate family members, then we cannot avoid the question of who should count as an immediate family member and thus qualify for this exceptional immigration status.[28] It is certainly possible, and in my view desirable, to extend the concept of family beyond current conventional limits, for example, by counting long-term cohabiting relationships without formal marriage ties as constituting a family, but there will still have to be legal criteria and definitions. The criteria for family relationships that give rise to a legal right of family reunification cannot mirror the fluidity and variability of real relationships in the contemporary world.

The dominant model is clearly the nuclear family: parents and minor children. Children who have already grown to adulthood often do not qualify for family reunification, especially if they themselves have married, thus forming their own nuclear units. (As the father of two grown—though unmarried—sons, I have to say that I am troubled by this implicit picture of the family relationships that really matter.)

The focus on the nuclear family is clearly the product of a particular cultural tradition. As more immigrants arrive from different places, we cannot avoid questions about alternative conceptions of the family and of family responsibilities. In some traditions, adult children have strong responsibilities to care for their aging parents (a norm that seems more compelling to me today than it did forty years ago). Should democratic states permit citizens and residents to bring in their parents? Some states (but not all) do, and permission to do so becomes more likely if the parents are elderly or dependent or without other children outside the receiving country, despite the predictable economic costs associated with care for the elderly. On the other hand, this is usually regarded as an act of discretionary generosity by the state and is sometimes constrained by requirements to prove that the parents are not (yet) suffering from medical problems that will be expensive to treat.

So far as I know, no democratic state pays attention to cultural differences between groups that may affect the character of the relationship between adult children and their parents. In some cultures, relatives who are not the biological parents may have roles and responsibilities that are comparable to the ones normally undertaken by parents in Europe and North America. Should these relationships entitle them to bring in the children for whom they are responsible? Most states resist extending the rights of family reunification on the basis of distinctive cultural commitments, an approach that seems both understandable (because of concerns about opportunistic abuse and perceptions of fairness) and troubling.

There is a tension between an approach to the definition of family (for purposes of claiming a right to family reunification) that is fixed and relies on criteria from the dominant culture and an approach that is open to analogies, to cultural variability, and to functional equivalents. The merits of the alternative approaches are intimately connected to contemporary debates over multiculturalism, the neutrality of the state, and the moral relevance of minority cultures. In my view, it is too restrictive to say that the only understanding of the family that matters is the one held by the majority in the receiving state, but too expansive to say that the understanding of the family held by actual or potential immigrants is the only one that counts in assessing their claims to family reunification. I don't think there is an easy solution to this issue, and I don't have the space to pursue it in more detail.

As I noted above, democratic states do generally acknowledge the claims of family reunification, although some limit these claims or undermine them in ways that are morally problematic. For example, the United States gives a higher priority to citizens than to noncitizen residents with regard to the admission of spouses and minor children, and even sets a numerical limit on the number of noncitizen immediate family members who are permitted to come.[29] Given the importance of family reunification, I do not think that numerical limits on the entry of immediate family members of either citizens or residents are morally defensible. As I have argued in chapter 5, there is no justifiable basis for distinguishing between citizens and residents with respect to fundamental rights outside the realm of political participation. Family reunification is a fundamental right that all members of society should possess.

Often the obstacles to family reunification are not formal restrictions but administrative and procedural barriers. It is useful to draw attention to such limits as a reminder that a formally just policy may be deeply unjust in practice because of the way it is implemented. In Canada, for example, there are frequent complaints that people with spouses and children in some areas of the world (e.g., South Asia) have to wait years for permission for their family members to immigrate because there is a huge backlog of applications. States have a moral obligation not only to respect the right of family reunification in principle but also to develop administrative procedures that ensure that the right will be effective in practice.

Another example of an unjust obstacle to family reunification can be found in the ways that some states try to prevent the abuse of the right of family reunification. For many people in the world, admission to the states of Europe and North America is a scarce and valuable opportunity. Since the ways to obtain admission are limited, it is inevitable that some will try to take advantage of points of access to which they are not entitled. Some people enter sham marriages with citizens or residents with whom they neither have nor aspire to have any intimate connection, simply for the sake of gaining admittance.

Given the presupposition here that the state has the right to control immigration, the state is clearly entitled to take measures to prevent this form of fraud. It must do so within reason, however, and not as an excuse for denying entry to legitimate spouses. For example, until recently the United Kingdom pursued a policy of refusing admittance to people if the "primary purpose" of their marriage to a UK resident was to immigrate to the United Kingdom. It then put the burden of proof on those seeking family reunification to prove that immigration to the United Kingdom was not the purpose of the marriage, establishing a high standard that was difficult to meet.[30] As one commentator has noted, the upshot of this was that the right of family reunification in the United Kingdom was more secure for EU citizens who were not British (because their claims to family reunification were governed by EU law) than it was for the British themselves.[31] This sort of policy fails to respect the legitimate right of residents to family reunification. The claim that such a policy merely prevents fraudulent marriages undertaken for immigration purposes is a thin disguise for an attempt to prevent an immigration flow that is politically unpopular but grounded in claims of justice.

In a related vein, Denmark has adopted a rule denying family reunification to spouses under 24. The ostensible goal here is to prevent forced marriages of young women. That is certainly a legitimate objective, but it is not reasonable to consider all arranged marriages to be forced marriages, and not reasonable to deny all spouses under 24 the opportunity to live with their Danish partner in Denmark, simply to discourage forced marriages.[32] Again, this seems like a policy designed more to prevent a flow of unwanted immigrants than to achieve its stated goal, and it violates the moral right to family reunification.

Conclusion

Even if one accepts the widely accepted premise that states have a right to control immigration, there are still significant moral constraints on how that control may be exercised. In deciding whom to admit on a discretionary basis, states are morally obliged not to discriminate for or against applicants on the basis of such criteria as race, ethnicity, religion, and sexual orientation or to use criteria of exclusion like ideological views that conflict with democratic principles. Moreover, states are morally obliged to admit the immediate family (at least spouses and minor children) of people who are already citizens or established residents. These moral constraints are not merely a theorist's construction of the world as it ought to be. They are already widely, if imperfectly, reflected in the practices of most states in Europe and North America.

10

Refugees

Gustavo Gutierrez was a good cop, so good that he was used in public advertisements as a model for the Juárez police force: an honest officer whose only goal was to enforce the law. That is what got him in trouble. Drug gangs noticed the ads and offered him bribes. He refused. They threatened him and his family. The threats were credible since the gangs had killed dozens of police officers and justice officials in Juárez. Gutierrez quit his job and moved to another part of Mexico over 16 hours away, but he still did not feel safe. In 2008 he fled to Canada and asked for asylum. "I had a good life—house, car, relatives close by," he says. "I lost all of that. I'm glad I'm alive, but it's hard to start again."[1]

Should Canada admit Gustavo Gutierrez as a refugee? Should it send him back to Mexico? If he is sent back, he may be killed. If Canada admits him, is it obliged to take in the many thousands of other people threatened by violent drug gangs in Mexico, Jamaica, and other countries? What about others around the world facing threats to their lives and well-being? We have only to mention Bosnia, Sri Lanka, Rwanda, Iran, Iraq, Congo, Darfur, and Afghanistan to evoke some of the recent cases that have caused millions of people to flee their homes in a desperate effort to find safety. Do those of us who live in democratic states have a responsibility to admit these refugees if they want to find a new home in one of our communities? Are we justified in refusing them entry?

Refugees and the Holocaust

Contemporary reflection about refugees begins in the shadow of the Holocaust. In discussing the topic of refugees, we should remember one fundamental truth: Jews fleeing Hitler deserved protection, and most of them did not get it.

In July 1938, representatives from over thirty countries met in France to discuss how to respond to the refugees generated by Hitler's persecution of German Jews. Apart from the Dominican Republic, no state offered to take in more refugees. Some Jews were able to find an open door—leading intellectuals and scientists, people with financial resources or political connections, and a few other lucky ones. But many more were turned away.[2] In one famous case in 1939, Jewish refugees from Germany reached the shores of North America in a ship named the *St. Louis* and sought asylum. They were refused permission to land. The boat returned to Europe and many of its passengers perished in the Holocaust.[3]

Some may object that no refugee situation today compares with Hitler's Germany. There is a lot of truth in that, but we should be wary of taking easy comfort in such a view, imagining that we would never act as our predecessors did. If one looks at the responses to Jewish refugees in the late 1930s, it is striking how many echoes one hears of contemporary concerns and attitudes. Remember that, at this time, the death camps had not yet been built, and the Nazi regime had not yet committed itself to the Final Solution. Everyone knew that Jews were suffering but there were differing perceptions about the extent of their oppression. Some of those opposed to admitting Jewish refugees were overtly anti-Semitic but many people took a view that went more like this:

> What is happening to the Jews is too bad, but it's not our fault. We have our own problems. If we take in all the Jews who want to come, we will be overwhelmed. There are simply too many of them. Besides, while Jews may be subject to discrimination and occasional acts of violence, things are not as bad as their advocacy groups say. They exaggerate the problem. Many of the Jews really just want better economic opportunities than they have now at home. In fact, the ones who do manage to make it to North America to seek asylum cannot be among the worst off because they have enough economic resources to cross the Atlantic. Times are tough here. We have an obligation to look out for our own needy first. A large influx of Jews could be a cultural and political threat. They don't share our religious traditions or our democratic values. Some of them are communists and pose a basic security threat, but it's hard to be sure which ones, so it's better to err on the side of caution in restricting entry. Many of them have shown that they don't really respect the law because they have bribed officials abroad for exit permits and travel papers, they have purchased forged documents, they have hired smugglers to transport them illegally, and they have lied to our immigration officials. Finally, admitting Jewish refugees serves the Nazis' own goals and does not help to address the underlying problems that have given rise to the Nazi phenomenon.

In some respects, many of the concerns about Jewish refugees then were as reasonable as the concerns about asylum seekers are today. There was debate and uncertainty about the extent of the risks faced by Jews in Hitler's Germany even during the late 1930s. Those who were able to travel to North America were economically better off on average. Some Jews were communists. Some did bribe officials and use forged documents and hire smugglers in order to escape. Not all of the people who were turned away died in the Holocaust. The potential number of refugees was very large. Admitting Jewish refugees would not have solved the problem of the Nazis. Yet despite all of these facts, I take it to be incontestable that the response of democratic states to Jewish refugees during the 1930s was a profound moral failure, something that we should acknowledge as a shameful moment of our histories and resolve never to repeat.

We often gain our most important moral insights not from theory but from experience. As Rawls says, we have "considered convictions of justice" that we should use as a way of testing and criticizing our theoretical accounts.[4] I propose to use this terrible failure to accept Jewish refugees as a constraint upon our inquiry into the ethics of admitting refugees. Whatever principles or approaches we propose, we should always ask ourselves at some point, "What would this have meant if we had applied it to Jews fleeing Hitler?" And no answer will be acceptable if, when applied to the past, it would lead to the conclusion that it was justifiable to deny safe haven to Jews trying to escape the Nazis. This approach will not settle every question about refugees that we have to consider, but it will give us a minimum standard, one fixed point on our moral compass.

Refugees and Immigration: Framing the Inquiry

I approach the topic of refugees from the limited perspective of my concern with immigration into democratic states. This is only one of many normative issues raised by refugees, but I address these wider issues only to the extent necessary to address my more limited concerns.[5]

In this chapter, I will work within the familiar constraints of the conventional assumption about the right of democratic states to exercise discretionary control over immigration. This might seem surprising at first glance, but the idea that refugees have special moral claims to admission implicitly assumes the conventional view. It treats the obligation of states to admit refugees as an exception to the general rule that states are free to control entry and settlement.[6] This is not an unusual approach. Even those who most strongly defend the moral right of states to exercise discretionary control over admissions usually say that democratic states have a duty to accept at least some refugees.[7]

Treating the claims of refugees as a special case makes sense only if we presuppose that most people in the world cannot advance such claims. Some would object to that premise, arguing that the vast economic and political differences between states provide legitimate reasons for people from poor, authoritarian states to move to rich, democratic ones. I will consider that line of argument in the next chapter. In this one, however, I want to accept, as a premise, that what one might call the "ordinary inequalities of the modern world" do not give rise to a moral claim to admission as a refugee.

The Duty to Admit Refugees

Why should democratic states take in refugees at all? There are at least three kinds of reasons that can generate a duty to admit refugees: causal connection, humanitarian concern, and the normative presuppositions of the state system.[8]

The first rationale is causal connection. Sometimes we have an obligation to admit refugees because the actions of our own state have contributed in some way to the fact that the refugees are no longer safe in their home country.[9] Americans—whether supporters or opponents of the war—recognized this in the wake of the Vietnam War and took in hundreds of thousands of refugees from Vietnam, Cambodia, and Laos. The United States has the same sort of obligation toward Afghan and Iraqi refugees, especially those forced to flee because their lives were put in danger as a result of their cooperation with American troops, but, by comparison with the response to Vietnam, the country has done comparatively little to meet this responsibility so far.

We should already be starting to think about environmental refugees—people forced to flee their homes because of global warming and the resulting changes in the physical environment. One argument is that the rich democratic states bear a major responsibility for these environmental changes and so have a duty to admit the people who are forced to leave their home states because of these changes. Of course, there are counter arguments, as there are in the wider debate about how to allocate the costs of responding to climate change.

The general point is simply that causal connections can generate moral duties. I will not attempt an assessment of the competing accounts of the causes of refugee flows in this book.[10] That is beyond my competence. Obviously, the assignment of moral responsibility on the basis of causal connections will depend crucially on the interpretation of those causal connections.[11]

A second source of the duty to admit refugees is humanitarian concern. We have a duty to admit refugees simply because they have an urgent need for a safe place to live and we are in a position to provide it. This sort of moral view has many different sources, secular and religious. I won't try to identify those sources here. It is enough to note that they exist and that they converge here on a sense of obligation to help people in dire need.[12] When I advanced my claims at the outset about our obligations to Jewish refugees, I was appealing intuitively to this overlapping consensus, to a shared sense, with many different foundations, that we ought to have opened our doors to these refugees.

A third way to think about the duty to admit refugees is to see it as something that emerges from the normative presuppositions of the modern state system. The modern state system organizes the world so that all of the inhabited land is divided up among (putatively) sovereign states who possess exclusive authority over what goes on within the territories they govern, including the right to control and limit entry to their territories. Almost all human beings are assigned to one, and normally only one, of these states at birth. Defenders of the state system argue that human beings are better off under this arrangement than they would be under any feasible alternative. There are ways of challenging that view, and I will consider some of them in the next chapter. For the moment, however, let's assume that it is correct.

Even if being assigned to a particular sovereign state works well for most people, it clearly does not work well for refugees. Their state has failed them, either deliberately or though its incapacity. Because the state system assigns people to states, states collectively have a responsibility to help those for whom this assignment is disastrous. The duty to admit refugees can thus be seen as an obligation that emerges from the responsibility to make some provision to correct for the foreseeable failures of a social institution. Every social institution will generate problems of one sort or another, but one of the responsibilities we have in constructing an institution is to anticipate the ways in which it might fail and to build in solutions for those failures. If people flee from the state of their birth (or citizenship) because it fails to provide them with a place where they can live safely, then other states have a duty to provide a safe haven. Thus, we can see that states have a duty to admit refugees that derives from their own claim to exercise power legitimately in a world divided into states.

These three rationales are complementary. All three can be relevant at the same time, and any one of them is sufficient to create at least a prima facie duty to admit refugees.

Four Sets of Questions

Given this general sense that there is some duty to admit refugees, how can we clarify the nature and extent of that duty for democratic states? Refugees raise four basic kinds of questions for the ethics of immigration. First, who should be considered a refugee? For the purposes of my inquiry, a refugee is someone whose situation generates a strong moral claim to admission to a state in which she is not a citizen, despite the absence of any morally significant personal tie to those living there (as in family reunification). What gives rise to this sort of moral claim?

Second, what is owed to refugees? At a minimum, refugees need a place where they can be safe, but do they have a moral claim to more than that? Should they receive an opportunity to build a new life—jobs, education for their children, and so on? Are they entitled to a permanent new home rather than just a temporary shelter?

Third, how should responsibilities for refugees be allocated among different states? In particular, what is the nature and extent of the obligation of democratic states to admit refugees? This is the most crucial question from the perspective of this book.

Finally, are there limits to our obligations to refugees and, if so, what are they? Is there some point at which a democratic state is morally entitled to say to refugees: "We know that you face genuine and dire threats, but we have done enough. You are not our responsibility. We leave you to your fate."

The Current Refugee Regime

In exploring these questions, I proceed, as usual, through critical reflection upon current practices, beginning with a brief description of how things work now. Democratic states admit refugees in two ways today: resettlement and asylum.

Resettlement

Resettlement occurs when a state selects refugees who have found a safe haven elsewhere, usually under UN auspices, and offers them a permanent new home. Most of the states with significant resettlement programs (the United States, Canada, and Australia) are traditional immigration countries. (Sweden is an important exception to this pattern.)

For the purposes of this chapter, two things matter most about resettlement as it is currently practiced. First, the overall number of those resettled is very small relative to the needs of refugees. For example, in 2011, the UN High Commissioner for Refugees (UNHCR) had over ten million refugees under its care, over half of whom had been in exile for several years or more, but there were only about 80,000 places available for resettlement.[13] So, resettlement currently helps some refugees but is irrelevant to most.

Second, there is no generally recognized obligation to take in refugees for resettlement. States who accept refugees for resettlement may be seen as generous, but those who refuse to do so violate no generally acknowledged norm. For that reason, resettlement, as currently practiced, is not seen as a moral duty that constrains the state's discretionary control over immigration. I add the qualifier "as currently practiced" because I will argue in this chapter that we should see resettlement as a strong and extensive moral duty.

Asylum

The second way in which democratic states admit refugees is by granting them asylum. Asylum is far more significant and far more controversial than resettlement as a way of admitting refugees to democratic states.

Like Gustavo Gutierrez whose story opened this chapter, some people arrive in democratic states and ask to be allowed to stay there on the grounds that they are refugees. Under the Geneva Convention on Refugees, states may not return refugees to their state of origin or send them to any other state in which their lives or liberties would be threatened. This is the principle of non-refoulement. The Convention was originally adopted in 1951, but it applied then only to refugees in Europe whose plight was due to events prior to its adoption. In 1967, however, a Protocol was adopted that removed these geographical and temporal limits, making it a universal and ongoing commitment to assist refugees. Over one hundred states have signed the Convention including all democratic states in Europe and North America. The refugee regime created by the Geneva Convention establishes the normative principles that democratic states currently acknowledge as defining their responsibilities to refugees.

Every signatory state must pass legislation to make the Geneva Convention applicable within its own legal system. In principle, every person who arrives in a state and claims to be a refugee is supposed to be given a fair hearing to determine whether or not her claim is valid. If a state accepts the claim, it is obliged, roughly speaking, to grant the refugee asylum and to provide her with a fairly extensive package of legal rights.[14]

During the first decade or so after the 1967 Protocol was adopted, relatively few people came to affluent democratic states as asylum seekers, in part because communist countries restricted emigration and in part because there were relatively few claimants from the developing world. During the 1980s this changed rapidly. Requests for asylum grew dramatically in the industrialized states, from several thousand per year in the 1970s to a few hundred thousand in the early1980s, then to several hundred thousand in the late 1980s, peaking at over 850,000 in 1992. Although the breakup of the former Yugoslavia generated a significant portion of the refugee claimants in the late 1980s and early 1990s, hundreds of thousands of others came from all over the world. Rich democratic states began to fear that they would face a continually growing number of claimants as changes in transportation and communication made it possible for more people from Asia, Africa, and Latin America to seek refuge in Europe and North America. They also worried that many people from poor states had come to view asylum claims as a way to bypass normal immigration controls and gain temporary entry, with the hope of finding some way to stay on, even if they did not qualify as refugees under the Convention.

In response to these concerns, every state in Europe and North America adopted policies to prevent people from arriving and claiming refugee status. The most important technique was to impose more stringent visa controls on states whose citizens seemed likely to ask for asylum after arrival. To get a visa, people were required to provide supporting documentation about their lives that would convince immigration officials that they would want to return home and so would be unlikely to file a claim for asylum.[15] To enforce compliance with these visa restrictions, airlines and other carriers were subjected to heavy fines for transporting people without proper documentation. In addition, states adopted other policies to restrict the filing of asylum claims. One important tactic was to insist that any asylum claim must be filed in the first safe state in which an applicant arrived after leaving her home country. This had the effect of limiting claims in the rich democratic states, since refugee claimants usually travel over land and most refugee-generating states do not border Western Europe or the United States.[16] Some states declared the arrival area of their airports or other border entry points not to be part of their territory for purposes of asylum. This (legally problematic) move enabled them to assert that they were not violating their obligations under the Geneva Convention if they sent travelers back without a proper hearing to the state from which they had just arrived even if the travelers claimed to be refugees. In some cases, boats carrying potential refugees were interdicted at sea.[17]

As measures to reduce the number of asylum applicants, these techniques of exclusion were fairly effective. They stopped the exponential growth of claims and reduced the annual average to about 400,000 a year in the rich countries, a level that is well above what it was in the 1970s and early 1980s but also well below the peak years.

How does the current refugee regime answer the four questions that I posed above and what should we think of these answers?

Defining Who Is a Refugee

The Geneva Convention answers the question "who should be considered a refugee" by defining a refugee as any person who

> owing to a well-founded fear of being persecuted for reasons of race, religion, nationality, membership of a particular social group or political opinion, is outside the country of his nationality and is unable or,

owing to such fear, is unwilling to avail himself of the protection of that country; or who, not having a nationality and being outside the country of his former habitual residence, is unable or, owing to such fear, is unwilling to return to it.[18]

As with all legal definitions, each of its terms ("well-founded," "persecution," "membership of a social group") must be interpreted and then applied to particular cases.

People seeking asylum in democratic states often meet a skeptical and critical inquiry into the question of whether they are really refugees. Every democratic state has established a set of laws and institutions to determine whether particular asylum claimants meet the requirements of the Convention. The use of the term "persecution" is clearly intended in part to recognize the principle that we should not lightly override the normal rule that states are free to exercise discretionary control over entry and settlement by noncitizens. Given the premises of this chapter, that is a reasonable concern. No state is perfect. The ordinary failures of law enforcement, like the ordinary inequalities of the modern world, do not provide grounds for giving someone refugee status.[19] To deserve refugee status a person must be facing a serious threat to her fundamental interests, not simply the risks faced in ordinary life in a society that normally protects people's basic human rights.

There is some variation in the ways that democratic states interpret and apply the Convention definition. What should it take to establish that one qualifies as a refugee under this definition? Would being a Jew in Germany during the late 1930s be enough or should one have to show that one had been personally subjected to violence or threats by agents of the state? From my perspective, the former should clearly be sufficient, but some states interpret the Convention as requiring something like the latter. What about being a black in apartheid South Africa? Should that have been enough to qualify someone who escaped from South Africa as a refugee or should that person have been required to prove something more, such as that she had expressed anti-apartheid views and been punished or threatened as a result? Again, I take the former view.

As these examples suggest, I think the right approach is one that takes a more flexible and expansive reading of the Convention's requirements. Some democratic states have taken this sort of approach. For example, some states have accepted women fleeing domestic violence as refugees on the grounds that the state from which they were fleeing did not take this threat seriously and this amounted to persecution on the basis of gender.[20] Even on the most expansive interpretation of the Convention, however, people fleeing civil wars and famine are generally not thought to qualify, because they are not targets of violence or deprivation, despite the fact that their lives are in danger. On the other hand, someone who seeks asylum because she was thrown in jail for a few weeks for expressing political views would normally qualify as a refugee under the Convention.

In my view, this discrepancy reveals that the Convention embodies a misplaced set of priorities. To insist that a refugee must be deliberately targeted is a mistake. From a moral perspective, what is most important is the severity of the threat to basic human rights and the degree of risk rather than the source or character of the threat. Some regional associations of states and many scholars have endorsed the idea of adopting a more expansive definition of who is a refugee.[21]

UNHCR adopts just such an expansive definition in interpreting its mandate to protect refugees. I noted above that UNHCR was responsible for over ten million refugees in 2011.[22] Not all of these people would qualify as refugees under the Convention definition, but UNHCR also

> recognizes as refugees persons who are outside their country of nationality or habitual residence and unable to return there owing to serious and indiscriminate threats to life, physical integrity or freedom resulting from generalized violence or events seriously disturbing public order.[23]

There is normally not much worry that people under the care of UNHCR are taking advantage of the refugee regime simply to gain access to another country. Most of these are people living in states next to their country of citizenship, often in refugee camps. Very few people pretend to be refugees in order to gain the opportunity to live in a refugee camp.

Note that even an expansive definition like the one used by UNHCR falls well short of treating the "ordinary inequalities of the modern world" as giving rise to a claim to be a refugee. Nevertheless, most democratic states have resisted this sort of expansion. Some object that if we were to define "refugee" this broadly for purposes of asylum, too many people would qualify as refugees. Then democratic states would no longer be willing to support the refugee regime and it would collapse.[24]

It is certainly appropriate to worry about feasibility, especially if one is making recommendations for action. We should not push to change the official definition of "refugee" if we think that will create a backlash that will lead to less actual protection for refugees. Nevertheless, in an academic inquiry like this one, it is important to get clear first about what we think is right in principle before moving to the question of what we should do in practice. If one moves too quickly to the question of feasibility, one risks confusing elements of analysis that should be kept distinct. In thinking about how to define the category of refugee, we should focus above all on the seriousness of the moral claim that is being advanced in an effort to overcome the normal rule about the state's right to exercise discretionary authority over immigration. The seriousness of the claim is not affected, at the level of principle, by the number of claimants.[25]

One common way to try to find a principled basis for limiting the number of people who might qualify as refugees is to say that refugee status should be reserved for those who can only be helped through relocation. Those who can be helped where they are should not be considered refugees.[26] In my view, this approach implicitly confuses two distinct sorts of questions. The first is "What is the best solution to a particular problem?" The second is "Should a person who has fled because of this problem be granted asylum as a refugee?"

It is certainly true that expanding the refugee regime would not do much to solve problems like global poverty, civil war, or ethnic conflict. We can normally do more to assist people suffering from deprivations of their basic human rights by improving the situation where they are rather than by enabling them to move somewhere else, and that is what we should do. Human beings need physical security, peace, food, shelter, medicine, education, and economic opportunities. It is normally better for everyone if they can satisfy these needs in their home states, rather than by finding a new home in another country. But the question we are faced with when someone arrives seeking asylum is not what is the best way to address these broad problems but rather whether this particular person deserves to be considered a refugee with a right to start a new life in our state or whether we should send her back to her home state.[27]

Think again of Gustavo Gutierrez. The best solution to the problem that has forced him to flee would be for the Mexican state to succeed in asserting its authority so that the drug gangs were no longer in position to threaten the lives of police officers on a routine basis. That is clearly the solution that Gutierrez himself would prefer. As he says, he did not want to leave Mexico. He had a good life there. But while that is a preferable solution, it is not one that is actually on offer. The choice that Canada faces is whether to grant Gutierrez asylum or whether to send him back under circumstances in which his life will be in grave danger.

Some may object that granting people asylum will undermine local resistance to injustice and oppression by giving people an easy way out. But that sort of objection understates the costs of leaving (as Gutierrez's story reminds us) and overstates what it is reasonable to ask people to bear in an effort to bring about change. We can admire those who risk torture and death for the sake of freedom and justice but we should not require it of anyone.

Consider another case. In the Congo over the past decade five million more people have died than we would normally expect and several hundred thousand women have been raped.[28] These terrible ills have been produced by the collapse of any stable political order and by a series of ongoing, mutating civil conflicts linked in part to external actors and interests. The international community has been unable or unwilling to find a solution to the humanitarian disaster there. If one were to ask what other states should do to protect the basic human rights of the inhabitants of the Congo, no one would suggest that the best course would be to move tens of millions of Congolese to other states. To recognize people fleeing the Congo as refugees will do little or nothing to solve the underlying problems or to improve the situation of those who remain. Nevertheless, we do have to decide how to respond to those who escape.

Suppose that some Congolese women make their way out of the Congo and into a neighboring state. No one doubts that UNHCR should provide them with assistance, shelter, and a safe haven. But suppose that instead of reaching a neighboring state, they made their way onto a plane that took them to a democratic state in Europe or North America. Should they be given an opportunity to stay in that state or should they be sent back to the Congo where they would be in danger of being raped or killed or starved to death? I think the answer to that question is just as obvious, and that is the kind of question we have to answer in deciding who is a refugee. The fact that protecting these few women will not solve the underlying problem in the Congo is irrelevant. As I noted at the outset in discussing the case of Jewish refugees, protecting refugees almost never solves the underlying problem that has given rise to their flight. But that is not a reason to refuse them refuge. The question of whether or not some person deserves to be considered a refugee is distinct from the question of what is the best solution for a larger problem.

What Is Owed to Refugees?

In thinking about the second question, what is owed to refugees, we have to distinguish between the immediate aftermath of flight and the longer term. The existing refugee regime reflects such a distinction in practice. The first priority is to secure the safety of the refugees and to protect their basic human rights. For these purposes, emergency arrangements such as refugee camps are often appropriate. But this is not sufficient as a permanent solution. In the long run, if refugees are unable to return home safely, they need a new home.

The Convention adopts this approach. It asserts that, in principle, people who are recognized as refugees and who cannot return safely to their country of origin within a reasonable time should be given a new home and an opportunity to make a new life on the same terms as the members of the society they have joined. In effect, the Convention says that it is not enough to provide refugees with physical safety. People have a right to membership in a society. If they cannot any longer be members of their country of origin, they must be given access to membership in some other state.

The idea of a right to membership implicitly accepts the principle that rights are relative to the regime. A refugee who settles in a poor state will have many fewer rights and opportunities than one who settles in a rich one, even if both are treated as full members of the society where they have settled. Given the premises of this chapter, these differences are not unjust. As I noted at the outset, we are presupposing in this chapter that the ordinary inequalities of the modern world do not give rise to a right to refugee status with its moral claim to entry to a new society. Refugees are treated fairly (except by their country of origin) so long as they enjoy safety, protection of their basic human rights, and the same rights as other members of the society where they live.

The idea that refugees have a moral right to membership in some society is distinct from the arguments about social membership advanced in Part I of this book. The arguments about social membership become relevant, however, once refugees have been admitted and have settled in a new society. The Convention's approach fits well with the arguments I advanced in earlier chapters about the rights that democratic states ought to grant to those whom it admits and about the ways in which membership claims grow over time. Refugees normally have no membership claims in their new state at the outset, but they acquire them over time. Moreover, a democratic state cannot legitimately try to keep people from becoming members by isolating them from others in society. A rich democratic state cannot create camps where refugees are prevented from having contact with the rest of the population and are provided only with basic levels of food, clothing, and shelter, even if the provision of such basic levels of support would be equal to what the refugees could have expected if their membership rights had been respected in their country of origin. If a democratic state admits refugees, it must provide the refugees with most of the rights that others living in the society enjoy. Over time, it must accept them as members.

One implication of this idea of a right to membership is that there is a limit to how long refugees can be kept in a temporary status. The basic justification for granting someone admission as a refugee is that it is not safe for her to go home. Sometimes circumstances change, and an unsafe situation becomes safe. That removes the original justification for granting the refugee entry. If this transformation takes place relatively soon after the refugee's arrival, it may be reasonable to expect the refugee to return home.[29] But over time, that changes. When the communist regimes in Eastern Europe collapsed and those states adopted democratic institutions, it would not have been reasonable to expect all those who had fled over previous decades to return home just because it was now safe to do so. As is the case with immigrants admitted on a temporary basis, refugees become members over time. Within a few years at most, what happens in their country of origin should become irrelevant to the question of whether refugees have a right to remain in the place where they have started a new life. If things become better in their country of origin and they want to go home, they should be free to do so. But no one should force them to leave.

I have been focusing so far on people recognized as refugees. Not all of those who arrive as asylum claimants gain such recognition. Indeed in most democratic states, the majority of asylum claimants do not. What then?

In principle, if people don't qualify as refugees, they have no basis for a moral claim to stay. After all, we are presupposing the moral legitimacy of the state's discretionary control over immigration and are only considering here how that might be constrained by a duty to admit refugees.

In practice, this greatly oversimplifies the issue, in part because restrictive interpretations of the Convention can generate moral complications. Democratic states often determine that an asylum claimant does not qualify for refugee status under the Convention, because she does not meet all of its formal requirements, but also that she cannot be returned to her country of origin because she would face serious threats to her life or freedom if she were sent back. The principle of non-refoulement sets a much broader constraint on the ability of democratic states to return people to their home countries than the principle that states should grant asylum to people recognized as refugees under the Convention.

Most democratic states have some sort of quasi-refugee status that they grant to people from countries with high levels of internal armed conflict or countries devastated by a natural disaster. In that sense, they often implicitly endorse the UNHCR's more expansive definition of who is a refugee. These people don't qualify for refugee status under the Geneva Convention, but it is not safe for them to go home. In such cases, people are permitted to remain but often with fewer rights than those officially recognized as refugees. From a normative perspective, we can see that one function of this sort of alternative refugee status is to compensate for the limitations of an overly restrictive formal definition of who is a refugee under the Convention.

Leave aside the legal technicalities for a moment. From a normative perspective, it is the non-refoulement constraint that matters morally. Whenever a state acknowledges that it would be wrong to send someone back to her home country, it is implicitly recognizing that person as a refugee in my sense of the term, that is, someone whose situation generates a strong moral claim to admission (or continuing presence in) a state in which she is not a citizen, despite the absence of any morally significant personal tie to those living there. As with recognized refugees, those who are allowed to stay under one of these more restrictive designations become members over time and should be recognized as such.

Sometimes states indicate that those permitted to stay on some basis other than the Convention's definition are being allowed to remain only on a temporary basis. In the United States, for example, one alternative to formal refugee status is actually called "temporary protected status." But the arguments advanced above about the moral relevance of the passage of time apply just as much to people who have a real need for refuge that does not meet the Convention definition as it does to people who do qualify as refugees under the Convention. If we let them stay long enough, they become members and should be allowed to remain. No one should be expected to live in limbo indefinitely.

Allocating Responsibilities for Refugees

I have been discussing what democratic states owe to the refugees whom they admit, but most refugees do not seek asylum in rich democratic states or get resettled there. They flee to states near their country of origin. They often wind up in refugee camps. Some are able to gain some sort of membership status in the state to which they have fled, but most cannot. Many stay in the refugee camps for years. This clearly represents a terrible failure to meet the moral claims of refugees. So, one of the questions we have to consider is whether democratic states ought to admit more refugees.

What is the nature and extent of the obligation of democratic states to admit refugees? That is the crucial question for this book, but we can address that question effectively only in the context of a broader discussion of how responsibility for refugees should be assigned.

Let's start again with the way the current refugee regime assigns responsibility to take in refugees. As we have seen, it imposes no duty on states to accept refugees for resettlement. The principle of non-refoulement, however, forbids a state from sending refugees back to their country of origin so long as they would be at risk there or to any other state where they are likely to face persecution. Thus, the current regime places the obligation to care for a refugee on the state where the refugee first arrives and claims asylum.[30] That state remains responsible for the refugee, unless it can find another state that is willing to take her in for resettlement.

Is there a moral logic behind this way of assigning responsibility for refugees? I think there is. In my view, the non-refoulement principle is an indispensable element in any just refugee regime, though, as we shall see, it is not a sufficient principle by itself and it generates certain problems.

The Moral Logic of Non-refoulement

One crucial background presupposition of the current refugee regime is the principle of state sovereignty. As we saw in chapter 6, the principle of state sovereignty entails that states are normally responsible for what goes on in their own territory and not responsible, or at least not nearly as responsible, for what goes on in the territory of other states. From this perspective, it is precisely the fact that a person seeking asylum has made it to our territory that matters morally. Her physical presence creates a degree of moral responsibility that did not previously exist. The arrival of the refugees implicates us directly and immediately in their fate. They will no longer be at great risk, if we do not return them.[31]

Given the principle of state sovereignty, the Convention is right to insist that every state has a special responsibility to make sure that no one within its jurisdiction is sent to a place (including her home country) where she will be at great risk. This does not mean that non-refoulement is adequate as the sole basis for allocating the responsibility to care for refugees, but it does set a constraint upon the morally acceptable alternatives.

What are the problems with non-refoulement? The most obvious objection is that it does not assign the responsibility to take in refugees on the basis of equitable principles but instead allows the allocation of refugee admissions to be determined by where people seek asylum. This clearly has the potential to create disproportionate burdens if the refugees cluster their asylum requests on a relatively few states. Some states may be expected to take in more than their fair share. We find concerns expressed about excessive burdens for two sorts of states: neighboring poor ones and distant rich democratic ones.

Disproportionate Burdens and Neighboring States

Let's start with the former. As an empirical matter, we know that the vast majority of refugees flee to neighboring states simply because that is the easiest way to escape. This means that relatively poor states are being expected to bear the burden of accommodating large numbers of refugees in addition to dealing with their own problems. Is that fair?

No, although to a certain extent it may be unavoidable, and it makes moral sense in some respects to expect nearby states to bear a disproportionate share of the responsibilities of sheltering refugees in the short run. First, the neighboring states are the only ones that most refugees are able to reach immediately. Second, other things being equal, having refugees stay nearby (at first) increases the likelihood that they will be able to return home.

The underlying normative assumption of the modern international order is that a person should be living in a state where she is a citizen, unless some other state invites her in. So, the first and strongest moral claim that refugees have is against their home state. That state has a duty to change its policies or to get its affairs in order so as to make it possible for the refugees to return home and to live there free from fear of persecution.

That does happen sometimes. A crisis breaks out and people flee but within six months or a year, things settle down. They are able to return home, and they do. Repatriation is always the preferred solution of the United Nations and of other states, so long as the refugees can return home safely. As a general rule, it is easier for refugees to return home if they have not gone too far away.

Thus, the moral justification for expecting nearby states to bear a disproportionate share of refugee admissions is twofold. First, refugees are most likely to flee to a neighboring state, and this triggers the state's responsibility not to return the refugees to a place where they will be at great risk. Second, repatriation is the morally preferable solution and the likelihood of repatriation is increased if refugees settle nearby, at least initially.

This justification is limited in two ways, however. First, the underlying moral responsibility for refugees falls upon the international state system as a whole, since the problem of refugees is a byproduct of this way of organizing the world politically. While neighboring states can reasonably be expected to bear a disproportionate share of the burden of providing refugees with an initial place to stay, it is not reasonable to expect them to bear a disproportionate share of the economic costs of caring for refugees. Indeed, their provision of territorial shelter should arguably free them from any expectations of further contributions. The economic costs of caring for refugees should be borne by other states or international organizations.

Second, the fact that a state has a moral responsibility not to return a refugee who has arrived on its territory back to a dangerous situation does not mean that it should be the one to provide that refugee with a new home. The contemporary refugee regime lumps these two responsibilities together (except for voluntary resettlement), but as we shall see, there are good reasons in principle for separating them. Furthermore, even though geographical proximity is quite relevant to the question of what state should provide a temporary shelter for refugees, it is not as relevant to the question of what state should provide a new home to refugees who have no reasonable prospect of returning to their country of origin in the near term. As the likelihood of repatriation diminishes, the moral case for keeping the refugees nearby also weakens. Thus, while it may be reasonable to expect neighboring states to bear a disproportionate share of the responsibility for admitting refugees in the short run, it is unjust to extend that disproportionate expectation to the long run. Leaving non-refoulement as the only normative principle governing the allocation of refugee admissions does precisely that. That is why relying on non-refoulement alone is unfair to the neighboring states.

Disproportionate Burdens and Rich Democratic States

Turn now to the second concern. Why might the principle of non-refoulement create disproportionate burdens for rich democratic states? For two reasons, the first involving refugees and the second involving asylum claimants who do not qualify as refugees.

Too Many Genuine Refugees?

First, refugees might reasonably say to themselves that if they have to start life over somewhere new it would be better to do so in a place with more long-term opportunities for themselves and especially for their children. Many refugees would not have the resources to act upon this sort of calculation, but the principle of non-refoulement creates incentives for refugees to seek asylum in a rich democratic state rather than somewhere else. If enough did so, it would mean that rich democratic states would be asked to admit more than their fair share of refugees (at least if we assume that a fair distribution would have some basis other than relative wealth and the refugees' own preferences for determining where refugees should go).

I use the hypothetical tense in my discussion of this issue because in my view this concern about rich democratic states being unfairly burdened with too many refugees is only a potential problem rather than an actual one (in contrast to the actual burden borne by neighboring states who clearly do admit and shelter a disproportionate share of refugees). As I observed in my initial discussion of asylum, all of the rich democratic states have adopted techniques of exclusion to make it much more difficult for people to get to their territory and claim asylum. Given the general effectiveness of these techniques, it is not plausible to claim that the actual distribution of refugees burdens rich states unfairly, though many people probably believe that it does.

While many people in democratic states worry about being expected to admit more than their fair share of refugees, the much more important issue is the moral wrong involved in the use of techniques of exclusion to keep the numbers within bounds. Visa controls, carrier sanctions, and the other techniques of exclusion are indiscriminate mechanisms. They are just as likely to exclude genuine refugees as those without valid claims. These techniques fail the fundamental test that I set out at the beginning of the chapter that no policy is justifiable if it would have led to the exclusion of Jewish refugees fleeing the Nazis. (Indeed, visa controls played an important role in preventing Jewish refugees from reaching safety in the late 1930s.) Democratic states cannot meet their moral responsibilities to refugees by establishing a system to protect refugees that they then prevent refugees from using.

The Problem of Failed Asylum Claimants

Some will argue that the use of the techniques of exclusion is unavoidable because of the high number of requests for asylum from people who do not qualify as refugees under the Geneva Convention. This is the second potential source of disproportionate burdens for rich democratic states. Strictly speaking, this does not involve a disproportionate share of refugee admissions, but it is an issue that is directly connected to the question of the responsibility of democratic states to admit refugees, so it is important to discuss it here.

As I noted earlier, the number of asylum claims in Europe and North America increased dramatically in the 1980s and declined only after the techniques of exclusion had been adopted. Many, indeed most, of the people who seek asylum in rich democratic states are not recognized as refugees under the Geneva Convention.

Some people are tempted to leap from the fact that most asylum claimants do not succeed in gaining recognition as refugees to the conclusion that the real problem with non-refoulement is that it creates incentives for people to file asylum claims that they know have little merit in an attempt to gain entry to democratic states with the goal of using the time during which their cases are being considered to gain a foothold in society and to find some way to stay on after their claim for asylum is denied.

This is the classic picture of the "asylum abuser," someone who is really just an economic migrant with no strong moral claim to entry and who is seeking to get into a rich democratic state through a mechanism that is supposed to be reserved for refugees. This picture informs much of the popular discourse around refugees in democratic states, especially in Europe, and it generates a great deal of moral outrage.

There are undoubtedly some claimants who fit this picture of the asylum abuser, and, given the conventional assumption (which I am not challenging in this chapter) that states are morally entitled to restrict the entry of those who are only suffering from the "ordinary inequalities of the modern world," the moral outrage against them is, in a certain sense, understandable. They are taking spaces that should be reserved for real refugees and making it more difficult to maintain a system that is to provide refugees with protection. If only the asylum abusers refrained from their opportunistic behavior, many will say, there would be no need to use the techniques of exclusion to limit the number of asylum claimants.

While these concerns are understandable, it would be a mistake to suppose that most people whose claims for asylum fail fit this picture of asylum abusers or that better behavior by asylum claimants would eliminate the pressures to use the techniques of exclusion. Most people seeking asylum are not lawyers. They often have little idea about what legal principles govern the refugee system and whether the reasons that have led them to flee their country of origin will be considered sufficient to qualify them for refugee status under the Convention.[32] The fact that an asylum claim is rejected does not prove that the application was fraudulent.

Consider again the case of Gustavo Gutierrez. Under some interpretations of the Convention, he does not qualify as a refugee because the kind of threat he faces does not meet the Convention's requirements. Indeed, that is why his claim was initially denied. But even if that legal interpretation prevails, it would be absurd to describe him as an asylum abuser. His fears are real. He could not reasonably be expected to anticipate the ruling. Even if he did, would he be obliged to stay home in Mexico and wait to be killed?

Most asylum applications have some basis in dangers and hardships that the claimant faces. Most people do not leave their home country and file an asylum claim lightly. There are almost always push factors, things driving them out, as well as pull factors, things attracting them to the new place. So, the picture of the failed claimant as ipso facto an asylum abuser is a gross distortion of reality.[33] As I noted before, democratic states often feel obliged not to deport failed asylum claimants because of the risks those claimants would face if they were sent home. From a normative perspective, people like this should be considered genuine refugees, not asylum abusers, whatever their legal status under the Geneva Convention.

What about applicants who lie in their applications and destroy documents to make it harder to deport them? Can't we at least say that people who do this are abusing the asylum system? Not necessarily. Real refugees are rightly terrified of political authorities. How can they be expected to trust the authorities in the state in which they are seeking asylum, especially in a context in which they know there is a general suspicion of asylum applicants? They correctly perceive many of the officials with whom they interact to be hostile and suspicious. They are afraid, not without reason, that if they say the wrong thing, their application will be denied and they will be sent back. They do not know what the wrong thing might be in a complex determination process filled with legal technicalities. So, they talk with other applicants, trying to learn what works and shaping what they say to fit what they think the authorities want to hear.

Recall again my initial suggestion that we measure our approach to refugees today against the standard of how we should have responded to Jews fleeing Nazi Germany. Would it have been reasonable to expect Jewish refugees not to lie or destroy documents if they thought that it was necessary to do so to gain safety elsewhere? Should their lying have been grounds for denying them refuge? Real refugees whose lives will be in danger if they are sent home have stronger incentives than economic migrants to lie and destroy documents. It is wrong to assume that such behavior is proof of a character flaw. In sum, outrage about asylum abusers is largely misplaced.

Some people suggest that the solution to the large volume of asylum applications that are ultimately denied is to streamline the process in which asylum claims are heard and to find other ways to reduce the incentives to file claims with little chance of success. If those who do not qualify as refugees could be identified quickly and sent home, it would reduce the incentives for those with weak claims to apply and might ultimately eliminate the need for the techniques of exclusion.[34]

While some procedural reforms may be appropriate and may help to eliminate a few extreme cases, the obstacles to reducing the incentives to apply for asylum have deep roots in democratic norms and principles. Let me mention just three such constraints.

First, in every democratic state there are standard legal procedures for assessing contested claims. These legal procedures are complex, costly, and time-consuming because of the need to permit the parties to gather evidence, construct arguments, and press appeals. The democratic understanding of due process means that we have to allow asylum claimants to use the same sorts of processes.

Second, the opportunity to work while one's claim is being considered is itself a powerful incentive to apply for asylum even for people with little hope of success. One could reduce this incentive by detaining asylum claimants but that is very expensive. Even more important, it conflicts with the democratic commitment to human freedom which makes it hard to justify lengthy pre-determination detention, simply as a method for deterring asylum seekers.

Third, it is extremely difficult to deport people who do not qualify under the Convention. This, too, reinforces the incentives for applicants to try.

In sum, there is no way to reform the current asylum process that will substantially reduce the incentives to apply, at least not without violating deep democratic norms.[35] Yet it was the large volume of asylum claims that led democratic states to adopt the morally objectionable techniques of exclusion.

Reallocating Responsibilities for Refugees

So far in this section we have seen that there is a moral logic to the principle of non-refoulement but also that the almost exclusive reliance on this principle in the current refugee regime generates two problems with respect to the allocation of responsibilities to admit refugees. The primary problem is that the vast majority of refugees wind up in neighboring states, not only in the short run which would be acceptable, but also over the long term. This places an unfair burden on the neighboring states and also means that the moral claims of long-term refugees to membership in some society are rarely met. The second problem concerns the incentives for people to seek asylum in rich democratic states. I do not think these incentives actually result in rich democratic states taking in more refugees than they should, but fear of this possibility does have a number of pernicious consequences. First and foremost, it has led these states to adopt techniques of exclusion that prevent many genuine refugees from being able to gain asylum. Second, it makes it easier to construct everyone seeking refugee status as an asylum abuser. Third, it requires rich democratic states to spend significant resources on refugee determination processes.

These are two different problems, and they require different solutions, although perhaps the solutions would be combined in an ideal refugee regime. The first problem could be addressed by making it a strict duty for states to take in an appropriate number of refugees for resettlement. The second problem could be addressed by breaking the link between where one requests asylum and where one receives it. Let me say something more about each proposed solution.

Resettlement as a Strict Duty

As I mentioned at the outset of the chapter, it is a sad fact that repatriation is not a realistic possibility for many refugees. So, one crucial component of a better refugee regime would be to make resettlement a formal duty with the binding character that non-refoulement has now rather than a discretionary option for states that choose to be generous. The duty of non-refoulement would continue, of course, for reasons discussed above.

The principle of non-refoulement generates relatively clear guidelines for the allocation of responsibility for admitting refugees (even if some issues at the margins can be contested). Seeking to allocate responsibility for long-term refugees more fairly creates many more complications and ambiguities. Let me briefly mention some of the relevant considerations that we would have to take into account if we wanted to allocate the responsibility for refugee admissions fairly among states.[36]

I noted at the outset that sometimes states are causally responsible in some way for the fact that people need to leave their homes and become refugees. That sort of causal connection is obviously a relevant consideration in thinking about who should admit the refugees for resettlement.

Still another factor is what the refugees themselves want. They are not just passive victims to be assisted in whatever way the receiving states deem best. They are human beings whose agency deserves respect. Respecting their agency does not mean that they are entitled to gain refuge wherever they choose, however.[37] They are certainly entitled to expect that immediate families will not be divided in the process of relocation. Moreover, most refugee movements involve groups rather than isolated individuals, and in such cases the refugees will normally want to be able to share the challenges of adjusting to a new social context with others who have similar backgrounds and experiences and who can provide mutual support and a sense of community.

It is clearly appropriate to take into account the receiving state's absorptive capacity (that is, its ability to take in refugees and to settle them effectively). What affects this absorptive capacity?[38] One obvious factor is the size of the existing population in the receiving state. It would certainly not be fair to expect the Netherlands with its population of several million to take in the same number of refugees as the United States with its population of 330 million. But it is easier to see what is extremely unfair than it is to say precisely what fairness requires.

Population density may be a relevant factor because of its effect on housing and the environment, though it is much less salient in the modern world where most people live in cities than it was in a world where most people were agricultural workers. From an ecological perspective, dense urban patterns of human living may be less harmful than ones in which people are more dispersed.

Another important consideration is the state's economic capacity. This is partly a function of a state's overall wealth and partly a function of its economic dynamism (that is, of its ability to generate jobs and education for refugees and the housing and other goods that they will need to live). Some argue that rich states should be expected to take in more refugees than poor ones because they can more easily afford it. Others object that what it will cost to care for refugees depends in part on the circumstances of the host country and its normal standard of living, since refugees are supposed to live as members of the receiving society. So, it will be more expensive to care for refugees in rich states than in poor ones. This opens the door to discussions of whether it would be morally preferable for rich states to fulfill at least part of their responsibilities to refugees through resource transfers to poor receiving states rather than through admitting refugees to rich states. Some object that this idea denigrates refugees.[39]

What about similarities or differences between refugees and the existing population with respect to things like culture, religion, and ethnicity? As an empirical matter, it is almost certainly the case that a state's willingness to take in refugees will depend in part on the extent to which the current population identifies with the refugees and their plight. Moreover, other things being equal, it will be easier for the refugees themselves to adapt to the new society and for the receiving society to include them, the more the refugees resemble the existing population with respect to language, culture, religion, history, and so on. It would serve no one's interests to ignore the question of fit. It is important, however, not to elevate this consideration into something that justifies exclusion or marginalization of refugees on the basis of race, culture, or religion, and as we saw in earlier chapters this is a significant danger when such factors become principles of selection.

In the same vein, it seems reasonable to say that states like the United States, Canada, and Australia which have a long history of admitting immigrants and of coping with diversity can be expected to take in more refugees (other things being equal) than states which do not have such a history. As I have argued earlier in the book, however, every democratic state will receive some immigrants and has a responsibility to include those immigrants as full members of society. So, it would be wrong to use a history of insularity as a justification for refusing to resettle any refugees.

The discussion so far shows that there are a number of considerations that ought to be taken into account in allocating responsibility to resettle refugees. Doubtless there are others that I have not mentioned. Determining the relative weight to be given to these various considerations is bound to be complex and contested. I will not attempt to offer any synthesis here. One might wonder whether agreement on concrete guidelines to allocate responsibility would ever be possible given the range of issues and possible disagreements, but the challenges to reaching agreement are no worse in this case than they are in reaching agreement on many complex issues which almost always involve a variety of contested and competing considerations.

Would the adoption of a formal duty to take in refugees for resettlement in accordance with the sorts of criteria I have mentioned require an international body with enforcement powers? Not necessarily. For resettlement to be established as a formal duty like non-refoulement, states would certainly have to agree to some sort of formal covenant. But it need not entail anything more than that. Individual states could be responsible for interpreting and enforcing the commitments in a covenant on resettlement, just as they are responsible for the interpretation and enforcement of the existing Geneva Convention on Refugees. I leave open the question of whether it would be preferable to create an international body with stronger powers to promote the resettlement of long-term refugees. At this point, it would be a tremendous advance for most states even to acknowledge that they have a binding responsibility to resettle refugees and for them to engage in public debates about the appropriateness of different criteria. I doubt very much that any rich democratic state would be able to make a plausible case that it is taking in its fair share of refugees for resettlement today under any theory of fair shares that was subjected to public scrutiny and debate.[40]

The deepest obstacles to implementing a better allocation of responsibility for the resettlement of refugees do not derive from our uncertainty about how to resolve intellectual disagreements about what is fair but rather from our (collective) reluctance to do what fairness requires. I will explore this issue below. For the moment, the main point is to see that making resettlement a formal duty and taking into account the sorts of considerations I have identified (however those considerations were ultimately balanced), would provide a more just way of allocating responsibility for long-term refugees than the current refugee regime's exclusive reliance on non-refoulement, geographical proximity, and occasional generosity.

Breaking the Link between Claim and Place

What about the second problem, the incentives for people to seek asylum in rich democratic states and the negative consequences that flow from that? In principle, again, the solution is relatively simple. The key is to break the link between where a refugee initially files a claim for asylum and where she receives safe haven, both in the short term and in the long run.[41]

The state where a refugee claims asylum has a responsibility to ensure that the refugee is not sent back into danger but not necessarily a responsibility to provide her with a new home. Refugees have a moral right to a safe place to live, but they do not have a moral entitlement to choose where that will be. As we have just seen, this does not mean that refugees' preferences about where they relocate carry no moral weight, but rather that their preferences should not be regarded as the only relevant consideration.

People have incentives to seek asylum in places where they will be better off economically than they were at home, regardless of the strength of their refugee claims.[42] If there were no connection between the place where one requests asylum and the place where one receives protection, however, these incentives would disappear. Why travel thousands of miles to file a refugee claim if that does not enhance one's chances of being able to live in the state where the claim is filed? Moreover, if the connection were broken, rich states would no longer have any reason to try to prevent people from filing asylum claims on their territory because filing a claim would not gain the applicant a foothold on residence. If rich states stopped using the techniques of exclusion that they employ now, it would eliminate one of the biggest moral objections to the current asylum regime—that many refugee claimants cannot access it.

If there were no clear advantage to be gained from acquiring refugee status beyond the acquisition of a right to live safely in a new country (and not necessarily the place where one sought asylum), people would have fewer incentives to make opportunistic use of the system. As a result, there would be much less reason to worry about defining who is a refugee. (The poor states who now receive most of the world's refugees rarely expend any effort in determining whether the new arrivals in their states are really refugees.) Rich democratic states would have no need for elaborate determination systems designed to keep people from acquiring refugee status without proper justification, if gaining that status did not guarantee residence in their own state. In principle, the money now spent on determination could be reallocated to assist refugees.

While this sort of approach sounds attractive in theory, there are good reasons to be wary of it in practice. In breaking the link between the place where one files for asylum and the place where one receives it, the proposed changes would take away the rights refugees now enjoy when they qualify for asylum in Western states to receive protection in those states. Because their presence in our community makes us responsible for their fate (for reasons discussed in relation to the principle of non-refoulement), we should not send refugees elsewhere for protection unless we can be confident that their basic human rights will be adequately protected wherever they wind up. The asylum claimants may not have a moral claim to enjoy the perquisites of living in a wealthy society, but they do have a right to not to suffer any deprivation in their basic human rights. In a world in which state sovereignty is still the key principle, how are we to ensure that the human rights of the refugees are protected in some other state?

Even if we could be confident of the destination state's good intentions, who will provide the material resources and the supervision of the treatment of refugees needed to ensure that their basic human rights are met on an ongoing basis? In principle, states in North America and Europe should be able to use the money saved on determination systems to meet the material requirements. The reforms would require fundamental changes in the Geneva Convention, however. Once freed of the commitments and constraints created by the Convention, why would the rich states continue their promised level of support? It is nice to imagine that the billions now spent on refugee determination systems would be spent instead on food, clothing, and shelter for refugees, but why wouldn't the money be used to reduce taxes instead? In a world where a billion people live in absolute poverty without rich states being moved to respond to their needs in any significant way, why imagine that they would respond to the needs of refugees in a more adequate way?

It is possible to imagine a refugee regime that incorporates the protections provided by non-refoulement in the current regime but that distributes the responsibility to admit refugees for resettlement more fairly and that removes the incentives to file asylum claims in rich democratic states, thus eliminating the need for morally objectionable techniques of exclusion as well as expensive systems for evaluating asylum claims. Unfortunately, it would not be easy to create such a regime. As we have just seen, any attempt to separate the place where a person files a claim for asylum from the place where she receives asylum is likely in practice to undermine existing protections for refugees without delivering the promised benefits. The other proposed reform—making resettlement a formal duty—carries fewer risks of perversion but, I fear, even less likelihood of success. To see why that is the case, we have to consider our fourth question.

The Limits to Our Obligations to Refugees

The fourth and final question about our duties to admit refugees is the question of limits to obligation. One of the most striking features of the refugee regime created by the Geneva Convention is that it sets no limits to the obligation of states to protect refugees seeking asylum. States are permitted to turn away people who do not qualify as refugees, but not those who meet the Convention's standards, no matter how many of them there are. To be sure, even the commitments in the Geneva Convention are constrained by the responsibility of states to maintain public order. No one expects a state to admit so many refugees that it can no longer function. But this is a minimal constraint.[43]

I speak here of principle. In practice, as we have seen, democratic states use techniques of exclusion that they know will prevent real refugees (as well as others) from arriving, thus limiting the demands that are actually made of them to admit refugees. However, the techniques of exclusion do not technically violate the principle of non-refoulement (at least for the most part). Democratic states do not acknowledge openly that these techniques exclude refugees who would otherwise be entitled to admission, nor do they claim openly that there are too many refugees with valid claims.

My proposal to make resettlement a moral duty would add to the demands being made upon democratic states with respect to the admission of refugees. Are these demands more than it is reasonable to expect democratic states to bear? To put the question I am asking another way, when, if ever, is a democratic state morally entitled to say to refugees: "We have done enough. We have to protect the interests and needs of our own citizens and residents. We recognize that you have genuine claims, that your physical security and vital subsistence needs will be jeopardised if we do not admit you, but we are going to refuse to do so."

Many people think that there is some point at which a democratic state's concern for its own interests and its own population may make it legitimate to shut the doors, even on people who clearly qualify as refugees. David Miller acknowledges that refugees have strong moral claims to admission, but he argues that these claims have limits:

> There can be no guarantee…that every bona fide refugee will find a state willing to take her in.…At the limit, therefore, we may face tragic cases where the human rights of the refugees clash with a legitimate claim by the receiving state that its obligation to admit refugees has already been exhausted.[44]

When is this limit reached? When are we justified in turning away genuine refugees? This turns out to be a troubling question, to which neither Miller nor any other theorist I have read offers either clear guidance or a satisfactory answer. My own answer is "almost never."

Given the moral presuppositions of the state system, it is certainly reasonable for a state to give priority to securing the basic rights of its own citizens and residents, over comparably urgent basic rights of outsiders.[45] If one takes the moral claims of refugees seriously, however, it is not clear why their claims to an admission which is necessary to protect their most basic rights should be subordinated to much less vital interests of members of the receiving state.

People sometimes say that the question of legitimate limits to the duty to admit refugees must ultimately be left to states themselves to decide. Miller's statement is again typical:

> The final judgement must be left with the members of the receiving community who may decide that they have already done their fair share of refugee resettlement.[46]

The considerations that Miller says should go into determining a state's "fair share" are similar in many ways to the ones I advanced above in my discussion of the allocation of responsibility for admitting refugees. He seems to think, however, that we are obliged to take at face value a state's judgment about the extent of its responsibilities for refugees, about what constitutes its own fair share.

The difficulty with this sort of position, as we have seen repeatedly in this book, is that it conflates the question of who ought to make a decision with the question of whether a given decision is justifiable. The fact that a state has the moral right to make a decision does not entail the view that its decision is justifiable or that it is immune from criticism. Having the right to make a decision is not the same as having a right to act arbitrarily or with complete discretion. Even if no other party has or should have authority to overrule a decision, we may still be in a position to criticize it. For example, one may think that it is appropriate that the Supreme Court of the United States should have the final say on what the Constitution requires and still think that it has made a decision which is legally and morally indefensible in a particular case such as *Plessy v. Ferguson* or *Bush v. Gore.*

When the United States refused to admit Jewish refugees from the *St. Louis,* those who defended the decision asserted that America had already done its fair share of refugee resettlement, especially given the difficult economic circumstances of the time. When I criticize that decision and assert that the American response to Jewish refugees was a profound moral failure, I am not claiming that there ought to have been some supranational authority that decided how many refugees the United States would admit. I am simply saying that Americans should have made a different decision, that their collective moral judgment was deeply flawed. The mere fact that the members of a potential receiving society think they have already done enough to meet their obligations to refugees is not, in itself, sufficient to establish that they have done enough.

Recall the approach that I proposed at the outset, that we ask what any proposed principles would have implied for our response to Jewish refugees fleeing Hitler. I have assumed from the outset that my readers will agree that turning away those refugees was wrong, that no appeal to the limits to our obligations would have justified closing the door on them. If someone wants to accept that premise but still wants to defend the possibility that the exclusion of genuine refugees in some other case would be justifiable, that person should explain what distinguishes the legitimate case of exclusion from the indefensible one.

I do not claim that it is impossible to imagine circumstances in which the exclusion of refugees might be defensible. I have already acknowledged the public order constraint, and it is possible that there would be other circumstances in which admitting more refugees would bring such high costs to the basic interests of those in the receiving society that exclusion would be justifiable. As Hume reminds us, one of the background conditions for justice is limited scarcity. If everyone were in dire need, it might be unreasonable to expect people to do more than look out for their own.

In the real world, however, this is a purely hypothetical speculation. I do not see how any democratic state in Europe or North America today could make the case that it has taken in so many refugees that it is now morally entitled to turn real refugees away. Indeed, if the argument I have advanced is correct, all of these states have a moral duty to resettle (more) refugees and are failing to meet that duty.

As I have already pointed out, the vast majority of refugees find shelter in neighboring states. Those states would have a much stronger basis to cry "Enough!" and some have occasionally done so, though even then, generally without sufficient grounds. For the most part, however, they have let the refugees in. There is a certain irony here. Immigrants from poor, illiberal, authoritarian, and religiously conservative states are often constructed as threats to the admirable values and practices of democratic states. When it comes to the admission of refugees, however, the former states have made room for millions of human beings in desperate need while most of the latter have devoted their energies to keeping refugees out.

I do not mean to romanticize the refugee-receiving states. To some degree their openness to refugees has been a matter of their inability to keep the refugees out rather than their willingness to let them in (though even poor states have soldiers with guns). Some states allow refugees in for political reasons and some (like Iran) simultaneously admit large numbers of refugees from elsewhere and generate large numbers of their own refugees. Nevertheless, the contrast between the numbers admitted in North and South is stark.

The desire to set limits to our obligation to admit refugees is understandable, given the background presuppositions of the state system. Each state is supposed to protect the basic human rights of those within its own jurisdiction. If every state did this, we would not have to worry about admitting refugees at all. The responsibility to admit refugees is a secondary, derivative duty. Our state has a responsibility to admit refugees only because some other state has failed to carry out its own primary moral duty.[47] So, in a way, it makes sense that states resent being asked to take in refugees. This does not make it legitimate to exclude the refugees, however, or, worse still, to blame them. Anger at Nazis for creating a refugee problem should not have been transformed, as it sometimes was, into resentment of Jews.

Another concern that underlies the quest for limits is the fear that, without such limits, those states that are willing to fulfil their obligations to refugees could face an endless ratcheting up of their responsibilities. As we have just seen, admitting refugees is a secondary moral duty arising from the failure of some states to fulfil their primary moral duty. But suppose that we had a fairer allocation of responsibilities for refugees, including a formal duty to admit refugees for resettlement, and then other states failed to fulfil this duty (that is, failed to admit their fair share of refugees for resettlement). Would the states that were willing to meet their secondary responsibilities then be faced with a tertiary responsibility? Would they be obliged to take up the slack, admitting still more refugees for resettlement than required by their initial fair share, because the refugees' moral claims to membership in some society would otherwise go unmet? I see no clear answer to this question.

Some have tried to justify the adoption of the techniques of exclusion by rich democratic states along these lines, suggesting that it is a reasonable response to the dynamic of cascading moral failures that threatened to impose greater burdens on the ones who continued to fulfill their responsibilities. The problem with this line of argument is that there is little evidence that states adopting the techniques of exclusion have tried to ensure that they were receiving their fair share of refugees through the resettlement process. (Sweden may be the exception that proves the rule.)

Some will be inclined to view the ratcheting up issue as a collective action problem. While there are similarities with respect to the challenges of coordination, information, and enforcement that we face in dealing with collective action problems, there is one fundamental difference that makes the creation of a satisfactory refugee regime much more difficult: the absence of any common interest. Treating refugees justly serves relatively few state interests.

Morality and Self-Interest

What makes the issue of refugees especially difficult is that it involves a deep conflict between interests and morality. If we think about ordinary morality, it is striking how many moral principles, habits, and practices fit very well with self-interest, as conventionally understood, so long as one takes a long-term or "enlightened" view of self-interest.[48] Indeed, a lot of ordinary morality could be seen as an aid to self-interest in the sense that it prevents the emergence of the collective action problems that arise when people act only on the basis of a narrow and immediate view of self-interest. For example, it is a familiar point that capitalist market systems function much better in contexts where most people are honest most of the time, and the prevailing culture discourages graft, corruption, and theft. It is not necessary for there to be perfect compliance for people to see that these sorts of moral norms and habits are a public good, that they make everyone's lives better off. This recognition reinforces the norms, making it even more likely that honesty will be the best policy most of the time.

As a general matter, it is much easier to get people to follow a course of action recommended on moral grounds when it fits with self-interest in the way I have just outlined than when it does not. Finding ways to present moral arguments that draw attention to the links between morality and interest make it more likely that the moral arguments will be accepted. This approach is common in politics, and it can do a lot of good in guiding policies in ways that make them more ethical.

This applies to the ethics of immigration as well as to other areas. Take an example from one of the earlier chapters: providing public education and basic health care to the children of migrants who settle without authorization. This is the right thing to do from a purely moral perspective, but it is easier to persuade people to go along with the idea because it is so clearly in everyone's interest not to have children growing up in our society without a basic education or with medical conditions that might pose a risk to others.

One could make similar arguments about the collective interests served by adopting citizenship rules that include the children of immigrants in the political community, by providing the same economic and social rights to residents as to citizens, by creating a societal culture in which all feel included and respected, and by granting immediate family members a right to join citizens and residents. Even providing legal rights to irregular migrants is often in the interests of ordinary citizens for reasons I laid out in chapter 7. In all these cases, the requirements of justice and prudence largely coincide or, at least, correspond closely enough that it is possible to persuade people to do the right thing.

That is not always the case. Morality cannot be entirely reduced to enlightened self-interest. Sometimes morality and self-interest do not reinforce one another, even in the long run. Any morality worth the name will contain views of right and wrong, or good and bad that *may* clash with self-interest, even enlightened self-interest, under some circumstances.

I am afraid that refugee policy is today one of those areas where the gap between what morality requires and what serves even long run self-interest is so great that interest can do very little work in supporting morality. During the Cold War, this was somewhat different. The openness of the West to refugees from communism was often trumpeted as one of the marks of the superiority of capitalism over communism. The connection between morality and interest in this area was maintained in part by the fact that the communists rarely permitted people to leave so that the Western states did not have to take in many refugees, and in part by the fact that the movement of asylum claimants from poor to rich countries had not yet begun so that the West could not be accused of hypocrisy in excluding them.

Today, it is much harder to show what interests are served by openness to refugees. One can try to link concern for refugees with self-interest by appealing to a collective self-image. Both Canada and the United States pride themselves on being generous because they take in more refugees than most other states. This sort of appeal has some purchase but also significant limits. It is fine so long as the demands posed by the intake of refugees are perceived not to be too burdensome, but it is vulnerable to changes in both circumstances and perceptions. One can also appeal to a form of self-interest by encouraging identification with refugees, but this becomes harder the more the refugees are removed from most of the existing population by cultural or geographical distances.

I am not suggesting that discussions of refugee policy should ignore the connections between morality and self-interest. On the contrary, as I have pointed out, it is appropriate to try to think of ways to reduce the incentives to make opportunistic use of the asylum system and to reduce the incentives to employ techniques of exclusion. Where we can, we should seek a better alignment of interests and morality. The real problem, in my view, is that the admission of refugees does not really serve the interests of rich democratic states.

The fact that morality sometimes requires actions that do not contribute to self-interest does not matter very much so long as it does not require any great sacrifice of self-interest either. The admission of refugees raised few political issues when the numbers were small. When the number of asylum claimants increased, however, the tension between morality and self-interest became greater. In the modern world, there are many millions of people who clearly qualify as refugees under any reasonable definition of the term and many of them need permanent new homes outside their states of origin. There is now, I fear, a deep conflict between what morality requires of democratic states with respect to the admission of refugees and what democratic states and their existing populations see as their interests.

I have argued in this chapter that democratic states have a moral duty to provide refugees with a safe place to live in the aftermath of their flight and to provide them with a new home if they are unable to return safely to their state of origin within a reasonable time. I have argued further that the refugee regime created by the Geneva Convention meets some of these duties but also that it suffers from a number of important moral flaws. I have shown how it would be possible in theory to construct a better refugee regime that preserved the virtues of the Geneva Convention while remedying its flaws, and, in particular, one that allocated responsibilities for refugees more fairly. But this would require an expansion of existing commitments toward refugees, especially with respect to resettlement. That sort of expansion would not extend the obligations to refugees beyond reasonable limits, but given the ways in which it would conflict with the interests of states, we cannot be too optimistic that democratic states will be willing to do what they ought to do in admitting refugees. Needless to say, I hope that my pessimism is misplaced.

The Case for Open Borders

Borders have guards and the guards have guns. This is an obvious fact of political life but one that is easily hidden from view—at least from the view of those of us who are citizens of affluent democracies. If we see the guards at all, we find them reassuring because we think of them as there to protect us rather than to keep us out. To Africans in small, leaky vessels seeking to avoid patrol boats while they cross the Mediterranean to southern Europe or to Mexicans risking death from heat and exposure in the Arizona desert as they try to evade border patrols and enter the United States, it is quite different. To these people, the borders, guards, and guns are all too apparent, their goal of exclusion all too real. What justifies the use of force against such people? Perhaps borders and guards can be justified as a way of keeping out terrorists, armed invaders, or criminals. But most of those trying to get in are not like that. They are ordinary, peaceful people, seeking only the opportunity to build decent, secure lives for themselves and their families. On what moral grounds can we deny entry to these sorts of people? What gives anyone the right to point guns at *them*?

To many people the answer to this question will seem obvious. The power to admit or exclude noncitizens is inherent in sovereignty and essential for any political community that seeks to exercise self-determination. Every state has the legal and moral right to exercise control over admissions in pursuit of its own national interest and of the common good of the members of its community, even if that means denying entry to peaceful, needy foreigners. States may choose to be generous in admitting immigrants, but, in most cases at least, they are under no moral obligation to do so.

I want to challenge that view. In this chapter and the next, I will argue that, in principle, borders should generally be open and people should normally be free to leave their country of origin and settle in another. This critique of exclusion has particular force with respect to restrictions on movement from developing states to Europe and North America, but it applies more generally.

In the first part of this book, I examined questions about immigration, citizenship, and democracy within the framework of the conventional view that states are morally entitled to control admissions. In the past two chapters I have been exploring ways in which that right to control admissions is constrained by moral considerations that democratic states often acknowledge, at least in principle. Now, however, I want to pose a more fundamental challenge. I intend to call into question the assumption that states are morally entitled to restrict immigration. Let me begin by sketching the contours of this challenge.

The Basic Challenge of Open Borders

In many ways, citizenship in Western democracies is the modern equivalent of feudal class privilege—an inherited status that greatly enhances one's life chances.[1] To be born a citizen of a rich state in Europe or North America is like being born into the nobility (even though many of us belong to the lesser nobility). To be born a citizen of a poor country in Asia or Africa is like being born into the peasantry in the Middle Ages (even if there are a few rich peasants and some peasants manage to gain entry to the nobility). Like feudal birthright privileges, contemporary social arrangements not only grant great advantages on the basis of birth but also entrench these advantages by legally restricting mobility, making it extremely difficult for those born into a socially disadvantaged position to overcome that disadvantage, no matter how talented they are or how hard they work. Like feudal practices, these contemporary social arrangements are hard to justify when one thinks about them closely.

Reformers in the late Middle Ages objected to the way feudalism restricted freedom, including the freedom of individuals to move from one place to another in search of a better life—a constraint that was crucial to the maintenance of the feudal system. Modern practices of state control over borders tie people to the land of their birth almost as effectively. Limiting entry to rich democratic states is a crucial mechanism for protecting a birthright privilege. If the feudal practices protecting birthright privileges were wrong, what justifies the modern ones?

The analogy I have just drawn with feudalism is designed to give readers pause about the conventional view that restrictions on immigration by democratic states are normally justified. Now let me outline the positive case for open borders. I start from three basic interrelated assumptions. First, there is no natural social order. The institutions and practices that govern human beings are ones that human beings have created and can change, at least in principle. Second, in evaluating the moral status of alternative forms of political and social organization, we must start from the premise that all human beings are of equal moral worth. Third, restrictions on the freedom of human beings require a moral justification. These three assumptions are not just my views. They undergird the claim to moral legitimacy of every contemporary democratic regime.

The assumption that all human beings are of equal moral worth does not mean that no legal distinctions can be drawn among different groups of people, nor does the requirement that restrictions on freedom be justified mean that coercion is never defensible. But these two assumptions, together with the assumption that the social order is not naturally given, mean that we have to give reasons for our institutions and practices and that those reasons must take a certain form. It is never enough to justify a set of social arrangements governing human beings to say that these arrangements are good for us, without regard for others, whoever the "us" may be. We have to appeal to principles and arguments that take everyone's interests into account or that explain why the social arrangements are reasonable and fair to everyone who is subject to them.

Given these three assumptions there is at least a prima facie case that borders should be open, for three interrelated reasons. First, state control over immigration limits freedom of movement. The right to go where you want is an important human freedom in itself. It is precisely this freedom, and all that this freedom makes possible, that is taken away by imprisonment. Freedom of movement is also a prerequisite to many other freedoms. If people are to be free to live their lives as they choose, so long as this does not interfere with the legitimate claims of others, they have to be free to move where they want. Thus freedom of movement contributes to individual autonomy both directly and indirectly. Open borders would enhance this freedom.

Of course, freedom of movement cannot be unconstrained, but restrictions on freedom of movement require some sort of moral justification, that is, some argument as to why the restriction on freedom is in the interest of, and fair to, all those who are subject to it. Since state control over immigration restricts human freedom of movement, it requires a justification. This justification must take into account the interests of those excluded as well as the interests of those already inside. It must make the case that the restrictions on immigration are fair to all human beings. There are restrictions that meet this standard of justification, as we shall see, but granting states a right to exercise discretionary control over immigration does not.

The second reason why borders should normally be open is that freedom of movement is essential for equality of opportunity. Within democratic states we all recognize, at least in principle, that access to social positions should be determined by an individual's actual talents and effort and not limited on the basis of birth-related characteristics such as class, race, or gender that are not relevant to the capacity to perform well in the position. This ideal of equal opportunity is intimately linked to the view that all human beings are of equal moral worth, that there are no natural hierarchies of birth that entitle people to advantageous social positions. But you have to be able to move to where the opportunities are in order to take advantage of them. So, freedom of movement is an essential prerequisite for equality of opportunity.

It is in the linkage between freedom of movement and equality of opportunity that the analogy with feudalism cuts most deeply. Under feudalism, there was no commitment to equal opportunity. The social circumstances of one's birth largely determined one's opportunities, and restrictions on freedom of movement were an essential element in maintaining the limitations on the opportunities of those with talent and motivation but the wrong class background. (Of course, gender was another pervasive constraint.) In the modern world, we have created a social order in which there is a commitment to equality of opportunity for people *within* democratic states (at least to some extent), but no pretense of, or even aspiration to, equality of opportunity for people *across* states. Because of the state's discretionary control over immigration, the opportunities for people in one state are simply closed to those from another (for the most part). Since the range of opportunities varies so greatly among states, this means that in our world, as in feudalism, the social circumstances of one's birth largely determine one's opportunities. It also means that restrictions on freedom of movement are an essential element in maintaining this arrangement, that is, in limiting the opportunities of people with talents and motivations but the wrong social circumstances of birth. Again, the challenge for those who would defend restrictions on immigration is to justify the resulting inequalities of opportunity. As I will argue, that is hard to do.

A third, closely related point is that a commitment to equal moral worth entails some commitment to economic, social, and political equality, partly as a means of realizing equal freedom and equal opportunity and partly as a desirable end in itself. Freedom of movement would contribute to a reduction of existing political, social, and economic inequalities. There are millions of people in poor states today who long for the freedom and economic opportunity they could find in Europe or North America. Many of them take great risks to come. If the borders were open, millions more would move. The exclusion of so many poor and desperate people seems hard to justify from a perspective that takes seriously the claims of all individuals as free and equal moral persons.

This preliminary case for open borders will generate a host of questions and objections. In the rest of this chapter and in the next one, I will try to identify the questions and objections that I find most challenging and illuminating, using my responses to clarify, qualify, and deepen my defense of free movement.[2]

The Nature of the Inquiry

I want to start by clarifying the nature of my discussion in these two chapters. When I argue for open borders, I am not making a policy proposal that I think might be adopted (in the immediate future) by presidents or prime ministers or public officials charged with making immigration policy. I have noted at various points throughout this book that there can be a important differences between what one thinks is right as a matter of principle (which has been the primary focus of the book) and what one thinks is the best policy in a particular context, given existing political dynamics, the range of feasible options, the effects on other policies, and so on. As we saw in the last chapter, the gap between principle and policy is particularly wide when we focus on refugees. When it comes to the question of open borders, that gap becomes a chasm.

From a political perspective, the idea of open borders is a nonstarter. Most citizens of states in Europe and North America are already worried about current levels of immigration and about their states' capacities to exclude unwanted entrants. They assume that their states are morally entitled to control immigration (for the most part) and they would see open borders, if anyone actually proposed it, as deeply contrary to their interests. Any political actor advocating such a view would quickly be marginalized (and so none will).

Why make an argument that we should open our borders when there is no chance that we will? Because it is important to gain a critical perspective on the ways in which collective choices are constrained, even if we cannot do much to alter those constraints. Social institutions and practices may be deeply unjust and yet so firmly established that, for all practical purposes, they must be taken as background givens in deciding how to act in the world at a particular moment in time. The feudal system, whose injustice I have presupposed above, was once deeply entrenched. So was the institution of slavery in the seventeenth and eighteenth centuries. For a long time, there was no real hope of transcending those arrangements. Yet criticism was still appropriate. Even if we must take deeply rooted social arrangements as givens for purposes of immediate action in a particular context, we should never forget about our assessment of their fundamental character. Otherwise we wind up legitimating what should only be endured.

To be sure, most people in democratic states think that their institutions and policies have nothing in common with feudalism and slavery from a normative perspective. Democratic states, they suppose, are basically just. Some will acknowledge that democratic states should do more to protect basic human rights elsewhere and to bring those in desperate poverty up to some minimal level of well-being. But most people do not see discretionary control over immigration by democratic states as a restriction on freedom, or at least not a freedom to which noncitizens are morally entitled. Most people in North America and Europe also think that they are morally entitled collectively to what they have (in any given democratic state) and entitled to protect it by keeping others out. It is precisely that complacency that the open borders argument is intended to undermine. The control that democratic states exercise over immigration plays a crucial role in maintaining unjust global inequalities and in limiting human freedom unjustly.

The goal of this discussion then is to explore the implications of democratic principles for immigration when we treat the idea that states are entitled to control admissions as an open question rather than a presupposition. Any complex set of moral principles will contain tensions and trade-offs and will require a balancing of competing moral considerations, but even when these complexities are taken into account, the restrictions on immigration that we normally assume to be justifiable are in fact deeply at odds with our most fundamental moral principles.

In this chapter and the next, I will ask only what justice requires in principle. For the purposes of that discussion, I will set aside worries about what to do if some people or some states are unwilling to do what they should. So, I will not spend time discussing the question of whether one state should open its borders if others refuse to do so because the most important question of principle is whether democratic states should generally be open, not how some who seek to act justly should respond to the moral failures of others. In practice, as I have already acknowledged, no affluent democratic state in the contemporary world will open its borders. So, we are unlikely to gain much insight into practical matters of policymaking by working through a hypothetical question about how one imaginary democratic state should behave if its leaders (and population) were persuaded by my arguments about what justice requires with respect to open borders. I do not mean to suggest that my discussion of principles has no implications for action, however. I will explore these implications in chapter 13.

No inquiry can proceed without some presuppositions. Even though I am proposing to challenge some deep conventional assumptions, I do so only by presupposing others. In this chapter, as is the case throughout the book, I presuppose the normative validity of democratic principles, while offering a particular interpretation and analysis of them. This is still political theory from the ground up, even though it may seem strange to use that label for a line of argument that is so at odds with existing practices. The point is that I do not start with a general theory of human freedom or equality and try to deduce the case for open borders from that. I do not even start with a general theory of mobility and try to show why it is so important to human beings to be able to move freely across borders. I use no specialized language or technical arguments. Rather I begin as before with ordinary democratic principles and practices, examining each in light of the other. The only difference is that in this chapter that dialectic gives rise to a much deeper criticism of the way we do things now than it did in the earlier ones. Nevertheless, as should already be apparent, the case I am making for open borders is one that ordinary readers should be able to understand (whether they agree with it or not). It appeals to familiar, widely shared democratic principles and tries to show that these principles have unsettling implications.

An argument for open borders also presupposes that there are borders. Having borders that are open is not the same as having no borders. More specifically, I will assume that we are living in a world divided into separate, sovereign states in the way that the current world is. Each state governs a discrete territory, claims a legitimate monopoly on the exercise of violence within its territory, and has the legal right to control entry to its territory. This presupposition is not intended to preclude the more complicated relations of authority that we actually find in the world (e.g., federalism within states or institutional arrangements between states such as the European Union).[3] The presupposition also does not exclude questions about possible moral constraints on the ways in which states may exercise their sovereign powers, especially the power to control admissions. That, after all, is the main question I want to address in the chapter. I say more about the relationship between sovereignty and open borders in the next chapter.

Some will wonder whether I concede too much in assuming a world of sovereign states. Of course, one could explore the question of whether a world government or perhaps some more authoritative system of international law would be preferable to current arrangements. That is an important question for global justice, but one that is beyond the scope of this book. I want to explore the question of how our fundamental moral principles say that states should behave, leaving open the question of what the best way is to try to ensure that states actually follow these principles and whether that requires some new institutional arrangement.

Open Borders and Common Sense

Let me start with the objection that requiring states to open their borders cannot be right because it is so at odds with our basic moral intuitions and our practices. As one critic puts it, the idea of open borders "defies common sense."[4] Another critic points out that an open borders policy conflicts with the practices of all democratic states, even those that seem to approximate most closely democratic ideals.[5] In international law one can find support for the claims of permanent residents and migrant workers (even irregular migrants) and refugees, but all international law, even human rights legislation, treats the basic right of states to control immigration as beyond question.

I take these objections seriously. I have myself argued elsewhere that our practices may contain moral insights that our theories miss and that we have reason to be wary of moral theories that conflict with our normal moral intuitions.[6] On the other hand, as I noted in the same places, it sometimes takes the critical perspective of theory to bring to light what is wrong with our practices.

In making the argument for open borders, I am claiming that this is one of those cases in which the critical perspective of theory is right and conventional practices and intuitions are wrong. Unless readers are willing to accept the idea that what most people believe to be morally right can actually be wrong, there is no point in reading further. So, why should readers accept that possibility? Because we know from experience that we can come to view deeply embedded practices and institutions as unjust, even though these practices and institutions were seen as morally acceptable by people in previous generations. Institutionalized racism and sexism, in the form of segregation and the legal subordination of women to men, are only the most obvious examples. No one today thinks that these practices are compatible with democratic principles, although most people in the past assumed that they were. I am not claiming that the case against restrictions on immigration is as clear-cut as the case against racism and sexism, but I do think the basic analogy holds. Discretionary control over immigration is a deep injustice that does not seem unjust to most people today. It may be fair to say that the burden of proof lies upon a person (like me) who wants to make a claim about justice that departs radically from our ordinary moral understandings, but it would be wrong to dismiss this possibility out of hand.

If we accept the possibility that conventional morality may be wrong, it affects the kinds of arguments we can use. Criticisms of the argument for open borders should not appeal to conventional moral intuitions about the state, since the claim is precisely that these intuitions are faulty. This may seem self-evident, but the conventional understanding of the state holds such sway over our normative imaginations that we are often not even aware that we are deploying it. Many of the objections to open borders simply smuggle back in (usually unconsciously) the very assumptions that are supposed to be the subject of the inquiry. I will try to point out examples as I discuss the objections.

Of course, we cannot escape moral intuitions and moral assumptions altogether, especially in an approach like mine that works from the ground up. As I noted above, I am myself assuming the moral validity of democratic principles and my use of the analogy with feudalism implicitly assumes that contemporary readers would find feudal arrangements to be unjust.[7] In other words, I am using some parts of our moral traditions to argue against others, and I am claiming that our deepest principles have implications that those who first developed those principles did not foresee. This should be a familiar form of moral argument, analogous to ones deployed by critics of discrimination on the basis of race, gender, and sexual orientation. The broad claim is that the idea of open borders fits better with our most basic values—liberty and equality—and with our most deeply rooted intuitions about justice than the idea that the state should be able to restrict immigration at will. The values, principles, and intuitions that support the latter are ultimately far less compelling.

The Global Justice Challenge

My general argument for open borders has two components, one linking it to freedom and the other to equality. In this section I want to pursue the link between open borders and equality. One important objection to my argument for open borders is that it greatly overstates the moral importance of being able to move freely across state borders from an egalitarian perspective, at least in most circumstances.[8] Leaving aside special cases like family reunification or refugees, the critics say, the real problems to which my argument points are the vast inequalities between rich states and poor states, and especially the fact that so many people live in desperate poverty. These are the underlying conditions that make people want to move, and they cannot be addressed effectively by opening borders. Even if borders were open, the critics say, it would do little to help most of the poor because most of them could not and would not move. Indeed, one might object that there is something morally perverse in suggesting that the solution to the problems of the global poor and disadvantaged is to make it possible for them to come to rich states, especially if one sees the problems they face as due in no small part to the actions of rich states and the institutions they have created, as some critics insist is the case. Our most important moral priority, from this perspective, should be to transform the underlying conditions and, especially, to help the least well off emerge from extreme poverty. It is a matter of achieving global distributive justice. What global justice requires is a massive transfer of resources from rich states to poor states and a transformation of the international economic order, not open borders.

In many ways, I agree with this line of argument. I agree, for example, that reducing international inequalities and, especially, eliminating extreme poverty, are more urgent and more fundamental moral tasks than opening borders.[9] Of course, not everyone shares this view of global justice. In the next chapter, I will also consider arguments to the effect that the obligations that any political community has to outsiders are much more limited than this account of global justice or my own argument for open borders maintains. For the moment, however, let's proceed on the assumption that this egalitarian view of global justice has merit (as I think is indeed the case).

As I have explained above, I am concerned in this chapter, primarily with questions of fundamental principle rather than questions about strategies for action. At the level of principle, there is no conflict between open borders and a view of global distributive justice that requires great reductions in the inequalities between states. On the contrary, these ideals fit well together. Significant reductions in the inequalities between states would transform open borders from a critical but perhaps unrealizable ideal into a feasible arrangement, precisely because reducing inequality would reduce the pressure to move and eliminate fears of open borders creating vast dislocations.[10] For reasons that will become clearer as we proceed, open borders between states would be an important institutional feature of a just world. In principle, free movement is not in conflict with global justice but rather is part of what global justice requires.

Those who would dismiss the importance of open borders because of its secondary importance for the task of reducing international inequalities miss two important points at the level of principle. First, the argument for open borders makes a crucial contribution to the critique of international inequality because it makes it harder for rich states to claim that they bear no responsibility for the persistence of inequality and the plight of the poor. Second, in a context of international inequality, freedom of movement is an important moral goal because of its contribution to equality of opportunity, quite apart from its effects on the overall level of inequality.

Consider first the way the open borders argument brings home to us our own complicity in the maintenance of global inequality and poverty. The current division between rich and poor states can persist in its current form only because the rich states feel entitled to restrict the entry of people from poor states. Restrictions on migration are a linchpin of the modern state system. They enable it to function despite these vast inequalities.

One obstacle to getting agreement on the moral duty of rich states to address global poverty and to reduce international inequalities is that people disagree about the causes of these problems and about the viability of alternative ways of addressing them. How can we be sure that money spent on development will be well spent rather than wasted, that it will help poor people rather than line the pockets of corrupt elites, that it will improve conditions rather than make things worse? And to what extent are we really responsible, either causally or morally, for the difficulties people elsewhere face? Questions of this sort are sometimes self-serving rationalizations for avoiding constructive action, but not always. There are serious critics of almost every approach to development and genuine disagreement about the causes of, and moral responsibility for, inequalities.[11]

In the context of this dispute over the causes of and cures for global inequality, arguing for open borders draws attention to the fact that at least some of the people who are poor remain poor because we will not let them in. We use coercion every day to prevent people from achieving a better life. We cannot evade our responsibility for that.[12] We know how to admit immigrants. Despite occasional political rhetoric that the boat is full, no democratic state in Europe or North America can pretend that it could not take in many, many more immigrants than it does now without collapsing or even suffering serious damage. Opening borders might not be the best way to address these problems, but the open borders argument takes away any justification for complacency and inaction.[13]

What about the possibility that opening borders will actually increase international inequality rather than reduce it? That is an important question that usually focuses on the claim that letting talented and well-educated people move from poor states to rich ones harms the efforts of poor states to develop themselves (the so-called "brain drain" argument). I have already discussed this argument in chapter 8. Let me just say here that it would not be plausible to suggest that rich states are keeping their borders closed in order to help poor states or that closure is the best form of assistance.

Second, even if free movement did little or nothing to reduce overall inequality (though I think that is implausible), it would still be an important moral goal. To return to my initial analogy, defenders of feudalism could plausibly have argued (and indeed some did) that opening careers to talents would do nothing to benefit most peasants. Vast social inequalities persisted after the end of feudalism, but that did not make the abolition of feudal birthright privileges morally unimportant. This change made positions in social hierarchies less dependent on the social circumstances of an individual's birth and more dependent on the individual's personal capacities and efforts.[14] Ending the formal barriers to equality of opportunity created by restrictions on immigration would not be a cure-all either, but it would clearly contribute to global equality of opportunity and so would be a significant moral advance over current arrangements.

Some people would challenge this claim on the grounds that equality of opportunity is an incoherent idea when applied at a global level. They say that the concept of equal opportunity presupposes that we know what sorts of opportunities matter and how to weigh them against one another. In a global context, cultural differences are too great to make that feasible. If we do not know what equal opportunity really means, how can we know whether open borders would really contribute to this goal?[15]

In my view, these concerns are greatly exaggerated. Equality of opportunity is a complex and contested idea, of course, but the conceptual difficulties of interpreting it and applying it at the global level are not radically different from the difficulties of interpreting it and applying it at the domestic level.[16] In any event, when it comes to the question of whether open borders would contribute to enhancing equal opportunity, the argument about cultural variability collapses because the migrants who are seeking to move to rich democratic states clearly want the sorts of opportunities those states provide. They think those opportunities are better than the ones at home or they would not move. So, we cannot deny *them* admission and access on the grounds that we don't know what they really want or value. Restrictions on entry are a clear obstacle to equal opportunity for those who want to migrate.

Open Borders and Human Freedom

In this section I want to deepen my defense of the claim that open borders would contribute to human freedom. In some respects, I find it puzzling that it is necessary to make the case that it is an important restriction on human freedom to require people to get permission to enter a territory and reside there, especially when political authorities are almost entirely free to deny that permission. I am inclined to think that it should be intuitively obvious to those who value freedom that this is a serious constraint on freedom, even if they judge the constraint to be justifiable. I know from many conversations, however, that people often do not see it that way, even political philosophers professionally committed to elaborating liberal ideas. One common response I have heard goes something like this: "I can see why preventing people from poor states from moving to rich ones is a serious constraint on their freedom because they have such strong reasons to want to move. But why should I have a right to move from Canada to Sweden or from the U.S. to Norway? It is not a serious limitation of my freedom not to be able to do that."

What is interesting about this response is the way it reverses the normal presuppositions of democratic thinking. My interlocutors do not ask why Sweden or Norway should be able to refuse to admit an immigrant from Canada or the United States who wants to enter their territory. They ask why someone from Canada or the United States should be free to immigrate to Norway or Sweden. From a democratic perspective it should be restrictions on freedom that require justification, not the exercise of freedom.[17] When it comes to freedom of movement across state borders, however, that expectation tends to be reversed.

In the movie *The Shawshank Redemption*, the character played by Morgan Freeman is released on parole after forty years in prison and goes to work in a grocery store. In one scene, he asks the store manager for permission to go to the bathroom. The manager assures him that he does not need to ask permission to take a bathroom break. Later, reflecting on this incident, Freeman's character realizes that he has so internalized the constraints of prison life that he no longer understands what it is to think as a free person (though this motivates him to seek a fuller freedom than he has on parole). I think that something similar occurs in our approach to immigration. Discretionary state control over immigration is such a well established and pervasive practice that it seems unquestionable to many people. Because assumptions about the state's right to control entry and settlement pervade our consciousness, we reverse the normal assumptions about the justifications of freedom and constraint. I intend to challenge that way of thinking.

In this chapter, I want to focus exclusively on the reasons we have for thinking that the ability to move freely across borders might be the sort of vital interest that could deserve protection as a human right. This is only one side of the argument, of course. For a fair assessment, we have to consider not only the reasons why freedom of movement across borders is an important freedom but also the reasons why states might want the right to limit that freedom. That is the focus of the next chapter. As we shall see in that chapter, there are plausible reasons for restricting immigration under some circumstances, though these reasons are far more limited than people normally assume. I will argue in that chapter that the morally acceptable reasons for restrictions on immigration do not justify discretionary state control over immigration and do not prevent us from viewing the freedom to move across borders as a human right. For the moment, however, I want to focus only on the positive side—the case for seeing the freedom to move and reside wherever one wants as a vital human interest.

In developing my argument, I will proceed through reflective engagement with existing practices of mobility and freedom. This section proceeds in three steps. In the first, I argue that treating the freedom to move across state borders as a human right is a logical extension of the well-established democratic practice of treating freedom of movement within state borders as a human right. In the second, I explain why seeing the freedom to move across borders as a human right makes sense given our normal democratic understanding of human freedom and its importance. In the third I explain why treating the freedom to move across borders as a human right is compatible with the concern for reducing inequality discussed in the previous section.

The Cantilever Argument: Extending the Right to Freedom of Movement

At the moment no state or international body recognizes a general human right to enter a state and settle there without the state's permission. Citizens have a right to enter their own state, and, as we have seen in the last chapter, those seeking asylum from persecution have some rights to enter a state and stay there so long as they are at risk. But there is no generally recognized human right to go where one wants and live where one chooses. Should there be? How might one go about answering such a question?

One way to make a normative argument in favor of recognizing a new human right is to show that the proposed right is closely analogous to something that we already recognize as a human right. David Miller has called this the cantilever strategy.[18] The basic idea is that we start with some existing human right that everyone who accepts democratic principles recognizes as a human right. We can normally assume, for example, that those committed to democratic principles will accept the standard list of human rights articulated in major human right documents. We don't have to develop arguments for these rights. Rather we can use them as the starting point of an argument.[19]

This way of arguing for a moral view is common in philosophy and in ordinary life (even if most people would not think to apply the word "cantilever" to it). One takes certain commitments for granted and tries to show that these commitments have implications for another, more contested issue. For example, when someone claims that discrimination on the basis of sexual orientation is morally objectionable because it is similar to discrimination on the basis of race, she is not usually challenged (these days) to defend the view that discrimination on the basis of race is itself morally objectionable. That is taken as a settled issue. She may be challenged, however, to defend the claim that there is a relevant similarity between race and sexual orientation. As this example suggests, cantilever arguments have played a major role in debates about extending rights to marginalized or excluded groups. They have been often been used to challenge the exclusion of immigrants from citizenship and from other rights.

There is a powerful cantilever argument in favor of seeing the right to move freely across borders as a human right, namely that this is a logical extension of the right of free movement within states. Freedom of movement within a state is widely recognized as a human right. It is listed as a human right in prominent international documents. Here, for example, is the first part of Article 13 of the 1948 Universal Declaration of Human Rights:

(1) Everyone has the right to freedom of movement and residence within the borders of each state.

Article 12 of the 1966 International Covenant on Civil and Political Rights says something quite similar. Every democratic state in Europe and North America has endorsed these international documents, and many of them have constitutional provisions of their own guaranteeing internal rights of free movement. So, internal free movement is firmly established as a human right, at least at the level of principle.

That opens the door to the cantilever argument. If it is so important for people to have the right to move freely within a state, isn't it equally important for them to have the right to move across state borders? Every reason why one might want to move within a state may also be a reason for moving between states. One might want a job; one might fall in love with someone from another country; one might belong to a religion that has few adherents in one's native state and many in another; one might wish to pursue cultural opportunities that are only available in another land. The radical disjuncture that treats freedom of movement within the state as a human right while granting states discretionary control over freedom of movement across state borders makes no moral sense. We should extend the existing human right of free movement. We should recognize the freedom to migrate, to travel, and to reside wherever one chooses, as a human right.

Notice that in this cantilever argument for treating freedom of movement across state borders as a human right I take the moral importance of free movement within the state as a given. I assume that the fact that internal free movement is actually recognized as a human right by important international documents which have been endorsed by democratic states is sufficient to establish it as a firm foundation upon which I can build the extension that is the right of free movement across borders. I deliberately do not attempt to articulate the rationale for treating free movement within the state as a human right. Instead, I just claim that whatever that rationale is, the same rationale will apply to movement across borders because the reasons why people want to move from one place to another will apply in both cases. Indeed I mention specific reasons why people might want to move only as hypothetical examples to support my claim that the reasons for moving within and between states are quite similar. I do not suggest that these reasons for moving actually constitute the vital interests that make internal free movement important enough to be recognized as a human right. There might be a variety of ways to defend the idea that freedom of movement within the state should be a human right. I leave that open. Instead, my goal in this argument is to shift the task of explaining why freedom of movement within the state deserves to be a human right to those who want to resist the idea of treating freedom of movement across borders as a human right. Given the plausibility of my analogy between the two kinds of movement, the opponents have to offer a rationale for the human right they do accept (i.e., the right of free movement within the state) and then explain why that rationale does not apply to movement across borders.

There are two ways of resisting a cantilever argument, and both are relevant here. The first is to challenge the analogy itself. The second is to argue that the proposed new right has harmful consequences that the original right does not entail or violates entitlements that the original right respects. In this chapter,

I will consider only the first sort of objection: the claim that some of the key positive reasons for establishing freedom of internal movement as a human right do not apply to the proposed new right of freedom of movement across borders. In the next chapter, I will consider the second sort of objection: arguments that treating free movement across borders as a human right would have negative consequences that internal free movement does not have or violate entitlements that are respected by internal free movement.

I have encountered five ways of trying to draw distinctions between freedom of movement within states and freedom of movement across borders in order to challenge the analogy I have drawn. I will argue that none of them succeeds.

The first objection is that free movement within the state serves a nation-building function that has no analogue in free movement across borders. Freedom of movement for citizens within the state's territory helps to promote a sense of common national identity. That is why states embrace it.

The problem with this objection is that it provides no normative justification for establishing freedom of movement within the state as a human right. It may be true that internal freedom of movement has a nation-building effect, and that freedom of movement across borders does not. It may also be true that the nation-building effect is the reason why political elites in some states established internal free movement as a legal right.[20] But we are talking about why internal freedom of movement should be regarded as a human right. The fact that freedom of movement within states may contribute to a sense of common national identity is simply not a relevant reason for making it a human right. The same point applies if one wants to argue that freedom of internal movement is economically advantageous. There is no need to make a prudent policy into a human right. Human rights require a different sort of rationale.

Any plausible justification for making something a human right has to link it to the fundamental interests of human beings, not to the contingent benefits of a particular policy. Indeed, internal freedom of movement may not always be advantageous from the perspective of political elites. There can be good policy reasons for restricting mobility rights in some circumstances. A state may want to avoid an excessive pace of urbanization or to promote local or regional responsibility for social programs. For example, China has created the *hukou* system to restrict movement from rural to urban areas. The fact that this policy has been criticized as a violation of human rights illustrates my point.[21] If internal freedom of movement were merely a policy with certain advantages, there would be no reason for states to make it a human right, thus limiting their discretion. It would make more sense simply to leave the legal right to internal freedom of movement as a policy tool that states might (or might not) want to deploy, depending on the circumstances. Nevertheless, internal freedom of movement has been established as a basic human right that all states must respect, even when it is against their interests to do so. In sum, the nation-building effect of free movement provides no justification for treating internal free movement as a human right. It follows that the fact that freedom of movement across borders does not have a nation-building effect provides no reason for resisting the extension proposed in my cantilever argument.[22]

A second challenge to the analogy between internal free movement and free movement across borders seeks to show that internal free movement is linked to citizenship while free movement across borders is not. Some say that a right of internal free movement is a right that is owed to individuals because of their political relationship to the state.[23] If this line of argument does not intend to challenge the status of internal free movement as a human right, and that is what I am assuming here, the claim must be that free movement within the state is a membership-specific human right, to use my earlier terminology. Clearly, a general right to move across borders does not rest on any link to an already established membership. So if it were possible to show that the right of internal free movement rests upon membership claims, then it would be possible to challenge the analogy between internal movement and movement across borders and to defeat the cantilever argument.

The problem with this line of argument is that it is not easy to explain why the right of internal movement should be seen as a membership-specific human right rather than a general human right. Recall that general human rights like the right to personal security, the right to free speech, and the right to freedom of religion are rights that are owed to all human beings who are within the jurisdiction of a state, regardless of their legal status. As we saw in chapters 5 and 7, they are rights owed even to visitors and irregular migrants. At first glance (and, I will argue, upon closer scrutiny as well), freedom of movement within the state looks like this sort of general human right. That certainly corresponds to the practice of democratic states. Democratic states routinely claim a right to determine whether noncitizens may enter and reside in the state, but they do not normally claim a right to tell them where they may and may not go once they have been admitted or where they must reside once they have been given permission to stay.[24]

The major human rights documents do not limit the right of free internal movement to citizens (or even citizens and residents). As I noted above, Article 13 of the 1948 Declaration announces that *"Everyone* has the right to freedom of movement and residence within the borders of each state" (emphasis added).[25] There is nothing membership-specific about that. Article 12 of the 1966 Covenant is a bit more circumspect, establishing freedom of movement and residence within the state as a human right of all those "lawfully within the territory of a state."[26] The phrase "lawfully within" does not limit the right to members, however. It implies that even people who are only in a state on a temporary basis as visitors or tourists should enjoy freedom of movement and residence within the state while they are present, even if the conditions of their admission limit their activities in other ways. The "lawfully within" caveat seems intended to avoid providing irregular migrants with a legal foothold for moving within a state once they have gained entry.

Is there a case for seeing internal free movement as a membership-specific human right? Recall that a membership-specific human right is one that the state is morally obliged to grant to citizens and perhaps to residents as well, but not to others within its jurisdiction. In my original discussion of this distinction, I mentioned the right to enter one's own country as an example of a membership-specific human right for citizens. That right appears in both the 1948 Declaration and in the 1966 Convention. Of course, that specification simply presupposes that the state is normally entitled to restrict entry for those who are not citizens, and the whole point of the open borders argument is to challenge that limitation. But I am not claiming that every membership-specific human right is morally flawed in the way that this one is. For example, the right to vote is legitimately restricted to people with ongoing ties to the society whose laws they help to shape. We don't think that visitors and tourists ought to be able to vote, and that is not because we have failed to understand the implications of democratic principles. (By contrast, democratic principles do require that permanent members of a society have the right to vote, as we saw in chapter 3.) So, if we think of the right to participate in democratic elections as a human right, it is a membership-specific human right, one that is owed only to people who live in the society (or who have some comparable claim) and not to everyone who happens to be in the country during an election.

Can the right of internal free movement be linked to membership in this way? I don't see how. From the individual's perspective, freedom of internal movement is important for many reasons unrelated to membership or political participation. It contributes to personal, civil, economic, and social dimensions of freedom as well as to the ability to participate in politics. Of course, freedom of internal movement can be vital to political participation or can prove essential to protect other fundamental political rights, but that does not show that we should transform it from a general human right (as it is now) into a membership-specific right.[27] So, we can't use this as a basis for challenging the cantilever argument.

A third challenge to the cantilever argument is to say that the real goal of the human right to internal free movement is to prevent discrimination against groups within a state.[28] Discrimination against people seeking to cross borders does not raise the same concerns, according to these critics, and so the analogy between internal movement and movement across borders breaks down.

If this assertion about the purpose of the right to internal free movement is advanced as a historical claim about why it was originally established as a human right, there does not seem to be much evidence to support that interpretation in the sources I have read.[29] Supporters of this right in the 1948 Declaration were certainly conscious of and reacting to forced relocations of people by the Nazis, and some of the opponents of the right like South Africa were trying to preserve discriminatory practices, but the secondary sources suggest that the primary motivation for making freedom of movement within the state a human right was that it was seen as an important human freedom in itself, not merely that it would provide a bulwark against discrimination.

It is true, of course, that a right to freedom of internal movement can provide valuable protection against certain sorts of discrimination, but it is far too broad a right for that to be its primary purpose. There can be good public policy reasons for regulating movement in ways that are prohibited once freedom of movement is established as a human right. Indeed, that concern was reflected in the original debates on the issue. So, if the goal of free movement were only to prevent discrimination, it would make sense to tailor the right much more narrowly, for example, by prohibiting discriminatory restrictions on freedom of movement.

Finally, even if the goal of a right of free movement were to prevent discrimination on objectionable grounds, there would be just as much reason to adopt a right of free movement across borders as there would be to adopt a right of free internal movement. Racial and religious discrimination have played a major role in restrictions on immigration in the past. Think of the White Australia policy and the similar policies in the United States and Canada. Ironically, this is the one area where states have generally imposed some limits on their own discretion with regard to immigration. As I argued in chapter 9, despite the general claim to a right to discretionary control over admissions, no democratic state today treats it as morally acceptable to discriminate (openly) on the basis of race or religion in admissions.

In sum, the idea that the purpose of the right of free movement is to prevent discrimination is implausible as an account of the basic rationale of the right and would provide no basis for resisting an extension of the right even if the account were true.

A fourth way of challenging the cantilever argument is to say that what is really important is whether people have an adequate range of freedoms and opportunities, including freedom of movement, within their own state. So long as they have passed this threshold of adequacy within their own state, they normally have no vital interest in being able to cross state borders.[30]

The problem with this threshold argument is that it provides no normative basis for the human right of free movement within the state, which I am taking as the starting point in my cantilever argument. If the standard for vital interests is only that people have an adequate range of opportunities, and if adequate range is defined modestly, it is not clear why this range of opportunities could not be provided within subunits of large states. For example, many states within the United States and several provinces in Canada have a larger population and a wider range of internal economic and social opportunities than many independent states. American states and Canadian provinces have relatively strong jurisdictional powers and responsibilities. So there could be good policy reasons for restricting entry of people from other states and provinces, such as preventing people from other jurisdictions from taking advantage of more generous social programs. In fact, these policy reasons look a lot like the reasons that are sometimes offered for restricting immigration. On the threshold argument, it would appear that the vital interests of people could be met within these subunits. So, the threshold argument provides no reason to have a human right of internal free movement beyond the relevant subunit. Yet the existing human right guarantees a right of free movement across the entire territory of the country. The cantilever argument demands a rationale for the radical disjuncture between the importance accorded internal free movement and the importance accorded free movement across borders. Since the threshold argument cannot provide a rationale for internal free movement, it fails to meet that demand.

The final challenge to the cantilever argument is the claim that there is a fundamental difference between the interest a person has in moving within her own state and the interest she has in moving across borders. The former, some say, is a vital interest and so worthy of protection as a human right, while the latter is merely a minor interest, a matter of a preference. Note again that this argument does not challenge the original right of free movement within the state but seeks rather to distinguish the interests protected by internal free movement from the ones protected by movement across borders.

At first glance, this argument may look plausible, in part for the reasons discussed in my theory of social membership. Most people develop connections and relationships in the society where they live. They speak the language, they understand the informal norms, they know how things work, and they identify with the community. That's where they belong. So, it might seem plausible to say that it is more important for most people to be able to move around in the territory of the state where they live than to be able to move to some other state.[31]

As soon as one thinks about the differences between states, however, the argument looks much less persuasive. Consider the vast differences between states and the consequences of these differences for the lives of human beings. Fiji is a small, poor island state in the South Pacific with a population of less than a million people. The United States is a huge, rich state with a population of three hundred and thirty million people. From what perspective would it make sense to say that every American has a vital interest in being able to move freely within the entire territory of the United States, but that every Fijian only has a vital interest in being able to move freely within the territory of Fiji? On what grounds could one claim that the Fijian has no vital interest in having access to the much wider array of geographic, economic, social, and political options that access to the United States would provide? Why wouldn't the vast differences between states matter when it comes to the question of the extent and limits of our interests in freedom of movement?

Someone might object that this takes us back to the argument about open borders and global justice. It does, but in a somewhat different way and that difference matters. Now we are concerned not so much with the overall pattern of distribution or of opportunity and how that might be affected by open borders but with the moral claims of individual human beings to human rights that protect their vital interests. Remember that the challenge posed by the cantilever argument simply presupposes that freedom of movement within the state is a human right. That is not in question. The objection we are considering is one that seeks to distinguish between freedom of internal movement and freedom of movement across borders on the grounds that the former protects vital interests and there are no vital interests at stake in the latter. In the world as it is organized today, that is wildly implausible.

In sum, none of the five attempts to challenge the analogy between internal freedom of movement and freedom of movement across borders can withstand scrutiny. The cantilever argument stands. So long as we regard freedom of movement within the state as a human right, we should also regard freedom of movement across borders as a human right.

Why Freedom of Internal Movement Should Be a Human Right

Like an architectural cantilever, a cantilever argument is only as strong as the foundation on which it rests. When I began articulating the open borders argument, I was confident that no one committed to democratic principles would challenge the moral status of basic human rights articulated in major human rights documents. I was wrong. I have found that, faced with the choice between extending the right of free movement across borders and challenging the moral status of internal free movement as a human right, some people are willing to throw internal freedom of movement under the bus. They say (sometimes only implicitly and more often in conversation than in print) that perhaps freedom of movement within the state is not so important after all, not really something worthy of designation as a human right.

This takes us back to fundamentals. Why does freedom of movement, either within the state or across state borders, matter morally? To make the case that open borders would contribute significantly to human freedom, I will first show that freedom of movement within the state is an important freedom. Then I will show that if states were to control internal movement in the ways that they control movement across borders, this would constitute a significant restriction of this important freedom. This will enable us to see that treating movement across borders as we currently treat internal movement within democratic states would enhance human freedom, other things being equal. Remember that we are deferring consideration of any negative consequences of open borders until the next chapter.

As usual, I want to stick close to the ground, presenting a discussion of freedom of movement that fits with ordinary understandings of that idea, though also one that will have a place in any plausible theoretical account. So, I begin by giving an example of an ordinary experience of exercising the right of free movement within a democratic state.

Imagine the following scenario. Everything in the world is as it is today, except that you live in New York and want to go from New York to Los Angeles, perhaps for a visit, perhaps to move there permanently. Let's say you decide to drive. You have to rent or buy a car, and you have to get gas for the car. As you drive along, you may face tolls on some roads, and you will need food and lodging. When you get to Los Angeles, you will have to find a place to stay, whether temporarily or permanently.

Let me draw your attention to two features of the situation that in some sense limit your capacity to do whatever you want with respect to moving from New York to Los Angeles. First, you need certain resources to make the move: a car, gas, food, lodging, etc. Second, you have to obey two sets of laws in the course of the move: laws protecting private property (which prevent you from just taking whatever resources you need) and laws regulating traffic. For the moment, I won't say anything about whether these limits on your capacity to do whatever you want should be regarded as constraints on your freedom to move or perhaps as the background structures that make freedom possible or as something else. Roughly speaking, however, these are the only obstacles to your moving from New York to Los Angeles if you choose to do so.

Now think about the *absence* of other sorts of limits on your capacity to move. One obvious respect in which you are free to move is that you are moving because you have decided to do so. No public official has ordered you to move. Of almost equal importance is the fact that, with certain minor qualifications (such as a possible obligation not to leave the city because of your involvement in court proceedings), no official is entitled to prevent you from moving from New York to Los Angeles. You don't have to get the government's permission to make the move or to get on the highway or to buy gas or to set up residence in Los Angeles. Furthermore, you don't have to explain to any official why you have decided to move. You may (or may not) discuss your reasons for moving with your friends and relatives, and they may (or may not) think your reasons are good ones, but no official is entitled to a say in the matter. Indeed, you don't even have to notify any government official about your trip, though if you do decide to stay in Los Angeles you will eventually have to inform various government offices about that (e.g., in the course of filing taxes, getting a local driver's license, etc.). Finally, all of these facts about the ways in which the government may not hinder or even involve itself in your move from New York to Los Angeles are not just contingent features of the current situation which the government is free to change by passing new laws or changing its policies. The freedoms that I have identified are deeply integrated into the legal structure of the United States at the most fundamental constitutional level. They constrain public officials (at least in principle). The bottom line is that apart from requiring you to obey generally applicable property and traffic laws, the political authorities are not entitled to limit your ability to move from New York to Los Angeles in any way.

This freedom that you have to move from New York to Los Angeles is one commonplace example of what the human right to internal free movement entails in practice. Intuitively, this seems to me to be an important freedom. Let's consider some of the reasons people have offered for thinking that it is not.

First, some critics argue that internal freedom of movement is not a very important freedom because we restrict movement within countries for many different reasons: respect for private property, imprisonment and parole for criminal offenses, medical quarantines, prohibitions on settling on indigenous lands, traffic regulations, and so on. Some of these reasons, like traffic regulations, they say, do not involve any fundamental values. They are merely matters of efficiency or public convenience. If we can restrict free movement within countries for trivial reasons like traffic control, the critics ask, how could it be an important freedom, much less a basic human right?

The claim that freedom of movement cannot be important because it is subject to these sorts of constraints implicitly relies upon a conception of freedom that no friend of freedom would endorse. Even if we were to grant that laws regulating traffic and protecting private property can appropriately be described as constraints on freedom of movement, similar constraints apply to most important freedoms. The critics are invoking an implausible standard, one that could be used to discredit any claim to a freedom right.

Take the example of freedom of speech. That is widely acknowledged to be both an important freedom and a human right. A right to freedom of speech does not mean that you can say anything to anyone whenever and wherever you want. As everyone knows, free speech is subject to many different restrictions, regulations, and constraints even in democracies where it is acknowledged as a fundamental right. You cannot yell "fire" in a crowded theatre. You cannot normally enter someone else's house to express your ideas or set up a loudspeaker outside their house, even if the audience you are trying to reach with your speech is inside. All democracies have laws about libel and slander, and some have laws regulating hate speech. Often we make people take turns in expressing their ideas. We regulate speech through formal rules like Robert's Rules of Order and informal norms like expecting people to raise their hand to ask a question. Some ways of restricting free speech are contested (e.g., hate speech laws), but (almost) no one actually imagines that it makes sense to have no limits at all on speech. None of this means that freedom of speech is a meaningless concept or a trivial concern.

Likewise, the fact that freedom of movement is subject to various restrictions and qualifications does not mean that it cannot be an important freedom or a basic human right. In fact, it makes sense to see some restrictions on freedom of movement, like traffic regulations, as designed to increase overall freedom of movement, just as rules about taking turns should be seen as a contribution to, rather than a restriction of, free speech. It's a familiar point that the freedom of one individual must be compatible with a like freedom for others. Restrictions that serve the purpose of making everyone's freedom compatible with everyone else's freedom are freedom-enhancing. Traffic regulations are like that.

Other restrictions, like denying people the right to enter the property of others, do limit freedom of movement in the name of promoting other values, but freedom of movement is not alone in being restricted for the sake of these values. As we have just seen, freedom of speech is also constrained by the right to private property. And the right to private property, which is itself intimately linked to freedom, is constrained in its turn by rights to freedom of movement and freedom of expression.[32] Different freedoms can conflict and then they have to be balanced against one another. So, the existence of restrictions on freedom of movement for the sake of other forms of freedom or to enhance overall freedom does not prove that freedom of movement is unimportant or that it cannot be a human right.

A second objection to the idea that freedom of movement is important focuses on the idea of vital interests. Human rights, these critics say, are supposed to protect vital interests. So, if the freedom to move is to be regarded as a human right, it must be necessary to move to protect some vital interest. But it is rare that someone really needs to move to meet a vital interest, especially if the person is living in a democratic country where people's vital interests are usually not under threat. Furthermore, some versions of the objection insist, vital interests cannot be idiosyncratic. A vital interest must be a generic human interest like the need for subsistence rather than the need for a particular kind of food. This makes it even more unlikely that it will be necessary to move to satisfy a vital interest.[33]

In the context of my example above, this sort of objection would take the form of asking "What is so important about moving from New York to Los

Angeles? New York is a big city. You can meet your generic vital interests as well in New York as in Los Angeles (leaving aside the possibility that you need constant sunshine and warm weather). Moreover, the state of New York is bigger than many countries in both size and population. If you have to leave New York City, you can always go to Albany or Buffalo. Why can't you meet your vital interests within the boundaries of New York State?"

I think this objection misses the mark, and not just because of the limitations of Albany and Buffalo as alternatives to Los Angeles. The vital interest that is at stake here is not the specific move to Los Angeles but freedom itself. You have a vital interest in being free, and being free to move where you want is an important aspect of being free. It's not everything, of course. But it matters greatly. You have a vital interest in being able to go where you want to go and do what you want to do, so long as you do not violate anyone else's rights. Having your will matter is one important aspect of modern freedom. One of the classic ways of conceiving of freedom is in terms of not being subject to the will of another. From this perspective, it matters a lot that no political authority gets to decide whether or not it is important for you to go to Los Angeles. That is up to you. In my example, I deliberately did not say why you were going from New York to Los Angeles, because all that mattered was that you had decided to go. Perhaps it will be a difficult journey and when you get there you will find that the people have strange customs to which you will have to adapt. Perhaps you will regret the move. But it is your choice whether to go or not. It is not up to the government to decide what options are valuable and why. If that freedom were taken away or severely restricted, it would be an important loss.

A third objection to seeing freedom of movement within the state as an important freedom is that most people don't want to move. How important can a freedom be, the critics ask, if most people do not make use of it?

"Very important" is the correct answer. Once again the objection approaches freedom in the wrong way. We cannot assess the importance of having the freedom to move from New York to Los Angeles just by considering how many people actually make the move. Rights are not designed only with majorities in view. Indeed, one of the fundamental goals of rights is to protect the vital interests of minorities and individuals. So, the first question is not merely what proportion of a population wants to exercise their freedom to move but whether some individuals want to do so. The claim that a particular freedom is unimportant if most people don't take advantage of it is unpersuasive once one looks at individuals rather than numbers. To those who do want to move, the freedom is vital.

There is a second, deeper point. As with many rights and freedoms, freedom of movement can be an important right, even if one never actually exercises it. Simply knowing that you have the right to move contributes to your freedom. It matters greatly that every citizen is free to run for public office, rather than having that option legally restricted to a predetermined elite, even though most people never run for office or aspire to do so. Having a right to a fair trial is important, even though you will never make use of this right unless you are accused of a crime. Having a right to freedom of religion can be important, even if you live in a community in which your religion is shared by the vast majority so that your own religious practices are never actually under threat. Having a right of free speech is important, even if you never say anything controversial. So, too, having the right to move freely can be important, even if you always live in the same place.

There is a fourth objection to which I am more sympathetic, though this is not usually advanced in conjunction with the others. This is the objection that a formal freedom like the right to move is not very significant if one does not have the resources to make use of that freedom. As I noted in my story, you cannot drive from New York to Los Angeles unless you have access to a car and can pay for gas, food, and lodging. The same issue arises even more forcefully in the context of international migration. Even if people had a right to move across borders, many would not have the economic resources needed to do so. But the need for economic resources to make formal freedoms effective does not mean that formal freedoms do not matter. It simply means that formal freedoms are not sufficient. Indeed, that fits perfectly well with my argument in the earlier global justice section about the need for more economic equality between states, and it is one of the arguments for redistribution within democratic states. But redistribution within and between states raises other issues, and no book can discuss everything. The crucial point for my purposes is that having a right to move is an important aspect of freedom in and of itself. Without that right, you are not free to move even if you have the economic resources to do so. And we should not underestimate the ability of people to find the resources to move even under difficult circumstances.

So far, I have used a story about an ordinary decision to move from New York to Los Angeles to render vivid the importance of the freedom to move. Now I want to imagine the transformation in three stages of an individual's control over the decision to move from New York to Los Angeles so that in the end it looks like the kind of opportunity (or lack of opportunity) to move that faces most migrants. I do this for two reasons. First, this offers a way of making the absence of freedom in the immigration context more visible. As I have said at various points, we tend to take the state's control over immigration for granted and that distorts our thinking about freedom. Second, I want to bring home the point that freedom admits of degrees. While I am arguing that we should establish a human right to move freely across state borders, we are not limited to a choice between this and the status quo. As I will try to show, there are other ways of structuring the immigration process that would represent a great advance in human freedom even while falling well short of open borders.

So, let's return to our original example and modify it a bit. You want to move from New York to Los Angeles. Let's suppose first that instead of just being free to go whenever you want, you have to get permission to move to Los Angeles, but that the permission will be routinely granted if you request it. This is clearly a constraint on your freedom in some ways. For example, it can affect the timing of your move. You have to plan further in advance, wait for official approval, etc. Still, I'm assuming here that you have an entitlement to move once you have filed the proper papers. There is no official discretion. So, it is still appropriate to say that you enjoy a right to freedom of movement under this second scenario.

Now let's modify the example more significantly. In this third scenario, you don't enjoy a right to move even upon notification of your intent. You have to notify the authorities of your desire to move, but they are entitled to balance your desire to move from New York to California against various other considerations which might make it seem better from a public policy perspective if you are not allowed to make the move. These considerations might be concerned with your personal abilities and job prospects or with circumstances in the state to which you are seeking to move (e.g., its current unemployment level) or with the overall number of requests to enter. The details don't matter (on the assumption that they comply with the sorts of normative principles that I identified in chapter 9).

So, a big change has taken place. You are no longer simply free to move. You have to get the approval of the authorities and that approval may not be forthcoming.

Now let's restore the balance a bit. Let's also assume that the officials must show that denying you permission to move is necessary for the public policy goals that they are pursuing, that there is no other way to pursue the goal effectively that intrudes less on your freedom, and that the benefits gained by your exclusion outweigh the harm done to you by refusing you entry. Suppose further that the authorities have to establish these claims in an independent forum in which you are entitled to present evidence and arguments challenging their claims and that you have a right to appeal if the decision goes against you.[34]

Under this scenario, you are not simply free to move but you are not simply a passive subject, either. You are still treated as an agent whose will matters, you have a range of rights and your desire to move is a weighty consideration that must be taken into account in the final decision. In that respect your freedom still counts for a good deal, although clearly not for as much as it did under the first two scenarios. Obviously, it would be possible to adjust the rules and procedures to give your freedom to move more or less weight in this sort of process.

I introduced this latest scenario to bring home the point that there are degrees of freedom and that there are institutional arrangements well short of open borders that treat people as free agents whose will deserves respect even when it is constrained. There are familiar institutional practices that democratic states adopt when they restrict freedoms that they recognize as prima facie worthy of respect. These are the sorts of practices that I was trying to evoke above. They limit the arbitrary exercise of power and preserve some important elements of freedom.

Finally, let us modify the example one more time. In this final scenario, you have to notify the authorities that you want to move, but political officials in California (whom you have had no say in electing) are free to decide whether or not to let you in.[35] They may make the decision based on announced policies but they are not required to do so. They do not have to take your interests into account in their policy and they generally don't. They don't have to justify the policy to any independent forum or prove that it meets any criteria. They apply their policy to your case in whatever way they see fit, and you have no recourse or basis of appeal if you think that the policy has been misapplied. In this last scenario, you may still be permitted to move but your rights have almost completely disappeared. Your freedom to move is entirely at the discretion of the authorities.

Compared with the all of the other scenarios, the individual seeking to move from New York to California enjoys a lot less freedom in this last scenario. Of course, this last scenario roughly corresponds to the position of most immigrants seeking admission to democratic states (excluding various special arrangements such as the internal mobility provisions within the European Union). Under a regime of discretionary state control over borders, therefore, people have a lot less freedom to move compared with the freedom they would have under a regime of open borders or even than they would have under a regime modeled on the scenario that required authorities to justify exclusion to individuals on objective grounds in an independent forum and which gave the individual's desire to move significant weight. The freedom that people lack under the current discretionary regime is an important freedom for reasons that should be apparent from this everyday example of being able to move from New York to California.

Human Rights and Moral Priorities

As I have noted, my argument for open borders contains two components. The first is that open borders will contribute to the reduction of international economic inequality by removing the barriers that prevent people in poor states from coming to rich states to improve their lot. The second is that free movement should be regarded as a basic human right because of its intrinsic importance as a human liberty.

Some critics argue that these two components are fundamentally at odds with one another. They say that the concern for inequality implies giving priority to the poor in admissions to rich states, but treating free movement as a human right precludes this because it is owed equally to all.[36] Some who are sympathetic to the ideal of open borders suggest that I should focus on the goal of reducing international inequality, abandoning the idea that free movement should be seen as a human right.[37]

I reject this view. While I think that challenging international inequalities is one important function of my open borders argument, I also think that there are important independent reasons for seeing freedom of movement as a human right. In my view, these elements of my argument are mutually reinforcing and complementary. I want to continue to defend both.

I confess that I am puzzled by the objection that there is some tension between seeing free movement as a human right and giving priority to the poor in situations where all cannot be admitted.[38] There are many basic rights that can be fully respected only if most people are not seeking to exercise them at the same time. We all have the right to free speech, but we cannot all speak at once (and expect to communicate). Every citizen has the right to run for public office, but think of the chaos if everyone born in the United States and 35 years old decided to launch his or her own campaign for the presidency. We may all have a right to walk freely on the public sidewalks, but it is not possible for all of the inhabitants of a city to exercise that right at the same time on the same stretch of sidewalk. If more people want to use the same public street at the same time than are able to do so, we would presumably have to develop priority principles for the exercise of that right, and it would be plausible to do so by considering the relative urgency of the reasons why people want to exercise this right. (Think of the challenge of developing rules for mass demonstrations, parades, and so on.)

Most of the time we do not have to pay attention to the implicit constraints on the right to free speech or the right to run for public office or the right to use public streets or other basic rights because people spontaneously and for reasons of their own avoid exercising their rights in ways that lead to conflicts. Sometimes, however, conflicts emerge. Consider the example of emergency health care which I have described in previous chapters as a human right. Even under conditions in which all can be treated, emergency rooms routinely treat the most urgent cases first, making others wait. In conditions of extreme scarcity, such as one encounters in wars and catastrophes, medical officials go further and create a triage system that gives priority to those with urgent needs and a reasonable chance of survival, denying medical care not only to those with less urgent needs but also to those whom medical treatment is unlikely to save (even though some of these would be saved if treated). It seems to me that this question of how to allocate emergency health care to which all are entitled in principle provides a close analogy to the moral challenge we would face if we accepted freedom of movement as a human right but thought that there were compelling moral reasons for limiting entry to some extent. So long as one does not adopt an unreasonably narrow idea of human rights, there is no contradiction in principle between the idea of seeing freedom of movement as a human right and the idea that the poor should be given priority of entry, if not all can be immediately admitted.[39] In a just world, however, as I will argue in the next chapter, the demands of equality and freedom would be largely complementary rather than in conflict.

Conclusion

In this chapter I have presented the initial case for open borders. In the first half of the chapter, I argued that there are aspects of the contemporary international order that bear an uncomfortable similarity to feudalism. In a world with a few rich states and many poor ones, the state's right to exercise discretionary control over immigration plays a crucial role in maintaining the privileges of those who live in the rich states. Those of us who live in rich democratic states are complicit in a system of inequality which we are able to maintain only because of the ways in which we limit the freedom of others to enter our territories. In the second half of the chapter, I tried to show that the restrictions that we place on the freedom to move across borders are incompatible with our deepest democratic values. Freedom of movement within the state is rightly seen as a fundamental freedom, I argued, and the freedom to move across borders should be seen as a fundamental freedom as well. I turn next to challenges to this view.

12

The Claims of Community

In the previous chapter, I focused on the positive case for open borders, identifying the reasons for thinking that granting people the right to move and settle wherever they want would contribute greatly to human freedom and equality. I turn now to challenges to open borders that focus on the moral claims of the political communities that immigrants might seek to enter.

In this chapter, as in the previous one, I am not concerned with questions about the immediate feasibility of open borders but rather with its status as a moral ideal, a requirement of justice. Some will be impatient with this approach, dismissing it as utopian. But critiques of deeply entrenched injustices are always utopian. That is what it means to say the injustices are deeply entrenched.

Most people do not agree with my claim that justice requires free movement across borders. They do not regard open borders as something that is right in principle but unrealistic. Rather they share the conventional view that states are morally entitled, as a matter of principle, to exercise discretionary control over immigration or they think that open borders would have such bad consequences that the positive case for it no longer seems plausible once one takes these consequences into account. From this perspective, the deepest objection to open borders is not that it is unachievable but that it is wrong about what morality requires. That is the sort of criticism I want to consider.

When I speak in this chapter of "discretionary control over immigration" as the opposite of open borders, I am not using this phrase in an absolutist sense, just as I do not use the phrase "open borders" in an absolutist sense. It is the conventional view that I want to criticize, not some implausible caricature of that view. Most of those who want to grant the state wide latitude in decisions about admissions accept some constraints like the ones I have discussed earlier about nondiscrimination, family reunification, and so on.[1] As I argued before, those limits on discretion are quite compatible with the conventional view.

Despite the strong defense I offered of open borders in the previous chapter, I think there are few (if any) moral absolutes, especially when it comes to human action in the world. Freedom and equality are fundamental values but they are not the only values. Besides, the concepts of freedom and equality contain their own internal tensions and each stands in tension with the other. And so, as we shall see in this chapter, limits on free movement can sometimes be justifiable. But there is a vast difference between acknowledging qualifications to a right of free movement and rejecting open borders altogether.

Bounded Justice

One important challenge to the idea of open borders is that it exaggerates the moral claims that people outside a political community can make on those within. From this perspective, the demands of justice arise primarily within the context of a state, from common subordination to political authority and from the many ways in which that common subordination inevitably affects people's lives. In this view, freedom of movement, equality of opportunity and distributive justice are not moral principles that transcend borders. They are moral claims that people acquire from their participation in a political community and from their connections with the other members of that community. So, even if permitting free movement across borders would enhance human freedom and equality, democratic states are under no obligation to open their borders, especially if they see some costs to their own citizens in doing so. I will call this the bounded justice view.[2]

Most of those who take this view do not deny that we have some moral duties to people outside our political community. They recognize that states should not violate the human rights of outsiders. Beyond that, they think that democratic states have some obligations to respond to the moral failures and incapacities of other states. For example, they usually acknowledge that we have a duty to address the plight of refugees, at least in part by admitting some of them. Many of these theorists believe that every human being has a moral right to live in a political community that respects basic freedoms and that gives people a reasonable chance at a decent life. They also think that affluent democratic states have a moral obligation to assist those who are below this threshold. So, many of these authors do not defend the status quo, but criticize it sharply.

At the same time, these theorists think that arguments for global justice, including the argument for open borders, fail to recognize the limits to justice claims by nonmembers. Their view is that justice is primarily about relationships inside the state. There may be very significant differences between states in terms of the life chances that they offer their inhabitants, but this fact does not give rise to any strong moral claim for assistance from better off states to those less well off, or to a right for people to move from one state to another where prospects are better.

Like the advocates of bounded justice, I think that ongoing subjection within a political community has great moral significance. That is precisely why I argued in earlier chapters that those who settle permanently within a political community should be regarded as members and given access to citizenship. Not everyone is a member, and membership does matter morally. Even if borders were open, there would still be important and legitimate distinctions between a state's responsibilities for those within its borders and its responsibilities for those outside. I explore this point further later in the chapter. Where I part company with the advocates of bounded justice is when they say that justice is *only* concerned with our connections to our political community and to our fellow citizens and that therefore the exclusion of people who wish to join our community is not unjust.

One immediate problem with the bounded justice view is that it simply presupposes the moral legitimacy of the coercion that is used to exclude peaceful immigrants who want only to enter in order to build decent lives for themselves and their families. One of the virtues of the open borders argument is that it brings this problem into view. Refusal of entry is an exercise of coercive power.[3] (Borders have guards, the guards have guns.) Even on the bounded justice view, the exercise of coercion by a state raises questions of justice. Coercion must be justifiable to the person being coerced. To say that coercion must be justifiable to the person being coerced is not to say that we must persuade every individual that she is being treated fairly but rather that we must offer reasons for our use of coercion, that those reasons must respect the claims of all human beings to be regarded as moral agents, and that the reasons must be open to criticism and contestation.[4]

One theorist of bounded justice, Michael Blake, acknowledges that refusal of entry involves the exercise of coercive power but argues that this form of coercion is much less morally significant than the pervasive coercion to which those living within a state are subject and so requires much less justification.[5] I find this line of argument puzzling. While it is true that a state has no direct control over the daily life of a person whom it has excluded, it is hard to imagine an exercise of the state's coercive power short of imprisonment that has a more pervasive effect on a person's life than refusal of admission. This is what we might call a gateway decision. It has enormous implications for all the subsequent life choices a person can make.

Indeed, it is not only the direct refusal of entry that we should see as an exercise of coercive power but the background rules that make people believe there is no point in seeking entry. In the modern world, contemporary means of communication enable most people to know something about life in other states and contemporary modes of transportation would make migration physically and economically feasible for many, in the absence of coercive restrictions. The existence of these coercive restrictions is so well known that it often acts in a pre-emptive way, effectively removing migration as an option from the minds of people who might otherwise consider it. From this perspective, we might say that, for many people, even the ongoing exercise of state power in their daily existence does not have as pervasive an impact on their lives as this prior determination of where they belong and where they may (or may not) live.

My claim in the previous chapter that freedom of movement across borders should be seen as a general human right raises the stakes higher still. All of the advocates of bounded justice agree that it is unjust for states to violate the human rights of nonmembers. They extend the scope of justice that far. The advocates of bounded justice can, of course, deny that we should regard freedom of movement as a general human right, but they cannot do so simply by appealing to the idea of bounded justice, since bounded justice is, by definition, not concerned with general human rights. Moreover, since bounded justice advocates usually acknowledge that states may have a duty to admit refugees, it seems hard to imagine how they can justify routinely turning away nonrefugee immigrants on a discretionary basis without appealing, at least implicitly, to the moral legitimacy of the background arrangements that assign human beings to particular states and deny them a general right of entry to others. The bounded justice view thus rests ultimately on a claim about the moral legitimacy of the way the world is organized.

Most theorists of bounded justice do not confront this issue directly. They simply start with the claim that the primary problem of justice is the moral justification of the state's authority to those who are subject to it. That is certainly how democratic ideas emerged historically, but the inner logic of democratic commitments to human freedom and equality requires us to go deeper. It requires us to ask whether the way the world is currently organized is just or not, and, if not, what would be required to make it just.

Why does the way that the world is organized raise questions of justice? Because that structure itself is coercively imposed. Human beings enter a world in which they are subject to the authority of a particular state and have no right to move to any other state only because that is the way we human beings have organized the world. It is not the natural order of things. The current organization is maintained through the use of force, implicit and explicit. So, we are entitled, indeed obliged, to ask whether this coercively imposed structure can be justified to those who are subject to it.

Consider the billions of people who find themselves with limited life chances, given the way the world is organized. They live in an international system that divides the world into distinct political units. Most of these political units produce a highly restricted set of opportunities for most of their inhabitants; a few offer much more. Why should these billions regard this overall arrangement as morally legitimate? Aren't they entitled to ask whether there is an alternative way to organize the world that would serve their interests better? If there is, why they should be expected to submit to the current one?

One common objection to global justice arguments from a bounded justice perspective is that there is no institutional mechanism in place to secure compliance with the requirements of global justice. I find the objection puzzling. It seems to treat the absence of such institutions not as a challenge to be addressed and an obstacle to be overcome but as an explanation of why we are not obliged to try. If we have an obligation to maintain just institutions, we also have an obligation to create just institutions where they do not yet exist. The absence of an institutional mechanism should be seen not as an excuse for complacency but as a reason for action.[6]

At a deeper level, the question of institutional arrangements is secondary to, and derivative from, the question of principles. We want institutional arrangements that will enact and reflect our principles of justice, not principles of justice that simply reflect our institutional arrangements. I do not mean to deny that we may create just institutions first in the course of coping with particular practical problems and only articulate their moral logic later. Nor do I mean to deny that some moral obligations grow out of the creation of institutions and do not exist prior to those institutions. But we cannot simply assume that the institutions we have are sufficient from the perspective of justice. If we begin with the moral obligations that we have within existing institutions and arrangements and allow those to set limits to our moral horizons, we will simply reproduce and legitimate whatever moral defects they contain. This is obvious if we consider past institutional arrangements that we now consider unjust.

To return to the feudalism analogy, we would not consider it sufficient from a moral perspective for those living under feudal arrangements to have asked what nobles owed to one another or even to have asked what they owed to peasants (e.g., *noblesse oblige*). Like the modern state system, the feudal class structure was a complex social institution with a pervasive effect on the lives of those subject to it and with its own powerful internal norms. Nevertheless, that reality did not render it above criticism. In that case, we can clearly see that it was appropriate to ask whether feudal institutional arrangements were just and whether they should have been replaced with something better.

We must ask the same question of our own institutions, including the current arrangements for organizing the world politically. The mere fact that the modern state is a complex social institution with pervasive effects on those subject to it does not mean that we have to accept current norms about what is owed to outsiders or how one becomes a member. Of course, the fact that we have to ask questions about the justice of the current state system as we do about feudalism does not make the two morally equivalent. There are many salient differences between feudalism and current international arrangements. Perhaps the current arrangements are just or could be made so. But is there a way to make that case to those on the other side of the fence that separates the haves from the have-nots? In any event, we are obliged to consider that question. We cannot simply assume that one of the things the have-nots do not have is a right to ask such a question.

Much of the contemporary debate about global justice has focused on the question of whether different states are sufficiently interconnected to give rise to claims of distributive justice. It is a mistake, however, to imagine that questions of justice arise only if there are dense relationships across borders. In important ways, the international system itself establishes and limits the possibilities of such relationships. Through its initial assignment of people to states and its subsequent restrictions on movement, this system profoundly shapes the life chances and the relationships of human beings, all of whom are subject to this system.[7] This way of organizing the world is a human construction with tremendous consequences for those who live under it. Questions about the justice or injustice of this structure are unavoidable.

Social institutions, including the current norms governing the state system, are neither natural nor inevitable. We face questions every day about whether to affirm and maintain the institutions within which we live or whether to criticize and try to change them. If the institutions are just, we have a duty to maintain them. If they are unjust, we have a duty to try to change them.

Every day, through the use of force and the threat of force, democratic states help to maintain an international order that assumes that states may exclude potential immigrants without taking the aspiring migrants' interests into account and without offering them any justification for their exclusion beyond the state's perception of its own interests. Are democratic states acting justly when they do this? We have to address that question. We cannot simply rule it out of court, as the bounded justice approach attempts to do.

Communities of Character

One famous effort to justify discretionary control over immigration is offered by Michael Walzer.[8] In a seminal discussion of the topic, he contends that human communities need the capacity to make decisions about who will be admitted to the community and who will not. Without closure, he says, there can be no "*communities of character*, historically stable, ongoing associations of men and women with some special commitment to one another and some special sense of their common life."[9] In the modern world, Walzer says, closure should take place at the level of the state because modern democracies "probably require the kind of largeness, and also the kind of boundedness, that states provide."[10]

If we insist that states be open, Walzer contends, the result will be that neighborhoods will become closed—"a thousand petty fortresses" in another famous phrase—and if neighborhoods are required to be open, we will have "a world of deracinated men and women."[11]

Walzer's justification of discretionary control over immigration is probably the one that is most often cited in normative discussions of this question. His language certainly captures and reinforces the conventional assumption. Does his argument stand up to scrutiny? Does it explain why states should be morally free to admit or exclude immigrants as they see fit?

I don't think so. "Communities of character" sound attractive, certainly in comparison with "petty fortresses" and "deracinated" individuals, but what makes communities of character possible? What enables them to prosper or causes them to fail?

Walzer presents "closure" as a necessary condition for communities of character. If by that he means that it is not possible to sustain a community of character unless there are people in the community who have lived there for most of their lives and who identify with the community and have a sense of its distinctiveness, he is probably right. But if he means that it is not possible to sustain a community of character unless it actively exercises control over the entrance into the community of people who are not born there, he is certainly wrong. Everything depends on how many are trying to get it. If very few people try to enter a community (relative to its size), they will normally pose no threat to the maintenance of the community. Closure, in the sense of active, discretionary management of who gets in is not necessary to protect communities of character unless a lot of people are trying to get in (again relative to the size of the existing community).

Why would that happen? Why would a community of character ever be faced with more people seeking entry than it could easily accommodate? The implicit presupposition of Walzer's analysis is that communities of character are good for human beings. They provide the contexts in which human beings can flourish and lead the best lives (rather than by living in petty fortresses or as deracinated individuals).

Let's assume that he is right about this. In that case, the first question that we ought to ask is why significant numbers of people would ever want to move elsewhere, leaving the communities of character in which they were born and raised. Of course, a few might leave for personal reasons of one sort or another, but that would not pose any problems for the other communities that took them in. Why would large numbers abandon their own community of character if it is the best place for them?

Walzer himself asserts that people normally will not want to leave and will seek to do so (again, in large numbers) only if things are going very badly at home. Yet he also asserts that open borders between states will lead to "a world of deracinated men and women." He does not say why he expects this to happen, but the only plausible account is that he implicitly assumes that the differences between states will be so significant that many people will want to move despite the built-in attractions of staying at home. Despite his claims about the importance of communities of character, he is worried that too many people will be willing to leave their own community of character for an unfamiliar one that offers better life chances.

If that is an accurate description of the logic underlying Walzer's account, several more questions leap out. Why focus on the defensive measures (closure) needed to sustain a community under pressure from an unwanted influx of migrants rather than on the positive measures that would make closure unnecessary? Shouldn't our first concern be to identify the conditions that would enable all (or most) communities of character to flourish to such an extent that most members of those communities will have no desire to move elsewhere? Wouldn't that be the approach that would be best for most human beings? Wouldn't it be morally preferable for communities of character to flourish without closure (that is, without overtly excluding others)? Furthermore, if many people *are* seeking to leave their community of character to go somewhere else, don't we have to weigh their reasons for seeking entry elsewhere against the desires of those already present to maintain their community as it is? Walzer himself recognizes this elsewhere, setting almost no limits to entry in the case of refugees seeking asylum, as I noted in chapter 10. Why does he implicitly privilege the maintenance of communities of character above all else here?

Walzer's defense of discretionary control over immigration fails because he has no answer for these questions. Indeed, he does not even consider them. For arguments that attempt to do so, we have to look further.

Self-Determination and State Responsibility

Some defenders of discretionary control over immigration have tried to address this challenge directly, offering both a justification for inequalities between states and an account of why states must be morally free to restrict immigration. They argue that significant inequalities between states can be a legitimate outcome of collective self-determination. These inequalities can in turn give rise to a legitimate need for discretionary control over immigration. Let's call this line of argument the state responsibility thesis.[12]

David Miller and John Rawls defend this view, but Miller has developed it more fully. Miller invites us to imagine two contrasting societies named Affluenza and Ecologia.[13] These societies start out from an equal resource base, but Affluenza uses up its resources in immediate consumption while Ecologia devotes its resources to sustainable development. Over time, as a result of their different policies, Ecologia has higher per capita resource levels than Affluenza. Miller argues that it would be wrong to redistribute resources from Ecologia to Affluenza to bring these societies (and hence their members) back to a position of resource equality. First, he says, redistribution would create perverse incentives, rewarding profligacy (Affluenza) rather than responsibility (Ecologia). Second, he contends, redistribution would be unfair because the citizens of Ecologia made sacrifices for the sake of the long term. Their later advantages, and the disadvantages of Affluenza, are a direct product of the choices made by each society. So, the inequalities must be left in place for reasons of efficiency and fairness. Having established that self-determination will give rise to legitimate resource differences, Miller says that giving people the right to move from poorer societies to better endowed ones "would also undermine self-determination, in any world that we can realistically envisage."[14]

In sum, on Miller's account, it would be a mistake to think that a just world would necessarily be one in which there were no significant economic inequalities between states and no significant differences between the life chances of people born in different states. Justice requires community self-determination, and the different choices that states make may give rise to inequalities and make them morally legitimate. Discretionary state control over immigration is morally legitimate even in an ideal world, according to Miller, because it is a necessary corollary of these legitimate inequalities between states.

Does the state responsibility thesis hold up to scrutiny? I think not. The argument has three problems. First, it exaggerates the connection between self-determination and inequality. Second, it misses the ongoing importance of the connection between equal starting points and responsibility. Third, and most important, it subsumes the moral claims of human beings under the claims of the community into which they are born and gives participation in a self-determining community a moral weight that it cannot bear.

Consider first the question of how much inequality between states would be justified by the state responsibility thesis if that thesis were correct. Miller's story implicitly assumes that all of the differences between states are due to choices that the states have made. What if the inequalities between states are due more to the power relations between states than to the independent choices that particular states make? If we accept the state responsibility thesis, we should presumably try to eliminate inequalities that are a product of power rather than self-determination so that self-determination can have its proper impact. (I do not need to worry about how to do that because, like Miller with his hypothetical examples, I am only attempting to clarify principles here.)

How much of the inequality between states in the world today is due to power and how much to self-determination? That is an empirical and historical question to which I do not pretend to have an answer. To the extent that it is power rather than self-determination that explains actual inequalities, however, the inequalities are not morally justified by the state responsibility argument, and so restrictions on migration designed to preserve such inequalities are not justified either.

Power and self-determination are not the only options in explaining international inequality. Consider the role of luck which appears to play no role in Miller's story. Imagine Ecologia I and Ecologia II with the same collective values and goals and equal starting places. Because of external circumstances over which they have no control and could not reasonably have foreseen, Ecologia I winds up much better off than Ecologia II.

What if some of the people from Ecologia II decide that they would like to move to Ecologia I, thinking perhaps that they will find its basic values congenial but that it will offer better economic prospects? Is Ecologia I entitled to prevent them from coming? Well, not on the basis of the state responsibility thesis. The differences in outcomes between Ecologia I and Ecologia II do not derive from differences in collective self-determination as the earlier differences between Ecologia and Affluenza did, but from luck. So, why can the migrants from Ecologia II be refused entry to Ecologia I?[15]

In sum, the state responsibility thesis cannot justify all of the existing inequalities between states and offers no reason to restrict migration to protect inequalities that are not the product of self-determination.

In fairness to Miller, I should say that this first argument can be seen as a clarification of the state responsibility thesis rather than a critique of it. Miller does not claim that existing global inequalities are entirely the product of self-determination, only that self-determination may give rise to legitimate inequalities. Miller and Rawls both regard current inequalities between states as morally problematic and both argue that rich states have a duty to help poor states achieve a level of development that will enable their citizens to lead decent lives. Nevertheless, both Miller and Rawls make comments that suggest that they think state responsibility plays an important role in explaining current inequalities.[16] Both also clearly think that after the duty to help other states has been met, there will still be substantial inequalities between states that will justify discretionary control over immigration.

If the first problem with the state responsibility thesis can be seen as a clarification rather than a critique, the second cannot. The second problem is that this account drastically reduces the connection between human agency and responsibility for outcomes in all generations except the first. Consider how generations matter when thinking about individual responsibility. One common view is that it is reasonable to expect individuals to be responsible for the consequences of their choices, given a starting point of equal circumstances.[17] This is basically the same intuition as the one that underlies the state responsibility thesis, but applied to individuals rather than communities.

Notice the way that generations complicate the moral theory of responsibility for individuals. The choices that individuals make have consequences not only for themselves but also for their children. From one perspective, that is a good thing in terms of the responsibility thesis because people normally care a lot about what happens to their children. So, the fact that one's choices have consequences for one's children creates a strong incentive to make good choices. On the other hand, these consequences can affect the starting points of the children (for better or worse), and according to the responsibility thesis, every individual is supposed to have an equal starting point. There is an obvious tension here. If we reduce the effects upon children of the life choices made by their parents, we weaken the link between choice and responsibility for the parents. If we don't reduce these effects, however, then it is only in the first generation that the link really holds between choice and responsibility. In all subsequent generations, the fate of individuals is highly shaped, for good or ill, by the choices of their ancestors. I don't mean to suggest that there is a simple solution to all this. The underlying idea of responsibility for choices made from an equal starting point generates internal tensions and requires trade-offs between the goal of holding individuals responsible for their choices by making them live with the consequences of those choices and the goal of ensuring that individuals in every generation have an equal starting point. In the end, we have to aim only for relatively equal starting points, rather than completely equal ones.

If we think now about the problem of responsibility with respect to a self-determining political community, we face a problem that is similar in some respects but different in others. If we regard each community as a single agent, then it seems appropriate to say that each community should be responsible for the consequences of its choices, at least assuming some reasonably equal starting point. That is the basic logic of the state responsibility thesis. From this perspective, however, the problem of generations does not really arise, because each community exists (in principle) in perpetuity.

If we consider the human beings who make up each political community this neglect of the generational question is much less satisfactory. Over time, the entire human composition of the community changes. Why does this matter? Because the choices that we describe the political community as making are choices made by a particular set of human beings—the citizens alive at the time and their representatives. On a theory of community self-determination, it makes sense to hold those citizens responsible for their decisions and to expect them to live with the consequences of those decisions. But over time, those people die. The people who come after them are *not* responsible for the decisions that their predecessors made. So, it does not seem fair (from a perspective that emphasizes the responsibility of citizens as agents) to make them live with the consequences (good or bad) of those prior decisions. They have their own claim to a relatively equal starting point, not only as individuals but also as members of a self-determining community.

You may object (as Miller does) that the members of a political community do not come along in discreet generations. As Hume famously observed, human beings are not like butterflies, one generation entering and another leaving all at once. Every political community is a shifting, intergenerational community, with new members entering through birth and others leaving through death.[18] (Leave aside migration for the moment.) It is simply not possible to limit the consequences of a decision made in the name of a political community to the members of the community who participated in that decision.

There is considerable truth in this, but it is not the whole story. Recall that when it comes to individuals we think that we need to make some effort to limit the effects of previous generations on subsequent ones and to create relatively equal starting points for every person who comes along so as to maintain the link between choice and responsibility for everyone, even though this inevitably weakens the link between choice and responsibility in some respects by freeing parents of (full) responsibility for the effects their choices would otherwise have on the life chances of their children. We can see that weakening the link between choice and responsibility for parents is objectionable on grounds of incentives and fairness, but necessary to avoid the more fundamental unfairness of allowing grossly unequal starting points for individuals to emerge over time. (I write here of principle, not practice, since we know that in actual democratic states we do often permit grossly unequal starting points between individuals.) At the same time, we recognize that we can never make the starting points perfectly equal and that trying to do so would interfere too much with the choice-responsibility nexus and would also conflict with other values and principles such as respect for family life. So, we face trade-offs, but we do not abandon the effort to create equal starting points altogether just because the starting points can never be perfectly equal.

The same principles should apply to self-determining political communities. The choices that a self-determining community makes must have consequences for those who live in the community or the community would no longer be self-determining, and that includes consequences for later generations. But that does not mean that later generations ought to bear the entire burden (or ought to reap the entire benefit) of the decisions made by earlier generations. It is true that there is no neat distinction between generations, but that does not preclude the existence of redistributive mechanisms and structures that could keep inequalities from growing too large so that we would not have to abandon altogether the idea of equal starting places for communities over time.

The state responsibility thesis contends that redistribution would undermine self-determination. But the absence of redistribution neglects the preconditions that made the state responsibility thesis plausible in the first point, that is, that it is fair to hold communities responsible for the consequences of their choices *when the choices are made from an equal starting point.*

When Miller takes up the problem of later generations, he acknowledges that later generations may not enjoy an equal starting point but says first that the inferior starting point is due to the choices of their predecessors and then that the later generations have no complaint of justice against the earlier ones because no one is entitled to any particular level of resources so long as it is sufficient "to sustain the institutions that make a decent life possible."[19] So, in Miller's analysis the concern with equal starting points entirely disappears after the first generation, despite the fact that those equal starting points played a crucial role in his original justification of the state responsibility principle.

Miller asks rhetorically what charge of unfairness the second generation might level against the first. But the charge of unfairness that the second generation can raise is not directed against the first, as Miller assumes, but against the structure of relationships between communities. What is unfair is a structure that gives all the weight to a principle of community responsibility and none to the idea that those who come later should also enjoy equal starting points, even though the background condition of equal starting points played a crucial role in the initial justification of the principle of community responsibility. Without equal starting points for later generations, it no longer seems plausible to suggest that inequalities between communities are simply the consequences of the choices those communities have made. As a result, the principle of community responsibility loses much of its force as a justification for restricting immigration into more successful states. If there is enough redistribution to maintain roughly equal starting points for communities over time, the incentives to migrate will be greatly reduced and there will be no reason to regard immigration as a threat to community responsibility. If there is not, the background requirements for the community responsibility principle are not being met and so the principle cannot justify restrictions on immigration.

The final and most important problem with the state responsibility thesis is that, on this account, the moral claims of individuals become almost entirely mediated through their membership in the communities to which they have been assigned at birth. This dynamic is particularly evident in Rawls's version of the argument which parallels Miller's in most respects. Rawls speaks of political communities as "peoples" rather than "states." Having advanced the state responsibility thesis (using his language of "peoples" in place of "states"), Rawls makes this observation about immigration: "People must recognize that they cannot make up for failing to regulate their numbers or to care for their land...by migrating into another people's territory without their consent."[20] In this formulation, which is repeated almost verbatim later, individual human beings who are seeking to move from one society to another to pursue better lives for themselves and their families are seen, in effect, only as agents of the society they are trying to leave. The sentence suggests that a collective that has failed to care for its territory adequately is trying to offload its problems by sending migrants into the territory of other collectives. The migrants themselves are not seen as autonomous human beings, pursuing aspirations and trying to build better lives for themselves and for their children. The use of coercion to prevent them from doing so is not even identified as a regrettable constraint on human freedom.

Rawls goes on to say that in the theoretical context of his inquiry (i.e., in "a realistic utopia") many of the causes of mass migration in the modern world would disappear: religious and ethnic persecution, political oppression, starvation, and the subordination of women (which leads, he says, to population pressure). So, he concludes, "The problem of immigration is not, then, simply left aside, but is eliminated as a serious problem in a realistic utopia."[21]

Even though he says that immigration would not be a serious problem, Rawls is not in favor of open borders. Why not? The answer, I think, is that there would be considerable economic and other differences between societies even in his realistic utopia, as a result of differences in policy choices. Indeed some political communities would even be decent hierarchies rather than liberal democracies. In his only brief discussion of immigration later in the book, Rawls repeats his responsibility argument and says in a footnote that this entails "a least a qualified right to limit immigration" without saying what those qualifications are.[22] So, when Rawls says that immigration is "not a serious problem in a realistic utopia," he is saying in effect that using coercion to restrict migration raises no serious moral issues so long as those seeking to migrate are living in conditions above some minimum threshold in their original society.

This is puzzling. What if I don't like the "people" into whom I am born? Perhaps I reject all of their fundamental values (and accept those of some other "people"). If we recognize the moral equality of all human beings, we should presumably have to explain why assigning someone to a "people" at birth (with a right to leave but no right of admittance elsewhere) adequately respects this moral equality, given the vast consequences of such an assignment for one's life chances and one's life projects. Why can't one have the right to change "peoples"? Of course, one can if another "people" is willing to let one in, but why should it be entirely up to them? I think that the reason that Rawls does not see any of these issues as a serious problem, at least in the sense of something that requires discussion, is that he is implicitly seeing individuals as having moral claims only as members, not as human beings.

Miller is more careful in his language but winds up at the same point. For example, he claims that people have no fundamental moral right to migrate so long as they live in a society that provides them with "access to an *adequate* range of options ... defined in terms of generic human needs rather than in terms of the interests of any one person in particular."[23] He acknowledges that some people who would like to enter and settle will be prevented from doing so and that they have some moral claim: "They are owed an explanation for their exclusion."[24] But the explanation he requires is simply that their exclusion must serve the perceived interests of the society that they are trying to enter: "An adequate explanation will be one that links immigration policy to the general goals of the society in question."[25] So, the moral claim that potential immigrants have turns out to be very weak. Restricting entry requires a justification but not much of one.

As in Rawls's case, I find Miller's position puzzling. Why are the moral claims of ordinary migrants so weak? Unlike Rawls he sees that peaceful people are being excluded and that this exclusion must be justified to the person subject to it. But then the justification that he requires turns out to be minimal. Even if he has rejected the idea that free movement should be regarded as a human right, why doesn't he think that the interests of the potential migrant in getting in should at least be weighed against the costs to the state of admitting her? Why is any legitimate public policy goal sufficient justification?

Miller appeals to the idea of priority for compatriots here, but, as I will argue in more detail below, granting some priority to compatriots is not the same as making their interests a trump. He also appeals to the value of self-determination, but self-determination admits of degrees. Why is any hindrance to the state's plans, no matter how small, sufficient to justify exclusion? Indeed, as I suggested in the previous chapter, if we value human freedom, we might say that the fact that exclusion prevents peaceful human beings from going where they want should shift the burden of proof to the state. The state could be obliged to show both that it cannot achieve its policy goals in any other way than through restricting immigration (given that there are often many ways to pursue any given goal) and that the goal itself is important enough to justify restricting an important human freedom.[26]

In the end, the state responsibility thesis makes collectives morally fundamental and ties the fate of individuals not to the choices they make but to the circumstances of their birth. Even if we think states should be held responsible intergenerationally, we have no reason to hold later generations of individuals responsible. As I acknowledged, we cannot entirely avoid some bad consequences for descendants, but having a migration option mitigates those consequences to some degree. It does not eliminate all the bad consequences because migration normally has significant costs for the migrants, and having a right to migrate for the sake of opportunity is not the same as having the opportunities one wants in the community into which one was born. Nevertheless, it reflects a reasonable balance of these competing moral considerations.

Whether they would characterize it this way or not, theorists like Miller and Rawls are offering principles for organizing the world, that is, principles that justify a particular way of assigning rights and responsibilities both to political communities and to the people who live in those communities. Giving political communities a moral license to restrict immigration for the sake of self-determination goes too far in subordinating individuals to the communities to which they initially belong. It solves the problem of collective responsibility for collective choices only by denying individuals the opportunity to make important choices for which they can be personally responsible. It also limits the freedom of human beings much more than is necessary to prevent them from taking advantage of others' sacrifices. This way of organizing the world does not do justice to the moral claims that every human being has to be treated as a free and equal moral person.

Sovereignty

Another argument in defence of the state's discretionary control over immigration is that a norm of open borders would be intrinsically incompatible with state sovereignty. A general right of free movement, some think, would require a world government with the power to enforce such a right. A world government would be a bad idea (for everyone) for reasons of excessive centralization and risks of tyranny. So, we need to divide the world into independent political units like contemporary sovereign states. In a world divided into sovereign states, each state must have the power to control its own borders and so there can be no general right of free movement.

People often overstate the arguments against world government, but that is not an argument that I want to pursue here.[27] I indicated at the beginning of chapter 11 that I would develop the case for open borders in the context of the assumption of a world divided into independent, sovereign states, each of which (normally) has a right to exercise sovereign power within its territory and to control admission to its territory. As we have seen at a number of points in this book, however, we should not confuse the claim that states have a moral right to exercise sovereign power with the claim that every exercise of sovereign power must be regarded as morally right. Accepting (as a background assumption) the legitimacy of state sovereignty does not require us to abandon the idea of moral criticism of state behavior. The argument for open borders is one such criticism. It claims that it is morally wrong for states to exclude peaceful immigrants.

Some people, following Hobbes, think that any self-enforced limits on state power must be empty. So, they reject all talk of human rights or moral limits to state power. There are fewer who take that view today, however, and, unlike Hobbes, they rarely acknowledge that this also entails a rejection of constitutional democracy. As I observed in the introduction, the very idea of constitutional democracy is built upon the notion of self-limiting government (that is, that states have the capacity to restrict the exercise of their power in accordance with their norms and values). There is nothing in the nature of sovereignty that prevents a democratic state from recognizing that outsiders are morally entitled to enter and settle on its territory and that it has an obligation to permit them to do so, at least under normal circumstances. It may be unlikely that democratic states will agree to recognize such a claim, but that does not make the idea intrinsically incompatible with sovereignty.

The assumption that controlling borders is essential to sovereignty is actually of relatively recent vintage. For a long time, there was no connection between the idea of exercising political control over population flows and the sort of territorial jurisdiction that is the idea at the heart of modern sovereignty (namely, the state's monopoly over the legitimate use of violence within a particular geographical space).[28] States in the modern form date back to the seventeenth century, but they began to try to regulate entry and exit in a serious way only in the late nineteenth century. Passports were not introduced until World War I.[29] As I have said before, having open borders is not the same as having no borders.

Sovereignty and control over admissions are linked in the popular imagination and in political discourse, but they are often disentangled in actual political arrangements in the real world. Sovereignty itself is less simple than some assume. Federal systems often have complex separate and shared sovereignty arrangements.[30] Externally, in relation to other states, sovereignty may be unitary (though in a few cases even that power is divided). Internally, the central government has some powers and jurisdiction over some issues, and other units of government (provinces, states in the United States) have other powers and jurisdiction over other issues. The relationship between the central government and the other units is determined by constitutional arrangements. The central government does not have the final say in any simple or conventional sense. It is sheer dogma to insist that the sovereignty exercised by the component parts of a federal system is not real sovereignty. Like property, sovereignty is a bundle of rights that can be divided up in many different ways.[31]

Why does this complex picture of sovereignty matter? Because the sovereignty that federal units exercise coexists with open borders among the various units. People *are* generally free to change their membership in subnational political communities at will, despite the jurisdictional sovereignty that those subnational units exercise over many important issues. Of course, it is true that such openness has dynamic effects and that the various units may have to take migration incentives into effect in planning public policies, but in an interdependent world, political units have to take into account many different factors that are outside the jurisdiction they control.

The fact that citizens of European Union states are largely free to move from one member state to another reveals starkly the ideological character of the claim that discretionary control over immigration is necessary for sovereignty. No one can seriously doubt that the European states are still real states today with most of the components of state sovereignty. Indeed, every European state has a more effective actual sovereignty than most states elsewhere in the world. Nevertheless, with minor qualifications, European states that are members of the European Union do not claim that they may exercise discretionary control over the entry of immigrants from other EU states. They have agreed to limit their own sovereign power in this way. That is all that the open borders argument asks—only now in relation to the whole world and not just Europe. I recognize that the phrase "that is all" does not capture the practical significance of such a demand, but the point here is a conceptual one.

Someone may point out that European states did not adopt their open borders policy out of a commitment to justice or human rights but out of a concern for economic efficiency. In the first instance, they waited to implement the policy until the economies of the poorer states like Spain, Portugal, and Italy had improved sufficiently that the abolition of immigration restrictions within the EU would not lead to massive population movements from the poorer countries to the more affluent ones. For the same reason, they did not immediately grant the right of free movement within the EU to citizens of the states like Poland and the Czech Republic that joined later.

I accept these claims entirely. From my perspective, they simply confirm the fundamental point, namely that restrictions on migration are usually necessary to protect a community only when that community is so economically privileged relative to others that many outsiders would consider moving there. Hence, the absence of restrictions on immigration, even a legal commitment not to introduce restrictions, is not evidence of the absence of sovereignty.

Having a right to migrate across state borders does not require people to move, anymore than having a right to free mobility within a state requires people to move. Migration between states of the European Union is very low even though citizens of member states have a right to move (with minor qualifications).

Some people love novelty and adventure, but most people are not keen to leave home, family, and friends and to move permanently to a place where they don't speak the language and don't know their way about. Most consider doing this only when they think they have a lot to gain. So, restrictions on migration usually serve as a protection for economic and political advantage. If the economic and political differences among states in the world as a whole were no greater than the economic and political differences among states in the EU, there would be no reason to see a right of free movement as a threat to sovereignty under most circumstances.

In insisting that the principle of free movement is not intrinsically incompatible with state sovereignty, I do not mean to deny that there are circumstances under which immigration could threaten a state's capacity to govern itself. A massive inflow of migrants within a short time might indeed have this effect. But there is no necessary and inevitable link between sovereignty and restrictions on migration. Given the case I developed in the previous chapter on behalf of free movement, any justification of limits to free movement has to appeal to more than the simple concept of state sovereignty. As a concept, sovereignty only requires that states themselves be the ones to decide what their immigration policies will be. It does not entail the idea that their immigration policies must be morally unconstrained. In fact, as we have seen in chapters 9 and 10, almost everyone agrees that state sovereignty is morally constrained in certain ways in the area of immigration. I am simply arguing that those conventional limits are not the only ones democratic states are morally obliged to respect, when we reflect upon the ethics of immigration more deeply.

Priority for Compatriots

Some people try to justify both the inequalities between states and discretionary control over immigration as the morally legitimate result of our obligations to fellow members of our political community. These obligations, they say, rightly take precedence over the claims of strangers. To insist on free movement is to ask us to ignore these communal ties and to treat everyone in the world alike. It requires a degree of altruism that is unrealistic. Indeed it rests upon an inhuman sort of cosmopolitanism that fails to give the proper moral weight to particular attachments and memberships. We are morally entitled to favor family, friends, and, yes, our fellow citizens over those with whom we do not have such ties.[32]

I do not disagree with the claim that we are entitled to care more for our nearest and dearest than for distant strangers. There may be some cosmopolitans who think that the idea that all human beings are of equal moral worth requires us, individually and collectively, to give the same weight to the interests and concerns of all human beings, always and everywhere, regardless of our relationships with them, but I am not one of them.[33] I do not think that the principle of equal moral worth entails this sort of abstract universalism, and my argument for open borders does not entail this extreme form of cosmopolitanism.

I am not denying the moral relevance of particularistic attachments. Rather I am arguing that the moral claims of particularistic attachments are limited. They are constrained by considerations of justice.[34] The question is not whether we may favor compatriots over outsiders but rather in what ways we may do so. Some ways of favoring compatriots are morally permissible, while others are morally unacceptable. I am arguing that it is morally impermissible to favor current members of our community by excluding peaceful outsiders seeking to enter and settle. Many other ways of favoring compatriots may be morally permissible and some may even be morally required.

The Family Analogy

Consider the family. In many ways, I give priority to my sons over the children of other people. Most people do the same for their children. Indeed, a person would not be a good parent if she did not care much more for her own children than for the children of others. Should we think of states as extended families and of restrictions on immigration simply as a way of favoring our own?

There are many good reasons to be wary about drawing analogies between the family and the political community, not least the fact that the personal and intimate connections within the family (good and bad) are very different from the kinds of connections we can have with fellow citizens in a modern state. I will leave those sorts of worries aside here, however, and just draw attention to the moral limits on how we may favor family members over others.

The question is not *whether* one may favor one's own family members over others but *how* one may do so. The fact that I care most about my children doesn't mean I'd favor them over others no matter what. In many social contexts we think favoring family members is unfair (e.g., when calling balls and strikes in a baseball game). When the stakes are high (e.g., legal proceedings, decisions on appointments) we normally create institutional rules to try to prevent people from being able to favor their friends and relatives. In other words, our notions of justice constrain the extent and ways in which we think it is acceptable for us to favor family members, without implying, however, that every form of favoring them is unjust.

Even when existing arrangements favor our children, we may think that these advantages are unjust and want to change them. For example, as the children of upper middle class professionals, my sons have enjoyed a variety of advantages in their life chances, but I think justice requires (and I would support) a set of economic and social policies that would greatly reduce the advantages that accrue to this sort of social position. I don't want to live in a social order where class and race and gender give my children advantages, because I want to live in a social order that is just, and I want them to live in that sort of social order as well. That applies not only to the social order that exists within the state but to the social order constituted by the way the world as a whole is organized. So, even if we are morally entitled to favor compatriots in some ways, it does not follow that we are entitled to favor them in this particular way (that is, by excluding potential immigrants).

In sum, saying that opposition to discretionary control over immigration means that one is opposed to favoring compatriots over strangers is like saying that opposition to nepotism means that one is opposed to favoring family members over others. It inflates a particular moral limit into a global ban.

Special Responsibilities and Human Rights

No one would claim that we are entitled to favor our compatriots by invading (peaceful) foreign countries and robbing their inhabitants or, more generally, by violating the human rights of those who are not our compatriots. The idea that restricting entry is a reasonable and even necessary way to favor compatriots already presupposes that there is nothing deeply wrong with restricting entry, that it does not violate any important moral claims of those trying to get in. In other words, it presupposes the very issues that are supposed to be under consideration.

Do we have special responsibilities to the members of our political community? Of course. How could it be otherwise? Special responsibilities for those living within a political jurisdiction are a necessary corollary of having jurisdictions that make collective decisions, produce public services and collective goods, and collect taxes to pay for them. It is for the benefit of the people within our political community, not those living somewhere hundreds or thousands of miles away, that we operate schools and hospitals, maintain roads and sewers, collect garbage, and supply water. Our fellow members are the ones whose needs and interests have to be the primary focus of those entrusted with the political power of the community. That will remain true whether we have open borders or not. To say that we are entitled to care more for those on the inside than those on the outside, that we may legitimately give priority to our fellow members, is not, however, to say that we are entitled to keep people from entering and joining our community (nor is it to say that we have no obligations to those who remain outside, though that is a distinct question).

Saying that borders should be open is not a matter of ignoring particularistic ties, much less of demonstrating some sort of inhuman altruism. It is simply a question of recognizing the limits on the ways in which we can promote the interests of current members of our community. Clearly we cannot promote the interests of members by violating the fundamental human rights of people who are not (yet) members. If the freedom to move across borders and settle peacefully should be regarded as a human right, as I argued in the previous chapter, then it would be wrong to promote the interests of current fellow members by violating that right. The view that the priority due compatriots automatically justifies discretionary control over immigration simply ignores this sort of moral constraint.

National Security

I turn now to more qualified objections to open borders. These objections do not attempt to defend the conventional view about the state's right to exercise discretionary control over immigration as a fundamental principle. They accept that there is a persuasive general case for open borders and seek only to show that there are circumstances in which it is justifiable to restrict the right to freedom of movement to some extent. We might say that all of these qualified objections are contingent and self-limiting, in the sense that they justify restrictions on freedom of movement only if and to the extent that these restrictions are necessary to prevent harmful consequences that outweigh the moral claims to freedom of movement.

Let's start with the issue of national security. Earlier I said that I was presupposing, for purposes of this discussion, a world like our own, divided into separate states. Let's assume also that these states might face the possibility of violent threats from outsiders, whether state or nonstate actors. Can a concern for national security justify limits on freedom of movement?

Yes, if all the caveats from chapter 9 about the misuse of the national security rationale are included. My argument for open borders has been framed from the outset as an argument about the moral claims of ordinary, peaceful people seeking to build decent, secure lives for themselves and their families. It is not an argument for the admission of terrorists or invading armies.

Just as there can be moral limits on the exercise of sovereignty without denying sovereignty itself, there can be moral limits on the protection of national security without denying the fundamental importance of that goal. The national security rationale for restricting immigration is a contingent and self-limiting rationale, at least in principle. It is contingent because it comes into play only when immigrants actually pose a threat to national security and it is self-limiting because it only justifies the exclusion of immigrants who do pose a threat. Thus this rationale provides no justification for discretionary control over immigration.

I recognize the irony of describing national security as a self-limiting rationale, given the way it has been used in practice, but as I argued in chapter 9, it is entirely implausible to think of the vast majority of people seeking to migrate as threats to national security if one defines that concept in a reasonable way.

Public Order

Another familiar concern is public order. If too many immigrants came within a short period, they could overwhelm the receiving state, leading to chaos and the breakdown of public order. That would make everyone worse off in terms of both liberty and welfare. So, like protecting national security, preserving public order might provide grounds for limiting immigration under some circumstances. But is this a really serious concern? Would it entail a significant constraint on freedom of movement?

I think not, at least if we assume a background of greatly reduced inequality between states. Every human right and every liberty is subject in principle to some sort of public order restriction. It is a common qualification both in human rights documents and in liberal theories of rights.[35] Normally, this is not a very serious constraint on human rights and freedoms.

Whether the public order constraint would require significant limitations on freedom of movement would depend primarily on how many people were trying to move, relative to the size of the receiving state (and perhaps the country of origin). In a world in which the inequalities between states were much more limited than they are today, the incentives to move would be much more limited. As I have noted previously, citizens of the European Union have a right to freedom of movement among EU states, and this generates no public order problems. Migration rates are rather low in fact (around 3 percent of the population). So, in a more egalitarian world, it seems very unlikely that immigration would ever actually pose a threat to public order. For that reason we should see the public order constraint as only a minor qualification to the right of free movement, as it is for most other human rights.

The Background Assumptions

Some readers may object that in assuming a background of relative equality between states I am ignoring the strength of the public order objection. If rich democratic states today were to open their borders, the number of those coming might overwhelm the capacity of the societies to cope, leading to chaos and a breakdown of public order. One cannot assume that the potential immigrants would see the danger and refrain from coming because of the lag time between cause and effect, because of collective action problems, and so on. So, in the real world, the critics might say, concerns for public order would justify significant constraints on freedom of movement.

This objection is wrong in two different ways. First, the objection rests on a misunderstanding of the open borders argument. As I have tried to make clear from the outset of the previous chapter, the purpose of this argument is not to put forward a policy proposal but to make visible the deep injustice of existing global arrangements and to say what justice would require in principle. For that purpose, what is most important is to consider objections to my ideal of justice. That is what I have been doing in this chapter.

The ideal of justice that I have identified has two components: a right to freedom of movement across borders and relatively little inequality between states. Not everyone accepts this vision (to say the least), and I have been trying to explain in these two chapters why people committed to democratic values should accept this ideal.

Some people accept one part of my ideal but not the other. For example, some libertarians share my view that justice requires a human right to freedom of movement across borders but not limitations on the inequality between states. A public order constraint would involve a much more serious limitation on freedom of movement for this sort of libertarian view than it does for mine, precisely because the libertarian ideal would not require a relatively egalitarian background between states. For reasons of space I have not systematically discussed the libertarian alternative, but I have tried to make clear in both this chapter and the previous one why I think that justice requires a relatively egalitarian world.[36]

In contrast to the libertarian approach, some egalitarians think that justice requires relative equality between states but not freedom of movement. In the previous chapter, I tried to meet one aspect of that view by arguing that freedom of movement is an important value in its own right, thus making clear why it would still be morally significant in an egalitarian world. In this chapter I am trying to meet another aspect of that view by considering objections to freedom of movement against a background of relatively little inequality between states. Thus, I am trying to show why both components of my ideal matter from the perspective of justice and how they fit together.

Although I want to keep my main focus on questions about what justice requires in principle and although I am not recommending open borders as an immediate policy prescription, I do want to reject the view that the imagined consequences of opening borders today somehow provides a moral justification for existing patterns of closure, or worse still, for discretionary control over immigration.

This leads to the second way in which the objection I am considering is wrong. Let's accept the objection at face value and consider what the public order constraint would entail, if we were to consider the open borders issue against the background of current circumstances rather than in the context of a more egalitarian world. "Public order" is a minimalist standard, referring only to the maintenance of law and order. Let's notice its limitations.

First, in order for concerns for public order to provide a principled justification for restrictions on immigration, the threats to public order must arise directly from the numbers of immigrants, not from "backlash" (that is, the violent or antagonistic behavior of the current population toward the newcomers). In the latter case, it is the current members, not the immigrants, who are posing the threat to public order, at least from the perspective of justice. This might not settle the question of what policy to pursue, given the range of feasible options, but it would preclude using public order as a deep justification for restrictions on immigration.

Second, like the national security argument, the public order argument is contingent and self-limiting. It only justifies restrictions to the extent that they are necessary to preserve public order. It does not justify a policy of restricting immigration whenever that serves the interests of the current population. On the contrary, if we accept the general case for open borders and we are only concerned here with how concerns about public order might constrain openness, the state would be obliged to admit as many of those seeking entry as it could without jeopardizing public order.

In some ways, the public order argument is reminiscent of Garrett Hardin's famous lifeboat ethics argument.[37] It does no one any good to take so many people into a lifeboat that it is swamped and everyone drowns. Fair enough. On the other hand, people in a lifeboat are positively obliged to take in as many as they can without jeopardizing the safety of the boat as a whole. They cannot let people drown if they are able to save them without risking their own lives. This positive duty is a feature of the lifeboat situation that those fond of this analogy often neglect.

Like national security, public order is subject to expansive and problematic interpretations. Some people see a threat to public order in any new demand placed on a social system. We may need a safety margin in a lifeboat, but they want a safety margin of fifty empty places in a lifeboat built for sixty. Contrary to what some people claim, it is not plausible to say that the boat is full. Again, I think it would be a mistake to deny the moral relevance of public order in principle as a way of trying to prevent abusive interpretations. Instead, we should focus our critiques on the abusive interpretations themselves.

Rawls makes a similar point in *A Theory of Justice* when he acknowledges that liberties are always potentially subject to restrictions. He insists that the hypothetical possibility of a threat is not enough. Rather there must be a "reasonable expectation" that damage will occur in the absence of restrictions and the expectation has to be based on "evidence and ways of reasoning acceptable to all."[38] With that sort of standard, a public order constraint would set some limits to immigration under current conditions but would also clearly permit a vast expansion over current levels.

The Welfare State

Now consider the welfare state argument. Egalitarians sometimes worry that open borders would threaten the welfare state. They say that our first duty is to help the least well off in our own political community. For all of its limitations, the modern welfare state provides the least well off members of rich democratic states with much more security in the material conditions of their lives than they would otherwise possess. Egalitarian critics say that open borders would lead to an influx of so many poor people that it would be impossible to maintain the welfare state. Even if the immigrants came for work not for welfare, they would have needs (like health care) that would impose great costs and they would undercut the poorest current members in the labor market, driving many of them into greater reliance on welfare programs. The presence of so much cheap labor would benefit the rich and harm the poor. In sum, egalitarian critics contend that the corrosive effect of open borders on the welfare state is precisely why many conservative voices like the *Wall Street Journal* favor open borders and why egalitarians should oppose the idea.[39]

Notice that the welfare state argument, like the public order argument, gets much of its power from the assumption that we are talking about opening borders today without reducing the inequality between states, so that large numbers of poor people would have strong incentives to move to rich states. As I have just noted, that is not the assumption that underlies my inquiry. So, I want to ask first whether concern for the welfare state would provide any basis for an objection to open borders in a more egalitarian world.

Some might say that freedom of movement would pose a threat to the welfare state even in an egalitarian world, so long as we suppose that there is scope for legitimate variation in welfare provision among democratic states with similar levels of economic resources. Some states choose to have much more extensive welfare regimes than others, even if the others are comparably rich. The contrast between Scandinavia and the United States in today's world illustrates the point.[40] For various reasons, some people will have much greater need of the programs provided by welfare states than others. If borders were open, these people would have incentives to migrate to the countries with more extensive welfare regimes, even in a world of relatively equal states. So, some would argue, it would be justifiable for a democratic state to restrict immigration in order to preserve a more extensive welfare regime.

Note first that the welfare state argument is contingent and self-limiting (like the earlier arguments in this section). It is contingent because it depends on the actual facts about migration. It would provide a potential reason for restrictions on immigration only if people were actually migrating to take advantage of more extensive welfare provisions, rather than for other reasons. It is self-limiting because a concern to protect more generous welfare regimes would not justify restrictions if the amount of immigration (whatever its motivation) did not threaten the ability of the state to maintain its relatively generous welfare regime.

Because the concern here is to protect more generous welfare regimes, the argument provides no justification for restrictions on immigration into states with the least extensive welfare regimes. That may seem a minor point, but it matters because it draws our attention back to the fact that this argument does not directly challenge the positive case for open borders. It only offers considerations that may qualify the case for open borders under some circumstances.

Would immigration motivated by welfare state differentials rise to a level that would make it impossible to sustain more extensive welfare regimes in an egalitarian world? That is an empirical question to which we can only offer a speculative answer. In our highly inegalitarian world there is some evidence that welfare state differences play some role in motivating patterns of migration, although no one claims that it is a significant factor in the motivation of most immigrants or in the overall level of immigration into any rich state.[41] (Of course, migration options today are much more constrained than they would be in a world of open borders.) Another relevant indicator which I have mentioned before is the relatively low level of migration within the European Union, despite its internal open borders. Some will object that people are not free to move from one European state to another in order to take immediate advantage of the receiving state's more generous welfare programs. I see that not as an objection, however, but as a solution.

Suppose we accept the positive case for open borders but see welfare-motivated migration as a potential problem. Then we should consider whether the problem can be addressed by measures short of discretionary closure. For example, states with generous welfare provisions could establish waiting periods before immigrants were eligible for welfare state programs, as the EU does. This approach would be morally preferable to restrictions on immigration because waiting periods for eligibility do not infringe directly on the right to free movement. Indeed, I argued in earlier chapters that such waiting periods are morally defensible, at least for redistributive programs, even for immigrants who have been admitted as permanent residents. The same arguments would apply in a world of open borders. And for these purposes the experience of the European Union with its relatively low migration rates is quite relevant, since the EU has the sorts of differences between states both in terms of overall economic success and in terms of levels of welfare provision that we would expect to find in a more egalitarian world.

The welfare state argument rests implicitly on an assumption about the legitimacy of giving priority to compatriots, especially needy compatriots. In criticizing the priority for compatriots argument earlier in this chapter, I did not reject the idea altogether. In a world of relatively equal states, it is certainly reasonable, under normal circumstances, for states to limit the benefits of their welfare state programs to the members of the community. But that does not mean that it is legitimate to exclude potential immigrants from membership.

I accept that a concern for reciprocity is morally legitimate to some extent, and I have acknowledged the legitimacy of making people wait for access to some welfare state programs. But this does not justify restrictions on immigration. For most people, membership in the cooperative scheme of a particular political community is not the result of some choice that they made as individuals but is an accident of birth. That is acceptable as a basis for the initial assignment of membership, as I have repeatedly argued, but not for exclusion of those who want to join. If absence from the cooperative scheme is not the result of a decision not to cooperate, but of a denial of the opportunity to do so, the argument from reciprocity loses its force.[42]

Again, the open borders argument is particularly effective in exposing the flaw in claims about the moral relevance of reciprocity, connection, and mutual engagement. If we say that we have obligations to one another because we participate in common institutions that reflect our shared commitment to principles of justice or, in older language, because we have all signed the social contract, how are we to respond to the outsider (the aspiring immigrant) who says "OK. I'll be happy to participate and take on the same collective commitments to justice. I'll sign your social contract." What is the justification for saying, "No. We won't let you participate. You can't sign." If connection and consent provide the foundation for justice, then a refusal to permit people to establish the relevant connections or to give their consent requires more justification than appeal to existing arrangements. I am claiming that no such justification exists.

One variant of the welfare state argument focuses on the values and attitudes that sustain the welfare state. Some argue that the presence of newcomers can undermine the emotional preconditions of the welfare state: the sense of mutual identification, solidarity, and trust among the members of a society that makes people willing to sacrifice for one another and to support welfare state policies.

The first point again is that numbers matter. If there is relatively little immigration, as seems likely in an egalitarian world, and especially if people do not gain access to social welfare programs without contributing to them, immigration should have little impact on the willingness of current citizens to support the welfare state.

There is a much deeper issue here, however. To the extent that the willingness of current members to support the welfare state is eroded by the arrival of immigrants, we have to evaluate the moral legitimacy of this erosion. From a normative perspective, it matters enormously whether the unwillingness to support the welfare state grows out of morally objectionable attitudes such as racism or other forms of prejudice or simply out of what one might call legitimate indifference to the well-being of these new arrivals. Of course, as a practical matter, both sorts of attitudes may have the same effect on the viability of the welfare state, but from a principled perspective, concerned with moral justifications, the distinction is crucial. To the extent that the unwillingness of current members to support welfare programs once immigrants benefit from them is the product of morally impermissible attitudes and dispositions, then to that extent any negative effects on the welfare state cannot provide a deep justification for closure. If closure is to be justified at the level of principle, it cannot be on the basis of an underlying injustice.

Finally, my deepest objection to the welfare state argument is to the way it frames our thinking about immigration. This argument asks us to focus on a choice between the welfare state and freedom of movement. This way of presenting the issue prevents us from considering whether the choice is one that we ought to be expected to make. When a robber says, "Your money or your life," he presents us with a choice. (In a famous joke, Jack Benny responded to this demand, "I'm thinking.") When facing a robber, most people are under no illusion about the moral character of the choice they have to make. We have to make a choice, but it is wrong that the robber forces us to choose between our money and our life. In my view, the choice we are asked to make between the welfare state and freedom of movement is equally wrong.

The welfare state argument is implicitly asking us to choose between providing material support for needy members of rich states and providing material support for even needier people in poor states or giving those people the opportunity to move to rich states to acquire some means of subsistence. Why should we accept that trade-off? As a practical matter, that may sometimes be the choice that we face in the world today, but I want to argue that it's an illegitimate choice like the demand to choose between your money and your life. In a just world, there would be no such trade-off. Perhaps because there is no obvious agent (like the robber) constructing the trade-off, people are less likely to notice its morally problematic character, but that is precisely what the open borders argument is designed to bring into view. The need to choose between the domestic dispossessed and those abroad is the product of underlying structures which are the result of human constructions, not natural forces. Those structures are unjust.

Culture

Immigrants often come with national identities and cultural backgrounds that are different in important ways from those of most of the people in the society

they are entering. May a democratic state keep out immigrants in order to protect and promote the culture of the community against the changes that the
immigrants would bring?

In addressing this question we have to distinguish between ways in which
a democratic state may legitimately seek to preserve a collective cultural heritage and ways in which it may not. Consider a question that lurks in the background of discussions of immigration in both Europe and North America—and
sometimes not so far back. May a democratic state limit immigration so as to
preserve its European and Christian cultural heritage? The question presupposes that this cultural inheritance is likely to be weakened if significant numbers of immigrants who are neither European nor Christian are admitted. Even
if that presupposition were true—and it is problematic in a number of ways—
excluding immigrants because they are not European or Christian would not be
a morally legitimate way of seeking to preserve a democratic state's collective
culture because it would violate fundamental democratic commitments not to
discriminate on the basis of race or religion. We saw in chapter 9 that, even on
the assumption that states are generally free to control admissions, they are not
free to exclude on the basis of race, ethnicity, religion, or any of the other characteristics that we regard as discriminatory when used as a basis for exclusion
within the domestic context. So, a democratic state may not (legitimately) limit
immigration for the sake of cultural preservation, if it defines the culture in terms
of existing racial, ethnic, or religious patterns within the population.[43]

What sorts of public culture may a democratic state legitimately seek to
preserve? I have already addressed the question to some extent in chapters 3
and 4. The central theme of those chapters was that democratic commitments
to freedom and equality set severe limits to the kinds of cultural adaptations a
democratic state can demand or even expect of immigrants. If a democratic state
seeks to promote a national culture and identity, it must limit itself to versions
of culture and identity that are open to all of those within the state, regardless of
their ancestry, their race, their religion, their ways of dressing and eating and living so long as they do not harm others. If the state is limited in the kind of public
culture it can promote internally, it cannot justify restrictions on immigration
as a way of preserving some more extensive set of cultural commitments. If the
state is to restrict immigration for the sake of its public culture, it must be a public culture that it is morally entitled to pursue.

I do not have the space here to pursue a fuller discussion of what sorts of public culture are compatible with democratic commitments. Some theorists would
deny that democratic states should care about the public culture at all, but if that
is correct the problem I am trying to address disappears.[44] I want to consider the
claim that cultural preservation can offer a reason for restricting immigration,
and, for those purposes, I want to assume that democratic states can legitimately

be concerned with protecting certain aspects of the public culture such as the language of public life.[45]

Given this assumption, can the goal of cultural preservation provide a justification for restrictions on immigration? Again, we have to pay attention to the other background assumptions about the circumstances within which this question emerges. For reasons already explained, I want to assume a relatively egalitarian world as the background for this question. In that sort of context, it would very rarely be necessary to restrict immigration to protect the public culture. Small numbers of people may be flexible or whimsical enough to move for trivial reasons to a place whose national culture is very different from their own, especially one in which the language of public life is not their own native tongue. Most people, however, need a fairly serious reason to undertake such a challenge—either intimate personal ties or significant economic or professional opportunities that they cannot find at home. When the economic differences between states are not huge, relatively few people find such reasons to move.

If the migrants are few in number (relative to the established population), they can normally be easily absorbed and in any event will pose no serious threat to the existing public culture. Over time, their children will be educated in the language of public life and will come to see that language as their own native tongue. They will be integrated into the public culture in other ways as well. It is only if those seeking admission are numerous (relative to the settled population), that the newcomers could pose a serious cultural challenge. That is likely to happen only when there are very substantial differences between the material conditions in the migrants' country of origin and the one they are seeking to enter. So, the idea that immigration poses a cultural threat is almost always connected to the fact that closure is protecting noncultural advantages. Without those advantages, there would be no threat and no reason to fear open borders, at least under normal circumstances.

So far, I have been arguing that it is implausible to suppose that it would be necessary to restrict free movement for the sake of cultural preservation in a just world, that is, a world with only modest economic differences between states. But to clarify the issue further, let's suppose that even under just background conditions, some state did face an influx of immigrants that might swamp its national culture and transform its language from the language of the vast majority to the language of a minority. And let's assume further that keeping this from happening is a morally legitimate and important goal for the state. Would that justify granting the state discretionary control over immigration?

No. People often assume that we must choose between unconstrained open borders (come what may) and discretionary state control over migration where the state has no obligation to admit migrants unless it judges admission to be in the interest of current citizens. That seems plausible only if one is working with an implicit picture of what states may and may not do based on our current assumptions about what states are entitled to do. Here is an alternative principle. "People normally have the right to migrate and settle wherever they want, and to acquire the full rights of citizenship after some limited waiting period. States have the right to restrict migration only if they can show, on the basis of evidence in an impartial (but internal) forum, that further migration would endanger the survival of the national language and culture, and they may exercise this right of restriction only so long as and to the extent that the danger persists." This principle leaves the power with the state but not the discretionary moral authority to exercise that power for any reason that seems good to the state.

The position I have just outlined might be described as free movement with a cultural caveat. The cultural caveat is not so different from other sorts of caveats that limit every democratic freedom. Whether it is freedom of speech or freedom of religious practice or freedom of (internal) movement, every freedom that involves human action in the world is constrained by caveats for emergencies and crises where normal freedoms may be suspended.[46] So, the cultural caveat is like the public order constraint—a qualification of the commitment to open borders but a minor one.

My position takes culture seriously and gives it enough moral weight that it can justify limiting freedom of movement under some circumstances. It is possible to imagine cases in which, due to special circumstances, some groups (whether a small state or, more likely, some small substate group) would need to implement policies of closure (or partial closure) with respect to immigrants in order to protect a fragile, collective culture (and not some privileged economic position). Such cases are likely to be rare because we have to imagine that enough people want to move into a particular community to threaten the viability of its culture, despite the presumed distinctiveness of its language and its current use in public life, despite the absence of any strong economic advantages to living in the community, and despite the many alternatives available to the potential migrants. It is possible to imagine such a scenario, but it seems likely that it would be uncommon.

In sum, even if we accept the view that the preservation of a national culture is an important and morally legitimate state interest, it is unlikely to provide a justification for restricting immigration under just background conditions. Under some highly specific circumstances it might. We can allow for this possibility by adding a cultural caveat to the general principle of free movement. Like the other arguments in this section, the cultural caveat is contingent and self-limiting. It only justifies restrictions on immigration if they threaten the culture and only to the extent that is necessary to protect it. Under existing conditions, appeals to cultural preservation as a justification for restrictions on immigration serve mainly to disguise the ways in which such restrictions protect noncultural, and arguably illegitimate, interests.

Conclusion

I have tried to show in this chapter that there are no compelling arguments against open borders at the level of principle. There are some contingent and self-limiting arguments that justify restrictions on immigration under certain circumstances but no arguments that justify the discretionary control over immigration that states now exercise and that the conventional view endorses.

In defending open borders, I am not arguing for a world in which human beings move frequently from one political community to another, with no sense of home or belonging and no deep attachment to place or people. Political communities require relatively stable, intergenerational populations in order to function effectively over time. This requirement of intergenerational stability would be compatible with open borders, however, if the other requirements of justice were met. Modest migration does not threaten intergenerational stability. Most people find it more attractive to stay in their community of origin—a place where they know the language, have friends and family, and feel at home—than to move, so long as the differences in life chances between home and elsewhere are not too great. Having open borders would not lead to mass migration, if the differences between political communities were as limited as justice requires.

Political communities matter morally, but belonging need not entail exclusion. What would a just world look like? I'm not sure of all the particulars, but I am reasonably confident of this. If a just world had states, they would be states with open borders.

13

Conclusion

In the preceding two chapters, I critically examined the conventional view that states are morally entitled to exercise discretionary control over immigration. I argued that this view was wrong and that our deepest moral principles require a commitment to open borders (with modest qualifications) in a world where inequality between states is much reduced. The previous chapters of the book had operated with background assumptions that we lived in a world of very unequal states and that the conventional view was correct. In this concluding chapter, I want to consider how the open borders argument affects the analysis developed in the earlier chapters.

In broad outline, my position is this: the open borders argument does not conflict with my earlier conclusions in any important way. In some ways, it actually reinforces the central claims of the theory of social membership about the moral importance of belonging because it eliminates morally problematic claims advanced in the name of belonging, thus clearing space for the legitimate ones. In a world of open borders between distinct but relatively equal states, some of the issues I discussed previously, such as the problem of irregular migrants, would largely disappear, but many of the other questions about the ethics of immigration would remain salient. States would still have to determine how people should acquire citizenship, what legal rights ought to be enjoyed by noncitizens, and what sorts of social, economic, and cultural policies they should pursue with respect to immigrants. In general, the answers that I offered to these issues earlier in the book would still be valid in a world of open borders. States would be morally obliged to ensure appropriate access to citizenship for immigrants and their children, to secure the legal right of residents and temporary workers, and to create a political culture of inclusion and respect for migrants. Developing these claims in a bit more detail will enable me both to highlight the main arguments of the book and to show how well these earlier arguments fit with the argument for open borders.

Immigration in a Just World

Let's begin with citizenship, where the potential conflict between the earlier and later arguments seems strongest. In chapter 11, I said that "citizenship in Western democracies is the modern equivalent of feudal class privilege—an inherited status that greatly enhances one's life chances" while in chapter 2 I said that "birthright citizenship for the children of resident citizens makes moral sense as a practice . . . it is a moral imperative." How is it possible to reconcile these two statements? The answer is that it is not the practice of birthright citizenship per se that is being criticized in chapter 11 but its link to inherited inequality and closure. When that link is broken, the practice does make moral sense, indeed is a moral imperative, even in a world of open borders.

The critique in chapter 11 is concerned with the inequality between states and with the discretionary control over immigration that makes it possible to maintain that inequality. In that context, inherited citizenship in rich states does function as a form of illegitimate privilege. But as I explained in the last chapter, permitting free movement in a world of much less unequal states would not mean that most people moved from one state to another every few years, never setting down roots or establishing any deep attachments to a particular political community.[1] On the contrary, there is every reason to believe that most people would want to live in the state where they grew up and that migration pressures would be reduced. Nevertheless, some people would migrate and that would raise familiar issues. Even if states permitted free movement for peaceful visitors and settlers, they would still find it necessary to distinguish between citizens and others for some purposes (e.g., diplomatic protection, eligibility for voting and public office) and so would have to have ways of assigning citizenship. Citizenship as a status would not disappear in a just world of open borders and relatively equal states, but it would lose its character as an inherited privilege closed to outsiders.

But who should get citizenship in a world of open borders? This is where the arguments of chapters 2 and 3 are still relevant. I argued in those chapters that democratic principles require that citizenship be extended to all those subject to the laws on an ongoing basis in part because belonging matters and belonging comes primarily from living in a place and in part because the legitimacy of the laws rests upon the consent of the governed. I also argued that the appropriate mechanisms for implementing this principle would involve granting citizenship at birth to anyone born on the territory of the state with a reasonable expectation of growing up there, granting it automatically to anyone raised there for much of her childhood, and granting it (with at most modest requirements regarding language and knowledge of the country) to anyone who has lived there for an extended period and asks for it. These principles governing the allocation of citizenship would still apply in a world of open borders. So, even in a world of open borders, it would make sense to say that "birthright citizenship for the children of resident citizens makes moral sense as a practice...it is a moral imperative." Of course, the original statement in chapter 2 was deliberately bracketing the issues raised in chapter 11, but this just shows that the principles governing the allocation of citizenship are fairly robust. They apply both when those issues are on the table and when they are not. And, as we will see, that applies to most of the other arguments in the earlier chapters.

I also noted in chapter 2 that every democratic state provides for the automatic transmission of citizenship or a right to citizenship from parent to child, even if the family is not living in the parent's home state, so long as the parent himself or herself once lived there for some extended period. I argued that this pattern of granting access to citizenship flowed both from an obligation to protect the fundamental interests of the children of citizens and from an understanding of belonging. At the same time, I argued that this parental transmission of citizenship should not continue indefinitely. The most fundamental basis for belonging is living in the community. Membership should not be extended through multiple generations once that basis in residence is removed. Again, these arguments would still apply in a world where people were free to move from one state to another. It is true that in a world where people were free to move, the children would not need the parent's citizenship to have the right to move back to the parent's home state, but that is only one of the vital interests that are protected by parental transmission in the current world. Moreover, to the extent that a parent is motivated by her identities and attachments, she would have just as much reason to want to transmit her membership in her community of origin to her children in a world of open borders as she does in our world today.

Finally, I argued in chapters 2 and 3 that democratic states should permit dual or multiple citizenships in cases where individuals had genuine connections to the political communities, including not only the connections created by residence, which I treat as the strongest form of connection, but also connections deriving from their parents whose identities and attachments may have been formed by previous residence in another state. For reasons similar to the ones just discussed, in a world of open borders individuals might still want to maintain dual or multiple citizenships whether they acquired these though birth in one state to parents from another, or through birth to parents with different nationalities, or through retention of a citizenship after naturalization. Dual citizenship might be less important in a world of open borders, but, by the same token, states would have even less reason to oppose dual citizenship in such a world than they do today.[2]

What about the questions about the social inclusion of immigrants that I discussed in chapter 4? If we proceed from the understanding of a just world that I developed in chapters 11 and 12, in which free movement would be part of a wider transformation that involved a significant reduction in the economic inequalities between states, then one might expect that the problems of social inclusion would not be as great in a just world as they are in our world today. People would be less likely to feel that they had to move out of economic necessity and so would presumably be less inclined to move to a society with a very different culture and way of life, unless they were attracted by these differences. Nevertheless, it would be a mistake to assume away the questions and problems that I discussed in chapter 4. In a world of open borders, there would still be migration, in part for economic reasons. In that world, as in ours, migrants would bring various forms of cultural and religious diversity with them. So, in that world, as in ours, states would still have an obligation to construct and maintain a democratic ethos of inclusion. The points made in chapter 4 about the need for mutual adaptation with respect to rules, informal norms, incentives, practices of recognition, and national identity would all apply even in a world of open borders.

Now consider the questions raised in chapter 5 about how the rights of residents should resemble or differ from the rights of citizens. In a world of open borders, as in the world today, some people would move to states in which they were not citizens, and they might not become citizens for an extended period, if ever, even if citizenship were available to them. In chapter 5, I said that residents should generally enjoy the same legal rights as citizens, with a few modest qualifications. I argued that some of the rights that noncitizens enjoy are general human rights that ought to be extended to anyone subject to a state's jurisdiction but that many other legal rights are appropriately restricted to people living in the society. They are membership-specific rights.

Those arguments and the broad distinction between general human rights and membership-specific rights would apply just as fully in a world in which people were free to move across state borders. In a world of open borders, as in our world today, permanent residents should have basically the same rights as citizens, except for the right to vote and run for office, and many rights would remain tied to membership.

The open borders argument does bring one important qualification to the analysis in chapter 5. An important conceptual contribution of chapter 5 was the distinction between general human rights and membership-specific human rights. People often conflate the idea that human rights must be universal with the idea that they must be general. As I showed in chapter 5, that is not the case. A human right can be universal in the sense that it is a right that every human being has simply in virtue of her humanity but the content of the right may be tied to a person's social location, and in that sense the right is membership-specific. The example of a membership-specific human right that I used in chapter 5 was the right to enter one's own country. In a world of open borders, that would no longer be a good example of a membership-specific human right. The right to enter a country would be a general human right, largely replacing the membership-specific right to enter one's own country.[3] Recognition of a general human right of free movement would not mean that the distinction between general human rights and membership-specific human rights would no longer be relevant, however. As I point out in chapter 11, in a world of open borders, the right to participate in the democratic political process in the place where one lives would still be a membership-specific human right. Similarly, another membership-specific human right is the right to a nationality. It would be a mistake to see that as a right to whatever nationality one prefers, even in a world of open borders. Rather it is arguably best seen as a right to nationality in the state with which one has the strongest connections, mainly from living there, and this is reflected in the international rules for attributing citizenship to those who would otherwise be stateless at birth.

In chapter 6, I discussed the rights of those allowed to stay and work only on a temporary basis. I argued that temporary workers should be seen as temporary members of society and should enjoy most of the economic and social rights that citizens and permanent residents enjoy, with the exception of redistributive programs and with some qualifications for pensions and unemployment compensation. Even in a world of open borders, many people might choose to live and work in a state other than their own only for a limited period of time (as they often do now even in cases where they have a right to stay on). The arguments I advanced in chapter 6 about how temporary workers should be treated would still apply in a world of open borders. States might choose to make arrangements that would facilitate such temporary stays (e.g., ensuring that pension benefits would be transferable to the state of origin), but they would not be obliged to do so.

There is one important difference between the conclusions of chapter 6 and the principles that would govern temporary workers in a world of open borders: temporary workers could not be obliged to return home. I argued in chapter 6 that temporary workers who stay long enough should be regarded as full members of society, and that would still apply in a world of open borders.

In chapter 7, I discussed the rights of irregular migrants. I argued that irregular migrants were entitled to general human rights and that states were obliged to create a firewall between immigration enforcement and the protection of general human rights in order to ensure that the human rights of irregular migrants would actually be respected. I also said that irregular migrants should be given a range of other rights as well and that it often made sense to protect those rights with a firewall, but I said that the case for some of these other rights and for a firewall to protect them was less securely grounded in democratic principles. Finally, I argued that over time irregular migrants became members of society and acquired a moral right to have their legal status regularized.

In a world of open borders, states would normally have no right to prevent people from coming for peaceful purposes and no right to set time limits to how long they could stay after they arrived. So, the problem of irregular migration would disappear and the issues discussed in chapter 7 would largely be moot.

In chapter 8, I presented a theory of social membership that I said emerged from the answers offered to the various questions in the previous chapters. The central theme of that theory is that living in a society over time makes one a member and being a member generates moral claims to legal rights and to legal status. Nothing in the argument for open borders challenges that theme. Indeed, one of the main messages of this book is that it is possible to reconcile deep respect for the moral claims of belonging with a commitment to open borders. Particularism and universalism are not in such fundamental conflict as people often assume.

Chapter 9 dealt with admissions under the assumption that the state had a general right to exercise discretionary control over admissions. I considered arguments about criteria of selection and exclusion, as well as the duty of democratic states to permit family reunification.

In a world of open borders states would normally have no right to select among potential immigrants. That part of the discussion in chapter 9 would no longer be relevant. The arguments advanced in the chapter would not be refuted but rather superseded. Normally, in a world of open borders, there would be no need to grant priority based on family reunification either. I did acknowledge, however, that the principle of free movement across borders was not absolute and that there could be some circumstances under which states might be entitled to restrict entry, even of people who posed no threat. In such a context, for the reasons laid out in chapter 9, family reunification would still set a limit to the state's exercise of control over immigration, even under the exceptional circumstances that might otherwise justify some restrictions in a world of generally open borders.

When it comes to questions about the criteria of exclusion, the issue is more complicated. I acknowledged in chapter 12 that even in a world of open borders there might be some legitimate criteria of exclusion. For example, in chapter 9, I mentioned national security as a common criterion of exclusion that had often been abused but was legitimate in principle, and in chapter 12 I made the same argument, referring explicitly to the discussion in chapter 9. But most of the other criteria of exclusion that are legitimate under the assumption of discretionary immigration control in the discussion in chapter 9 would be either clearly impermissible or much more problematic in a world of open borders for reasons explained in chapter 12.

Chapter 10 dealt with questions about the responsibility of democratic states to admit refugees. I offered three complementary reasons why democratic states have a moral duty to admit refugees and then sought to clarify that duty by exploring questions about who should qualify as a refugee, what kinds of assistance refugees need, who should provide that assistance, and whether there are limits on what could be asked of states in assisting refugees. I argued that, in principle, we should expand the definition of refugee to include anyone fleeing serious threats to basic rights, regardless of the source; that refugees need only a safe haven at first but are entitled to full membership in a new society eventually if they cannot go home safely; that it is reasonable to expect those nearby to provide the initial shelter but that all states had duties to admit long-term refugees in accordance with their capacities to absorb them and other factors; and that ultimately there was almost no justification for refusing to admit refugees. I also argued, however, that there is such a big gap between the ideal refugee regime identified by these answers and what democratic states are actually willing to do, that there is no realistic chance of the ideal refugee regime being implemented. Any attempt to do so would make matters worse by undermining the protections for refugees provided by the existing refugee regime.

One might hope that in a relatively egalitarian world with open borders there would be no refugees, but it would be a mistake simply to assume this question away. Even in a world that was basically just, there could be extreme natural disasters that forced large numbers of people to move, and there can always be failures of particular states. To the extent that the problem of forced migration persisted in a world of open borders, the principles identified in chapter 10 would still be relevant. They might also be more realistic because the principle of open borders would make it impossible for states to confine refugees to wherever they first arrived as happens today and the relative equality between states would reduce the incentives for refugees to focus on a few states as the ideal places to start over. On the whole, however, these points about refugees and the related points about discretionary admissions in chapter 9 are minor qualifications to the general conclusion that the concerns of these chapters would be largely superseded in a world of open borders.

Overall then, some of the questions about the ethics of immigration that I discussed in the first ten chapters would largely disappear in a world of open borders, but most of the questions would still be relevant, and the arguments that I developed in the earlier chapters about what justice requires would still apply. In sum, the open borders argument does not challenge the findings of the first ten chapters, although it renders some of those findings moot.

Theory and Practice: What Is to Be Done?

We do not live in a just world. Does the argument for open borders have any bearing on what we ought to do in the here and now?

If I am right about the compatibility between the argument for open borders and the arguments in earlier chapters, we can look at the claims advanced earlier in the book as partial and practical steps toward a just world. Pursuing the goal of a just world does not require us to reject everything in the world as it is. My arguments about access to citizenship, the rights of residents and temporary workers, the full social inclusion of immigrants, and the principles of nondiscrimination and family reunification in admissions are not radical challenges to the status quo. On the contrary, they articulate the moral logic underlying the general trends of the last several decades toward more inclusive rules for the acquisition of citizenship and more expansive rights for residents and away from an assimilationist model of public culture and a discriminatory approach to admissions. There is no reason for advocates of open borders to oppose these principles or these policies, since they are also part of the ideal of a just world of open borders, as I have just shown. So, in these areas the open borders argument fits well with my previous claims about what ought to be done and with what is actually being done, for the most part.

Consider now my arguments in chapter 7 for responding to the moral claims of irregular migrants by creating an enforcement firewall to protect their legal rights and by granting them legal status after a period of residence. From an open borders perspective, this approach is clearly insufficient because it still treats the migrants as subject to constraints to which they would not be subject if the right of free movement were respected.

What if it is not politically feasible to get states to accept open borders? That is clearly the reality today. There are degrees of injustice, and from the same open borders perspective, granting irregular migrants some rights and some opportunity to acquire legal status would be less unjust than denying these things altogether. It would at least be a step in the right direction. An open borders perspective might also make it less likely that irregular migrants would be seen as people who have done something morally wrong in entering without legal permission, since the law that excludes the migrants is unjust from this perspective. I do not present this as an inevitable difference, however, because one can take the view that even if a law is unjust it should be obeyed until it is changed. Conversely, some may take the view that the state is entitled to restrict immigration but that this does not imply that people who enter without permission are acting immorally. These are complex questions that I cannot pursue here but they have some bearing on whether or not people think that any regularization of status should be accompanied by a fine or some symbolic acknowledgment of guilt. My own view is that, in principle, regularization should not entail either a fine or an acknowledgment of guilt, but this is the sort of issue on which I would be willing to compromise if it would lead to an effective reform.

As I showed in chapter 7, even those who think that states are entitled to exercise discretionary control over immigration have good reasons to support firewall and regularizaton policies (although they may disagree among themselves about what rights should be protected in this way and how long irregular migrants should have to wait for legal status). Those who accept the open borders argument should support the same policies. They can also press to minimize the time that irregular migrants would have to wait for regularization of their status and to maximize the legal protections in the meantime, within the constraints of what is politically feasible in a particular context. The firewall and regularization proposals are idealistic in relation to the status quo, but they have some chance of being adopted, at least in part. They are not utopian in the way that the open borders ideal itself is under current conditions. So, the analysis in that chapter also offers relatively concrete guidance about how to act in the world, guidance that should be helpful not only for those who accept the state's right to control immigration but also for those who believe in a more demanding vision of justice (i.e., open borders) but want to promote justice as much as possible within the limits of what is feasible.

Fundamentally, however, the open borders argument itself is not intended to advance a specific program of action. While I do think that a just world will be one in which people are largely free to live where they choose and in which there is relative economic equality among places and people, I am not certain that the best way to move in the direction of that world is to increase immigration to rich democratic states as much as possible. That is a much more contingent question whose answer depends on strategies of transformation, a topic that I have not tried to address for the most part. The goal of the open borders argument is to challenge complacency, to make us aware of how routine democratic practices in immigration deny freedom and help to maintain unjust inequality. If I can persuade some people to think more critically about the way the world is organized and about the way it ought to be organized, the open borders argument will have done its job.

Appendix

PRESUPPOSITIONS AND POLITICAL THEORY

How should political theorists think about immigration? I don't think there is a single correct answer to that question. The answer will depend in part on the audience we are addressing, on the goals of our inquiry, and on the substantive questions that we want to ask. In this appendix I want to discuss the approach that I adopted in this book. I hope that talking about my approach will give rise not only to a discussion of its merits and demerits (though that is perfectly appropriate) but also to reflection by readers about how their ways of thinking about immigration resemble or differ from mine and about whether the differences in approach, if any, reflect substantive intellectual disagreements or simply differences of focus. I hope also that this methodological appendix will provide a helpful model for scholars working on other topics in the field of applied political philosophy and, indeed, that it will be of interest to any theorists concerned with the relation between theory and practice. I repeat the caution that I offered in the introduction that this appendix is likely to be of interest only to political theorists.

In the introduction I mentioned two key elements in my approach: (1) my attempt to construct a theoretical account by applying widely shared democratic ideas and principles to particular questions about immigration ("political theory from the ground up"); (2) my decision to adopt the conventional view of the state's right to discretionary control over immigration as a presupposition in the first ten chapters and then to criticize that view in chapters 11 and 12. I will assume that readers of this appendix are familiar with that section of the introduction, and I will try to avoid repeating the points I made there, though there is bound to be a bit of overlap.

My primary goal in this book was to explore what justice requires, permits, and prohibits with respect to immigration in contemporary democratic states. What are the options available to someone with such a goal? I'm sure that I could not list them all, but let me mention three approaches that I decided not to pursue, as a way of framing the one that I actually chose.

First, I might have tried to construct a general theory of justice in order to build my analysis of immigration upon that foundation. That would have had the advantage of providing a systematic and comprehensive approach to the topic. I decided not to take this approach for two related reasons. First, it seemed to me unlikely that I would be able to come up with a general theory of justice that most people would find persuasive. Better minds than mine have tried that already, and the most successful—perhaps John Rawls is the most obvious example in the twentieth century—have attracted plenty of persuasive critiques, however much one admires their achievement.[1] Second, in any general theory of justice, there are many more important topics than immigration. I feared that if I started with the question "What is justice?" I would never get to questions about immigration. In ordering dinner, it is wiser to start with a menu than with the Cartesian *cogito*, and it seemed to me that something like that also applied to the task of thinking about the ethics of immigration.

The second possible approach that I considered was to start from some existing political theory, like that of Rawls, and to try to work out the implications of that theory for the question of immigration. That's an approach that can be helpful. Indeed it is the approach that I adopted in my first foray into this field many years ago when I tried to trace out the logic of Rawls's theory for immigration.[2] That approach also has drawbacks, however. First, it, too, limits the pool of those likely to be persuaded (if not quite as drastically as constructing one's own general theory). Many people do not agree with Rawls (or with any other theorist I might have chosen). If my analysis of the ethics of immigration were too closely tied to a particular philosopher's general theory of justice, those who objected to the general theory might have good reason to object to my account as well. Second, those who accept a theory often disagree about its interpretation and application to particular topics. I wanted to spend my time debating the merits of different views on immigration rather than debating the correct reading of Rawls (or anyone else).[3] Finally, I found in my early work that Rawls's theory (as I interpreted it) was very illuminating when thinking about some topics, such as the fundamental question of whether states ought to be able to restrict immigration, but not much help in thinking about other topics such as the question of what rights residents or temporary workers should have or what cultural claims should be respected and accommodated, in part because Rawls himself had assumed away questions about immigration. Other important topics in immigration like what policies to adopt with respect to irregular migrants and refugees seemed to disappear altogether in Rawlsian ideal theory, where everyone acted in accordance with the principles of justice, and it was far from clear to me how to apply what he said about nonideal theory to such topics. I think that this difficulty is characteristic of other general theories of justice as well.

The third approach that I considered was to focus on questions about justice and immigration as they emerge from some particular historical, cultural, and political context. I might have explored the relationship between justice and immigration in Canada or the United States (or Germany or France, though those would have been harder for me). That is a perfectly appropriate way to pursue a discussion of justice and immigration. It is the sort of approach that is often used by those who study immigration from a legal perspective. They take their normative bearings from the fundamental values of a specific, historically situated constitutional order and explore the ways in which questions about immigration and justice emerge and can be addressed within that framework. Alternatively, one can take a contextual approach to normative inquiry without relying much on the legal order. Elsewhere I have argued that political theorists can learn a lot by taking a contextual approach and I have tried to do so myself.[4] Questions about immigration often involve competing normative considerations, and these can sometimes be explored most effectively by thinking about how to weigh and apply these competing considerations in relation to some specific context.

One drawback of a contextual approach is that it is, well, contextual. Even if one's analysis and conclusions are persuasive in the particular case, one has to wonder to what extent they rely upon particular, idiosyncratic features of the case and to what extent we can generalize from the particular case we are studying to others. I had another worry as well, namely that a contextual approach to immigration might be too conventional. I wanted to find some way to at least consider the possibility that deeply embedded and widely accepted views about immigration were morally problematic. That required some means of gaining more critical distance than is readily provided by a contextual approach.

For these reasons, I wanted to find a way of thinking about justice and immigration that was less ambitious than grand theory but that applied to more than one case, an approach that could be connected to real questions about immigration as people experience them in ordinary life but that would also be able to take a critical step or two back from the parameters of current debates.

The approach that I settled upon starts by recognizing that any inquiry will inevitably rest upon and be limited by presuppositions about what sorts of considerations are to be taken into account and what are to be left off the table. I have tried to bring to consciousness the most important assumptions that frame my own inquiry, and to modify some of those assumptions in the course of the analysis so as to bring into view questions and perspectives that my initial assumptions exclude. I have adopted presuppositions that I think enable me to address a range of questions about what justice entails for immigration, and, in some cases, I have changed those presuppositions in the course of my discussion in order to see how that affects the arguments. I call this way of proceeding the "shifting presuppositions" approach.

Let me first say something about the way that adopting specific presuppositions and then shifting them opens up different possibilities for framing an inquiry into the ethics of immigration. Then I will say more about the choices I made among these possibilities and the implications of those choices.

Shifting Presuppositions

All inquiries have presuppositions or background assumptions. In order to investigate some issues we must take other things as given: the meanings of words, moral norms, facts about the world, and so on. For example, when I say that I am interested in justice and immigration, I am assuming that the concepts "justice" and "immigration" will be intelligible, at least in a preliminary way, to my readers. I do not mean to suggest that anything is entirely beyond investigation, including the meaning of concepts that one uses as a starting point. We may start with some presupposition that we choose to challenge in another context or even later in the course of the same inquiry. Nevertheless, we cannot challenge everything at once. In any particular inquiry, we have to start with some background assumptions that are treated as given, at least at first. Often we adopt presuppositions in order to limit an inquiry to a few manageable issues, not because we imagine that the topics that are assumed away are not worth investigation in their own right. I do that at several points in this book.

There are many different possible presuppositions that we could adopt in framing an inquiry into the ethics of immigration. The presuppositions that we adopt can have a big impact on the kinds of questions that we ask and the sorts of answers that we find. To see why that is the case, let's focus for a moment on just one aspect of the presuppositions that may shape an inquiry about justice and immigration: a concern for feasibility. There is an old slogan in philosophy: ought implies can. But what does "can" mean in this slogan? If we accept the principle that ought implies can and if we make a claim about what justice requires with respect to immigration, whatever we say justice requires has to be possible in some sense. But in what sense must something be possible in order for it to be a requirement of justice? Must it be something that has a chance of passing the legislature this year? That is clearly too restrictive for any plausible conception of justice. Must it conform to conventional views of right and wrong, justice and injustice, no matter how contradictory and unreflective they may be? Again, that is clearly too constrained. But then what is the nature of the feasibility constraint? Perhaps there is no single correct answer to that question.

Imagine a continuum of possible presuppositions that stretches from the way things are now to the way things ought to be. I want to show how it is possible to position oneself at different points along such a continuum in thinking about justice and immigration and why there are advantages and disadvantages to whatever point we pick.

The Just World Presupposition

First, moving toward the "way things ought to be" end of the continuum, we might want to ask simply "What does justice require, permit and prohibit with regard to immigration?" In posing the question that way, we implicitly invoke the idea of justice in some sort of unqualified or absolute sense. We locate the inquiry at a point where we are setting to one side obstacles to justice that might be posed by the existing order of things: particular histories, established institutions, the distribution of power, conventional (but problematic) moral norms, the unwillingness of agents to act justly, and so on. Of course, this kind of inquiry cannot be *entirely* detached from reality. It is still constrained by the principle that "ought" implies "can." But it treats the constraints of "can," of what is possible, in a minimalist light. What justice demands must be humanly possible, under ideal circumstances. It need not be immediately feasible.

Adopting a background assumption that seeks to minimize the constraints upon moral reflection is a familiar way for philosophers to proceed. It is the approach many people took Rawls to be adopting in *A Theory of Justice* when he talked about ideal theory (though the nature of Rawls's ideal theory looks somewhat different when read in the light of his later work). In the *Politics* Aristotle talks about the best regime as a regime without presuppositions under circumstances that one would pray to the gods for. That is another variant of this approach.

Both Rawls in *A Theory of Justice* and Aristotle in the *Politics* implicitly take a single regime as their focus, presupposing a division of the world into regimes and saying little about what justice entails for the claims of outsiders (individual or collective) on those within the regime.[5] By contrast, an exploration of what justice ideally entails with respect to immigration should take the whole world order into account.

Let's use the label "the just world presupposition" for an inquiry that proposes to discuss justice and immigration against the background assumption of a world where all institutions are just, everyone is acting justly, we don't have to worry about overcoming past injustices, and so on. What are the advantages and disadvantages of adopting such a framework of inquiry?

On the one hand, it clearly has many advantages. The just world presupposition provides a context that is open to an independent and critical evaluation of the status quo. It opens up the possibility of our gaining a critical perspective on unjust arrangements and flawed moral views that are deeply entrenched and not easily subject to change.

Take, for example, the way the world is currently organized. The just world presupposition gives us room to criticize the modern state system as unjust, even if we concede that it is here to stay for the foreseeable future. The point here is not that the modern state system is unjust, but rather that it can be important to have the intellectual space to consider that issue. We should not always simply assume that the modern system of states cannot be challenged or changed.

Taking the general idea of unqualified justice as a presupposition also opens up space for challenging conventional normative views. The way we think is often as deeply entrenched and difficult to change as our institutions. We might want to think about immigration in the light of conceptions of justice that are quite different from the ones that are dominant today. We could use Plato, for example, to think about justice and immigration from a perspective that is radically at odds with contemporary conventional views of ethics. Or we could construct an entirely new theory of justice that isn't confined to concepts provided by a tradition of thought overwhelming shaped by elite heterosexual white males. In any event, this presupposition sets no a priori limits on what counts as justice and where immigration as a topic fits in an overall account of justice.

This sort of critical openness has many advantages. Even if we do not have a realistic chance of bringing about a fundamental transformation of our social arrangements or of ourselves, we should still assess current reality in the light of our highest ideals. If we are forced to choose between the lesser of two evils, it is essential not to delude ourselves into thinking that the lesser evil is really a good. Approaching moral questions with something like the just world presupposition avoids legitimating policies and practices that are morally wrong. It gives the fullest scope to our critical capacities.

On the other hand, adopting a just world presupposition has disadvantages as well. It detaches us from so many familiar landmarks that it is easy to lose our bearings and easier still to lose sight of the issue of immigration. There are many considerations that would have to come into play in any fundamental exploration of what a just world would require, all of them highly contestable. Questions about a just world must be related to and derived from a wider set of moral considerations, like our understanding of the human good, the moral standing of humans (and other beings), the relevance of different forms of political community to the achievement of this good, and so on. The most basic questions of philosophy are implicated. Even in a more restricted focus, the challenge is daunting. For example, suppose we asked what differences in language, culture, and identity would exist in a just world and how these differences would matter in social and political institutions. We know that some versions of these differences make justice (as many of us understand it) impossible to achieve, and others make it difficult. But would we assume them away altogether in a just world? Or should we treat such differences as givens in a just world, as if they were natural facts like climates and soils (which are themselves no longer simply natural facts in the real world). What sort of history is required by a just world? It will be immediately apparent that these sorts of questions only scratch the surface of the questions one might ask about a just world, and that many of these contestable features would be relevant to the question of immigration in a just world. In an inquiry into the nature of a just world, questions about immigration are bound to play a subordinate role. One has to worry whether one would ever reach them at all. This takes us back to the reasons why I chose not to approach the topic of justice and immigration by constructing my own theory of justice.

The just world presupposition is pretty far along the continuum toward the way things ought to be, but it does not go all the way to the end (if there really is an end). The just world assumption constrains our inquiry into what ought to be in some ways. It embodies limits that some might want to challenge. For example, Nietzsche rejects the language of justice and morality itself, and so a Nietzschean would not readily accept the just world presupposition as an appropriate framework for inquiry into what ought to be in some more fundamental sense, a sense that goes beyond the conventional moral categories of just and unjust, good and evil. We could certainly ask whether Nietzsche's philosophy has any implications for the way we think about immigration, but it would not be easy to do so starting from the just world presupposition.

Others might object to the just world presupposition on different grounds. This way of framing the discussion relies implicitly upon modes of reasoning and styles of rhetoric that are characteristic of the Anglo-American analytical tradition of philosophical thought but less congenial to, sometimes even in conflict with, other philosophical approaches such as, say, postmodernism. Those whose normative views are not derived from European philosophical and religious traditions might want to challenge the just world presupposition as a framework that implicitly excludes normative considerations or perspectives that they regard as relevant. For example, one might argue that a Confucian perspective on migration would want to resist the language of justice in talking about this topic.[6] So, the just world presupposition is not actually the end point on a continuum of normative inquiry. Of course, one might also ask whether "continuum" is really the right metaphor here and whether the phrase "normative inquiry" is not itself inappropriately confining.

The Real World Presupposition

The just world presupposition can help us to clarify fundamental principles, if only, as we have just seen, within certain parameters. Even within those parameters, however, the just world presupposition is often not very useful in helping us to decide how to act in a world where our options are constrained in a wide variety of ways. As an alternative to the just world presupposition therefore, we might want to position ourselves toward the other end of the continuum, the one anchored by "the way things are now." We might decide to focus on what justice requires of us with respect to immigration policies here and now. In this approach, the main question we are asking is "How should we act and what policies should we adopt, all things considered?"

Again, this is a familiar way to engage in normative reflection. It is what policymakers do, to the extent that they turn their minds to questions of justice. It is also the approach that is adopted by most of those who engage in moral arguments in public debates: editorialists, public intellectuals, NGOs, and ordinary citizens. Here the challenge is to determine the best course of action from the perspective of justice among the ones that have some chance of being adopted. Feasibility becomes a major consideration because we want to be effective, not utopian. This approach situates our inquiry in a context where we must take into account many of the factors that we excluded with the just world presupposition: particular histories, established institutions, the distribution of power, conventional moral norms, the unwillingness of agents to act justly, and so on. All of these factors affect the feasibility of alternative courses of action.

Let's call this way of thinking about what justice requires with respect to immigration in the context of the world as we find it, both morally and institutionally, "the real world presupposition." If we adopt the real world presupposition as the framework for our discussion of justice and immigration, the idea that "ought implies can" will act as a much more serious constraint on our inquiry. We have to take much of the world as given because it is not subject to our control or easily changed. For example, in this approach, the division of the world into states with vastly different amounts of power and wealth must be treated simply as a background assumption in our inquiry, because whatever one thinks of this fact from some ideal perspective, it is a feature of our world that is not likely to change in the immediate future. Similarly, we may have to work with deeply rooted conventional understandings of justice, even if these would look problematic from a more open-minded and critical perspective, because we are not likely to be able to persuade most people to adopt some radically new view of morality and justice. Furthermore, we cannot assume that others would be willing to adopt a just policy on immigration simply because it is just and without regard for how it affects their interests. And we may want to ask not what justice requires of states generally, but what justice requires of a particular state in dealing with immigration at this moment in time, given its history, the circumstances it faces, and the possibilities open to it.

What are the advantages and disadvantages of thinking about what justice requires with respect to immigration within a framework provided by the real world presupposition? Adopting this presupposition for our inquiry makes it much more likely that we will be grappling with the problems that people actually face. These problems often arise from the fact that states and individuals do not act justly and from particular circumstances that would be assumed away by the just world presupposition. More generally, this sort of approach makes it much more likely that our arguments and conclusions will be relevant to whatever policy debate is going on. The disadvantage, of course, is that we may not be able even to see deep injustices. Indeed, we may wind up affirming them as legitimate.

The real world presupposition, as I have described it, is pretty far along the normative continuum toward the way things are, but it is not at the endpoint of that continuum. The point of the presupposition is still to frame an inquiry into what *justice* requires, permits, and prohibits with respect to immigration, and so it does not preclude criticism, even sharp criticism, of the status quo.

In contrasting the just world and real world presuppositions, I do not mean to imply that the meaning of either is self-evident or uncontested. On the contrary, people disagree deeply both about the nature of justice as an unqualified ideal and about what is possible in the here and now. Indeed, it is probably fair to say that people sometimes disagree more about what the real world is (i.e., about the set of feasible options for various issues) than they do about what a just world would look like. Nevertheless, I hope that it is already intuitively clear that adopting one of these background assumptions rather than the other can have a considerable effect on the kinds of questions we ask, the evidence we consider, and the arguments we advance. How great that effect is will depend in large part on what we think justice is and how wide we think the gap is between what justice would require with respect to immigration in a just world and the set of feasible policy options today. The wider the gap, the greater the effect of adopting one presupposition rather than the other.

The just world presupposition and the real world presupposition do not exhaust the alternatives we can adopt by way of background assumptions for an inquiry into immigration. As I said, they mark out two points on a continuum, and there are many other points along the way. We may want to abstract from some of the constraints of the real world but not others for purposes of a particular moral inquiry. For example, we might want to ask (as I do in this book) what a just refugee regime would look like, assuming some things about the obligations of states toward refugees and challenging others. That question requires more abstraction from the real world than the question of what some particular state's refugee policy should be in the here and now, but it does not go all the way to the just world presupposition. After all, in a world in which everyone was acting justly the problems posed by refugees would be dramatically reduced and so much easier to solve.

This last observation illustrates why we should not assume that the just world presupposition always offers a superior perspective on moral questions. Some of the most urgent moral questions simply disappear from view in a just world.

For example, as I noted in the concluding chapter, if a just world requires open borders (as I contend), the problem of irregular migration disappears in a just world. But what to do about irregular migration is one of the most urgent practical moral issues that we face today. Moral reflection about justice requires more than simply constructing an ideal picture of justice and then seeing how closely we can approximate that picture in the real world.

Let me be clear. I am not arguing now that the just world presupposition has no merit and that we should always focus instead on practical alternatives. If I thought that I would not have spent so much time on the open borders debate. The point is rather that we should be conscious of the inevitability of adopting some background assumption with respect to the role (if any) that feasibility is playing in our discussion. We should also be aware that there is no single correct position on this spectrum. Whatever position we choose will have advantages and disadvantages for reflections about justice.

Where does my book fit on this spectrum that I have drawn? Well, it is not at either extreme, and it does not stay in one place. A book that argues for open borders is obviously not completely constrained by the real world presupposition. On the other hand, in the first several chapters I presuppose the conventional view about the state's right to exercise discretionary control over immigration, and even in the final chapters, I am working with institutional and normative presuppositions that stop my inquiry well short of the just world presupposition as I have described it here.

Rather than try to position my project precisely on an imaginary continuum (which itself captures only some aspects of the background presuppositions of any inquiry), let me talk about the various limiting presuppositions that I have adopted and explain why I have adopted them. That will help to reveal the advantages and disadvantages of the approach I have taken. I will also return to the question of why I shift presuppositions in the course of the discussion.

The Democratic Principles Presupposition

Perhaps the most important limiting assumption that I adopt is my commitment to democratic principles broadly defined. I explained in the introduction that I would use the term "democratic principles" to refer to the broad moral commitments that underlie and justify contemporary political institutions and policies in states in Europe and North America and that I would identify specific principles in the course of my engagement with particular questions and issues. I won't repeat my elaboration of those points here, and I leave it to readers to judge how well that way of articulating democratic principles works in the book. My focus here is on the way the presupposition of a commitment to democratic principles limits my inquiry.

When I talk about what justice requires, I am already presupposing that it is justice as understood in the contemporary democratic tradition. I know that lots of people don't accept these principles, and I am not claiming that we should not engage with critics of democracy. After all, I teach courses in the history of political thought which includes Plato and Nietzsche, no friends of democracy. I am aware that I am not addressing important intellectual challenges both from within the Western tradition and from outside it. But no book can address every possible challenge. Assuming a commitment to democratic principles is a way of keeping my inquiry within manageable bounds. It also makes it more likely that my arguments will appear relevant to the audience that I am trying to reach. Finally, and perhaps most importantly, this presupposition does correspond to my own actual views and enables me to engage with the questions and arguments that I care most about (though there is always a little corner of my mind interested in engaging with the more fundamental challenges to which I have just alluded).

Adopting this assumption of a commitment to democratic principles does not entail my taking a position on questions about the extent to which those who do not accept democratic principles ought to do so. I am endorsing neither universalism nor relativism. Instead, one purpose of treating the commitment to democratic principles as a background assumption is to set that question aside, for this book. I want to explore the implications of democratic values for immigration, not to assess the merits of those values in comparison with others.

At the outset of the book I said that I am only claiming that my arguments apply to the United States, Canada, Australia, New Zealand, and democratic states in Europe. (As I explain in a note to chapter 1, for stylistic reasons, I do not usually mention Australia and New Zealand and I use the term North America to refer only to Canada and the United States even though Mexico is also a North American country.) Think of this as another restrictive assumption. I adopt this restrictive assumption because I think that context often matters morally. Significant differences in circumstances may require us to qualify normative generalizations. Claiming that we can say anything meaningful about what justice requires with respect to immigration in both North America and Europe is already controversial because many people think that differences in history, culture, and circumstances preclude meaningful comparisons between the Old World and the New World when it comes to immigration. I am consciously challenging that claim. I think I know enough about both contexts to be able to defend my claim that the normative arguments I advance apply to both, in part because I have been engaged in scholarly exchanges with academics from Europe for many years. I feel less confident, however, about my knowledge of other democracies such as Mexico, Japan, India, and Israel, to name only a few whose circumstances differ in ways that might be thought to be morally relevant from the circumstances in the states on which I focus.

Do democratic states outside Europe and North America actually differ in ways that affect the reach of my normative arguments? On that question I am agnostic, at least for now. I suspect that many of my arguments about access to citizenship, the rights of residents, the treatment of irregular migrants, and so on will apply just as much to democratic states elsewhere as they do to states in Europe and North America (or will be wrong for the same reasons in all these cases). Nevertheless, I would feel obliged to learn more about these cases before making any strong assertions. Again, I want to make clear that I am not endorsing a relativistic view. The purpose of my limiting presupposition is to restrict the inquiry for the purposes of the book, not to assume a particular answer or preclude further discussion.

What about the applicability of my arguments to states that do not claim to be democratic? Again, I did not have the space in the book to explore that issue. It is important to see, however, that the fact that my arguments rest upon democratic presuppositions does not entail the conclusion that they can only tell us about the moral obligations of democrats.

One of the interesting puzzles within the democratic tradition is how to reconcile various values like pluralism and equality or individual autonomy and collective self-determination with one another. All democrats, no matter how universalistic, have to leave some room for differences between people because not to do so would require us to suppress freedom altogether. At the same time, all democrats, no matter how communitarian and relativistic, have to set some limits to acceptable variations in individual and collective behavior, because not to do so would be to undermine the basis upon which we say that the traditions, values, and choices of individuals and communities should be respected. Different theorists will mark off these boundaries in different ways, but almost all of them will say that some practices are morally unacceptable, whether or not the people who engage in these practices accept democratic moral norms.[7]

To advance a claim in the name of human rights is to say that people are morally entitled to be treated (or not treated) in a certain way, regardless of the cultural commitments of the society where they live, their own moral views, or the views of their political authorities. I have restricted my argument to Europe and North America for reasons of analysis and exposition, but many of the claims advanced in the book have a potentially wider reach. The reach of a claim may be universal even if the source of the argument is particularistic (in the sense that it is rooted only in the democratic tradition).

Some people might find this possibility worrisome. Contemporary debates about human rights often find democrats (in Europe and North America) taking the ostensibly high ground in promoting and defending human rights against people (usually in Asia and Africa) whose practices and values allegedly conflict with these rights. I say "ostensibly" and "allegedly" as a caution that we should not always accept such claims at face value, but I don't mean to deny that the charges of human rights violations are often warranted or that we have a moral responsibility to pursue them. Nevertheless, these sorts of arguments always have a whiff of neo-colonialism and neo-imperialism about them, as those of us who live in the affluent West stand in judgment upon the morally inferior behavior and values of people from other societies and cultures.[8]

One advantage of the open borders argument as I construct it is that its critical thrust is directed more at those who live in the affluent societies of Europe and North America than at those who live elsewhere. Even if we expand the reach of this argument and see the right to move freely across state borders as a human right, it is the rich democratic states who are the worst offenders in preventing people from exercising this right today (though, of course, all states violate it as they try to control their borders). So, it should be possible to present the open borders argument to those who do not start from democratic premises without it coming across as a challenge from accuser to accused. The open borders argument may have the potential to open more space for a fruitful exchange of views with people who do not share democratic presuppositions than some familiar forms of engagement across this divide, even though the open borders argument does presuppose a commitment to democratic principles.

The general approach to moral inquiry that I espouse here is to recognize that all moral arguments must begin from presuppositions but that we adopt different presuppositions for different purposes and that it may be appropriate to adopt something as a presupposition in one context that we want to subject to critical examination in another. That general approach can be used to open up my own arguments to other forms of criticism and exchange. My open borders argument starts from democratic presuppositions, but I would be happy to engage with people who do not share those democratic presuppositions in a discussion about what a just world requires, especially with regard to migration. For such a conversation to get off the ground we would have to search for some other shared presuppositions, but what form those would take, how we might proceed, and where we would end up is something that could be determined only in the course of an exchange. It is quite possible that the resulting conversation would not look anything like the discussion in this book.

The Conventional View Presupposition

The commitment to democratic principles is a presupposition that governs the entire book. Let's turn now to another major presupposition in the book, but one that plays a role only in the first ten chapters: the assumption that states normally have a right to exercise discretionary control over immigration or, what I call throughout the book, the conventional view. I explained in the introduction that I adopted the conventional view as a presupposition in the first ten chapters in order to explore a range of ethical questions about immigration in a normative context that would seem plausible to most people. I won't repeat here the arguments that I offered previously in defense of that strategy, but I do want to present some related ideas.

Starting out with the assumption that states have a right to control borders served an important intellectual function in the book. It enabled me to bring to light some moral considerations about immigration that would have been harder to see if I had begun with the question of whether borders should be open (especially given my positive answer to that question). As I emphasized in chapter 8, my arguments in the first half of the book rest to a considerable extent on the claim that immigrants who are present have moral claims because they are members of the political community and their membership claims deepen over time. The first half of the book is, above all, an argument about belonging and the moral importance of membership. I don't think that line of argument is inconsistent with my argument for open borders, and I have explained why that is the case in chapter 13, but I do think that it would have been more difficult to elaborate the theory of social membership simultaneously with the argument for open borders. Adopting the initial assumption of discretionary closure allowed me to develop the two arguments sequentially and then to explain why they are not in conflict as many would assume.

In adopting the conventional view as a presupposition together with the related presupposition of the existing, highly inegalitarian international order, I was positioning the first several chapters of the book relatively close to what I have called the real world presupposition (though perhaps not close enough for some). In abandoning that presupposition in chapters 11 and 12, I was consciously moving away from questions about what is immediately feasible and positioning my discussion further along the continuum toward the just world presupposition.

The way that I posed the open borders challenge in chapter 11 deliberately started by leaving the presupposition about the existing institutional background in place: the division of the world into states with vast differences of power and wealth between them, the absence of adequate human rights protections in some states, and so on. I simply removed the constraint of presupposing the conventional view and abstracted from any questions about the immediate feasibility of the conclusions in order to focus on moral principles. This enabled me to open up the question of how the conventional principle affirming the state's right to control its borders was connected to more fundamental moral commitments.

Adopting a presupposition that leaves the world order as it is today while focusing on the question of control over borders makes it possible to examine existing arrangements more critically. What becomes sharply visible within the framework provided by this presupposition is that restrictions on migration usually serve as a protection for economic and political privilege. I freely acknowledge that pointing this out will not change it. I do not imagine that moral criticism moves the world, at least not often. But one function this sort of criticism can perform is to unmask (for a moment) the pretensions to moral legitimacy that are supplied by the conventional view that every state has an inherent right to control its own borders.

Later in chapter 11 and in the following two, I moved closer to the just world presupposition. Still, I did not ever simply adopt the just world presupposition as the framework for my inquiry. As I have already noted, I simplified the inquiry into justice and migration by presupposing a commitment to basic democratic principles, thus setting to one side (for these purposes) the various issues raised by undemocratic views. And to simplify the inquiry further, again in order to keep the focus on migration, I assumed that a just world might still be composed of different political communities with differences of language, culture, and history. With those presuppositions in place, I was able to argue that a just world would with be one with roughly the same level of economic development and basic freedoms protected in each state, but with the right to move freely across state borders. That is a plausible, though of course contestable, picture of a just world from a democratic perspective. Adopting these presuppositions is what made it possible to paint that picture.

Presuppositions as Controls

I want to conclude my discussion of presuppositions by drawing attention briefly to another, quite different way in which I used presuppositions in the book, namely as controls. In the sciences and social sciences, if researchers want to understand the relationship between two variables, they have to control for other variables that might affect the ones under study, directly or indirectly, even though those other variables might also be very important in some respects. Philosophers do not seek to explain cause and effect as empirical researchers do, but we are sometimes interested in isolating particular issues. In my case, I was particularly interested in questions about justice and immigration. So, whenever possible I tried to separate out the question of what justice required or permitted with respect to immigration from questions about what justice required or permitted with respect to other issues in economics, politics, or society, even though I recognized that those other questions were very important in their own right, in some cases even more important than questions about immigration.

At several points in the book, I pursued this goal by framing the inquiry into what justice required with respect to immigrants with the presupposition that the rights and duties of citizens could be used as a standard against which the rights and duties of immigrants should be measured. Rather than asking directly what justice required with respect to the rights and duties of this or that category of immigrants, I asked whether justice required that immigrants have the same rights and duties as citizens.

I adopted this presupposition to keep the focus on immigration. It is not that I actually think that whatever rights and duties citizens have in contemporary democratic states automatically meet the requirements of democratic justice. For example, I think that democratic justice requires that all citizens (and residents) in a rich state have access to adequate health care, a standard that is clearly not met (at the time of writing) in one notable democratic state.[9] But a debate on what justice requires with respect to health care would be a distraction in a book on the ethics of immigration. By simply presupposing the citizen's bundle of rights and duties as a standard and focusing on the comparison between that bundle and the bundle of rights and duties granted immigrants, I was able to keep the focus on questions directly related to immigration. The same presupposition permitted me to generalize the normative argument to all democratic states without worrying about the fact that citizens in one state had different rights from citizens in another. The comparison between the citizen's rights in any given state and the immigrant's rights in the same state is all that matters for the purposes of my inquiry.

This way of proceeding means that the conclusions of my analysis are always qualified and limited. An immigrant who has the same social rights as a citizen but no access to health care is not being treated unjustly in virtue of her status as an immigrant but she is being treated unjustly (in my view) in not being provided with adequate health care. It may be little consolation to her that native-born citizens are just as badly off. From an analytical perspective, however, it is important to understand the nature of the injustice, and using presuppositions as controls can contribute to that analytical clarity.

Conclusion

Let me conclude with a caution. I do not think that the way I have addressed the topic of immigration is the only way for political philosophers to do so. I write from within the Anglo-American analytic tradition of political philosophy, particularly as that has been shaped over the past four decades by responses to John Rawls. This is a tradition that emphasizes certain sorts of intellectual virtues: clarity, structure, precision, logical argument. In this tradition, when you meet an ambiguity, you try to clarify it; when you encounter a contradiction, you try to resolve it; when you see that something is implicit, you try to make it explicit. And that is generally what I try to do in my writing. For the most part, the other authors with whom I engage in this book take the same sort of approach. We have our disagreements, even methodological disagreements, but our basic approach to the discussion of immigration is similar.

This way of thinking has its strengths but also its weaknesses (which others probably see more clearly than I). The emphasis on structure and argument makes it harder to see some problems and more difficult to be aware of what is suppressed. The pursuit of precision and clarity can create the illusion of certitude and obscure the ways in which our knowledge depends upon our leaving things out or taking things for granted.

There are other forms of philosophical reflection that seek to highlight contradictions rather than resolve them, to embrace ambiguities rather than clarify them, and to take as their primary focus whatever is left out in conventional discussions. They aim to be critical but they resist the impulse to evaluate and prescribe. They emphasize the dangers of drawing distinctions and offering justifications. There is an extensive literature on immigration that is shaped by this sort of approach.[10] And there are many other possible approaches as well. These other approaches may enable to readers to gain insights into immigration that my book does not provide and to see questions that are not visible in my book.

I mention the limitations of my approach to immigration and what can be learned from alternative approaches as a caution about, not a repudiation of, what I have done in this book. After all, if I did not think that the virtues of my way of thinking about immigration outweighed its limitations, I would not have written the book. Every alternative approach has its own limitations and problems. Every way of thinking that illuminates some aspects of a topic simultaneously casts other aspects into the shadows with that same illumination. I hope that readers find my book illuminating. I do not imagine that it casts no shadows.

NOTES

Chapter 1

1. Bennhold 2008.
2. I will use the terms "moral" and "ethical" interchangeably in this book.
3. In saying that I am addressing people in North America and Europe, I do not mean to exclude readers elsewhere but only to limit the reach of my claims. In fact, I assume that my arguments apply just as much to Australia and New Zealand as they do to North America and Europe, and I occasionally cite examples from those cases. It would be cumbersome to keep mentioning this, however, and so for stylistic reasons I will just refer to North America and Europe (with apologies to my friends in Australia and New Zealand). What about Mexico which is a democratic state in North America but not a rich one or Japan which is rich and democratic but not in Europe? I actually think the arguments in this book apply to both of those cases, though there are challenges and objections to that view that deserve consideration and that I don't have the space to work through. So, leaving them out is partly stylistic, partly pragmatic. When it comes to other states and other regions of the world, the reasons for my restraint are even more substantive. Again, I do think that many of the arguments in this book will be relevant in other parts of the world, but at least some of my claims might need to be modified to take account of contextual considerations. I simply don't have the space to pursue those complications. That is one reason why I generally try to avoid explicit consideration of the case of Israel in this book, for example. I want to keep the focus on general principles, not on the applicability of those principles to a particular case. I discuss this issue of how far the analysis extends in a bit more detail in the appendix.
4. See Hailbronner 1989 for an explicit articulation of this view, which is, however, a common presupposition of many discussions of immigration. For a sophisticated critique of the view that sovereignty and self-determination shield states from moral criticism with respect to the exclusion of immigrants, see Fine, forthcoming.
5. Rawls 2005.
6. For a discussion of the virtues and limitations of realistic approaches to immigration and other policy issues, see Carens 1996. In the appendix, I develop a related but slightly different line of argument.

Chapter 2

1. Kinzer 1993.
2. See Triadafilopoulos 2012 for a discussion of the evolution of German citizenship policy. The German law requires those who acquire citizenship from being born on German territory to choose between German citizenship and any other that they have acquired at birth by

the age of 23. For reasons that will become apparent in the last section of the chapter, I regard this requirement as morally indefensible.

3. My discussion in this chapter and the next owes a great deal to Rainer Bauböck (1994) whose work remains today the most sophisticated and subtle analysis of these issues. Ruth Rubio-Marin (2000) also provides an excellent treatment to which I am greatly indebted. William Barbieri's (1998) book is thoughtful and underappreciated. Michael Walzer's chapter on membership in *Spheres of Justice* (1983) is widely recognized as the pioneering discussion of the topic among contemporary political theorists and greatly influenced my own thinking. My own initial forays into the area can be found in Carens 1987b and 1989. I returned to the topic in Carens 1998, 2004a, 2005, and 2007.

4. In some states, people acquire permanent resident status only after some years with temporary but renewable permits, as distinct from residence permits that are genuinely temporary and include the expectation that the permit holder will leave by the time the permit expires. I intend to include the former, but not the latter in the main discussion of access to citizenship for the children of immigrants.

5. Citizenship as a legal status is called "nationality" in international law and in some academic discussions. I prefer to use the term "citizenship," despite its other connotations because that is the word used most often in public discussions of the questions I am considering here, at least in the English-speaking world. I will occasionally use "nationality" for stylistic reasons when the context makes the meaning clear. The term "nationality" has its own complexities in a world in which many states contain more than one nation, sometimes ones that receive official recognition of some sort.

6. See Legomsky 1994 for a discussion of how the legal functions of citizenship could be fulfilled in other ways. See Spiro 2008 for an argument about how globalization has transformed what citizenship can be and can do.

7. Two recent works that seek to make the practice of birthright citizenship and the questions it raises much more visible are Shachar 2009 and Stevens 2010. See also the earlier critique of birthright citizenship in Schuck and Smith 1985 on which these more recent books build. I criticize Schuck and Smith's book in Carens 1987b.

8. For criticism of birthright citizenship as a form of inheritance, see Shachar 2009 and Stevens 2010. I have myself drawn an analogy between contemporary practices of birthright citizenship and the role of inherited social statuses under feudalism. See Carens 1987a. I explain why the sympathetic treatment of birthright citizenship in this chapter does not conflict with that claim in chapter 13 of this book and in a bit more detail in Carens 2013.

9. For discussions of how these factors affect the question of who should be included in the demos, see Whelan 1983, Dahl 1989, and Bauböck 1994. Rubio-Marin (2000) provides an excellent overview of these issues. My own earlier discussions of this topic, cited in note 3, focused on similar considerations.

10. In the text, I use the generic feminine in asserting the right of individuals not to be deprived arbitrarily of their nationality. There is a certain irony in this formulation, since in many states women were routinely deprived of their nationality upon marriage, even after the adoption of the convention.

11. At this point in the argument I am deliberately avoiding discussion of whether the children of resident citizens acquire legal citizenship at birth through a legal rule that focuses on descent (*ius sanguinis*) or one that focuses on birthplace (*ius soli*). Both are forms of birthright citizenship, and the children of resident citizens always qualify under both sorts of rules. Later in the chapter, I take up the different kinds of rules and discuss how the differences matter.

12. For a discussion of why it is important to think about relationships when talking about rights and justice, see Nedelsky 2011.

13. Federal arrangements complicate this picture but for the sake of simplicity I will leave that complication aside.

14. People in the children's rights movement argue that some of the limitations on minors are unjust and that minors should have more say about how their lives go and should gain more legal rights at a younger age than is now the case. These are often good arguments, but they do have limits. No one claims that infants should be entitled to vote.

15. In the text, I am implicitly assuming that the citizens in question (child and adult) reside in the state where they hold citizenship. I explore some of the complications of nonresidence later in the chapter.

16. Bauböck makes a similar point about the inevitability of some variation in degrees of connection: "citizenship status and rights cannot be tailored to fit individual interests and circumstances, but must apply in a wholesale way to categories of individuals whose relation with a political authority creates a presumptive interest in membership" (Bauböck 2009b: 484).

17. The arguments for birthright citizenship for the children of resident citizens imply that any child who was born in another country but is adopted by resident citizens should be granted citizenship at the moment of adoption because that is the moment (rather than birth) when the child enters the family. From a moral perspective, a child who is adopted into her family automatically becomes a member of her new parents' political community. She has just as strong a moral claim to official recognition of that membership through a grant of legal citizenship as a child who is born into her family. The fact that the adopted child may have another citizenship is entirely irrelevant from a moral perspective for reasons that will become apparent in the discussion of dual citizenship later in the chapter.

18. See Weil 2001. For updated and more detailed versions, see Howard 2009 and Dumbrava 2012. Citizens who live abroad can be described as emigrants (from their home country's perspective) but their children are not emigrants, since they have never lived in their parents' country of origin, just as they are not properly described as immigrants in the country of their birth if they have never lived anywhere else, even though their parents are immigrants.

19. The best philosophical discussion of the issues raised by emigrants (and external citizenship generally) is Bauböck 2009b. See also Bauböck 1994.

20. The idea that the general duty to avoid statelessness explains why children of emigrant citizens receive citizenship at birth implicitly presupposes what it is supposed to explain. Why should the parents' country of origin be the one that should grant citizenship to a child who is born and lives elsewhere? The parents have left their state's territory and are subject to its jurisdiction only in limited ways. Indeed, the international convention on statelessness assigns the responsibility to avoid statelessness first to the state of birth at least when that is also the state of residence. It is only if that state fails to adopt appropriate rules regarding the acquisition of nationality that the convention imposes a duty upon the state of parental citizenship to extend that citizenship to children born abroad. If meeting the duty to avoid statelessness were the real motivation for the normal practice of granting citizenship to the children of emigrant citizens, one would expect a much more contingent and qualified policy that granted this citizenship only when the children did not receive another at birth. Note also that the duties assigned to states by the convention on statelessness presuppose the moral relevance of social connections between particular individuals and particular states.

21. One objection to the argument that the children of emigrants have a moral claim to citizenship in their parents' country of origin because of the ways in which their interests and identity may depend upon their recognition as members of that community is that others may have much more vital interests at stake in gaining recognitions than the children of emigrants do. For example, people from a poor state might have a much more vital interest in gaining American citizenship than my children who, after all, are already in a privileged position as Canadian citizens. This objection implicitly rests upon a challenge to the presuppositions that I adopted at the beginning of this chapter regarding the moral legitimacy of the existing international order and the rights of states to control admissions. I do not want to consider that challenge here for reasons laid out in the introduction (and, in more detail, in the appendix). I do think that the challenge introduces an important line of inquiry, and I will consider that challenge in later chapters of the book, though I will argue that this way of framing the issue is ultimately misguided.

22. Shachar (2009) explores the implications of seeing citizenship as a form of property.

23. Like almost every principle, the one I have enunciated in the text about limiting the transmission of citizenship is subject to qualification under certain circumstances. For example, if the original emigrants have been forced into exile and their children have been unable to return, a newly established (or restored) democratic state might be justified in extending access to citizenship to later generations born abroad. Some states in Eastern Europe adopted policies

of this sort in the wake of the collapse of the Soviet Union. Similarly, if descendants of emigrants were subject to persecution because of their ancestral origins, the state of (ancestral) origin might be justified in extending to the descendants offers of admission and access to citizenship. Again this reflects real historical circumstances, though the question of what would be justifiable in any particular case would require a detailed analysis that I cannot provide here.

24. See Dumbrava 2012: 212–213.

25. For a discussion of the historical context within which France and other European states adopted *ius sanguinis*, see Weil 2008.

26. France made this change because it had a substantial immigrant population. The motivation for the change was not primarily a desire to include the immigrants into the French community but a desire to make them subject to military conscription. Nevertheless, the idea that being French is a matter of will rather than blood and that anyone can become French has long been an important rhetorical component of French republicanism. See Weil 2008 for the full complicated story.

27. For overviews of this history, see Rogers 1985, Sassen 1999, Joppke 1999, and Howard 2009.

28. While excluding generation after generation of the descendants of immigrants from citizenship conflicts with any plausible account of democratic legitimacy, people often find it possible to ignore or put up with this sort of contradiction in their principles for decades or even generations. Think of the history of racial segregation in the United States. So, the fact that the citizenship laws were wrong did not make it inevitable that they would be changed. It is still necessary to tell the specific story of why living with this contradiction proved impossible in various European states. For the German story, see Triadafilopoulos 2012.

29. The EUDO Citizenship website of the European University Institute is an excellent source for information about ongoing developments with respect to citizenship policies in Europe. See http://eudo-citizenship.eu.

30. Some of those who seek to explain these changes emphasize the crucial role of political parties or courts or interest groups (see Joppke 1999 and Howard 2009). It is certainly appropriate to pay attention to these sorts of actors, but that just pushes the explanatory puzzle back a bit. Why did these actors seek to pursue this sort of policy? In most cases, it is hard to appeal to material or even political considerations. Churches, courts, and even political parties have ideas about what is just or fair when it comes to the inclusion of immigrants. I do not think that the transformation of citizenship policies in Europe can be explained without reference to the role of moral ideas.

31. The situation of the children of irregular migrants is a bit more complicated. Often their parents are settled in the sense of having resided within the state for a number of years but they are there without authorization. I take up questions about access to citizenship for irregular migrants and their children in chapter 7.

32. I say that birthplace does not normally give rise to a strong moral claim to citizenship, rather than that it never does, because the international convention on statelessness places the first responsibility for preventing statelessness on the country where a person is born. Thus birthplace alone does give rise to a strong moral claim to citizenship, if a person would otherwise be stateless, even if this moral claim can be seen as the product of a convention.

33. Technically, the rule is not universal in its reach. The relevant passage reads, "All persons born or naturalized in the United States, and subject to the jurisdiction thereof, are citizens of the United States and of the State wherein they reside." Traditionally, the phrase "subject to the jurisdiction thereof" was interpreted to exclude (1) the children of foreign diplomats, (2) the children of a hostile, occupying army, and (3) native Americans living as members of a recognized tribal group. Some scholars have argued that it is possible to interpret this phrase more broadly so that the *ius soli* rule applies only to citizens and legal permanent residents (see Schuck and Smith 1985). This is clearly a minority view among constitutional scholars, however. I criticize this argument in Carens 1987b. Smith himself (1997) has modified his view on the wisdom of reinterpreting the Constitution in this way.

34. It is possible for people to acquire multiple citizenships at birth. I refer only to dual citizenship for convenience of exposition. The arguments for recognizing dual citizenship at birth

apply just as much to cases in which individuals have comparable moral claims at birth to more than two citizenships.

35. Whether the children of immigrants gain citizenship in their parents' country of origin or not is entirely dependent on the citizenship laws in the parents' country of origin. The state where the children actually live has no control over that. If the children do not inherit their parents' citizenship, the state where they were born will have to grant them citizenship or they will be stateless. In practice, almost every state allows children born abroad to inherit their parents' citizenship, if both parents have the same citizenship. States are often more restrictive about inheritance when only one parent is a citizen, especially if the child is born abroad, and this sometimes does leave children stateless at birth.

36. See, for example, Hammar 1989, Bauböck 1994, Spiro 1997, Rubio-Marin 2000, Hansen and Weil 2002, Faist 2007, Faist and Kivisto 2007, Macklin and Crepeau 2010.

37. See, for example, Martin 2002, Schuck 2002, and Renshon 2005. The proposed regulations and constraints apply to adult activities and commitments like military service or participating in politics. They also have some bearing on the acquisition of citizenship through naturalization as I will discuss below.

38. The greater involvement of women in the military has also begun to challenge the idea that the "real" soldier is a man, though that transformation still has a long way to go.

39. The term "mixed marriage" was frequently used in the past as a category for marriages between spouses with different racial, ethnic, or religious identities, often with the connotation that this sort of marriage was a problem. With the erosion of that normative view, the term itself is used less often these days. In the context of citizenship status, however, I do not think that the term carries a pejorative connotation. It can be purely descriptive. At least, that is what I intend.

40. Indeed, in some states, a woman lost her own citizenship when she married on the assumption that she would acquire her husband's and that it was desirable for the family to have a single citizenship. But since not all states granted their citizenship automatically upon marriage, this sometimes left women stateless—even when they were living in a state in which they had acquired citizenship at birth and which they had never left.

41. For an illuminating discussion of the relationship between gender and nationality, see Knop 2001.

42. See, for example, Martin 2002 and Schuck 2002. For a defense of participation in more than one political community, see Bauböck 2009b.

43. This objection applies to the recent German reform that grants birthright citizenship to the children of settled immigrants but requires these children to choose between their German and their parental citizenship at the age of 23. No such demand is made of children who hold dual citizenship because one parent is a German citizen and the other holds another nationality. For a discussion of the German policy on dual nationality, see Naujoks 2009.

Chapter 3

1. The story and the quotations are from Harnischfeger 2008. There was some dispute about whether the town council was within its legal rights to reject Arifi. The focus of the story was a forthcoming referendum, which would have affirmed the legality of such decisions. The referendum was defeated. I have no further information on Arifi's fate, but it seems plausible to assume that after the defeat of the referendum, she gained her Swiss citizenship.

2. The rights of citizenship are sometimes made contingent on good behavior, but not the status of citizenship itself. For example, in some jurisdictions, criminals are not allowed to vote while in prison and in some cases even after they are released. There are reasons to object to such policies but I won't pursue them here.

3. See Weil 2008.

4. For a lucid and fair-minded overview of this question, see Hampshire 2011. Hampshire is more sympathetic to requirements of linguistic competence and civic knowledge than I am, but our positions are not far apart. Miller (2008a) also has an excellent discussion of the issue.

5. My categories of social membership and democratic legitimacy correspond closely to Rubio-Marin's categories (2000) of deep affectedness and subjection. Bauböck (1994, 2005) has articulated similar arguments. He now prefers the concept of stakeholdership to social membership as the foundation for claims to citizenship (Bauböck 2009b). While I understand the concerns that prompt this switch, I am not persuaded that it really solves the difficulties that he identifies with the idea of social membership. Every term has its limitations.

6. I adopt the assumption that full voting rights and the right to seek high public office are reserved for citizens because most people and most states think of voting rights and citizenship as going together. As an empirical matter, the vast majority of democratic states restrict voting rights in national elections to citizens. There are a few exceptions, however. See Waldrauch 2005 for the details. Seglow (2009) uses the fact that voting rights are in principle (and occasionally in practice) detachable from citizenship status to challenge the claim that democratic legitimacy requires access to citizenship for long-term resident immigrants. Technically, it is true that the arguments about consent and participation can be met by granting immigrants voting rights and other political rights such as the right to run for public office rather than formal citizenship status, but then one has to ask what reason a state would have to withhold citizenship status from people entitled to vote, at least if they want citizenship status, and whether those reasons are compatible with democratic principles. This is one of those questions that is interesting but too technical for this book.

7. The majority of Swiss people themselves seem to have concluded that it would be a mistake to allow a decision about national citizenship to be determined on the basis of local preferences, despite a long tradition of strong local democracy. In the referendum anticipated in the *New York Times* article discussed in note 1 of this chapter, they rejected a proposal that would have explicitly authorized local authorities to exercise discretionary control over naturalization.

8. Bennhold 2008. My thanks to Holly Mann for drawing my attention to this case.

9. As Christian Joppke puts it, "Ever since Kant, it is a key precept of liberalism that law and public policy can regulate only the external behavior of people, not their inner motivations. And this is not just philosophical wish but hard legal fact in the constitutional state" (2010: 2). See Miller 2008a for a similar emphasis on the important difference between behavior and beliefs with respect to what can be demanded of immigrants.

10. See Bleich 2011 for a thoughtful comparative exploration of the various ways in which democratic states seek to restrict racism, even at the level of speech and motivation, while respecting commitments to freedom of thought and expression. As Bleich shows, it is not possible to address these topics in practice without recognizing the existence of conflicting considerations. Different states find different ways to balance the tensions.

11. In 2011 France made it illegal to wear clothes that cover the face (like the niqab or burka) in public. That law clearly violates democratic principles in my view. In any event, the law was not in effect when Silmi was denied citizenship, so one cannot claim that the refusal to grant her citizenship was connected to her own refusal to obey a law.

12. Accessed on April 23, 2011, at http://usgovinfo.about.com/od/immigrationnaturalizatio/a/oathofcitizen.htm. There are provisions for those who have conscientious objections to swearing oaths to be able to "affirm" this content instead.

13. See, for example, Miller 2008a, Hampshire 2011, Joppke 2010, and Hansen 2010. My discussion of the arguments for and against tests of civic competence draws in large part on ideas articulated in the exchanges compiled in Bauböck and Joppke 2010, including the Joppke and Hansen articles cited in this note.

14. See Miller 2008a, Joppke 2010, Hansen 2010 (despite his claim to provide an 'unapologetic' defense of citizenship tests), and Hampshire 2011.

15. Even tests that are not actually designed to exclude people from citizenship may be set at too high a level, however. People who are highly educated or already citizens often exaggerate how easy it is to pass these tests.

16. The one exception to this, as I observed in note 2, is that some states deprive criminals of their right to vote.

Chapter 4

1. Parekh 2000: 204, emphasis in original.
2. I use the term "inclusion" in this chapter to discuss issues that others sometimes treat under labels like "assimilation" or "integration." I prefer the term "inclusion" because at least in normative discussions of immigration the term "assimilation" usually implies that it is only immigrants who have to change, and sometimes the term "integration" carries the same connotation. As will become clear, that is not my view. People use such terms in different ways, however, and I don't want to make any strong claims about the implications of terminology. I have myself used the term "integration" in the past without intending this connotation of one-sided adaptation, and sociologists sometimes use the term "assimilation" without intending any normative implications. In any event, I hope that "inclusion" will be seen as a reasonable label for the issues that I want to discuss. For helpful discussion of the terminological issues, see Parekh 2000 and Modood 2007.
3. The issues to which I am drawing attention in this chapter have been widely and deeply discussed in the philosophical literature on multiculturalism, and I cannot hope to do justice to the complexity of these issues in a single chapter. My goal here is only to gesture in the direction of that wider discussion and to show why it matters for the ethics of immigration. Among the many authors that I have found helpful in thinking about this topic are (in alphabetical order) Veit Bader, Rainer Bauböck, Seyla Benhabib, Will Kymlicka, Cecile Laborde, Jacob Levy, David Miller, Tariq Modood, Bhiku Parekh, Anne Phillips, Jeff Spinner-Halev, Charles Taylor, and Iris Marion Young. See the list of references for some of their works. My own previous discussions of some of the issues can be found in Carens 2000a, 2004a, 2006, and 2009a.
4. For an elaboration of this view that has received a lot of attention, see Barry 2001.
5. Simon Caney (2002) develops this point carefully and fully in a response to Barry.
6. I deliberately use the word "place" rather than "state" in this sentence because some states have more than one public language, and the language of public life may vary from one geographical region to another.
7. See Crawford 1992 for an account of the debate at its most heated point. Countries like Canada which have more than one official language sometimes have debates about whether immigrants should be free to choose the language in which their children are educated, but this is a debate about whether they have a right to choose between official languages not whether they should be able to educate their children in their native tongue. I have discussed and defended Quebec's requirement that the children of immigrants be educated in French in Carens 1995.
8. For a careful examination of some of the ways that questions about the construction of mosques have emerged in Europe and of the varying responses to these questions, see Maussen 2004 and 2009.
9. See Bouchard and Taylor 2008, especially chapter 8. The report as a whole is a model of the sort of thoughtful contextual engagement that I am advocating in this chapter.
10. The commission called the informal process I am describing here "concerted adjustment" in contrast to "reasonable accommodation," which it treats as involving a formal process. I prefer to use the term "reasonable mutual adjustment" or "reasonable mutual accommodation" to characterize both the formal and informal processes. In contrast to the commission, I do not think that formal processes preclude compromises or even citizen agency, though I agree with the commission that informal processes are often preferable in this regard.
11. The proverb, "When in Rome, do as the Romans do," is variously attributed to St. Augustine and St. Ambrose. When the early Christians would not do as the Romans did in one way, that is, by worshipping Roman gods, the Romans were so miffed that they threw the Christians to the lions. Worshipping Roman gods was probably not the sort of conformity to Roman practices that was being recommended by St. Augustine and St. Ambrose (who were writing in a later era when Christianity had been established as the dominant religion). To the Romans who demanded it, however, asking people in Rome to worship Roman gods seemed to be a very reasonable request, involving little more than polite behavior. The Christians' refusal to do this marked them in Roman eyes as religious fanatics who threatened

governmental authority. This might give one pause about invoking such a proverb without careful qualification.

12. I do not mean to criticize the Toronto schoolchildren who use this phrase. It is the responsibility of the schools to educate students about why they should not use this phrase.

13. Translated from the German and quoted in footnote 3 in Baubӧck 2003.

14. Huntington 2004: 61.

15. See, for example, Gutmann 1987, Callan 1997, Levinson 1999, and Macedo 2000.

16. Roberts 2010.

17. Why do I not characterize the decline in the practice of changing names as an unambiguously positive development? Because some scholars attribute the reduced incentives to change names not to a reduction in discrimination against those of immigrant origin but to the fact that changing names is simply no longer a very effective strategy for avoiding discrimination because so many more immigrants are now what Canadians call "visible minorities" (that is, people whose physical appearance indicates that they are probably not of European origin). If all that had changed in recent decades was the effectiveness of the name-changing tactic and not the underlying discrimination, there would be nothing to cheer about. The truth is probably somewhere in between. See the discussion in Roberts 2010.

18. The term "multiculturalism" is in scare quotes because those who claim that multiculturalism leads to separatism almost never point to any actual policies adopted under the rubric of multiculturalism, as I point out below. The general position that I defend in this chapter could certainly be described as a version of multiculturalism, on any reasonable definition of that term, and I have characterized it that way myself in the past. Nevertheless, I have generally avoided the use of that term in my exposition, because the term itself has become so contentious that using it may obscure more than it clarifies. If people agree with my views here, I do not care whether they label them "multicultural." If they disagree, I want it to be for substantive reasons and not because of this label.

19. Will Kymlicka (1995 and 1998) has argued forcefully that the point of most multicultural policies is to enable minorities to participate in mainstream institutions, and that it is the refusal to recognize and respect their distinctive concerns and commitments that is more likely to lead them to want to live separate lives. I agree though I would add one nuance to his general argument. Some multicultural policies, like permitting Sikhs to wear their traditional turbans rather than the usual headgear required by an official uniform, are designed to make it more likely that immigrant minorities will participate in mainstream institutions. Other multicultural policies, like funding optional courses in languages of origin (in addition to the required education in the official language) or other cultural initiatives of that sort, serve the interests of immigrant minorities, but do not directly enhance their participation in mainstream institutions. On the other hand, these sorts of policies communicate to citizens of immigrant origin that their identities and cultural commitments are accepted by the wider society. This can make them feel included and so increase the likelihood of their committing themselves in turn to the wider community.

20. For an analysis and critique of this phenomenon, see Modood 2007.

21. Cumming-Bruce and Erlanger 2009.

22. In rare cases, there may be a fundamental individual right to receive communications in some language other than the official language(s). When one is accused of a crime, one has a fundamental right to understand the accusation and the proceedings. This generates a right to communication in one's own language (or at least in a language that one understands), if the accused person does not understand the official language. In most other circumstances, justice does not require translation services as an individual right.

23. For the importance of having minorities visible in the public sphere, see Young 1990, Phillips 1995, and Williams 2000.

24. Sometimes states contain more than one national identity, as in multinational states like Canada, Belgium, the United Kingdom, Spain, and so on. Those cases raise complicated questions about the relationship between particular national identities and the national identity of the state as a whole, but I won't pursue those complexities here.

25. For the American story, see Smith 1997. For the Canadian one, see Kelley and Trebilcock 2010.

Chapter 5

1. When I speak of the rights of citizens I mean to refer to *resident* citizens because, of course, some of the citizens of the country to which the immigrants come will be emigrants living elsewhere, and citizens who live abroad often have a somewhat different package of legal rights and duties from those who live at home. As a shorthand, I'll normally use the term "citizens" to refer to resident citizens and the term "residents" to refer to noncitizen residents.

2. The major exception to this pattern in the past was compulsory military service, which now has been abolished in most democratic states. Indeed, in the United States, even the duty to serve in the Army did not distinguish (male) citizens from (male) residents, because the latter were also subject to the military draft, and, like citizens, are still required to register. This is unusual, however. Most states have limited conscription to (male) citizens. (Indeed, as I mentioned in chapter 2, this was one reason why France adopted a *ius soli* law in the late nineteenth century, extending automatic birthright citizenship to the children of immigrants.) The most notable exception today to the practice of imposing the same legal duties on residents as on citizens is the policy of requiring citizens, but not residents, to serve on juries if summoned. This affects only a fraction of the citizen population, and I see no reason why jury duty could not also apply to long-term residents. A few democratic states also impose a legal duty to vote and impose a fine for not doing so.

3. In North America immigrants often (but not always) acquire permanent resident status at the time of entry; in Europe it has been more common to have a series of steps in which immigrants' right of residence becomes more secure over time, even when they are admitted on the grounds of family reunification, and so, with an expectation of ongoing residence. Tomas Hammar, whose path-breaking work on this topic appeared more than two decades ago, calls long-term, securely established residents *denizens*, using this archaic English term as a way to distinguish them from legal citizens, on the one hand, and from immigrants whose arrival is more recent or whose legal rights remain more tenuous. I prefer the term residents. See Hammar 1990.

4. For more on both of these points, see Carens 2000a: chapter 1.

5. The generalization should be qualified by recognition of the fact that noncitizens enjoyed local voting rights in the nineteenth century in some jurisdictions and these were gradually eliminated.

6. Numerous scholars have commented on this process. See, for example, Soysal 1994, Hammar 1990, Hollifield 1992, Jacobson 1996, Joppke 1999, Layton-Henry 1991, Schuck 1984. Yasemin Soysal, in particular, has drawn attention to the way this pattern of development differs from Marshall's famous account of the evolution of the rights of citizens, in which political rights preceded, and were instrumental in securing, social rights (1994: 131).

7. See Soysal 1994, Jacobson 1996.

8. See Freeman 1995, Joppke 1999 and 2001.

9. See Martin 2002 and Schuck 1998: chapter 8.

10. See European Council 2003.

11. I don't mean to suggest that the practices cannot be contested because, in principle, anything can be contested.

12. The actual passage from Arendt refers to the problem of statelessness in the interwar period. See Arendt 1958; chapter 9.

13. Not having citizenship status renders people vulnerable to investigation regarding their compliance with immigration law, and those laws are often subject to fewer procedural constraints than other laws. Authorities are sometimes able to take actions against people that would be prohibited in normal legal contexts (e.g., extended detention, questioning without lawyers) under the cover of enforcing immigration law. A particularly vivid illustration of the phenomenon was the roundup and extended detention of young Arab and Muslim males in the United States in the aftermath of 9/11 and the subsequent deportation of many of them for technical violations of immigration laws that would normally have been overlooked. For any noncitizens who become entangled with legal authorities, however, the threat of deportation looms in the background and affects their capacity to enjoy and exercise their rights.

14. I add the phrase "at least for ordinary criminal cases" in this sentence because when issues of national security are said to be at stake, states do sometimes distinguish, and sharply, between citizens and noncitizens. I criticize this below.

15. Treating criminal suspects differently on the basis of citizenship status might be a violation of international law, but states do not always respect international law in their domestic legislation. Furthermore, even if this sort of differential treatment is a violation of international law, that still leaves open the question of whether that particular rule of international law simply reflects calculations of mutual advantage by states or some deeper principle of justice. I claim that it is the latter.

16. This aspiration to pursue justice may well be unfulfilled in practice. At least in North America, we know that the criminal justice process is deeply affected in practice by class and race. See, for example, Cole 1999 and Neugebauer 2000. It would not be surprising if citizenship status, or more broadly the perception that someone is "not really one of us" also plays an important role. But not even the harshest critic of the way things work in practice would advocate a return to legal systems (as under feudalism) that constructed formal differences among the categories of people subject to ordinary laws.

17. In later chapters, I consider noncitizens who do not fit into these two categories (that is, noncitizens who are living in a society but who are are neither visitors nor authorized permanent residents).

18. Some scholars argue that states should provide residents with most of the rights that citizens enjoy because we should regard the residents as on a path to citizenship and the granting of these rights recognizes that status. See Motomura 2006. I am sympathetic to this view but I develop a different line of argument in the text. As should be clear from chapter 3, I agree that it is appropriate to see residents as on a path to citizenship but I think that there are other reasons that explain why residents would be morally entitled to these rights, even if they were not on a path to citizenship. The approach that I emphasize in the text helps to explain the moral logic behind the extension of rights to residents in Europe even in states where it was assumed that the residents would not become citizens. It also helps to explain why so many of these rights should be extended to immigrants who are not permanent residents and so not on a path to citizenship, as we will see in the next two chapters.

19. Later in the book, I will consider the argument that we should challenge this conventional understanding. For the moment, I accept it as a corollary of the background presupposition that states are entitled to exercise considerable discretionary control over immigration. Of course, some people come as tourists and then seek work without authorization from the state. I will explore the issues raised by such cases in chapter 7.

20. To make the categorization complete, we might note that states can also create general discretionary rights (that is, legal entitlements that are given to everyone who happens to be physically present but that do not protect interests vital enough to warrant calling them basic human rights). (For example, in many places anyone may wander in off the streets and use a public library without charge.) I mention these sorts of rights for the sake of analytical completeness. They play no role in the argument.

21. The salience of these remaining distinctions would be significantly reduced if states accepted the principles governing access to citizenship that I outlined in chapters 2 and 3. Nevertheless, they would still be relevant.

22. For analyses of the principles underlying the right to leave, see Whelan 1981 and Dowty 1987.

23. The name Victor Castillo is a pseudonym, but the other details of the case are accurate. See Coutin 2009.

24. I persist with my use of the generic feminine even though the vast majority of criminals are male. The vast majority of CEOs are male as well, but using the generic feminine helps to challenge conventional assumptions about social roles. Will it be an indicator that we are actually approaching gender equality when we have as many female criminals as males? In any event, there are women who are convicted of crimes and deported, so this is not an empty category.

25. In fact, it is not always true that those deported for criminal violations are hardened criminals. People are frequently deported for relatively minor, nonviolent crimes, often drug related. Others who are convicted may not be guilty at all. In the text I have assumed that

the convicted noncitizens were in fact guilty, as a way of taking up the harder challenge to my case against deportation. But, at least in North America, it is not uncommon for people accused of crimes, especially racial minorities, to be held without bail for several months and then offered an official plea bargain in which they will be sentenced only to the time already served if they plead guilty and will face the risk of years of incarceration if they insist on their innocence but are subsequently convicted by a criminal justice system that has already indicated its doubts by keeping them in jail for an extended period. They receive legal counsel from greatly overworked lawyers who have their own incentives for settling quickly. The clients, and sometimes even the lawyers, do not always understand that a guilty plea will make them liable for deportation. I set this sort of problem aside in my discussion in the text because there is no doubt that many of those convicted are in fact guilty, and my aim is to show that even they do not deserve to be deported. Nevertheless, we should not lose sight entirely of the way the legal system actually works.

26. See Supreme Court of Canada 2002. I should perhaps reveal that I appeared as an expert witness at the trial level in this case—on the losing side. This book gives me another (tiny) kick at this particular can.

Chapter 6

1. I'm not concerned in this chapter with people who fly in for a few days on business and stay in a hotel, but rather with people who come to live for months or years and who participate in ongoing economic activities. Foreign students constitute another important and distinct group of people who are neither permanent residents nor tourists, but I do not have the space to discuss the specific questions they raise with respect to the ethics of immigration. There is a burgeoning normative literature on temporary workers. For examples of some recent work in the area, see Chang 2008a, Stilz 2010, Lenard 2012, Lenard and Straehle 2012a, 2012b, Ottonelli and Tirresi 2012, Owen 2013. For an earlier critique of a Canadian program, see Macklin 1992.

2. In the text that follows in this section I construct a synthesis of the arguments for more limited rights for temporary workers. I draw on Bell 2006, Bell and Piper 2005, Pritchett 2006, Miller 2008a and 2008b, Ruhs and Martin 2008, and Stilz 2010. I try to construct the strongest case for a position fundamentally different from my own. I do not mean to imply that each of these authors would accept all of the arguments for that alternative position. Some of them would clearly endorse some intermediary view.

3. See Miller 2008a and 2008b. Motomura 2006 also defends the ideal of extending most of the rights of citizenship to permanent residents on the grounds that they should be seen as citizens "in waiting" but does not discuss the implications of this approach for temporary workers.

4. Miller 2008b: 196.

5. In other writings (2008a), Miller indicates that he would set stronger limits on morally acceptable terms of admission than the passage I have quoted implies. Even in the quoted article he makes it clear that this principle of consent applies only to workers who are present on a truly temporary basis. Other authors take a more expansive view of the legitimating power of consent. See, in particular, Bell 2006. For a critique of Bell, see Carens 2008a.

6. I say "normally" to leave open the possibility of something happening during their stay that gives them a different moral claim to remain, but I will not pursue that complication here. I am also assuming that they have been notified of this constraint at the time of admission.

7. Many of the programs that are intended to provide strict limits to how long workers remain are still relatively new. It remains to be seen how many temporary workers will go home at the end of their authorized stays, how many will find a way to convert a temporary status to a permanent one, and how many will simply remain as irregular migrants once their visas have expired.

8. European Council 2003.

9. One can criticize some of the practices of democratic states with respect to the least well off among citizens and residents on the same grounds. I think those criticisms are often well founded but again I am keeping the focus only on immigration in this book.

10. In most insurance arrangements—pensions are an exception—one hopes that one will never need to collect the benefits, since these compensate for a hardship one would prefer not to face.

11. This issue would become more complicated if the society provided no direct link between workforce participation and income support for those who have lost their jobs, but instead simply guaranteed an adequate level of basic income for all members of society. Certainly no human being within the jurisdiction of an affluent state like those in Europe or North America should be allowed to die from starvation or exposure to the elements, regardless of the legal terms governing her presence.

12. Often the injury or illness is not literally unavoidable but rather something that it would be costly to try to prevent. There is some level of risk associated with almost every human activity, of course. To eliminate every risk associated with production would be to eliminate almost all production. The public policy debate is always about what level of risk is reasonable, all things considered.

13. The effectiveness of this check on power varies, depending on the alternatives available to the employee. So, the degree of tightness in the relevant labor market, the kinds of social support available to workers who quit their jobs, and related factors determine whether this is a significant check or only a nominal one.

14. See Ruhs and Martin 2008.

15. In Carens 2008a, I have discussed two Canadian temporary worker programs that illustrate the general points made in this section. One is for live-in caregivers and another for seasonal agricultural workers. I leave them out here for reasons of space.

16. For a complementary analysis of the unfair character of guestworker programs, see Attas 2000. For a critique of this perspective, see Mayer 2005.

17. This is a key theme in Pritchett 2006.

Chapter 7

1. Berinstein et al. 2006: 23.

2. For critical discussion of the terminological issues and related matters, see De Genova 2002.

3. The scholarly literature on irregular migrants is relatively thin and explicitly normative discussions are rare. The most important exception to this that I have found is the discussion in Rubio-Marin 2000, which develops an argument for individual regularization based on claims of social membership that is very similar to the one I advance in the second half of this chapter. Hammar (1994) also offers a brief but cogent argument about the moral relevance of the passage of time for the inclusion of those present without legal authorization. Legal studies often include normative dimensions, though these are usually tied to particular legal traditions. In my view, the best work on irregular migrants in American law is by Linda Bosniak (see, e.g., Bosniak 1988, 1996, 2006, and 2007). Owen Fiss (1998) has an important argument about the implications of the American constitutional commitment to equality for the issue of irregular migration. Some studies focus on the rights of irregular migrants under human rights laws, whether national, regional, or international (see, e.g., Bogusz et al. 2004). There are also a number of sociological and policy studies that, while primarily empirical, include critical analyses and normative claims (see, e.g., Hayes 2001; Jordan and Düvell 2002; van der Leun 2003). Matthew Gibney (2000) makes some brief but explicit normative claims in the final section of his report synthesizing empirical research on irregular migrants in three European states. There are also a few important historical studies with normative implications, notably Ngai 2004. The positions that I defend in this chapter were first articulated in Carens 2008b and 2009b. Both articles were accompanied by a range of critical responses which I have tried to take into account here. For a more recent critique of my position, see Blake 2012b.

4. One of the objections to the popular terms "illegal aliens" and "illegal immigrants" is that such terms may be taken to imply that migrants in these categories have no legal rights whatsoever. Hence, the counter-slogan, "No one is illegal." As I observe in the text, however, even the strongest critics of unauthorized migration will not actually defend the claim that irregular migrants have no legal rights, if they address the question directly.

5. The treatment of detainees at Guantanamo Bay and the US administration's public defense of that treatment arguably constitute an exception to this general rule that, in a democratic

state, no one is outside the pale of the law's protection. On the other hand, this treatment has been widely criticized throughout the world as a violation of the rule of law, American courts have (at last) set some limits on what the government can do to the detainees, and even the defenders of Guantanamo normally claim that it is an exception, justified by the extreme danger of terrorism, rather than a legitimate exercise of a routine governmental power. I will not pursue here the deeper debate about the claim that this sort of exception reveals the true nature of democratic regimes, though it is probably apparent that I do not share that view. See Agamben 2005.

6. Berinstein et al. 2006: 22.
7. For the text of the convention, see Brownlie 1992.
8. The well-being of the child is also the focus of the international covenant, so one might argue that there are principles of international law that support the claim that the children of irregular migrants should receive a free public education, but as I noted earlier, I am concerned with moral rather than legal arguments.
9. To say that irregular migrants are not morally entitled to a legal right to look for work does not necessarily imply that irregular migrants are doing something morally wrong when they look for work without legal authorization. That further claim depends on arguments about the obligations of foreigners to obey the laws of a state in which they are not members and the conditions, if any, under which they are morally entitled to act contrary to the laws of such a state. That leads in turn to a much wider set of issues about the relation between legal and moral obligation that I do not have space to discuss here.
10. Carens 2008b.
11. Ibid.
12. As I observed in note 9, it is not self-evident that irregular migrants have a moral duty not to seek employment just because they have no moral claim to a legal right to work. The two issues are asymmetrical.
13. Bosniak 2007.
14. People disagree about what term to use to characterize the movement of migrants from unauthorized to authorized status. Critics of irregular migrants tend to use the term "amnesty," while those more sympathetic to their position normally prefer terms like "regularization" or "earned legalization." In earlier versions of this argument I used the term "amnesty," deliberately embracing a term that others see as pejorative in order to bring to consciousness the strength of the moral case for granting irregular migrants legal status after the passage of sufficient time. I have come to think, however, that this rhetorical move makes it harder to view the argument dispassionately and so in this version I adopt the term "regularization." For the earlier version, see Carens 2009b and 2010.
15. BBC News 2007a.
16. BBC News 2007b.
17. Grimmond also had a husband and children in the United Kingdom, and so I could have used her story for this point about family connections as well, but I wanted to add some variety in the exposition.
18. If marriage to a citizen provides a bar to deportation, it creates an incentive for sham marriages, but that is a familiar and manageable problem. I discuss this issue in chapter 9 in connection with the issue of family reunification.
19. Acosta 2011.
20. See Ngai 2004.
21. See Sassen 1999.
22. See, for example, Cornelius 2001 and especially Weber and Pickering 2011.
23. See Aleinikoff 2009.
24. See the magisterial analysis in Smith 1997.
25. See the discussion in Rubio-Marin 2000: 88–89.
26. Some argue that we establish statutes of limitations because the reliability of evidence erodes over time. If that were the primary motivation, however, it would make no sense to distinguish between less serious and more serious crimes, making more serious crimes subject to longer limits and having no limits at all on the most serious crimes like murder.
27. For suggestions along this line, see Callan 2009, Schuck 2009, and especially Swain 2009.

Chapter 9

1. For attempts to shield states from external criticism of their immigration policies, see Meilaender 2001 and Walzer 1983. For a helpful discussion of this issue that is generally compatible with the positions I take here, see Miller 2008a; section IV.

2. To speak of a state as having a particular view of its interests is implicitly to treat the state as a unitary actor. In fact, what counts as the interest of the state is inevitably the product of internal political contestation, driven in part by more limited interests. In the area of immigration, as in other areas, the concentrated interests of a few are often more politically effective than the diffuse interests of many in shaping public policy. Treating the state as a unitary rational actor can obscure that political reality. For my normative purposes in this chapter, however, I don't think that this complication matters very much. For the role of political interests in shaping immigration policy, see Freeman 1995.

3. For the history of exclusion on the basis of race in the United States, see Smith 1997, Tichenor 2002, and Zolberg 2006. For the Canadian story, see Kelley and Trebilcock 2010. For Australia, see Jupp 2007.

4. For those not satisfied with taking the unacceptability of racial discrimination in admissions as a starting point for reflection, see Carens 1988 for an explicit critique of the use of racial criteria in admissions with specific reference to the White Australia policy. See also Blake 2002 and Miller 2008a.

5. My thanks to Jacob Levy for pressing me to address this question.

6. A sophisticated variant of the argument in the text might incorporate the points I made in chapter 4 about the fact that many citizens who are *not* of immigrant origin fail to live up to democratic principles. Their failures, one could say, reveal the fragility of the underlying democratic culture. We are stuck, as it were, with the limitations of current citizens' commitments to democratic values, and we have only limited means to strengthen their commitments. Since we have to worry about sustaining a democratic regime that is only imperfectly supported by the existing population, it is important that we not add to this strain by taking in immigrants who are not themselves committed to democracy.

   Whatever the merits of this democratic fragility argument as an assessment of political realities in particular states, it is an argument that is external to the analysis of democratic principles. In discussions of immigration policy (and of many other policy areas as well), it is common to hear the assertion that following moral principles will lead to worse outcomes (from a moral perspective) than an alternative course because other actors will not accept or follow those same moral principles. The classic statement of this view is Machiavelli. This sort of argument is often plausible, though perhaps not so often as political realists like to believe. In any event, I agree that it is something that we have to take into account in deciding what course to pursue in political life. That sort of challenge is quite different from the one I am trying to undertake in this book, however. I am trying to unpack the moral logic of democratic commitments in the area of immigration, taking the commitments themselves as a given. As I have observed at a number of points already, one cannot leap directly from an understanding of what moral principles should govern immigration policy to conclusions about how to act in the world.

7. For original sources, see Wilkins 1892 and the thirty entries in Buenker and Burckel 1977: 208-210. For scholarly discussion, see Divine 1957, Gainer 1972, Garrard 1967, Higham 1963 and 1975, Smith 1997, Tichenor 2002, Zolberg 2006.

8. For a discussion of the role that concerns about economic self-sufficiency have played in American immigration policy, see Tichenor 2002 and Zolberg 2006.

9. See, for example, Borjas 1990 and 1999.

10. See Tichenor 2002 and Zolberg 2006.

11. See, for example, Brimelow 1995.

12. See Joppke 2005.

13. For a helpful (and critical) discussion of the ways in which co-ethics are favored by European states in matters of immigration and access to citizenship, see Dumbrava 2012.

14. See Kanstroom 1993, Barbieri 1998, and Triadafilopoulos 2012.

15. See Rubio-Marin 2000 and Triadafilopoulos 2012.

16. To be more precise, there are two selection processes for immigrants to Canada, one for immigrants who identify Quebec as their destination and another for those planning to settle elsewhere in Canada. For the rest of Canada, knowledge of French and English are given equal weight. Quebec has its own selection process and gives much greater weight to knowledge of French than of English. The basic principle is the same in both cases, however, namely that knowledge of an official language of the receiving society is given weight. I defend the legitimacy of the differential weight given to knowledge of French in the selection of immigrants bound for Quebec in Carens 1995: 25–33.

17. These statistics are cited in Brock 2009: 198–199.

18. See Kapur and McHale 2005.

19. For recent normative discussions of this issue, see Ypi 2008, Brock 2009, and Oberman 2013. I discuss the brain drain as a basis for objecting to more open migration in Carens 1992: 32–34. For an empirical assessment of the problem, with some policy recommendations for addressing it, see Kapur and McHale 2005.

20. For the view that the movement of the talented from poor to rich countries is less harmful than sometimes assumed, see Stark 2004 and Pritchett 2006.

21. If we were to probe this issue further, we would have to pay attention not just to the effects on poor states as a whole but to the effects on different categories of people in poor states. (Not every person living in a poor state is poor.) This refinement is unnecessary, however, since I am not going to pursue the topic further for reasons given in the text.

22. See, for example, Pogge 2008, Tan 2004, Caney 2005, and Brock 2009.

23. The phrase "reunification" implies that the family was once together and that family members have been separated from each other as a result of migration. In fact, admissions often involves family unification, that is, enabling people who have just become married to live together for the first time. For simplicity of exposition, I ignore this (and related) complication in the text and use the term reunification to cover all these cases. The best recent discussions of family reunification by political theorists are Honohan 2009 and Lister 2010. For very helpful earlier discussions, see Motomura 1997 and Meilaender 2001.

24. It may no longer be purely self-imposed. Meilaender cites evidence in support of the view that there is actually an emerging norm in international law that requires this (see Meilaender 2001: 180–181). But even if this is a norm, it is one that has emerged from practice and so it does not really change the question in the text.

25. Meilaender, who is generally a defender of the state's discretionary control over immigration, argues that this control is rightly limited by the claims of family: "We are bound to our family members through a more richly complex web of relationships, a mixture of love and dependence, than we share with any other people. These relationships give rise to especially intense feelings of mutual affection and concern. To deprive someone of these relationships is to deprive him of his richest and most significant bonds with other human beings. That is something we should do only in rare circumstances" (Meilaender 2001: 182).

26. For a helpful discussion of this issue, see Lister 2007.

27. Besides the issue of family reunification, which I explore here, the fact that different states have different systems of family law can create serious complications about the status of family relationships in a context of immigration. For an interesting exploration of some of these complications, see Foblets 2005.

28. Stevens (2010) takes a consensual view of the family but opposes state restrictions on immigration, so she escapes this problem, but not everyone who favors a consensual view of the family is likely to embrace this solution.

29. See Motomura 1997.

30. Originally, this policy applied only to non-British males seeking to join their British wives. When this was struck down by an EU court as a form of discrimination on the basis of gender, the British extended the policy to British husbands bringing in non-British wives, making the policy both gender neutral and more restrictive.

31. See Joppke 1999.

32. See Phillips 2009 for a helpful discussion of this issue.

Chapter 10

1. I draw my information on Gutierrez and the quotation from Kennedy 2010.
2. The literature on the failure of European and North American states to respond to Jewish refugees is vast. See, among others, Abella and Troper 1983, Breitman and Kraut 1987, Caestecker and Moore 2010, Cohen 1985, Feingold 1970, Gilbert 2007, London 2000, Marrus 1985, Morse 1968, Rosen 2007, Sherman 1970. For evidence of both the anti-Semitism and the national security worries of high officials in the US Army with respect to Jewish refugees, see Bendersky 2000.
3. For the story of the *St. Louis* and details about what happened to its passengers, see Ogilvie and Miller 2006. Canada's role in this tragedy is discussed in Abella and Troper 1983.
4. Rawls 1971: 19.
5. The best work on refugees by a political theorist is Gibney 2004. Other important recent works include Schuster 2003, Boswell 2005, and Price 2009. The literature on refugees in international law is vast. Two of the leading works are Hathaway 2005 and Goodwin-Gill and McAdam 2007. I unavoidably ignore many of the nuances and complexities that have been discussed in the legal literature.
6. If borders were open and everyone had the right to migrate anywhere, states might still have special responsibilities for refugees, but the problem would look quite different.
7. See, for example, Walzer 1983, Meilaender 2001, Miller 2007. Wellman 2008 is an exception.
8. For a fuller discussion of these three rationales, see Carens 1991.
9. See Walzer 1983 for an initial articulation of this line of argument. Shacknove (1988) and, more recently, Souter (2013) develop the argument in more detail. For a more qualified analysis of the connection between causality and moral responsibility, see Blake 2013.
10. For a particularly helpful exploration of the causes of refugee movements, even if now a bit dated, see Zolberg et al. 1989.
11. In some cases, like Vietnam and Iraq, the causal connection between our action and the existence of refugees is relatively clear and can be linked to particular states, although even in those cases there is still disagreement about the extent to which we are obliged to admit refugees. In other cases, like global warming and environmental refugees, the causal connection is more diffuse and contested. In still others, the cause of a particular refugee flow is even more disputed. For example, someone who sees existing refugee movements primarily as a byproduct of the world capitalist order or, slightly more narrowly, as a byproduct of efforts by dominant powers to maintain their hegemony, will assign moral responsibilities differently from someone who sees these refugee flows as the outgrowth of internal conflicts within particular states. Similarly, one might consider the extent to which contemporary refugee flows in Africa and Asia are attributable to the legacy of colonialism and the extent to which they are due to independent, intervening causes. How one assesses that issue would affect one's sense of the moral responsibility of the former colonial powers for these refugees.
12. I am appealing here to a parallel to Rawls's idea of the overlapping consensus that undergirds commitment to democratic principles. See Rawls 2005.
13. UNHCR 2011. This *Resettlement Handbook* not only provides a detailed report on UNHCR's resettlement programs and policies but also a lucid description and analysis of the issues related to resettlement.
14. The summary in the text leaves aside a great many legal complications. See Hathaway 2005 and Goodwin-Gill and McAdam 2007 for a more detailed discussion.
15. The visa controls and related documentation were largely designed to exclude people who might overstay a visa, becoming irregular migrants rather than temporary visitors. However, exclusion of refugee applicants was also a clear and explicit goal of these policies. If it were not, the likelihood that one might have a strong claim for asylum would be a reason for granting a visa rather than denying it.
16. The Balkans crisis in the 1990s was an obvious exception to this generalization.
17. For a more complete description and critique of these techniques of exclusion, see Gibney 2006.
18. Brownlie 1992: 65.

19. Gustavo Gutierrez's claim rests on the supposition that the danger he faces goes far beyond what we can reasonably call the ordinary failures of law enforcement.

20. For a discussion of this approach in Canada and of some of its limitations in practice, see MacIntosh 2010.

21. For an excellent recent discussion of the history of such efforts and a suggested definition of his own, see Gibney 2004. Shacknove (1985) provides a classic, highly influential scholarly defense of this sort of approach. Zolberg et al. (1989) offer another important example. For thoughtful attempts to defend the Convention's definition against its critics, see Martin 1991 and Price 2009.

22. This figure of ten million refugees does not include almost five million registered Palestinian refugees who are the responsibility of another agency, the United Nations Relief and Works Agency for Palestine Refugees in the Near East (UNRWA).

23. UNHCR 2011: 19.

24. The attempts by Martin (1991) and Price (2009) to defend the current Convention definition are motivated to an important extent by the desire to maintain political support for the admission of refugees by keeping the numbers within bounds that democratic publics are willing to accept. Later in the chapter I explore further some of the problems with setting such limits to our obligations to refugees.

25. This point is developed very effectively in Shacknove 1985.

26. For various formulations of this view, see Zolberg et al. 1989, Martin 1991, Price 2009, Lister 2013.

27. Some think that reducing extreme global poverty is a more urgent moral priority than protecting refugees. That is a position that I am inclined to accept, for the most part, but that is no reason not to think about our responsibilities to refugees.

28. Most of the deaths have resulted from disease and malnutrition generated as byproducts of the violence.

29. Whether it is actually reasonable to expect a refugee to return home will depend not only on whether it is safe there and how long she has been away but also on what the refugee suffered before escaping and what she will face upon her return. I leave those complications aside in the text.

30. The formulation in the text collapses two criteria that are often distinct: first arrival and first claim. Technically, the Convention requires those seeking asylum to submit their claim in the first state in which they arrive where they can be safe and can get a fair hearing for their claim under the Convention. European states have made great efforts to send potential asylum claimants back not to their country of origin but to another country that the potential claimant has passed through, the so-called safe third country. This has led to debates about what countries are "safe," especially given huge variations in recognition rates and in procedural practices. Germany has invested substantial amounts of money in building up the refugee determination systems in Eastern Europe so that Germany could claim that potential refugees can receive a fair hearing in those Eastern European states.

31. Singer and Singer (1988) contend that this argument about the moral responsibility created by the filing of an asylum claim within a state's borders rests on a false distinction between acts and omissions. I think their argument implicitly and inappropriately denies the relevance of institutional arrangements (like state sovereignty) in the assignment of moral responsibility. At the same time, I would agree with Singer and Singer that existing institutional arrangements sometimes unduly limit the extent of our moral responsibilities. For a critique of Singer and Singer's position on asylum, see my earlier, but limited, discussion in Carens 1992.

32. For a sensitive imagining of the complexities of actual cases from the agent's perspective, see Martin 1990.

33. For an examination of the determinants of asylum migration to Western Europe, see Neumayer 2005.

34. See Zolberg et al. 1989 and Martin 1991 for typical statements of this view.

35. For a much more detailed elaboration of this claim, see Carens 1997.

36. A helpful recent overview of some of the issues considered in the following sections can be found in Kritzman-Amir 2008. For other discussions of some of the relevant considerations

on which I have drawn, see Carens 1994, Hathaway and Neve 1997, Schuck 1997, Gibney 2007, and Miller 2007.

37. See the discussion in Gibney 2007.

38. For an excellent discussion of some of the factors that affect a state's capacity to take in refugees, see Gibney 2004.

39. For an illuminating discussion of these issues, see Gibney 2007.

40. I should leave open the possibility that Sweden would be an exception.

41. In developing this line of argument I draw upon ideas from Hathaway and Neve 1997 and Schuck 1997.

42. This migratory logic applies to the flow of asylum seekers to Europe and North America, as I have discussed in the text, but it also contributes to the increasing movement of people from poor states to those in the middle.

43. It is striking that the Convention's almost absolute prohibition on the exclusion of refugees seeking asylum is echoed by Michael Walzer one of the foremost advocates of the state's right to exercise discretionary control over immigration. Walzer discusses the case of the forcible return of over a million displaced people to the Soviet Union in the wake of World War II. These people asked to be allowed to remain in the West, but their pleas were ignored, largely for political reasons having to do with the relationship between the Western allies and the Soviet Union. Most of them were either executed immediately upon their return or sent to gulags where they perished. Walzer argues that the Western allies knew or should have known what fate lay in store for these refugees and that they should have permitted them to stay, despite the high political and economic costs this would have entailed in a context where relations with the Soviet Union were of vital importance and European states faced enormous economic difficulties in the wake of the war. When it comes to requests for asylum then, Walzer rejects the idea that the obligation to take in refugees is legitimately constrained by the receiving state's interests. Like the Geneva Convention, Walzer treats the claim of asylum as virtually absolute, even in the face of very high costs. He says that there may be some limit to the duty to admit refugees seeking asylum but also that he does not know how to specify what that limit would be. See Walzer 1983: 51.

44. Miller 2007: 227.

45. Miller suggests that we think in terms of a hierarchy of a state's duties with the "negative duty to refrain from infringing basic rights" by its own actions at the top, followed by the "positive duty to secure the basic rights" of it own citizens and residents. Below these two duties come the "positive duty to prevent rights violations by other parties" and finally "the positive duty to secure the basic rights of people when others have failed in their responsibility" (Miller 2007: 47). I have implicitly accepted a version of this hierarchy in the text, but the question remains why an acknowledged duty to secure the basic rights of people whom others have failed should ever be overridden by the state's duty or perhaps mere goal of advancing interests of its members that are not comparably fundamental.

46. Miller 2007: 227.

47. Ironically, it is a state's failure to protect the basic rights of its own citizens rather than those of noncitizens within its jurisdiction that triggers this new responsibility for refugees. Noncitizens who are forced to flee are entitled to return to their home state and so no other state normally has any special responsibility for them.

48. I qualify self-interest by the phrase "as conventionally understood," because it is always possible to define self-interest in terms of what morality requires or permits. Given such a definition, there could never be a conflict between self-interest and morality. This is a philosophical move with a pedigree that stretches back to Plato, and it has a good deal to be said for it, but it would simply define away the issues that I want to explore, so I set it aside here.

Chapter 11

1. Some people may wonder how I can reconcile this claim with my defense of birthright citizenship in chapter 2, but I think the two positions are perfectly compatible for reasons I will explain in chapter 13.

2. I first defended the idea of open borders in Carens 1987a and 1992a. My critique of the conventional view was anticipated by Nett 1971, Ackerman 1980, and Lichtenberg 1981. There is now a very substantial literature on this topic. Among the many important contributions to this debate, in addition to works cited subsequently in this chapter and the next, are Bauböck 2006, Blake 2005 and 2012a, Chang 1997 and 2008b, Cole 2000, Dummett 2001, Fine 2010 and forthcoming, Miller 2005, Pevnick 2011,Wellman 2008, Wellman and Cole 2011, Whelan 1988. Unfortunately, I cannot address all of the nuances and complexities of this debate. I focus on the challenges to my position that I think it is most important for me to address. In some cases, for reasons of space, I do not discuss issues that I think have been adequately addressed by others with whom I agree. For example, I do not address the freedom of association debate where I do not think I have anything to add to Fine 2010 and I do not address the debate about asymmetry between entry and exit where I do not think I have anything to add to Bauböck 2006.

3. Bauböck (2007) raises interesting questions about whether the actual arrangements of the contemporary world correspond, as an empirical matter, to this picture of independent states with control over immigration.

4. Isbister 2000: 632.

5. Woodward 1992.

6. See Carens 2000a and 2004b.

7. In assuming that feudalism is unjust, I have left aside the complex problem of historical anachronism and the questions about when it is appropriate to make critical judgments about the past and when not. Feudal arrangements certainly look unjust from the perspective of a liberalism which grew out of a rejection of feudalism.

8. Variants of this argument can be found in Kymlicka 2001b, Pogge 1997, Seglow 2005, and Oberman 2011.

9. This point is emphasized in Oberman 2011.

10. See Bauböck 2010 for an elaboration of one version this argument.

11. Thomas Pogge is the leading advocate of the view that rich states are causally and morally responsible for global poverty and inequality and that there are feasible ways of addressing these problems. See, for example, Pogge 2008. I am in general agreement with Pogge, although I disagree with some of his formulations about the links between individual moral responsibilities and these injustices. But Pogge (like all of us) has many critics, and a number of scholars have challenged his claims about our responsibilities and about the possibilities for transforming the conditions of the global poor. I see my argument as complementary to Pogge's and, in some respects at least, harder to challenge.

12. For a similar argument, see Kukathas 2005.

13. See Abizadeh 2006. For other arguments that support the idea that opening the borders of rich states at least somewhat to immigrants from poor states ought to be one element in an overall global justice strategy, see Bader 1997a, Sangiovanni 2007, Bauböck 2009a. For a more skeptical view, focusing on the negative consequences for those left behind, see Ypi 2008.

14. There are also many reasons for criticizing equality of opportunity, especially in a version that is limited to an elimination of formal barriers, but I will not pursue that issue here. For a classic discussion of this issue, see Rawls 1971.

15. For advocates of this view, see Miller 2007, Rawls 1999. For defenders of the view that there is a link between global justice and equality of opportunity, see Caney 2005 and 2008, Moellendorf 2002.

16. See Jacobs 2004 and Mason 2006 for good overall discussions of the ideal of equal opportunity. Some say that states can deal with the issue of equal opportunity because citizens within a single state share enough common views about what matters to resolve questions about the importance of various goods and the appropriateness of trade-offs among them (Miller 2007: 66). In fact, however, most contemporary democratic states contain internally the same range of cultural values and differences that we find in the world at large, even if not in the same proportions. As we saw in chapter 4, democratic states have to leave considerable room for people to make differing judgments about what is important in life. Moreover, it is easy to exaggerate the extent of cultural differences with respect to the desirability of

some of the goods that rich democratic states produce at such high levels: physical security, health care, education, material prosperity, longer life expectancy. These are things most contemporary human beings want for themselves and for their families, whatever country they come from.

17. See Bauböck 2010, Kukathas 2005 and 2010.

18. Miller 2013. I draw heavily on Miller's helpful account of cantilever arguments in my elaboration of the idea. I especially like this label because I once suggested that we should think of political theory as analogous to architecture (Carens 2000: 23).

19. Someone might object that there is no point in deploying cantilever arguments because we will ultimately be driven back to the foundation itself, that is, to the reasons that support the original right. There is something to that concern, but I think it underestimates the power of cantilever arguments. It is not always necessary to appeal to foundational reasons to establish an analogy. Sometimes the analogy itself seems intuitively obvious, even if one might not be able to articulate the reasons for the original right. In effect one can then say to the critic, "You claim to accept this original right, but not the extension. Given the power of the analogy, it is now up to you to explain what you think justifies the original right and why that justification does not apply to the extension. I will show you either that your alleged justification of the original right is not really a justification of the right at all or, if it is, that it also applies to the proposed extension." In other words, the task of excavating the foundation of the original right shifts to the person who wants to resist the extension. That is important because there are likely to be many different ways of justifying the original right, all of which may be vulnerable to some criticism or other. It is often easier to defend the extension than it is to defend the original right itself. In other words, if one can establish a plausible analogy between the original right and the proposed extension, the burden of proof shifts to critics of the proposed extension to show why the analogy does not hold or why the proposed right will have harmful consequences or violate entitlements that the original one did not.

20. See, for example, Maas 2007.

21. See Zhu 2003.

22. As an empirical matter, the contribution of internal free movement to nation-building may help to explain why states would be less inclined to resist the idea of making freedom of movement within the state into a human right than they are to resist the idea of making freedom of movement across borders into a human right. However, that does not affect the argument about the irrelevance of nation-building as a rationale for making internal freedom of movement into a human right.

23. See Blake 2006. In another article Blake makes a related claim. He says that citizens (and residents) are morally entitled to freedom of movement within the state precisely because they are subject to the pervasive coercive authority of the state while those seeking to enter the state are not subject to its pervasive coercive authority and so not entitled to this freedom. See Blake 2001. I find this line of argument perplexing (though I know that others find it persuasive). Why should the fact that I am not generally subject to a state's authority make it legitimate for that state to restrict my freedom to enter, especially when, by entering, I would render myself subject to its authority? I think the argument seems persuasive only if one presupposes what the argument is supposed to prove, namely that the state is entitled to use its coercive power to restrict entry. I discuss questions about justifications of the state's right to restrict entry more fully in the next chapter.

24. Programs that admit agricultural workers on a temporary basis and limit their occupational and geographic mobility provide an important exception to the generalization in the text that democratic states do not tell noncitizens where they may go or reside after admission, but that is why I used the qualifier "normally." I have discussed (and criticized) such programs in Carens 2008a. See also the discussion and the references in chapter 6 of this book.

25. Brownlie 1992: 23.

26. Brownlie, 1992: 129.

27. For a contrary view, see Miller 2013. Oberman (2012) points out that freedom of movement across borders can also be crucial for forms of political participation that we regard as important.

28. Miller 2013. I have heard others advance the same view in conversation.

29. See, for example, Glendon 2001, Grahl-Madsen 1992, Jagerskiold 1981, McAdam 2011, Morsink 1999. It is worth noting that establishing internal free movement as a human right was a controversial issue. The USSR defended the idea that states should be able to regulate internal movement on grounds of sovereignty. Its proposal on this issue was defeated in committee, and this was one of the reasons why the USSR refused to ratify the Declaration. See McAdam 2011: 48–49.

30. See, for example, Kymlicka 2001b, Miller 2007 and 2008a, Rawls 1999.

31. Since I developed the theory of social membership to explain why immigrants belong, I would not be happy to see it used to justify exclusion, but that does not prove that the argument is incorrect. For more on the relationship between social membership and freedom of movement, see chapter 13.

32. Even a strong advocate of private property rights like Robert Nozick acknowledges that property rights must be constrained in some respects by a right to freedom of movement. See Nozick 1974.

33. See Miller 2013.

34. For a discussion of how these sorts of practices might be incorporated into contemporary legal regimes regulating immigration and an argument about why such procedures are required by the rule or law, see Schotel 2012.

35. For an argument about the importance of the right of those excluded to participate in decisions about exclusion, see Abizadeh 2008.

36. See Woodward 1992: 61. Woodward's critique focuses on the immediate policy implications of the open borders argument. For reasons explained previously in the text, I think that is not appropriate at least for this current version of my argument. In fairness to Woodward, he was responding to an earlier version where my focus was less clear.

37. For this position, see Bader 2005, Seglow 2005. Bauböck (2010) takes the opposite position..

38. I am assuming in the text that the reasons why it is impossible to admit all who want to enter are themselves morally acceptable (for the sorts of reasons I discuss below). If the reasons for closure were themselves morally problematic the objection would collapse of its own weight.

39. Some readers who have thought about the triage analogy in medical care will undoubtedly want to ask whether we should have a comparable triage among immigrants applying for admission, giving priority to the needy but perhaps not taking the most desperate on the grounds that they won't be able to make it in the society they are trying to join (for reasons of lack of education, ill health, and so on). This is the sort of policy application of the open borders argument that I want to resist in this book, for reasons laid out earlier in this chapter. My use of triage in the text is intended only to point out that it is possible to attribute human rights to people even under conditions of scarcity and that scarcity can make it necessary to establish priority rules in satisfying those rights. Whether triage is a morally appropriate approach in this or other cases is a question I leave open here. I do not mean to deny that this can actually emerge as a real question in various ways for those dealing with immigration issues. For example, there is a debate over whether it is morally appropriate in selecting among refugees seeking resettlement from camps abroad to use criteria that measure their likelihood of successful integration into the society where they are to be resettled.

Chapter 12

1. David Miller's position is typical of those defending the state discretion view, and he recognizes various moral limits. See Miller 2007: 222.

2. Versions of the bounded justice argument can be found in Blake 2001, Macedo 2004, Miller 2007, Nagel 2005, Rawls 1999. For criticisms, see Abizadeh 2007, Caney 2008, Cohen and Sabel 2006, Julius 2006.

3. For an argument that ordinary state control over admissions does not normally involve coercion, see Miller 2010. For a critique of that argument, see Abizadeh 2010. I agree with Abizadeh, but I am skeptical that anything important can hinge on a definitional dispute. In any event, my own critique of Miller later in this chapter does not depend on questions about what counts as coercion.

4. Nagel (2005) may be an exception to my claim that everyone recognizes that coercion must be justified to the one being coerced.

5. Blake 2001. I am persuaded by and indebted to the critique by Abizadeh (2007). In a later article (2008), Blake refines his original position, but I think his argument still assumes away the fundamental problem of how the existing international order can be justified to those subject to it.

6. For a fuller articulation of this argument, see Abizadeh 2007.

7. For a recent work developing this point, see Shachar 2009.

8. I provide a different, but complementary, critique of Walzer's defense of closure in Carens 1987a and an appreciation of his strengths as a theorist in Carens 2000a.

9. Walzer 1983: 62, emphasis in original.

10. Walzer 1983: 39.

11. Ibid.

12. David Miller (2007) is the one who has developed this line of argument most fully, but similar themes can be found in Rawls 1999 and Macedo 2004. Miller prefers the language of national responsibility and draws a distinction between state and nation, while Rawls and Macedo prefer to speak of peoples and distinguish between states and peoples. These distinctions are relevant to some issues but not to the ones I am pursuing here. All of these authors defend both discretionary control over immigration and economic inequality between political communities and do so in the name of collective responsibility and the self-determination of the political community. For my purposes in this chapter, therefore, it is simpler to speak of state responsibility.

13. Miller 2007: 68–75. (Miller's 2007 treatment draws on an earlier article published in 1999.) Miller's example and his overall argument are quite similar to the discussion in Rawls (1999: 117–118), including the names used for the contrasting societies. I focus primarily on Miller because his argument is a bit more fully developed. Miller and Rawls both actually compare two contrasting pairs of societies, but I don't think the second pair adds anything essential to the argument and it is simpler for purposes of exposition to consider only the first.

14. Miller 2007: 73.

15. A related but different question is whether there is a moral duty to reduce the differences between Ecologia I and Ecologia II. That will depend in part on one's judgment about the proper role of luck in human affairs. There is a vast literature on luck egalitarianism. For an illuminating overview that links this issue to questions about global justice, see Tan 2012. Beyond the luck egalitarian debate, discussions of the moral relevance of luck can be found in a number of places. See, for example, Nussbaum 2001, Pitkin 1999, Stone 2007, Williams 1982. I will not try to say anything here about this wider discussion.

16. At one point Miller rejects Thomas Pogge's claim that the position of poor states today is largely due to historical injustice on the grounds that some former colonies like Malaysia have managed to succeed economically (Miller 2007: 251). Rawls uses similar examples. This rebuttal is unpersuasive. The occasional success of African Americans in the United States in the first half of the twentieth century does not show that racism and discrimination had no ill effects on African Americans as a group. Similarly, the fact that a few former colonies have succeeded does not prove that colonialism had no ill effects overall. Of course, this does not prove the opposite either, but given the role played by equal starting points in the state responsibility thesis (which I elaborate in the next section), the burden of proof should rest upon those defending inequality to establish that departures from equality are properly attributed to self-determination rather than to other factors. That would require empirical and historical evidence that neither Miller nor Rawls supplies. My defense of open borders does not rely on such contestable claims about the impact of history.

  Neither Miller nor Rawls explicitly makes any connection between contemporary states and the names used in their stories about Affluenza and Ecologia, but, given their criticism of views like Pogge's, I think it is hard not to read them as attributing Affluenza-like profligacy to poor states and Ecologia-like wise stewardship to rich ones. That seems ironic, to say the least.

17. The choice/circumstances formulation is usually traced to Ronald Dworkin's influential 1981 two-part article "What Is Equality?" which is reprinted in Dworkin 2000, although Dworkin does not take up the issue of generations which I discuss in the next paragraphs. There is a lot of debate about the adequacy of the choice/circumstances approach for a theory of individual responsibility, including questions about what would count as a starting point of (relatively) equal circumstances, but I leave such complexities aside here.

18. The combination of generational change and collective continuity is not a unique feature of political communities but is a characteristic of every social institution (e.g., corporations, universities, public bureaucracies) that endures through time, though membership in other social institutions does not usually change primarily as a direct result of births and deaths.

19. Miller 2007: 72.

20. Rawls 1999: 8.

21. Ibid., 9.

22. Rawls also adds, "Another reason for limiting immigration is to protect a people's culture and its constitutional principles" and endorses Walzer's discussion of this issue (Rawls 1999: 39). I take up the question of whether protecting culture provides a basis for limiting immigration later in this chapter.

23. Miller 2007: 207, emphasis in original.

24. Miller 2007: 222.

25. Ibid.

26. I am focusing on the question of principle here but one should not assume that it would be practically impossible to balance the interests of the potential immigrant in getting in against the interests of the state in keeping her out. Laws and policies often require such balancing judgments even in current immigration regimes. See Schotel 2012.

27. People who dismiss the idea of world government as naively utopian often forget that only a few centuries ago it seemed equally preposterous to suggest that a large political community could be organized as a democratic republic with equal legal rights for all citizens, protections for minorities, and effective limits on the powers of government. Every person with knowledge and experience of the world knew that such an arrangement was a chimera. As it has turned out, however, the United States was only the first of many relatively stable states that have been built upon that model and that come close to realizing it, if always imperfectly. Even the difficulties posed by the size of the world population and the vast differences of language, culture, and religion are often overstated. Consider the case of India which by itself contains almost one-sixth of the world's population, hundreds of linguistic communities, and deep divisions along lines of religion and culture. Despite these challenging circumstances, India has functioned as a relatively stable federal democracy for over sixty years. Is it certain or even likely that peace and justice for the people in that territory would have been better served by dividing the region into smaller, more homogeneous independent states? If one-sixth of the world can be organized as a single political community without all of the terrifying consequences that some assert would inevitably follow from a world government, perhaps that should give pause to confident assertions about the necessary consequences of world government. I do not mean to suggest, however, either that India is a utopia or that world government is a feasible or desirable prospect in the immediate future.

28. See Bauböck 2010.

29. See Torpey 2000.

30. For more on this point, see Bauböck 2004 and 2007, Norman 2006, Carens 2000: chapter 7.

31. Some people suggest that we should think of the territory over which a state exercises jurisdiction as property owned by the state. They assume that it will follow that the state is morally entitled to exclude potential immigrants from its territory just as any property owner may exclude unwanted individuals from land that she owns. This conception drastically oversimplifies the concept of property and neglects the complications that follow from thinking of a state's territory as property. For example, thinking of the state's territory as collective property might imply that the state would be entitled to use that property as it chooses, including for purposes of redistribution, something that advocates of the property conception rarely embrace. On the other hand, if one wants to defend a private property approach, it is far from clear why the state should be entitled to interfere with individual owners' choices about

whom to hire or otherwise engage with on their property. For more on this point, see the discussion of Nozick in Carens 1987a, Kukathas 2010, Steiner 1992. As I suggest in the text, property is always a bundle of rights which can be constructed and constrained in many different ways, both morally and legally. In the real world, private property owners are not always entitled to exclude those who want to enter their property, especially if the owners are using the property for commercial purposes. Moreover, property owned by a political unit is public property, not private property. While this does not necessarily guarantee that every citizen may enter that property—think of military bases—it is the case that the state's ability to restrict access to public property, if it is held for the use of the public, is often constrained in many ways even in relation to people who are neither citizens nor residents. For a critique of the use of the property model in immigration, see Bauböck 2010 and Shachar 2009.

32. For the claim that free movement is incompatible with priority for compatriots, see Gibney 2004, Isbister 2000, Macedo 2004, Miller 2007, Tamir 1993.

33. This extreme form of cosmopolitanism is rare—I do not say nonexistent—even among those who identify themselves as cosmopolitans.

34. In criticizing open borders as insufficiently attuned to the claims of our fellow members in a political community, people often cite the work of Samuel Scheffler, the philosopher who has done the best work on the moral relevance of particular attachments (see Scheffler 2001). But Scheffler himself explicitly recognizes that the moral claims of our particularistic attachments are always open to what he calls "the distributive objection" (Scheffler 2001: 4). In other words, particularistic claims may be constrained by considerations of distributive justice. So, this just takes us back to the question of what distributive justice requires. Ironically, Scheffler himself suggests that one way to meet the distributive objection is to show "those who are not members of the putatively duty-generating groups and relationships are given the opportunity to join and voluntarily decline to do so" (Scheffler 2001: 74). If we apply this logic to the international order, we might say that, from Scheffler's perspective, significant economic differences between states would be justifiable only if borders were open. See the illuminating discussion in Abizadeh 2006. I do not know whether Scheffler himself would accept this extension and application of his analysis.

35. See, for example, Article 4 of the 1966 International Covenant of Civil and Political Rights (Brownlie 1992: 127) and Rawls 1971: 213.

36. For one version of the libertarian commitment to open borders, see Kukathas 2005 and Kukathas 2010.

37. See Hardin 1974.

38. Rawls 1971: 213.

39. For a good articulation of this argument, see Isbister 2000.

40. Some may think that the United States provides less (or Scandinavian countries more) in the way of welfare state support than justice requires (or permits), but for the argument in the text to get off the ground we have to assume this sort of variation to be legitimate.

41. For an overview of the empirical effects of migration on the welfare state today, see Soroka et al. 2006. Some of the literature discussed in that article draws attention to the effects of migration on the attitudes and values of the established population. Later in this section of the chapter I explain why it is important to exercise caution in invoking such effects to justify restrictions on immigration.

42. See the discussion of Scheffler in note 34 for a related point.

43. What about Israel? The idea that Israel can be both a Jewish state and a democratic one at the same time faces a number of deep tensions that have been explored most fully by Israeli scholars themselves, not all of whom affirm its possibility. If it is to be defended, however, it has to be on the grounds that special historical circumstances make the identity of Israel as a Jewish state legitimate and that this does not entail the subordination of non-Jewish citizens of Israel. For a recent effort at such a defense, see Gans 2008. I take no position here on the merits of that argument. In any event, Gans is clear that his argument only applies to Israel proper and not to the Occupied Territories. I hope that no one will imagine that the case for open borders can be used to legitimate Israeli settlements in Palestine, since the settlements take place against a background of political domination and strict limits on other forms of movement within and across Israel's borders. That is just one illustration of a general limit

on the proper use of the open borders argument. The case for open borders is an argument about the structural arrangements required by a just world. It cannot be used to defend (or criticize) particular policies regarding movement and settlement in contexts that otherwise leave in place the conventional background presupposition about the normal legitimacy of discretionary state control over immigration. Frankly, I do not think that the open borders argument helps much in thinking about issues like those involved in the Israeli-Palestinian debate. Those sorts of issues require a much more contextually sensitive approach of the sort I advocate in Carens 2000a and 2004b.

44. See, for example, Barry 2001 and Scheffler 2007.

45. In the text I simply assume that democratic states are morally entitled to protect some aspects of public culture, but that is in fact my view. See Carens 2000.

46. Some people suggest that these caveats reveal that those freedoms are not genuine. See, for example, Agamben 2005. That is not my view.

Chapter 13

1. For an exploration of the normative and political implications of a hypothetical world in which migrants are a majority and there are few long-settled people in the population of any state, see Bauböck 2011. As he shows, democracy requires a considerable amount of stability in the population that governs and is governed.

2. For reasons of space I have not pursued questions about the political participation of people who hold more than one citizenship. I think that it is possible to treat those questions as largely distinct from the question of whether dual or multiple citizenships make moral sense.

3. I say in the text that a human right to free movement would "largely" replace the current human right to enter one's own country because being able to enter one's own country is normally a more fundamental interest than being able to go where one chooses. The open borders argument does admit some limitations on the right of free movement, but it seems unlikely that justifiable limitations would extend to restrictions on a person's right to enter her own country.

Appendix

1. For an example of someone whose admiration and criticism of Rawls are equally profound, see Cohen 2008.

2. Carens 1987a. The same article explored the implications of Robert Nozick's libertarian theory and of a generic sort of utilitarianism for immigration, but it was the analysis of Rawls that attracted the most attention, presumably because of his stature in the field of contemporary political theory.

3. As it turned out, Rawls himself rejected the extension of his reasoning in *A Theory of Justice* that I used in my early article (and that others like Charles Beitz and Brian Barry had used before me). Rawls argued in later work that it was inappropriate to think of the original position as applying to (representative) individuals throughout the world. I was disappointed, of course, that Rawls did not agree with my approach, but, in my view, his later position was not dispositive because like other critics I thought the important question was not what Rawls himself said in his later work but what he ought to have said given the principles he had so cogently articulated in his earlier work. In any event, I had long since changed my approach to the topic to rely less upon Rawls for reasons explained in the text.

4. Carens 2000.

5. Both Rawls and Aristotle adopt a number of other presuppositions as well—different ones, of course. Some of their presuppositions are explicit, some are implicit, and all are contestable. But examining those presuppositions is a task for another day.

6. See Tu 1996.

7. Even a theorist like Michael Walzer who often defends a communitarian and relativist position that grants political communities wide moral latitude to set their own policies is prepared to say that it is wrong for a state to expel long-term residents simply on the basis of their

nationality or ethnic origin. He bases this position not on an appeal to the supposed norms of the political community itself but on a universal standard that he attributes to Hobbes. This is not an isolated misstatement but something with deep roots in Walzer's own political philosophy. For a fuller account of this universalistic streak in Walzer, see chapter 2 of Carens 2000.

8. Of course, some human rights advocates are much better at avoiding or minimizing this stance than others.

9. One could argue that the adoption of Obamacare reflects acceptance by the United States of the principle that universal access to health care is a requirement of democratic justice, a principle already accepted in most other rich democratic states. Of course, no democratic state entirely succeeds in meeting this requirement in practice.

10. For two books that illustrate in different ways the strengths of this sort of approach, see Honig 2001 and Bosniak 2006.

REFERENCES

Abella, Irving, and Troper, Harold. 1983. *None is Too Many*. New York: Random House.

Abizadeh, Arash. 2010. 'Democratic Legitimacy and State Coercion: A Reply to David Miller'. *Political Theory* 38 (1): 121–130.

Abizadeh, Arash. 2008. 'Democratic Theory and Border Coercion: No Right to Unilaterally Control Your Own Borders'. *Political Theory* 36 (1): 37–65.

Abizadeh, Arash. 2007. 'Cooperation, Pervasive Impact, and Coercion: On the Scope (not Site) of Distributive Justice'. *Philosophy & Public Affairs* 35 (4): 318–358.

Abizadeh, Arash. 2006. 'Liberal Egalitarian Arguments for Closed Borders: Some Preliminary Critical Reflections'. *Ethics & Economics* 4 (1). http://ethique-economique.net/.

Ackerman, Bruce. 1980. *Social Justice in the Liberal State*. New Haven: Yale University Press.

Acosta, Diego. 2011. 'The Returns Directive: Possible Limits and Interpretation'. In *The Returns Directive: Central Themes, Problem Issues, and Implementation in Selected Member States*, ed. Karin Zwaan, 7–24. Nijmegen: Wolf Legal Publishers.

Agamben, Giorgio. 2005. *State of Exception*. Translated by Kevin Attell. Chicago: University of Chicago Press.

Aleinikoff, T. Alexander. 2009. 'Legalization has its Costs, but They are Outweighted by the Benefits'. *Boston Review* 34 (3): 11.

Anderson, Bridget. 2008. 'Migrants and Work-Related Rights'. *Ethics & International Affairs* 22 (2): 199–203.

Arendt, Hannah. 1958. *The Origins of Totalitarianism*. 2nd edition. Cleveland: World Publishing Company.

Attas, Daniel. 2000. 'The Case of Guest Workers: Exploitation, Citizenship and Economic Rights'. *Res Publica* 6 (1): 73–92.

Bader, Veit. 2007. *Secularism or Democracy? Associational Governance of Religious Diversity*. Amsterdam: Amsterdam University Press.

Bader, Veit. 2005. 'The Ethics of Immigration'. *Constellations* 12 (3): 331–361.

Bader, Veit. 2001. 'Associative Democracy and the Incorporation of Ethnic and National Minorities'. *CRISPP* 4 (1): 187–202.

Bader, Veit. 1997a. 'Fairly Open Borders'. In *Citizenship and Exclusion*, ed. Veit Bader, 28–62. Basingstoke: Macmillan.

Bader, Veit. 1997b. 'The Cultural Conditions of Transnational Citizenship: On the Interpenetration of Political and Ethnic Cultures'. *Political Theory* 25 (6): 771–813.

Bader, Veit. 1995. 'Citizenship and Exclusion'. *Political Theory* 23 (2): 211–246.

Barbieri, William A. 1998. *Ethics of Citizenship: Immigration and Group Rights in Germany*. Durham, NC: Duke University Press.

Barry, Brian. 2001. *Culture and Equality*. Cambridge, MA: Harvard University Press.

Bauböck, Rainer. 2011. 'Temporary Migrants, Partial Citizenship and Hypermigration'. *Critical Review of International Social and Political Philosophy* 14 (5): 665–693.

Bauböck, Rainer. 2011. 'Citizenship and Freedom of Movement'. In *Citizenship, Borders, and Human Needs*, ed. Roger Smith, 343–376. Philadelphia: Pennsylvania University Press.

Bauböck, Rainer. 2009a. 'Global Justice, Freedom of Movement and Democratic Citizenship'. *European Journal of Sociology* 50 (1): 1–31.

Bauböck, Rainer. 2009b. 'The Rights and Duties of External Citizenship'. *Citizenship Studies* 13 (5): 475–499.

Bauböck, Rainer. 2007. 'Political Boundaries in a Multilevel Democracy'. In *Identities, Affiliations and Allegiances*, ed. Seyla Benhabib and Ian Shapiro, 85–112. Cambridge: Cambridge University Press.

Bauböck, Rainer. 2006. 'Free Movement and the Asymmetry between Exit and Entry'. *Ethics & Economics* 4 (1). http://ethique-economique.net/.

Bauböck, Rainer. 2005. 'Expansive Citizenship: Voting beyond Territory and Membership'. *PS: Political Science and Politics* 38 (4): 683–687.

Bauböck, Rainer. 2004. 'Territorial or Cultural Autonomy for National Minorities?' In *The Politics of Belonging, Nationalism, Liberalism and Pluralism*, ed. Alain Dieckhoff, 221–258. Lanham, MD: Lexington Books.

Bauböck, Rainer. 2003. 'Public Culture in Societies of Immigration'. In *Identity and Integration*, ed. Rosemarie Sackmann, Bernhard Peters, and Thomas Faist, 37–57. Aldershot: Ashgate.

Bauböck, Rainer. 1994. *Transnational Citizenship: Membership and Rights in International Migration*. Aldershot, UK: Edward Elgar.

Bauböck, Rainer, and Joppke, Christian, eds. 2010. *How Liberal Are Citizenship Tests?* EUI Working Papers. RSCAS 2010/41. European University Institute: Robert Schuman Centre for Advanced Studies. EUDO Citizenship Observatory.

BBC News. 2007a. 'Pensioner in Deportation Threat'. June 15. http://news.bbc.co.uk/2/hi/uk_news/scotland/tayside_and_central/6756341.stm (accessed December 19, 2012).

BBC News. 2007b. 'Pensioner Wins Deportation Fight'. June 20. http://news.bbc.co.uk/2/hi/uk_news/scotland/tayside_and_central/6223440.stm (accessed December 19, 2012).

Bell, Daniel A. 2006. *Beyond Liberal Democracy*. Princeton: Princeton University Press.

Bell, Daniel A., and Piper, Nicola. 2005. 'Justice for Migrant Workers? The Case of Foreign Domestic Workers in Hong Kong and Singapore'. In *Multiculturalism in Asia*, ed. Will Kymlicka and He Baogang, 196–222. Oxford: Oxford University Press.

Bendersky, Joseph W. 2000. *"The Jewish Threat": Anti-Semitic Politics of the U.S. Army*. New York: Basic Books.

Benhabib, Seyla. 2004. *The Rights of Others: Aliens, Residents, and Citizens*. Cambridge: Cambridge University Press.

Benhabib, Seyla. 2002. *The Claims of Culture: Equality and Diversity in the Global Era*. Princeton: Princeton University Press.

Benhabib, Seyla. 1996. *Democracy and Difference: Contesting the Boundaries of the Political*. Princeton: Princeton University Press.

Bennhold, Katrin. 2008. 'A Veil Closes France's Door to Citizenship'. *New York Times*. July 19. http://www.nytimes.com/2008/07/19/world/europe/19france.html (accessed February 19, 2012).

Berinstein, Carolina, Nyers, Peter, Wright, Cynthia, and Zeheri, Sima. 2006. *Access Not Fear: Non-Status Immigrants and City Services*. Report prepared for the 'Don't Ask, Don't Tell' Campaign, Toronto, Canada.

Blake, Michael. 2013. 'Immigration, Complicity, and Causality'. In *Citizenship, Plural Citizenships, and Cosmopolitan Alternatives*, ed. Rogers Smith. Philadelphia: University of Pennsylvania Press.

Blake, Michael. 2012a. 'Immigration, Association, and Anti-Discrimination'. *Ethics* 122: 1–16.

Blake, Michael. 2012b. 'Equality without Documents: Political Justice and the Right to Amnesty'. *Canadian Journal of Philosophy* Supplementary Volume 36: 99–122.

Blake, Michael. 2006. 'Universal and Qualified Rights to Immigration'. *Ethics & Economics* 4 (1): http://ethique-economique.net/.

Blake, Michael. 2005. 'Immigration'. In *The Blackwell Companion to Applied Ethics*, ed. Christopher Wellman and R. G. Frey, 224–237. Oxford: Blackwell Publishers.

Blake, Michael. 2002. 'Discretionary Immigration'. *Philosophical Topics* 30 (2): 251–273.

Blake, Michael. 2001. 'Distributive Justice, State Coercion, and Autonomy'. *Philosophy & Public Affairs* 30 (3): 257–296.

Bleich, Erik. 2011. *The Freedom to Be Racist? How the United States and Europe Struggle to Preserve Freedom and Combat Racism*. New York: Oxford University Press.

Bogusz, Barbara, Cholewinski, Ryszard, Cygan, Adam, and Szyszczak, Erika. 2004. *Irregular Migration and Human Rights: Theoretical, European and International Perspectives*. Leiden: Martinus Nijhoff.

Borjas, George J. 1999. *Heaven's Door: Immigration Policy and the American Economy*. Princeton: Princeton University Press.

Borjas, George J. 1990. *Friends or Strangers: The Impact of Immigration on the U.S. Economy*. New York: Basic Books.

Bosniak, Linda S. 2007. 'The Undocumented Immigrant: Contending Policy Approaches'. In *Debating Immigration*, ed. Carol M. Swain, 85–94. New York: Cambridge University Press.

Bosniak, Linda S. 2006. *The Citizen and the Alien: Dilemmas of Contemporary Membership*. Princeton: Princeton University Press.

Bosniak, Linda S. 1996. 'Opposing Prop. 187: Undocumented Immigrants and the National Imagination'. *Connecticut Law Review* 28 (3): 555–619.

Bosniak, Linda S. 1988. 'Exclusion and Membership: The Dual Identity of the Undocumented Worker under United States Law'. *Wisconsin Law Review* 6: 955–1042.

Boswell, Christina. 2005. *The Ethics of Refugee Policy*. Aldershot, UK: Ashgate.

Bouchard, Gérard, and Taylor, Charles. 2008. 'Report: Building the Future: A Time for Reconciliation'. Quebec: Government of Quebec.

Breitman, Richard, and Kraut, Alan M. 1987. *American Refugee Policy and European Jewry, 1933–1945*. Bloomington: Indiana University Press.

Brimelow, Peter. 1995. *Alien Nation: Common Sense about America; Immigration Disaster*. New York: Random House.

Brock, Gillian. 2009. *Global Justice: A Cosmopolitan Account*. Oxford: Oxford University Press.

Brownlie, Ian, ed. 1992. *Basic Documents on Human Rights*. 3rd edition. Oxford: Oxford University Press.

Buenker, John, and Burckel, Nicholas. 1977. *Immigration and Ethnicity: A Guide to Information Sources*. Detroit: Gale Research Company.

Caestecker, Frank, and Moore, Bob, eds. 2010. *Refugees from Nazi Germany and the Liberal European States*. Oxford: Berghahn Books.

Callan, Eamonn. 2009. 'All Things Considered, We Might Have to Choose between Competing Evils'. *Boston Review* 34 (3): 21.

Callan, Eamonn. 1997. *Creating Citizens: Political Education and Liberal Democracy*. Oxford: Oxford University Press.

Caney, Simon. 2008. 'Global Distributive Justice and the State'. *Political Studies* 56 (3): 487–518.

Caney, Simon. 2005. *Justice Beyond Borders*. Oxford: Oxford University Press.

Caney, Simon. 2002. 'Equal Treatment, Exceptions and Cultural Diversity'. In *Multiculturalism Reconsidered: 'Culture and Equality' and its Critics*, ed. Paul Kelly, 81–101. Cambridge: Polity Press.

Carens, Joseph H. 2013. 'In Defense of Birthright Citizenship'. In *Migration in Political Theory*, ed. Sarah Fine and Lea Ypi. Oxford: Oxford University Press.

Carens, Joseph H. 2010. *Immigrants and the Right to Stay*. Cambridge, MA: MIT Press.

Carens, Joseph H. 2009a. 'Fear vs. Fairness: Migration, Citizenship and the Transformation of Political Community'. In *Nationalism and Multiculturalism in a World of Immigration*, ed. Kasper Lippert-Rasmussen, Nils Holtug, and Sune Lægaard, 151–173. Houndmills, UK: Palgrave Macmillan.

Carens, Joseph H. 2009b. 'The Case for Amnesty'. *Boston Review* 34 (3): 7–10, 24.

Carens, Joseph H. 2008a. 'Live-in Domestics, Seasonal Workers, and Others Hard to Locate on the Map of Democracy'. *Journal of Political Philosophy* 16 (4): 419–445.

Carens, Joseph H. 2008b. 'The Rights of Irregular Migrants'. *Ethics & International Affairs* 22 (2): 163–186.

Carens, Joseph H. 2007. 'Wer gehört dazu? Migration und die Rekonzeptualisierung der Staatsbürgerschaft'. In *Bürgerschaft und Migration: Einwanderung und Einbürgerung aus ethisch-politischer Perspektive*, ed. Simone Zurbuchen, 25–51. Münster: LIT. A revised version of this article appeared in English as Carens, Joseph H. 2008. 'Immigration, Democracy, and Citizenship'. In *Of States, Rights, and Social Closure: Governing Migration and Citizenship*, ed. Oliver Schmidtke and Saime Ozcurumez, 17–36. New York: Palgrave Macmillan.

Carens, Joseph H. 2006. 'Free Speech and Democratic Norms in the Danish Cartoons Controversy'. *International Migration* 44 (5): 32–41.

Carens, Joseph H. 2005. 'On Belonging: What We Owe People Who Stay'. *Boston Review* 30 (3–4): 16–19.

Carens, Joseph H. 2004a. 'La Integración de los Inmigrantes'. In *Inmigración y Procesos de Cambio: Europa y el Mediterráneo en el Contexto Global*, ed. Gemma Aubarell and Ricard Zapata, 393–420. Barcelona: Icaria-Institut Europeu de la Mediterrània. A revised version of this article appeared in English as Carens, Joseph H. 2005. 'The Integration of Immigrants'. *Journal of Moral Philosophy* 2 (1): 29–46.

Carens, Joseph H. 2004b. 'A Contextual Approach to Political Theory'. *Ethical Theory and Moral Practice* 7 (2): 117–132.

Carens, Joseph H. 2000a. *Culture, Citizenship, and Community: A Contextual Exploration of Justice as Evenhandedness*. Oxford: Oxford University Press.

Carens, Joseph H. 2000b. 'Open Borders and Liberal Limits: A Response to Isbister'. *International Migration Review* 34 (2): 636–643.

Carens, Joseph H. 1998. 'Why Naturalization Should Be Easy: A Response to Noah Pickus'. In *Immigration and Citizenship in the 21st Century*, ed. Noah M. Jeddiah Pickus, 141–146. Lanham, MD: Rowman and Littlefield.

Carens, Joseph H. 1997. 'The Philosopher and the Policymaker: Two Perspectives on the Ethics of Immigration with Special Attention to the Problem of Restricting Asylum'. In *Immigration Admissions: The Search for Workable Policies in Germany and the United States*, ed. Kay Hailbronner, David Martin, and Hiroshi Motomura, 3–51. Oxford: Berghahn Books.

Carens, Joseph H. 1996. 'Realistic and Idealistic Approaches to the Ethics of Immigration'. *International Migration Review* 30 (2): 156–170.

Carens, Joseph H., ed. 1995. *Is Quebec Nationalism Just? Perspectives from Anglophone Canada*. Montreal: McGill-Queen's University Press.

Carens, Joseph H. 1994. 'The Rights of Immigrants'. In *Group Rights*, ed. Judith Baker, 142–163. Toronto: University of Toronto Press.

Carens, Joseph H. 1992a. 'Migration and Morality: A Liberal Egalitarian Perspective'. In *Free Movement: Ethical Issues in the Transnational Migration of People and of Money*, ed. Brian Barry and Robert E. Goodin, 25–47. University Park: University of Pennsylvania Press.

Carens, Joseph H. 1992b. 'Refugees and the Limits of Obligation'. *Public Affairs Quarterly* 6 (1): 31–44.

Carens, Joseph H. 1991. 'Refugees and States: A Normative Analysis'. In *Canadian and American Refugee Policy*, ed. Howard Adelman, 18–29. Toronto: York Lanes Press.

Carens, Joseph H. 1989. 'Membership and Morality: Admission to Citizenship in Liberal Democratic States'. In *Immigration and the Politics of Citizenship in Europe and North America*, ed. William Rogers Brubaker, 31–49. Lanham, MD: University Press of America.

Carens, Joseph H. 1988. 'Nationalism and the Exclusion of Immigrants: Lessons from Australian Immigration Policy'. In *Open Borders? Closed Societies: The Ethical and Political Issues*, ed. Mark Gibney, 41–60. Westport, CT: Greenwood Press.

Carens, Joseph H. 1987a. 'Aliens and Citizens: The Case for Open Borders'. *Review of Politics* 49 (2): 251–273.

Carens, Joseph H. 1987b. 'Who Belongs? Theoretical and Legal Questions about Birthright Citizenship in the United States'. *University of Toronto Law Journal* 37 (4): 413–443.

Chang Howard. 2008a. 'Guest Workers and Justice in a Second Best World'. *University of Dayton Law Review* 34: 3–14.

Chang, Howard. 2008b. 'The Economics of International Labor Migration and the Case for Global Distributive Justice in Liberal Political Theory'. *Cornell International Law Journal* 41 (1): 1–25.

Chang, Howard. 1997. 'Liberalized Immigration as Free Trade: Economic Welfare and the Optimal Immigration Policy'. *University of Pennsylvania Law Review* 145 (5): 1147–1244.

Cohen, G. A. 2008. *Rescuing Justice and Equality*. Cambridge, MA: Harvard University Press.

Cohen, Joshua, and Sabel, Charles. 2006. 'Extra Rempublicam Nulla Justitia?' *Philosophy & Public Affairs* 34 (2): 147–175.

Cohen, Michael Joseph. 1985. *Churchill and the Jews*. London: Routledge.

Cole, David. 1999. *No Equal Justice: Race and Class in the American Criminal Justice System*. New York: New Press.

Cole, Phillip. 2000. *Philosophies of Exclusion: Liberal Political Theory and Immigration*. Edinburgh: Edinburgh University Press.

Cornelius, Wayne A. 2001. 'Death at the Border: Efficacy and Unintended Consequences of US Immigration Control Policy'. *Population and Development Review* 27: 661–685.

Coutin, Susan Bibler. 2009. 'Migrants Complex Affiliations'. *Focus on Law Studies* 24 (2): 2–3, 10.

Crawford, James, ed. 1992. *Language Loyalties: A Source Book on the Official English Controversy*. Chicago: University of Chicago Press.

Cumming-Bruce, Nick, and Erlanger, Steve. 2009. 'Swiss Ban Building of Minarets on Mosques'. *New York Times*. November 29. http://www.nytimes.com/2009/11/30/world/europe/30swiss.html (accessed on July 26, 2011).

Dahl, Robert A. 1989. *Democracy and its Critics*. New Haven: Yale University Press.

De Genova, Nicholas P. 2002. 'Migrant "Illegality" and Deportability in Everyday Life'. *Annual Review of Anthropology* 31: 419–447.

Divine, Robert. 1957. *American Immigration Policy*. New Haven: Yale University Press.

Dowty, Alan. 1987. *Closed Borders: The Contemporary Assault on Freedom of Movement*. New Haven: Yale University Press.

Dumbrava, Costica. 2012. 'Nationality, Citizenship, and Ethno-Cultural Membership'. Ph.D. thesis, European University Institute.

Dummett, Michael. 2001. *On Immigration and Refugees*. New York: Routledge.

Dworkin, Ronald. 2000. *Sovereign Virtue: The Theory and Practice of Equality*. Cambridge, MA: Harvard University Press.

EUDO Citizenship website: http://eudo-citizenship.eu.

European Council. 2003. 'Status of Non-EU Member Country Nationals who are long-Term Residents'. European Union Council Directive 2003/109/EC. L 16/44. November 25. http://europa.eu/legislation_summaries/justice_freedom_security/free_movement_of_persons_asylum_immigration/l23034_en.htm (accessed March 20, 2013).

Faist, Thomas, ed. 2007. *Dual Citizenship in Europe: From Nationhood to Societal Integration*. Aldershot, UK: Ashgate.

Faist, Thomas, and Kivisto, Peter, eds. 2007. *Dual Citizenship in Global Perspective: From Unitary to Multiple Citizenships*. Houndmills, UK: Palgrave Macmillan.

Feingold, Henry. 1970. *The Politics of Rescue*. New Brunswick, NJ: Rutgers University Press.

Fine, Sarah. 2014. *Immigration and the Right to Exclude*. Oxford: Oxford University Press.

Fine, Sarah. 2010. 'Freedom of Association Is Not the Answer'. *Ethics* 120: 338–356.

Fiss, Owen M. 1998. 'The Immigrant as Pariah'. *Boston Review*. 23 (October/November). http://bostonreview.net/BR23.5/Fiss.html (accessed March 20, 2013).

Foblets, Marie-Claire. 2005. 'Mobility versus Law, Mobility in the Law? Judges in Europe are Confronted with the Thorny Question "Which Law Applies to Litigants of Migrant Origin?" ' In *Mobile People, Mobile Law: Expanding Legal Relations in a Contracting World*, ed. F. von Benda-Beckmann et al., 297–316. Aldershot: Ashgate.

Freeman, Gary. 1995. 'Modes of Immigration Politics in Liberal Democratic States'. *International Migration Review* 29 (4): 881–902.

Gainer, Bernard. 1972. *The Alien Invasion: The Origins of the Aliens Act of 1905*. London: Heinemann Educational Books.

Gans, Chaim. 2008. *A Just Zionism*. Oxford: Oxford University Press.

Garrard, John T. 1967. 'Parallels of Protest: English Reactions to Jewish and Commonwealth Immigration'. *Race* 9 (1): 47–66.

Gibney, Matthew. 2007. 'Engineered Regionalism, Forced Migration, and Justice between States'. In *New Regionalism and Asylum Seekers*, ed. Susan Kneebone and Felicity Rawlings-Sanei, 57–78. Oxford: Berghahn Books.

Gibney, Matthew. 2006. 'A Thousand Little Guantanamos: Western States and Measures to Prevent the Arrival of Refugees'. In *Migration, Displacement, Asylum: The Oxford Amnesty Lectures 2004*, ed. Kate Tunstall, 139–169. Oxford: Oxford University Press.

Gibney, Matthew. 2004. *The Ethics and Politics of Asylum*. Cambridge: Cambridge University Press.

Gibney, Matthew. 2000. 'Outside the Protection of the Law: The Situation of Irregular Migrants in Europe'. *Refugee Studies Centre Working Paper*. 6 (December).

Gilbert, Sir Martin. 2007. *Churchill and the Jews: A Lifelong Friendship*. London: Henry Holt and Co.

Glendon, Mary Ann. 2001. *A World Made New: Eleanor Roosevelt and the Universal Declaration of Human Rights*. New York: Random House Publishing.

Goodwin-Gill, Guy, and McAdam, Jane. 2007. *The Refugee in International Law*. 3rd edition. Oxford: Oxford University Press.

Grahl-Madsen, Atle. 1992. 'Article 13'. In *The Universal Declaration of Human Rights: A Commentary*, ed. Asbjorn Eide, Gudmundur Alfredsson, Foran Melander, Lars Adam Rehof, and Allan Rosas, 203–216. Oslo: Scandinavian University Press.

Gutmann, Amy. 1987. *Democratic Education*. Princeton: Princeton University Press.

Habermas, Jürgen. 1998. *Between Facts and Norms: Contributions to a Discourse Theory of Law and Democracy*. Cambridge, MA: MIT Press.

Hailbronner, Kay. 1989. 'Citizenship and Nationhood in Germany'. In *Immigration and the Politics of Citizenship in Europe and North America*, ed. William Rogers Brubaker, 67–79. Lanham, MD: University Press of America.

Hammar, Tomas. 1994. 'Legal Time of Residence and the Status of Immigrants'. In *From Aliens to Citizens: Redefining the Status of Immigrants in Europe*, ed. Rainer Bauböck, 187–198. Aldershot: Avebury.

Hammar, Tomas. 1990. *Democracy and the Nation State: Aliens, Denizens and Citizens in a World of International Migration*. Aldershot, UK: Avebury Publishing.

Hammar, Tomas. 1989. 'State, Nation, and Dual Citizenship'. In *Immigration and the Politics of Citizenship in Europe and North America*, ed. William Rogers Brubaker, 81–95. Lanham, MD: University Press of America.

Hampshire, James. 2011. 'Liberalism and Citizenship Acquisition: How Easy Should Naturalisation Be?' *Journal of Ethnic and Migration Studies* 37 (6): 953–971.

Hansen, Randall. 2010. 'Citizenship Tests: An Unapologetic Defense'. In *How Liberal Are Citizenship Tests?* ed. Rainer Bauböck and Christian Joppke, 25–27. EUI Working Papers. RSCAS 2010/41. European University Institute. Robert Schuman Centre for Advanced Studies: EUDO Citizenship Observatory.

Hansen, Randall, and Weil, Patrick, eds. 2002. *Dual Nationality, Social Rights and Federal Citizenship in the U.S. and Europe: The Reinvention of Citizenship*. New York: Berghahn Books.

Hardin, Garett. 1974. 'Living on a Lifeboat'. *Bioscience* 24 (10): 561–568.

Harnischfeger, Uta. 2008. 'Swiss to Decide on Secret Votes by Public on Citizenship Candidates'. *New York Times*. June 1. http://www.nytimes.com/2008/06/01/world/europe/01swiss. html?_r=2&emc=eta1. (accessed February 21, 2012).

Hathaway, James C. 2005. *The Rights of Refugees under International Law*. Cambridge: Cambridge University Press.

Hathaway, James C., and Neve, Alexander. 1997. 'Making International Refugee Law Relevant Again: A Proposal for Collectivized and Solution-Oriented Protection'. *Harvard Human Rights Journal* 10: 115–212.

Hayes, Helene. 2001. *U.S. Immigration Policy and the Undocumented: Ambivalent Laws, Furtive Lives*. Westport, CT: Praeger Publishers.

Higham, John. 1975. *Send These to Me: Jews and Other Immigrants in Urban America*. New York: Atheneum.

Higham, John. 1963. *Strangers in the Land: Patterns of American Nativism*. New York: Atheneum.

Hollifield, James F. 1992. *Immigrants, Markets, and States: The Political Economy of Postwar Europe*. Cambridge, MA: Harvard University Press.

Honig, Bonnie. 2001. *Democracy and the Foreigner*. Princeton: Princeton University Press.

Honohan, Iseult. 2009. 'Reconsidering the Claim to Family Reunification in Migration'. *Political Studies* 57 (4): 768–787.

Howard, Marc Morjé. 2009. *The Politics of Citizenship in Europe*. Cambridge: Cambridge University Press.

Huntington, Samuel. 2004. *Who Are We?: The Challenges to America's National Identity*. New York: Simon and Schuster.

Isbister, John. 2000. 'A Liberal Argument for Border Controls: Reply to Carens'. *International Migration Review* 34 (2): 629–635.

Jacobs, Lesley. 2004. *Pursuing Equal Opportunities: The Theory and Practice of Egalitarian Justice*. Cambridge: Cambridge University Press.

Jacobson, D. 1996. *Rights Across Borders: Immigration and the Decline of Citizenship*. Baltimore: Johns Hopkins University Press.

Jagerskiold, Stig. 1981. 'The Freedom of Movement'. In *The International Bill of Rights: The Covenant on Civil and Political Rights*, ed. Louis Henkin, 166–184. New York: Columbia University Press.

Joppke, Christian. 2010. 'How Liberal are Citizenship Tests'. In *How Liberal Are Citizenship Tests?* ed. Rainer Bauböck and Christian Joppke, 1–4. EUI *Working Papers*. RSCAS 2010/41. European University Institute. Robert Schuman Centre for Advanced Studies: EUDO Citizenship Observatory.

Joppke, Christian. 2005. *Selecting by Origin: Ethnic Migration in the Liberal State*. Cambridge, MA: Harvard University Press.

Joppke, Christian. 2001. 'The Legal-Domestic Sources of Immigrant Rights: The United States, Germany, and the European Union'. *Comparative Political Studies* 34 (4): 339–366.

Joppke, Christian. 1999. *Immigration and the Nation State: The United States, Germany and Great Britain*. Oxford: Oxford University Press.

Jordan, Bill, and Düvell, Franck. 2002. *Irregular Migration: The Dilemmas of Transnational Mobility*. Northampton: Edward Elgar.

Julius, A. J. 2006. 'Nagel's Atlas'. *Philosophy & Public Affairs* 34 (2): 175–192.

Jupp, James. 2007. *From White Australia to Woomera: The Story of Australian Immigration*. 2nd edition. Cambridge: Cambridge University Press.

Kanstroom, Daniel. 1993. 'Wer Sind Wir Wieder? Laws of Asylum, Immigration, and Citizenship in the Struggle for the Soul of the New Germany'. *Yale Journal of International Law* 18: 155–211.

Kapur, Devesh, and McHale, John. 2005. *Give Us Your Best and Brightest: The Global Hunt for Talent and Its Impact on the Developing World*. Washington, DC: Center for Global Development.

Kelley, Ninette, and Trebilcock, Michael. 2010. *The Making of a Mosaic: A History of Canadian Immigration Policy*. 2nd edition. Toronto: University of Toronto Press.

Kennedy, Brendan. 2010. 'Former "Murder City" Cop Seeking Safe-Haven in Canada'. *The Toronto Star*. May 23. http://www.thestar.com/news/gta/article/813527--former-murder-city-co p-seeking-safe-haven-in-canada.html (accessed March 20, 2013).

Kinzer, Stephen. 1993. 'Germany's Young Turks Say "Enough" to the Bias'. *New York Times*. June 6. http://www.nytimes.com/1993/06/06/world/germany-s-young-turks-say-enough-to-the-bias.html (accessed April 19, 2011).

Knop, Karen. 2001. 'Relational Nationality: On Gender and Nationality in International Law'. In *Citizenship Today: Global Perspectives and Practices*, ed. T. Alexander Aleinikoff and Douglas Klusmeyer, 89–124. Washington, DC: Carnegie Endowment for International Peace.

Kritzman-Amir, Tally. 2008. 'Not in My Backyard: On the Morality of Responsibility-Sharing in Refugee Law'. http://works.bepress.com/tally_kritzman_amir/1/ (accessed March 20, 2013).

Kukathas, Chandran. 2010. 'Expatriatism: The Theory and Practice of Open Borders'. In *Citizenship, Borders and Human Needs*, ed. Roger M. Smith, 324–342. Philadelphia: University of Pennsylvania Press.

Kukathas, Chandran. 2005. 'The Case for Open Immigration'. In *Contemporary Debates in Applied Ethics*, ed. Andrew I. Cohen and Christopher Heath Wellman, 207–220. Malden: Blackwell Publishing.

Kymlicka, Will. 2001a. *Politics in the Vernacular: Nationalism, Multiculturalism, and Citizenship*. New York: Oxford University Press.

Kymlicka, Will. 2001b. 'Territorial Boundaries: A Liberal Egalitarian Perspective'. In *Boundaries and Justice*, ed. David Miller and Sohail H. Hashmi, 249–275. Princeton: Princeton University Press.

Kymlicka, Will. 1998. *Finding Our Way*. Toronto: Oxford University Press.

Kymlicka, Will. 1995. *Multicultural Citizenship*. New York: Oxford University Press.

Laborde, Cécile. 2008. *Critical Republicanism: The Hijab Controversy and Political Philosophy*. Oxford: Oxford University Press.

Layton-Henry, Zig. 1991. 'Citizenship and Migrant Workers in Western Europe'. In *The Frontiers of Citizenship*, ed. Ursula Vogel and Michael Moran, 107–124. Houndmills and Basingstoke: Macmillan.

Legomsky, Stephen H. 1994. 'Why Citizenship'. *Virginia Journal of International Law* 35 (10): 279–300.

Lenard, Patti. 2012. 'Why Temporary Labour Migration Is Not a Satisfactory Alternative to Permanent Migration'. *Journal of International Political Theory* 8 (1–2): 172–183.

Lenard, Patti, and Straehle, Christine. 2012. 'Temporary Labour Migration, Global Redistribution and Democratic Justice'. *Politics, Philosophy and Economics* 11: 206–230.

Lenard, Patti, and Straehle, Christine, eds. 2012. *Legislated Inequality: Temporary Labour Migration in Canada*. Montreal-Kingston: McGill-Queens University Press.

Levinson, Meira. 1999. *The Demands of Liberal Education*. Oxford: Oxford University Press.

Levy, Jacob. 2000. *The Multiculturalism of Fear*. Oxford: Oxford University Press.

Lichtenberg, Judith. 1981. 'National Boundaries and Moral Boundaries: A Cosmopolitan View'. In *Boundaries: National Autonomy and Its Limits,* ed. Peter G. Brown and Henry Shue, 79–100. Totowa, NJ: Rowman and Littlefield.

Lister, Matthew. 2013. 'Who Are Refugees?'. *Law and Philosophy* forthcoming.

Lister, Matthew. 2010. 'Immigration, Association and the Family'. *Law and Philosophy* 29: 717–745.

Lister, Matthew. 2007. 'A Rawlsian Argument for Extending Family-Based Immigration Benefits to Same Sex Couples'. *University of Memphis Law Review* 37: 763–764.

London, Louise. 2000. *Whitehall and the Jews, 1933-1948: British Immigration Policy, Jewish Refugees, and the Holocaust*. Cambridge: Cambridge University Press.

Maas, Willem. 2007. *Creating European Citizens*. Lanham, MD: Rowman & Littlefield Publishers, Inc.

Macedo, Stephen. 2004. 'What Self-Governing Peoples Owe to One Another: Universalism, Diversity and the Law of Peoples'. *Fordham Law Review* 72 (5): 1721–1738.

Macedo, Stephen. 2000. *Diversity and Distrust: Civic Education in a Multicultural Democracy*. Cambridge, MA: Harvard University Press.

MacIntosh, Constance. 2010. 'Domestic Violence and Gender-Based Persecution: How Refugee Adjudicators Judge Women Seeking Refuge from Spousal Violence—and Why Reform Is Needed'. *Refuge* 26 (2): 147–164.

Macklin, Audrey, and Crépeau, François. 2010. 'Multiple Citizenship, Identity and Entitlement in Canada'. *Institute for Research on Public Policy* (6). http://papers.ssrn.com/sol3/papers.cfm?abstract_id=1646483 (accessed March 20, 2013).

Macklin, Audrey. 1992. 'Foreign Domestic Worker: Surrogate Housewife or Mail Order Servant?' *McGill Law Journal* 37 (3): 681–760.

Marrus, Michael R. 1985. *The Unwanted*. New York: Oxford University Press.

Martin, David. 2002. 'New Rules for Dual Nationality'. In *Dual Nationality, Social Rights and Federal Citizenship in the US and Europe: The Reinvention of Citizenship*, ed. Randell Hansen and Patrick Weil, 34–60. New York: Berghahn Books.

Martin, David. 1991. 'The Refugee Concept: On Definitions, Politics, and the Careful Use of a Scarce Resource'. In *Refugee Policy: Canada and the United States,* ed. Howard Adelman, 30–51. Toronto: York Lanes Press.

Martin, David. 1990. 'Reforming Asylum Adjudication: Navigating the Coast of Bohemia'. *University of Pennsylvania Law Review* 138 (5): 1247–1381.

Martin, Susan. 2002. 'The Attack on Social Rights: US Citizenship Devalued'. In *Dual Nationality, Social Rights and Federal Citizenship in the US and Europe: The Reinvention of Citizenship*, ed. Patrick Weil and Randell Hansen, 215–232. New York: Berghahn Books.

Mason, Andrew. 2006. *Levelling the Playing Field: The Idea of Equal Opportunity and Its Place in Egalitarian Thought*. Oxford: Oxford University Press.

Maussen, Marcel. 2004. 'Policy Discourses on Mosques in the Netherlands 1980–2002: Contested Constructions'. *Ethical Theory and Moral Practice* 7 (2): 147–162.

Maussen, Marcel. 2009. *Constructing Mosques: The Governance of Islam in France and the Netherlands*. Amsterdam: Amsterdam School for Social Science Research.

Mayer, Robert. 2005. 'Guestworkers and Exploitation'. *The Review of Politics* 67 (2): 311–334.

McAdam, Jane. 2011. 'An Intellectual History of Freedom of Movement in International Law: The Right to Leave as a Personal Liberty'. *Melbourne Journal of International Law* 12 (1): 27–56.

Meilaender, Peter C. 2001. *Toward a Theory of Immigration*. New York: Palgrave Macmillan.

Miller, David. 2013. 'Is There a Human Right to Immigrate?' In *Migration in Political Theory: The Ethics of Movement and Membership*, ed. Sarah Fine and Lea Ypi. Oxford: Oxford University Press.

Miller, David. 2010. 'Why Immigration Controls Are Not Coercive: A Reply to Arash Abizadeh'. *Political Theory* 38 (1): 111–120.

Miller, David. 2008a. 'Immigrants, Nations, and Citizenship'. *Journal of Political Philosophy* 16 (4): 371–390.

Miller, David. 2008b. 'Irregular Migrants: An Alternative Perspective'. *Ethics and International Affairs* 22 (2): 193–198.

Miller, David. 2007. *National Responsibility and Global Justice*. Oxford: Oxford University Press.

Miller, David. 2005. 'Immigration: The Case for Limits'. In *Contemporary Debates in Applied Ethics*, ed. Andrew I. Cohen and Christopher Heath Wellman, 193–206. Malden: Blackwell.

Moan, Marit Hovdal. 2008. 'Immigration Policy and "Immanent Critique"'. *Ethics & International Affairs* 22 (2): 205–211.

Modood, Tariq. 2007. *Multiculturalism: A Civic Idea*. Cambridge: Polity Press.

Moellendorf, Darrel. 2002. *Cosmopolitan Justice*. Cambridge: Westview Press.

Morse, Arthur D. 1968. *While Six Million Died: A Chronicle of American Apathy*. New York: Random House.

Morsink, Johannes. 1999. *The Universal Declaration of Human Rights*. Philadelphia: University of Pennsylvania Press.

Motomura, Hiroshi. 2006. *Americans in Waiting: The Lost Story of Immigration and Citizenship in the United States*. New York: Oxford University Press.

Motomura, Hiroshi. 1997. 'The Family and Immigration: A Roadmap for the Ruritanian Lawmaker'. In *Immigration Admissions: The Search for Workable Policies in Germany and the United States*, ed. Kay Hailbronner and David Martin, 79–119. Oxford: Berghahn Books.

Nagel, Thomas. 2005. 'The Problem of Global Justice'. *Philosophy & Public Affairs* 33 (2): 113–147.

Naujoks, Daniel. 2009. 'Dual Citizenship: The Discourse on Ethnic and Political Boundary-Making in Germany'. Focus Migration Policy Brief No. 14. Hamburg: Hamburg Institute of International Economics (HWWI).

Nedelsky, Jennifer. 2011. *Law's Relations: A Relational Theory of Self, Autonomy and Law*. New York: Oxford University Press.

Nett, Roger. 1971. 'The Civil Right We Are Not Ready For: The Right of Free Movement of People on the Face of the Earth'. *Ethics* 81 (3): 212–227.

Neugebauer, Robynne Susan, ed. 2000. *Criminal Injustice: Racism in the Criminal Justice System*. Toronto: Canadian Scholars Press.

Neumayer, Eric. 2005. 'Bogus Refugees? The Determinants of Asylum Migration to Western Europe'. *International Studies Quarterly* 49 (3): 389–410.

Ngai, Mae M. 2004. *Impossible Subjects: Illegal Aliens and the Making of Modern America*. Princeton: Princeton University Press.

Norman, Wayne. 2006. *Negotiating Nationalism: Nation-building, Federalism, and Secession in the Multinational State*. Oxford: Oxford University Press.

Nozick, Robert. 1974. *Anarchy, State and Utopia*. New York: Basic Books.

Nussbaum, Martha C. 2007. *Frontiers of Justice: Disability, Nationality, Species Membership*. Boston: Belknap Press.

Nussbaum, Martha C. 2001. *The Fragility of Goodness: Luck and Ethics in Greek Tragedy and Philosophy*. Cambridge: Cambridge University Press.

Oberman, Kieran. 2013. 'Can Brain Drain Justify Immigration Restrictions?' *Ethics*: 123 (3): 427–455.

Oberman, Kieran. 2011. 'Immigration, Global Poverty and the Right to Stay'. *Political Studies* 58: 253–268.

Oberman, Kieran. 2012. 'Immigration as a Human Right'. Available at SRRN: http://ssrn.com/abstract=2164939.

Ogilvie, Sarah, and Miller, Scott. 2006. *Refuge Denied: The St. Louis Passengers and the Holocaust.* Madison: University of Wisconsin Press.

Ottonelli, Valeria, and Torresi, Tiziana. 2012. 'Inclusivist Egalitarian Liberalism and Temporary Migration: A Dilemma'. *Journal of Political Philosophy* 20 (2): 202–224.

Owen, David. 2013. 'Citizenship and the Marginalities of Migrants'. *Critical Review of International Social and Political Philosophy* (Forthcoming).

Parekh, Bhikhu. 2008. *A New Politics of Identity*. Houndsmills: Palgrave Macmillan.

Parekh, Bhikhu. 2002. 'Rethinking Multiculturalism: Cultural Diversity and Political Theory'. *European Journal of Political Theory* 1 (1): 107–119.

Parekh, Bhikhu. 2000. *Rethinking Multiculturalism*. Cambridge, MA: Harvard University Press.

Pevnick, Ryan. 2011. *Immigration and the Constraints of Justice: Between Open Borders and Absolute Sovereignty*. Cambridge: Cambridge University Press.

Phillips, Anne. 2009. *Multiculturalism without Culture*. Princeton: Princeton University Press.

Phillips, Anne. 1995. *The Politics of Presence*. Oxford: Clarendon Press.

Pitkin, Hanna Fenichel. 1999. *Fortune Is a Woman*. Chicago: University of Chicago Press.

Pogge, Thomas. 2008. *World Poverty and Human Rights: Cosmopolitan Responsibilities and Reforms.* 2nd edition. Cambridge: Polity Press.

Pogge, Thomas W. 1997. 'Migration and Poverty'. In *Citizenship and Exclusion*, ed. Veit Bader, 12–27. Basingstoke: Macmillan.

Price, Matthew. 2009. *Rethinking Asylum: History, Purpose and Limits*. Cambridge: Cambridge University Press.

Pritchett, Lant. 2006. *Let Their People Come: Breaking the Gridlock on Global Labor Mobility.* Washington, DC: Center for Global Development.

Rawls, John. 2005. *Political Liberalism. 2nd edition.* New York: Columbia University Press.

Rawls, John. 1999. *The Law of Peoples*. Cambridge, MA: Harvard University Press.

Rawls, John. 1971. *A Theory of Justice*. Cambridge, MA: Harvard University Press.

Renshon, Stanley. 2005. 'Reforming Dual Citizenship in the United States: Integrating Immigrants into the American National Community'. Washington, DC: Center for Immigration Studies. http://www.cis.org/articles/2005/dualcitizenship.pdf.

Roberts, Sam. 2010. 'New Life in U.S. No Longer Means New Name'. *New York Times*. August 25. http://www.nytimes.com/2010/08/26/nyregion/26names.html (accessed December 10, 2012).

Rogers, Rosemarie. 1985. *Guests Come to Stay: The Effects of European Labour Migration on Sending and Receiving Countries*. Boulder, CO: Westview Press.

Rosen, Robert N. 2007. *Saving the Jews: Franklin D. Roosevelt and the Holocaust.* New York: Thunder's Mouth Press.

Rubio-Marin, Ruth. 2000. *Immigration as a Democratic Challenge*. Cambridge: Cambridge University Press.

Ruhs, Martin, and Martin, Philip. 2008. 'Numbers vs. Rights: Trade-offs and Guest Worker Programs'. *International Migration Review* 42 (1): 249–265.

Sangiovanni, Andrea. 2007. 'Global Justice, Reciprocity, and the State'. *Philosophy and Public Affairs* 35 (1): 3–39.

Sassen, Saskia. 1999. *Guests and Aliens*. New York: New Press.

Scheffler, Samuel. 2007. 'Immigration and the Significance of Culture'. *Philosophy and Public Affairs* 35 (2): 93–125.

Scheffler, Samuel. 2001. *Boundaries and Allegiances*. Oxford: Oxford University Press.

Schotel, Bas. 2012. *On the Right of Exclusion: Law, Ethics and Immigration Policy.* New York: Routledge.

Schuck, Peter H. 2009. 'In Moral Argument, the Details Matter'. *Boston Review* 34 (3): 13.

Schuck, Peter H. 2002. 'Plural Citizenships'. In *Dual Nationality, Social Rights and Federal Citizenship in the US and Europe: The Reinvention of Citizenship*, ed. Randell Hansen and Patrick Weil, 61–99. New York: Berghahn Books.

Schuck, Peter H. 1998. *Citizens, Strangers and In-Betweens: Essays on Immigration and Citizenship*. Boulder, CO: Westview Press.

Schuck, Peter H. 1997. 'Refugee Burden-Sharing: A Modest Proposal'. *Yale Journal of International Law* 22: 243–297.

Schuck, Peter H., and Smith, Rogers M. 1985. *Citizenship without Consent: Illegal Aliens in the American Polity*. New Haven: Yale University Press.

Schuck, Peter H. 1984. 'The Transformation of Immigration Law'. *Columbia Law Review* 34: 1–90.

Schuster, Liza. 2003. *The Use and Abuse of Political Asylum in Britain and Germany*. London: Frank Cass.

Seglow, Jonathan. 2009. 'Arguments for Naturalisation'. *Political Studies* 57 (4): 788–804.

Seglow, Jonathan. 2005. 'The Ethics of Immigration'. *Political Studies Review* 3 (3): 3–21.

Shachar, Ayelet. 2009. *The Birthright Lottery: Citizenship and Global Inequality*. Cambridge, MA: Harvard University Press.

Shacknove, Andrew. 1988. 'American Duties to Refugees: Their Scope and Limits'. In *Open Borders? Closed Societies?* ed. Mark Gibney, 131–151. New York: Greenwood Press.

Shacknove, Andrew. 1985. 'Who Is a Refugee?' *Ethics* 95 (2): 274–284.

Sherman, Ari Joshua. 1970. *British Government Policy toward Refugees from the Third Reich, 1933-1939*. Oxford: Oxford University Press.

Singer, Peter, and Singer, Renata. 1988. 'The Ethics of Refugee Policy'. In *Open Borders? Closed Societies?* ed. Mark Gibney, 111–130. New York: Greenwood Press.

Smith, Rogers M. 1997. *Civic Ideals: Conflicting Visions of Citizenship in U.S. History*. New Haven: Yale University Press.

Soroka, Stuart, Banting, Keith, and Johnston, Richard. 2006. 'Immigration and Redistribution in a Global Era'. In *Globalization and Egalitarian Redistribution*, ed. Pranab Bardhan, Samuel Bowles, and Michael Wallerstein, 261–288. Princeton: Princeton University Press.

Souter, James. 2013. 'Towards a Theory of Asylum as Reparation for Past Injustice'. *Political Studies* (Forthcoming).

Soysal, Yasemin. 1994. *Limits of Citizenship: Migrants and Postnational Membership in Europe*. Chicago: University of Chicago Press.

Spinner, Jeff. 1994. *The Boundaries of Citizenship: Race, Ethnicity, and Nationality in the Liberal State*. Baltimore: Johns Hopkins University Press.

Spinner-Halev, Jeff. 2000. *Surviving Diversity: Religion and Democratic Citizenship*. Baltimore: Johns Hopkins University Press.

Spiro, Peter. 2008. *Beyond Citizenship*. New York: Oxford University Press.

Spiro, Peter. 1997. 'Dual Nationality and the Meaning of Citizenship'. *Emory Law Journal* 46: 1411–1486.

Stark, Oded. 2004. 'Rethinking the Brain Drain'. *World Development* 32 (1): 15–22.

Steiner, Hillel. 1992. 'Libertarianism and the Transnational Migration of People'. In *Free Movement: Ethical Issues in the Transnational Migration of People and Money*, ed. Brian Barry and Robert E. Goodin, 87–94. University Park: Pennsylvania State University Press.

Stevens, Jacqueline. 2010. *States without Nations: Citizenship for Mortals*. New York: Columbia University Press.

Stilz, Anna. 2010. 'Guestworkers and Second-Class Citizenship'. *Policy and Society* 29 (4): 295–307.

Stone, Peter. 2007. 'Why Lotteries are Just'. *Journal of Political Philosophy* 15 (3): 276–295.

Supreme Court of Canada. 2002. *Lavoie v. Canada*, 2002 SCC 23, [2002] 1 S.C.R. 769.

Swain, Carol M. 2009. 'Apply Compassion Offered Illegal Immigrants to the Most Vulnerable Citizens'. *Boston Review* 34 (3): 15.

Tamir, Yael. 1993. *Liberal Nationalism*. Princeton: Princeton University Press.

Tan, Kok-Chor. 2012. *Justice, Institutions, and Luck*. Oxford: Oxford University Press.

Tan, Kok-Chor. 2004. *Justice without Borders: Cosmopolitanism, Nationalism, and Patriotism*. Cambridge: Cambridge University Press.

Taylor, Charles, and Gutmann, Amy. 1994. *Multiculturalism: Examining the Politics of Recognition*. Princeton: Princeton University Press.

Tichenor, Daniel J. 2002. *Dividing Lines: The Politics of Immigration Control in America.* Princeton: Princeton University Press.

Torpey, John. 2000. *The Invention of the Passport.* Cambridge: Cambridge University Press.

Triadafilopoulos, Triadafilos. 2012. *Becoming Multicultural: Immigration and the Politics of Membership in Canada and Germany.* Vancouver: University of British Columbia Press.

Tu, Weiming. 1996. 'Beyond the Enlightenment Mentality: A Confucian Perspective on Ethics, Migration, and Global Stewardship'. *International Migration Review* 30 (1): 58–75.

UNHCR. 2011. *Resettlement Handbook.* Revised edition. Geneva: United Nations High Commissioner for Refugees.

van der Leun, Joanne. 2003. *Looking for Loopholes: Processes of Incorporation of Illegal Immigrants in the Netherlands.* Amsterdam: Amsterdam University Press.

Waldrauch, Harold. 2005. 'Electoral Rights for Foreign Nationals'. Workshops on Citizens, Non-Citizens and Voting Rights in Europe. Edinburgh. http://www.euro.centre.org/EdinburghPaperWaldrauch.pdf (accessed March 20, 2013).

Walzer, Michael. 1983. *Spheres of Justice.* New York: Basic Books Inc.

Weber, Leanne and Pickering, Sharon. 2011. *Globalization and Borders: Death at the Global Frontier.* Houndmills, UK: Palgrave Macmillan.

Weil, Patrick. 2008. *How to Be French: Nationality in the Making since 1789.* Trans. Catherine Porter. Durham, NC: Duke University Press.

Weil, Patrick. 2001. 'Access to Citizenship: A Comparison of Twenty-Five Nationality Laws'. In *Citizenship Today: Global Perspectives and Practices,* ed. T. Alexander Aleinikoff, 17–35. Washington, DC: Carnegie Endowment for International Peace.

Wellman, Christopher H., and Cole, Phillip. 2011. *Debating the Ethics of Immigration: Is There a Right to Exclude?* New York: Oxford University Press.

Wellman, Christopher H. 2008. 'Immigration and Freedom of Association'. *Ethics* 119: 109–141.

Whelan, Frederick G. 1988. 'Citizenship and Free Movement: An Open Admission Policy?' In *Open Borders? Closed Societies? The Ethical and Political Issues,* ed. Mark Gibney, 3–40. Westport, CT: Greenwood Press.

Whelan, Frederick G. 1983. 'Prologue: Democratic Theory and the Boundary Problem.' In *Liberal Democracy: Nomos 25,* ed. J. Roland Pennock and John W. Chapman, 13–47. New York: New York University Press.

Whelan, Frederick G. 1981. 'Citizenship and the Right to Leave'. *American Political Science Review* 75 (3): 636–653.

Wilkins, William Henry. 1892. *The Alien Invasion.* London: Methuen.

Williams, Bernard. 1982. *Moral Luck.* Cambridge: Cambridge University Press.

Williams, Melissa S. 2000. *Voice, Trust, and Memory: Marginalized Groups and the Failings of Liberal Representation.* Princeton: Princeton University Press.

Woodward, James. 1992. 'Commentary: Liberalism and Migration'. In *Free Movement: Ethical Issues in the Transnational Migration of People and of Money,* ed. Brian Barry and Robert Goodin, 59–84. London: Harvester Wheatsheaf.

Young, Iris Marion. 2002. *Inclusion and Democracy.* Oxford: Oxford University Press.

Young, Iris Marion. 1990. *Justice and the Politics of Difference.* Princeton: Princeton University Press.

Ypi, Lea. 2008. 'Justice in Migration: A Closed Borders Utopia?' *Journal of Political Philosophy* 16 (4): 391–418.

Zhu, Lijiang. 2003. 'Hukou System of the People's Republic of China: A Critical Appraisal under International Standards of Internal Movement and Residence'. *Chinese Journal of International Law* 2 (2): 519–565.

Zolberg, Aristide R. 2006. *A Nation by Design: Immigration Policy in the Fashioning of America.* New York: Russell Sage Foundation.

Zolberg, Aristide, Suhrke, Astri, and Aguayo, Sergio. 1989. *Escape from Violence: Conflict and the Refugee Crisis in the Developing World.* New York: Oxford University Press.

INDEX

Note: Endnotes are indicated by n or nn after the page number.